Knowledge Creation and Management

KNOWLEDGE CREATION AND MANAGEMENT
New Challenges for Managers

Editors-in-Chief
Kazuo Ichijo
Ikujiro Nonaka

OXFORD
UNIVERSITY PRESS
2007

OXFORD
UNIVERSITY PRESS

Oxford University Press, Inc., publishes works that further
Oxford University's objective of excellence
in research, scholarship, and education.

Oxford   New York
Auckland   Cape Town   Dar es Salaam   Hong Kong   Karachi
Kuala Lumpur   Madrid   Melbourne   Mexico City   Nairobi
New Delhi   Shanghai   Taipei   Toronto

With offices in
Argentina   Austria   Brazil   Chile   Czech Republic   France   Greece
Guatemala   Hungary   Italy   Japan   Poland   Portugal   Singapore
South Korea   Switzerland   Thailand   Turkey   Ukraine   Vietnam

Published by Oxford University Press, Inc.
198 Madison Avenue, New York, New York 10016

www.oup.com

Oxford is a registered trademark of Oxford University Press.

Library of Congress Cataloging-in-Publication Data

Knowledge creation and management : new challenges for managers / editors-in-chief,
Kazuo Ichijo, Ikujiro Nonaka.
p. cm.
Includes bibliographical references and index.
ISBN-13 978-0-19-515962-2
ISBN 0-19-515962-4
1. Intellectual capital—Management.   2. Knowledge management.   I. Ichijo, Kazuo.
    II. Nonaka, Ikujiro, 1935–
HD53.K593 2006
658.4'038—dc22   2006040120

9 8 7 6 5 4 3 2 1

Printed in the United States of America
on acid-free paper

Preface

This book presents the latest management ideas in knowledge creation and management in readable and non-technical chapters. Knowledge continues to be a critical—perhaps *the* critical—factor for firms in today's competitive environment. The field of knowledge creation and management has been growing quickly as studies of firms that have successfully applied these tools have proliferated. As a result, far more is known about the field today than in the middle 1990s when the first books for managers began to be published.

We invited leading experts to contribute chapters in their fields of expertise. Each was asked to distil his or her subject in a chapter that would be accessible to managers who want to learn what can be applied to their organizations without the distracting details of research methodology. Each chapter, however, is based on careful research.

The book begins with an Introduction that describes the field in general. Part I presents chapters that describe how knowledge is created and communicated within and between firms. Part II focuses on specific applications of knowledge in strategic management, market research in product development, human resources, corporate finance, and research and development in innovation. Part III takes a broader view with chapters on globalizing knowledge, corporate governance of knowledge-based companies, enhancing social capital, and corporate renewal through knowledge management.

In addition, we have included a glossary keyed to the chapters. Though we have kept the use of technical terminology to a minimum, we believe that readers should become acquainted with the main terms that are used in the field.

An innovative feature is a website at Hitotsubashi University (where we teach) that offers updated examples of knowledge creation and management in practice, current research, and other useful information that we hope will facilitate our readers' application of the powerful tools described in this book: http//www.ics.hit-u.ac.jp/faculty/knowledge.html

We invite readers to explore this website as we continue to add information that we hope will be of value to them.

Acknowledgments

Our academic debts are large in completing and publishing this book. Above all, our biggest acknowledgments are due to the four advisory editors. Xavier Gilbert of IMD–International Institute for Management Development, Seija Kulkki of the Helsinki School of Economics, Dorothy A. Leonard of the Harvard Business School, and Laurence Prusak of Babson College helped us structure the chapters of this book and find the best authors for each chapter. Despite a very long editing process, these five editors were very patient and did not spare their time for giving us very professional and insightful advice. Without their advisory editorship, this book would not be published in this current form and with the current contents.

We are very grateful to all the authors who contributed to this book. It was academically exciting for us to read their innovative papers as enthusiastic readers. We also appreciate their patience and generosity since some of them had to wait quite long before seeing their chapters finally published in this book.

One dean and one president have been great supporters to this book. Hirotaka Takeuchi, Dean of Graduate School of International Corporate Strategy, Hitotsubashi University, has been a great influence on our thinking about knowledge-based management and organization. Peter Lorange, President of IMD–International Institute for Management Development has been very enthusiastic about this book and has always encouraged us to establish thought leadership in this field.

There are many acknowledgments due when a book is the results of research which has been conducted on a global basis. A book like this required tremendous cooperation from all the companies that participated in our research. We learned a lot from executives and managers we interviewed, who were forthcoming, candid, and generous with their time. The people who were excited by our ideas and supportive of our efforts helped us immeasurably. There are too many to name, and we hope they will forgive us if we do not to acknowledge them individually here.

Our colleagues at Hitotsubashi and IMD who directly and indirectly worked on this book were unbelievably committed, professional, and tolerant of our pace and style. We thank them for hanging in there on this project. Florian Kohlbacher has worked as a excellent research assistant for this book. Koko Sakata and Catherine Romagnan provided excellent administrative and secretary work and kept all the pieces together.

Last but not least, we would like to send our special thanks to the person who helped us find our words and worked so hard to bring them alive on the written pages. Herb Addison of Oxford University Press believed in the importance of this book, and in us. Through the lengthy process of planning the book and working with the contributors he was always patient, and kept us on track while encouraging us to fully explore the complexities and practical implications of the material. He provided very valuable comment and advice to us throughout all the editing and publication processes. Moreover, he carefully read all the drafts and provided valuable comments and excellent editing to all the authors. His partnership has been invaluable to us as he became a knowledge creator and a knowledge management expert himself. We are grateful to Herb for being enthusiastic about our concept from the beginning of this book project to its completion. Lastly we want to say "thank you" to our families for letting us concentrate on this book while having less time with them.

Personally, Ichijo especially wants to express his gratitude to his parents, who led him to this current academic career, and to his wife Kyoko and daughter Eri, who spent so many days in Switzerland living by themselves, without husband and dad. We thank our families for allowing us to complete this book, and for giving us a reason to hurry up and get it done.

Contents

Advisory Editors and Contributors

Advisory Editors

Xavier Gilbert
*IMD–International Institute for
    Management Development*

Seija Kulkki
Helsinki School of Economics

Dorothy A. Leonard
Harvard Business School

Laurence Prusak
Babson College

Contributors

Nicholas Athanassiou
*College of Business Administration
Northeastern University*

Mie Augier
Stanford University

Bettina Büchel
*IMD–International Institute for
    Management Development*

Bala Chakravarthy
*IMD–International Institute for
    Management Development*

Donald J. Cohen
*Research Associate
Babson College*

Thomas Davenport
*Technology Operations
    and Information
Management Division
Babson College*

Xavier Gilbert
*IMD–International Institute for
    Management Development*

Kazuo Ichijo
IMD–International Institute for
Management Development &
Graduate School of International
Corporate Strategy
Hitotsubashi University

Dorothy Leonard
Harvard Business School

Jay W. Lorsch
Harvard Business School

Martha Maznevski
IMD–International Institute for
Management Development

Sue McEvily
Katz Graduate School of Business
University of Pittsburgh

Makoto Nakano
Graduate School of International
Corporate Strategy
Hitotsubashi University

Ikujiro Nonaka
Graduate School of International
Corporate Strategy
Hitotsubashi University

Margit Osterloh
Institute for Organization and
Administrative Science
University of Zurich

Lawrence Prusak
Distinguished Scholar in
Residence
Babson College

David Teece
Institute of Management,
Innovation, and Organization
Haas School of Business
University of California,
Berkeley

Leigh M. Weiss
McKinsey & Company

Knowledge Creation and Management

Introduction

*Knowledge as Competitive Advantage
in the Age of Increasing Globalization*

KAZUO ICHIJO AND IKUJIRO NONAKA

This book reflects our contention that the knowledge-based management of corporations is at the center of what management has to do in today's fast-changing global environment. It is the fundamental purpose of the book to provide managers with the understanding and tools for successfully employing knowledge management in their organizations.

In this phase of globalization, much manufacturing and back office work is being transferred across geographical boundaries, often to countries with newly developing technological capabilities. At the same time, many firms are moving operations to the more developed world to create and offer knowledge and knowledge-based services that, at least at the present time, can be done only in these countries. This emphasis on change in the global environment puts knowledge management at the heart of what organizations need to do to cope with today's fast-changing environment. Therefore, the success of a company in the twenty-first century will be determined by the extent to which its leaders can develop intellectual capital through knowledge creation and knowledge-sharing on a global basis. Knowledge constitutes a competitive advantage. Knowledge creation and imagination have never been more important than in this age of globalization since, in the flat world described by Thomas L. Friedman, so many of the inputs and tools for collaboration are becoming commodities, available to everybody.[1]

To compete successfully, companies must hire, develop, and retain excellent managers who accumulate valuable knowledge assets. Attracting smart, talented people and raising their level of intellectual capabilities is a core

3

competency. In addition, the unique feature of knowledge as resource is that it can become obsolete in the future. Therefore, new knowledge has to be created continuously. At the same time, companies should encourage proficient managers to share the knowledge they develop across geographical and functional boundaries in an effective, efficient, and fast manner. In other words, to win in the competitive environment, companies need to be able to manage knowledge strategically. That means management of knowledge should constitute a core competency.

Despite the growing interest in knowledge management and the initiatives many organizations have taken to manage knowledge, few companies have succeeded in creating a knowledge-based competence to gain and sustain a competitive advantage. According to McKinsey, a global consulting company that has an excellent system for global knowledge management, there are only four companies that employ more than 200,000 people and deliver consistent profits per employee of $25,000 or more per year: General Electric, IBM, Toyota, and Citigroup.[2] This fact suggests that very few companies have been able to combine massive scale and complexity with consistently high profits.

In order to reduce complexity and make the most of size for competitive advantage, knowledge management is a must, especially for global companies. Sharing best practices across regions, functions, and businesses will help global companies increase profitability by reducing inefficient overlap of work and moving effectively and efficiently. For example, at GE and Toyota, knowledge management plays a strategically important role in gaining and sustaining their competitive advantage in the global market. Toyota widely articulated its crucial knowledge program for practicing *kaizen* (continuous improvement) so that people working in different Toyota subsidiaries can produce high-quality cars consistently. Their knowledge was summarized as the Toyota Way 2001 and was transferred across functional and regional boundaries. At GE, knowledge about best practices is actively shared through its famous operating mechanisms. Meetings that constitute GE's operating mechanisms—such as global leadership meetings, Corporate Executive Councils, and corporate officer meetings—are utilized for sharing knowledge. These operating mechanisms are based on GE's unique social architecture, which is enabled by GE values, the Work-Out system of giving all workers an opportunity to contribute ideas to improving the way the company operates, and boundaryless behaviors of GE employees. Knowledge-sharing is enabled by this social architecture. Given the small number of global companies that manage complexity effectively, we could say that knowledge management is still not easy to execute. But before we discuss the reasons for this, it would be useful to know something of the development of knowledge creation and management, and the contributions of some of its important thinkers.

The Development of Knowledge Creation and Management

Interest in knowledge as the source of a corporation's competitive advantage has a long history in several disciplines. For example, in economics, Adam Smith noted in *The Wealth of Nations* that workers learned from experience, and the Victorian economist Alfred Marshall highlighted knowledge as a productive resource. The Nobel Prize–winning economist Kenneth Arrow gave this phenomenon further expression in his 1962 article "Learning by Doing." All three men argued that if organizations can become better at learning by transferring what workers know, then they can become more efficient. Developing these learning strategies became an important theme of knowledge management.

In the field of management, as early as in 1959 Peter Drucker used the term "knowledge worker" for the first time in his book *Landmarks of Tomorrow*. Knowledge workers include those in the information technology fields, such as programmers, systems analysts, technical writers, academic professionals, researchers, and so forth. More recently, management of knowledge became a hot topic beginning in the 1990s. In 1991, Thomas A. Stewart introduced *Fortune* magazine readers to knowledge management and intellectual capital. His various articles were influential in making intellectual capital and knowledge become corporate buzzwords at that time. Then Ikujiro Nonaka and Hirotaka Takeuchi proposed a theory of organizational knowledge creation in their well-known 1995 book. Their book, *The Knowledge-Creating Company: How Japanese Companies Create the Dynamics of Innovation*, is one of the most cited books in the knowledge management literature.[3] In the same year, Dorothy Leonard-Barton published *Wellsprings of Knowledge: Building and Sustaining the Sources of Innovation*, in which she described knowledge as the crucial source for competitive advantage of a firm, and presented practical applications of knowledge for gaining and sustaining competitive advantage. In 1998, Tom Davenport and Larry Prusak published *Working Knowledge*, in which they shared lessons from knowledge management practices in over fifty firms and provided practical applications of knowledge management in organizational settings. By the end of the 1990s, articles on knowledge management were proliferating in academic and business journals all over the world.[4]

Like other management movements, the issue of managing knowledge-based competence of a corporation was in response to perceived changes in the larger economic environment. Changes are taking place in the external environment across a wide variety of dimensions at an accelerated pace. These include strategic alliances, open innovation, globalization of markets and of supply chains, technological breakthroughs, emergence of new industries, demographic trends, changes in the workforce, and geopolitical power games, to name a few. Such endemic changes in the external environment demand continuous and rapid change within the organization. Of all these changes, the drastic changes caused by globalization and the advancement of information technology are the key driving forces for increasing corporate interest in knowledge as a source of competitive advantage. Because of globalization and by means of effective information technologies, big corporations are now free to manufacture and sell their products in almost any countries they want, with very few rare exceptions. As Thomas L. Friedman pointed out in 1999:

> While there are a lot of similarities in kind between the previous era of globalization and the one we are now in, what is new today is the degree and intensity with which the world is being tied together into a single globalized marketplace and village. What is also new is the sheer number of people and countries able to partake of today's globalized economy and information networks, and to be affected by them.[5]

Globalization has been evolving since then, especially through the integration of emerging markets, such as India and China, into the global economy, and the global diffusion of productive knowledge that allows these and other developing nations, symbolically called BRICs (Brazil, Russia, India, and China), to compete with more developed nations because of much lower labor costs and by means of information technology. Computers have become cheaper and are dispersed all over the world, and there has been an explosion of software, e-mail, search engines such as Google, and proprietary software that can chop up any piece of work and send one part to the United States, one part to India, and one part to China, making it easy for anyone to do remote development. As a result of these changes, a new corporate global platform has been created "where intellectual work, intellectual capital could be delivered from anywhere."[6] Again according to Thomas L. Friedman, we are now entering the phase of globalization 3.0. The dynamic force in globalization 1.0, which lasted from 1492, when Columbus set sail, opening a battle between the Old World and the New World, until around 1800, was the beginning of countries being in global competition. In globalization 2.0, which lasted roughly from 1800 to 2000, interrupted by the Great Depression and World Wars I and II, companies were in global competition. In globalization 3.0, which started around 2000, the newfound power for individuals to collaborate and compete globally stands out. In this phase, work has become global knowledge work.[7]

It would be a serious mistake, however, to conclude that knowledge creation and management are important only to globally organized firms. Domestic firms, no matter what competitive environment they are in, can build a competitive advantage by developing and sharing knowledge within their organizations.

We return now to examining why knowledge management is so difficult to execute in practice.

Knowledge Management: Difficulty in Execution

We found that there are two main reasons for the difficulties that firms experience in developing effective knowledge creation and management programs.

First, the traditional disciplines of management do not lend themselves to knowledge management and should be revised so that the knowledge-based competence of a corporation can be managed effectively and efficiently. Traditional notions about strategy, human resource management, finance, and marketing should be reexamined and revised in order to manage knowledge for competitive advantage creatively, effectively, and efficiently. Knowledge is tacit as well as explicit, an important distinction that will be explored in more detail in this book. Tacit knowledge involves human processes in knowledge management—creativity, conversation, judgment, teaching, learning—and it is difficult to quantify; therefore, it is difficult to manage in the traditional disciplines, which are more quantitative than qualitative. Management of knowledge should rely on a new sense of emotional knowledge and care in the organization, one that highlights how people treat each other and that encourages creativity—even playfulness. It throws out new challenges to traditional disciplines.

Second, the business impact of the practical application of the knowledge management theoretical framework in actual business settings remains vague. This is partly due to the fact that there are too few research initiatives which analyze how knowledge management can specifically contribute to overcoming important management issues that corporate leaders are facing now. As a result, managers tend to discuss knowledge management per se, without applying it to actual business issues. This has had the effect of their overemphasizing information technology. As a consequence, they fail to learn how knowledge management can contribute to solving such important business issues as globalization, corporate governance, and corporate change management. Knowledge management ends up on the agenda for IT managers, not on the agenda for top management.

The Structure of the Book

The structure and organization of this book reflect our stated purpose to "provide managers with the understanding and tools for successfully employing knowledge management in their organizations." This purpose has guided the overall organization, the selection of contributors, and the writing style of the individual chapters.

We describe a knowledge-based view of organizations and show how to manage the knowledge-based competence of corporations to gain and sustain competitive advantage. We also show how important real-world business issues can be solved by the effective management of knowledge-based competence. The editors and contributors have coordinated their work to enable business practitioners to become familiar with the concepts and terminologies of knowledge-based management and organization, and to obtain practical guidelines about knowledge management in organizations. We hope that our readers can gain an understanding of new perspectives concerning functional disciplines, a major element of the knowledge-based view of a corporation.

Although the book is intended primarily for practicing business managers, we expect that academics will want to have the work in their libraries. But this book is not intended to be an academic review of the literature. It is written by experts in the field of knowledge management for managers who need to know the latest thinking about and applications of knowledge creation to use in their organizations.

We were assisted in the planning and preparation of this book by the advisory editors: Dorothy Leonard of the Harvard Business School, Seija Kulkki of the Helsinki School of Economics, Xavier Gilbert of IMD, and Lawrence Prusak of Babson College. The structure of the book is clear from the table of contents. In deciding this structure, and selecting the contributors for each chapter, we obtained valuable advice from the advisory editors.

Following this introduction, part I contains chapters describing the fundamentals of knowledge-based management and organization. In chapter 1, Ikujiro Nonaka and Ryoko Toyama describe Nonaka's theory of knowledge in the most current view of the organization. Then Laurence Prusak and Leigh Weiss describe knowledge in organizational settings. They describe their insights into how organizations generate, disseminate, and use knowledge for their competitive advantage. Bettina Büchel's chapter has as its topic knowledge creation and the transfer process across business functions, with a focus on innovation in product development and processes in organizations. Two chapters that further develop the knowledge transfer process follow Büchel's chapter. Dorothy Leonard focuses on knowledge transfer within organizations, and Martha Maznevski and Nicholas Athanassiou describe knowledge transfer across organizations, referring to learning networks within and across organizations. In the next chapter, Kazuo Ichijo describes the holistic view of knowledge management, paying attention to enabling conditions that support and sustain knowledge creation. The last chapter in part I, written by Thomas Davenport, describes the effective use of information technology to facilitate knowledge creation, externalization, sharing, and internalization.

In part II, functional applications of knowledge creation and management are described. Each author, who is a specialist in his or her topic, discusses how traditional approaches in each function should be changed so that the knowledge-based competence of corporations (an intangible asset) will be developed, utilized, and protected. Kazuo Ichijo examines corporate strategy from the knowledge-based view. Dorothy Leonard develops new insights into marketing, with a focus on the new concept of empathic design. Margit Osterloh describes new theories and practice for human resource management in the knowledge-based economy. Makoto Nakano demonstrates how the traditional notion of finance should be modified to make the most use of tacit intangible assets. Last, Mie Augier and David Teece explain how to organize and manage innovation in the global knowledge economy.

In part III, current important management issues and challenges are described, and authors who are experts on each issue reveal how the knowledge-based view of management and organization will help business leaders overcome those issues and challenges. Xavier Gilbert states how the knowledge-based view of organization and management will be effective in overcoming many of the challenges caused by globalization. In his chapter about corporate governance, Jay Lorsch develops his insights into how to audit knowledge assets (avoiding their deterioration), human resources, and corporate activities. Don Cohen analyzes the important issue of social capital—the good relationships among an organization's members—and proposes effective designs for this objective. This part is concluded by a chapter about corporate transformation written by Bala Chakravarthy (IMD) and Sue McEvily.

Following the articles is a glossary of key words and concepts in knowledge-based management and organization. The glossary should be an especially useful reference tool for practicing managers, who will often encounter the terms for the first time in the various chapters.

Finally, one of the innovative features of this book is that its readers will be able to read new cases about managing knowledge-based competence of a corporation on the Web site of the Graduate School of Corporate Strategy, Hitotsubashi University:

http//www.ics.hit-u.ac.jp/faculty/knowledge.html.

Four cases written by Dorothy Leonard-Barton, Kazuo Ichijo, Ikujiro Nonaka, and Laurence Prusak and Don Cohen have been uploaded. Each is a good supplement to the theories and practices discussed by each author in parts I and II. So that our readers can update their knowledge about knowledge-based management and organization, new cases will be continuously updated on this Web site.

All the chapters in this book are provocative. We asked each author, as an expert in the assigned field, to challenge the conventional theories and business practices from the viewpoint of seeing explicit and tacit knowledge as the most important source of competitive advantage. We hope this book will contribute to increasing the performance of organizations through the management of knowledge-based competence of corporations effectively, efficiently, and creatively.

Notes

1. Thomas L. Friedman, *The World Is Flat: A Brief History of the Twenty-first Century*. New York: Farrar, Straus and Giroux, 2005, p. 443.

2. *Financial Times*, November 2, 2005, p. 8

3. Chun Wei Choo and Nick Bontis, "Knowledge, Intellectual Capital, and Strategy," in their *The Strategic Management of Intellectual Capital and Organizational Knowledge*. New York: Oxford University Press, 2002, p. 11.

4. This introductory part is based on the description by Weiss and Prusak in their first draft for their chapter in this book.

5. Friedman, *The Lexus and Olive Tree*. New York: Anchor Books, 2000, p. xvii.

6. Friedman, *The World Is Flat*, pp. 6–7.

7. Ibid., p. 11.

PART I

FUNDAMENTALS OF KNOWLEDGE-BASED
MANAGEMENT AND ORGANIZATION

1

Why Do Firms Differ?

The Theory of the Knowledge-Creating Firm

IKUJIRO NONAKA AND RYOKO TOYAMA

Why do firms differ? This simple question is a central concern for scholars who study the theory of the firm (Nelson, 1991). Within the same industry there may be many different kinds of firms, all presumably competing with each other. Is this because some firms are doing the right thing and some are not? That cannot be the answer, for quite different firms in the same industry can be successful. We believe that the answer to the simple question lies at the heart of this book.

In this chapter we will examine the intellectual basis for viewing firms as knowledge-creating organizations and provide examples of successful knowledge-creating firms. The discussion must necessarily balance theory with applications, and the reader may want to read this chapter twice, first to get a sense of the theoretical underpinnings of knowledge creation, and again, after reading other chapters, to deepen his or her understanding of the subject.

Management thinkers have proposed a number of theories to explain differences in firms' structures and performances. The positioning school explains firm differences by pointing to the difficulties in entering an industry or a strategic group. Firms that want to move to a more profitable industry or segment are prevented from doing so by high entry or mobility barriers. The resource-based view explains firm differences in terms of the difficulties that firms have in imitating or acquiring resources. Firms that want to acquire the resources which give other firms a competitive advantage are prevented from doing so because such resources are impossible or too costly to acquire. Evolutionary economists explain that firms evolve differently due to managers' limited capabilities to foresee an uncertain future and their firms thus fall into path dependencies from which they cannot extricate themselves. Transaction cost economists explain that firms have different structures and boundaries due to the difficulties in transactions involving certain goods or services.

In short, contemporary theories basically explain the differences among firms *as a result* of profit-maximizing firms' inability to imitate successful firms. This implies that there is only one right way to solve the problem of profit maximization. Such differences among firms are viewed as market imperfections that should be competed away unless blocked by barriers, high cost, or limited capabilities of managers.

However, profits are not necessarily the sole purpose of a firm. If we ask managers why their firms exist, their answer would probably not be "to maximize profit." "Making a good car" is certainly a way to maximize profit, but it is also the goal itself, the reason to exist—for Honda, for example. To put it simply, firms differ because they *want and strive* to differ. They evolve differently because they envision different futures, which are based on their own dreams and ideals, and also because they adopt different strategies and structures to realize such futures. Even if they have the same goal, that does not necessarily mean that there is only one best way to achieve it. A "good car" probably means different things to Toyota and Honda, and their ways of making a good car also are different from one another.

This means that in order to explain why firms differ, we have to deal with the subjective elements of management, such as management vision, the firm's value system, and the commitment of employees. This position is well recognized by business historians such as Alfred Chandler (1977). However, many management scientists have avoided dealing with the subjectivity of humans. The pursuit of good science requires one to exclude subjectivity in the search for objective "facts" and universal rules concerning how these facts are connected. However, as Flyvbjerg (2001) has argued, social science is fundamentally different from natural science in terms of its need to deal with such subjectivity issues such as values, contexts, and power. Since humans are both objects and subjects of research at the same time, research in social sciences cannot be free from subjective factors.

Another assumption of some economists is that the firm is a passive entity which merely adapts to the environment and never tries to shape it (Teece, 2003). A firm is viewed as a static machine that takes information from the environment and processes it to set output levels (products, services, etc.).

The Firm as a Knowledge-Creating Entity

In this chapter we view the firm as a knowledge-creating entity, a dynamic entity that interacts with its environment, reshaping the environment, and even itself, through knowledge creation. This chapter establishes the theory of knowledge-creating firms in order to explain the complex process of creating knowledge organizationally. Based on epistemology (how to know) and ontology (what one exists for), the theory incorporates subjective issues such as values, contexts, and power, and captures the dynamic processes of knowledge creation through the interaction of subjectivities and objectivities both to shape and to be shaped by the business environment.

The Knowledge-based Theory of the Firm

These insights lead us to argue for a new way of understanding the firm: the knowledge-based theory of the firm. The theory rests on two essential elements: (1) a basic view of human beings and (2) the process of organizational knowledge creation.

Basic View of Human Beings

In neoclassical economic theory, the employees of a firm are generally undifferentiated and do not have specific knowledge. The firm is viewed as an information-processing machine to overcome the bounded rationality of human beings. Hence, for those who manage and research such a machine, human subjectivity is a noise to be carefully excluded. However, if we view the firm as an entity to create knowledge, we have to deal with the issues of human subjectivity.

In the long tradition of Western epistemology, knowledge has been defined as "justified true belief." Such a definition gives an impression that knowledge is something objective, absolute, and context-free. However, it is humans who hold and justify beliefs. Knowledge cannot exist without human subjectivity and the contexts that surround humans. "Truth" differs according to who we are (our values) and the point from which we look at it (our context). In organizational knowledge creation, it is these very differences in human subjectivity that help create new knowledge.

The differences in subjectivity are the differences in how we view the world. For example, when i-mode service (the Internet service via cellular phones developed at NTT DoCoMo in Japan) was conceived, it was viewed as just "another way to use a cellular phone" to increase revenues for phone companies as the existing voice transmission service entered the low growth period. However, the "outsiders" who were recruited to develop the service viewed it differently. A former magazine editor viewed it as "something interesting, something that young people can enjoy when they have a bit of time." A former Internet business entrepreneur viewed it as "Internet access via mobile phones." Through synthesis of these different views, i-mode service evolved into something totally different from a "useful information service for business people," in terms of price, content provided, and relationships with content providers. It became a new mode of communication.

Knowledge-based theories of the firm view humans not as replaceable parts of a machine but as beings who differ from each other and who are not satisfied with the current situation, transcending themselves to pursue new goals. Humans are purposeful beings who will act to realize their dreams and ideals—and these are beyond mere preferences (Rescher, 2003). An individual transcends himself or herself through knowledge creation (Nonaka, Toyama, and Konno, 2000; Nonaka and Toyama, 2003). In the organizational knowledge-creating process, individuals interact with each other to transcend their own boundaries and, as a result, change themselves, others, the organization, and the environment.

Viewing individuals as actively creating knowledge may resemble philosophical idealism. However, recent developments in brain science reveal that the essence of human brain activity is not passive processing of stimuli from the outside world, but active *creation* of contexts (Mogi, 2003). Peter Drucker (1993) emphasizes the importance of the individual's initiative for the productivity of knowledge workers. Maister (2000) empirically found a positive relationship between financial results and the ability of knowledge workers to make choices and to perceive that they are in control of their own destiny.

Organizational Knowledge Creation: The Synthesis of Subjectivity and Objectivity

The knowledge-creating theory that we advance is rooted in the belief that knowledge inherently includes human values and ideals. The knowledge creation process cannot be captured solely as a normative causal model because human values and ideals are subjective and the concept of truth depends on values, ideals, and contexts.

"Truth" as we define it becomes a truth through social interactions, instead of existing somewhere to be discovered. Unlike traditional views of knowledge, the knowledge-creating theory does not treat knowledge as something absolute and infallible. Any particular truth can be claimed to be incomplete, just as any current state of knowledge is fallible and influenced by subjective factors such as ideologies, values, and the interests of groups. However, our view of knowledge-creating theory does not view knowledge as being solely subjective. If knowledge stays within one's subjective world (or mind), it can expand only so far, since there is a limit to the world one can see or experience. In such a case, it is hard to create new knowledge or achieve the universality of knowledge.

Creating knowledge *organizationally* does not just mean that organization members supplement each other to overcome an individual's bounded rationality. It means that subjective, tacit knowledge held by an individual is externalized into objective, explicit knowledge to be shared and synthesized within the organization, and even beyond. (The difference between tacit and explicit knowledge is explained in the Introduction and is expanded in the chapters that follow.) The newly created knowledge is then used and embodied by individuals to enrich their subjective tacit knowledge. Hence, our knowledge-creating theory defines knowledge as a dynamic process of justifying personal belief regarding a "truth" that is never fixed.

Viewing the knowledge-creating process as the conversion from tacit knowledge into explicit knowledge means that the process is viewed as an ongoing social process of validating truth (Nonaka, 1994; Nonaka and Takeuchi, 1995). Knowledge is thus socially created through the synthesis of different views held by various people. Through the knowledge conversion process, called the SECI process, personal subjective knowledge is socially validated and synthesized with others' knowledge, so that knowledge keeps expanding (Nonaka, 1991; Nonaka and Takeuchi, 1995). In this process, tentative and partial knowledge created out of an individual's values and experiences is shared and justified by the members of the organization to create new knowledge. The knowledge created in the organization can then be tested through the justification process in the market, and new knowledge will be created by synthesizing views from the market.

For example, product development starts with *socialization*, the process by which tacit knowledge of customers is accumulated and shared. Such tacit knowledge is articulated into a product concept through *externalization*. The product concept is then systemized and made into a product through *combination*, in which explicit knowledge collected from inside and/or outside the organization is selected, combined, and processed to form more complex and systematic sets of explicit knowledge. The knowledge created in the form of a new product is then converted into tacit knowledge by market customers, who use it through *internalization*. The newly created tacit knowledge sets off a new spiral of knowledge creation (Nonaka and Takeuchi, 1995). Through this process of tacit and explicit knowledge conversion, subjective values are synthesized into more objective, socially shared knowledge to create a product that will meet the expectations and requirements of the customer.

The Dynamic Model of a Knowledge-Creating Company

We will now describe the basic components of a knowledge-based firm. Figure 1.1 shows the model of a knowledge-creating firm in which knowledge is created through dynamic interactions with the environment. The model consists of seven basic components: the SECI (Socialization, Externalization,

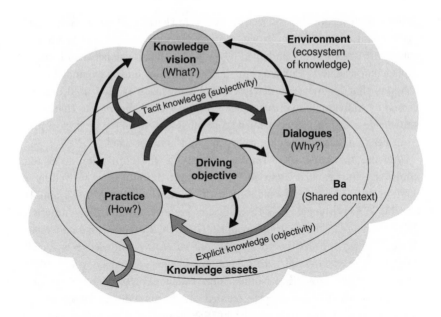

Figure 1.1 Basic components of a knowledge-based firm. *Source*: Adapted from Nonaka, Sasaki, and Senoo (2004).

Combination, and Internalization) process of *dialogues* and *practice*; the *knowledge vision* and *driving objectives*, which give direction and energy to the SECI process; *ba*, an existential place for the SECI process; *knowledge assets*, which are inputs and outputs of the SECI process; and the *environment* as an ecosystem of knowledge and multilayered *ba*. We will explain each of these components.

Knowledge Vision

The knowledge vision of a firm arises from confronting the fundamental question "Why do we exist?" By going beyond profits and asking "Why do we do what we do?" the mission and domain of the firm become defined. This knowledge vision gives a direction to knowledge creation. It also gives the firm direction with respect to the knowledge to be created beyond the firms' existing capabilities, and therefore determines how the firm evolves in the long term. While the strategy of a firm can change as the situation unfolds and uncertainty about the future decreases, the knowledge vision does not change so easily, since it stems from the fundamental ontological question of the firm's raison d'être.

The firm's knowledge vision inspires the intellectual passion of the organization's members so that they are encouraged to create knowledge. It also defines a consistent value system to evaluate and justify the knowledge created in the organization. The organization needs a value system to define what is truth, goodness, and beauty for the firm. Therefore, the firm's knowledge vision needs to be based on an absolute value that goes beyond financial matrices (Collins, 2001).

For example, the Japanese company Olympus has a vision of "Social-IN" that, it claims, is a more advanced concept than "Market-IN," since it is based on the idea that Olympus will create values based on the viewpoints of people who live in the society. At Honda, there is value to realizing "the joy of buying, the joy of selling, and the joy of creating" more than beating the competition. Eisai, a Japanese pharmaceutical company, has a vision of human health care. This vision makes the employees of Eisai recognize that the mission of the company is to be on the side of patients and their families, not on the side of doctors or pharmacists. This recognition has led to knowledge-creating activities designed to help patients and their families. For example, Eisai sent its employees to a nursing home to work as caretakers, in order to accumulate tacit knowledge about the elderly patients and their families. Such direct experience made them realize that the elderly often have difficulty swallowing their medicines. It led to the development of a type of tablet that dissolves quickly in the mouth.

Driving Objective

Without the actual effort to realize it, a firm's knowledge vision is little more than empty words. For knowledge to be created and justified on the basis of the firm's knowledge vision, the firm needs a concrete concept, goal, or action standard to connect the vision with the knowledge-creating process of dialogue and practice. We call such a concept/goal/action standard a *driving objective* because it drives the knowledge-creating process.

A driving objective triggers knowledge creation by questioning what the essence of things is. For example, Suzuki, a Japanese motorcycle company, set a goal of "1cc=1,000 yen" to develop a new scooter, a formula for the price. Hence, the goal was to sell a motorcycle with a 50cc engine for 50,000 yen. It was not simply a goal for cost-cutting. It was a concrete goal to help realize the vision of "inheriting a Japanese manufacturing culture." It drove the entire company to create knowledge by asking "What is the essence of a scooter?" To realize such a driving objective, it was not enough for Suzuki engineers to ask, "Is this part/work really necessary to make a scooter?" They needed to ask, "What is a scooter to begin with?" Such questioning led to the development of the Choinori scooter, which is based on the concept of adding only really necessary parts to a bare frame, instead of removing unnecessary parts from an existing model (Nonaka and Katsumi, 2004). The "really necessary parts" are not low- cost parts. The scooter uses some state-of-the art technologies, which have reduced the cost by cutting the number of parts.

The driving objective worked as an engine to synthesize the differences among various departments, such as research and development, manufacturing, and marketing. It made them focus, and strengthened their commitment to achieving such a demanding goal.

Seven-Eleven Japan uses "cut the opportunity loss" as its driving objective. To realize its vision of adapting to changing customer needs, the firm has to cut the opportunity loss by avoiding the situation of customers coming to a store and not finding what they want. Unlike the inventory cost from over-stocking, the concept of opportunity loss from unrealized sales is invisible and difficult to grasp absent such a mantra. With this driving objective, Seven-Eleven Japan has made a concerted effort to prevent items from going out of stock. Those responsible for placing orders, many of them part-time employees, have to build a hypothesis about next-day sales of each item by divining the essential reason why the item sold or did not sell well, and taking in the context, such as weather or school events in the neighborhood, that could affect the sales of the item. Orders are then placed on the basis of such hypotheses, which are immediately tested by objective data from the firm's state-of-the art, point-of-sales (POS) system that records each sale.

Seven-Eleven Japan also works closely with manufacturers to find the embedded needs and wants of customers, and to develop new products that customers really want. With such efforts, it has built a sustainable competitive advantage in offering its customers what they want when they want it. This goes well beyond traditional inventory management.

The driving objective of Canon is "cash flow." Despite its clear financial focus, the driving objective is not just about profit, but about making everyone in the organization think how he or she can improve the operation to increase cash flow. The concept of cash flow is relatively easy to grasp, and is therefore a good mantra to help everyone in the organization make the sources of competitive advantage visible in relation to his or her job.

Although it is a concrete goal, a driving objective such as "cutting opportunity loss" or "cash flow" has no clear end and requires relentless effort to achieve. It keeps moving the organization toward unattainable perfection. "Unattainable" sounds hopeless, but it actually serves the regulative function of driving the organization by preventing it from being defeated by imperfect realities (Rescher, 2003).

Dialogues: The Synthesis of Thoughts

Knowledge creation is guided through the synthesis of contradictions (Nonaka and Toyama, 2002, 2003). The world is filled with contradictions; duality is an essence of reality. By accepting such duality and synthesizing it, one can go beyond the simple dichotomy of either/or, and create new knowledge to solve contradictions.

Synthesis is achieved through dialectical thinking and action. However, we believe that "soft dialectic," which embraces contradictions and incorporates conflicting views, is more suited to synthesis in management than the Hegelian dialectic, which does not allow contradictions to remain in the synthesis. In soft dialectical thinking (which is an important part of Eastern philosophy), everything is put into a context, and understood in relation to the whole, instead of being considered as an absolute truth (Nisbett, 2003).

Synthesis in knowledge creation is achieved through *dialogues*. One can pursue the essence of seemingly contradictory things and accept others' views through dialogues. These allow one to discard presumptions and find a new solution to the contradiction. Dialogues are a method of learning others' views that are different from one's own, and to accept and synthesize them. To do that, one needs to articulate one's thoughts with both self-assertion and modesty.

What matters in dialogues is the meaning they create, rather than the form of logic they take. For example, a syllogism, a simple form of logic, leads to the conclusion "Socrates dies" from the premises "Every human is mortal" and "Socrates is a human." Despite its correctness, such logic cannot add any new meaning to the original premises. However, if we pursue the essence of being human or the essence of death, we might reach a new conclusion, such as "Socrates as a thought is immortal."

At Toyota, essential dialogues are encouraged in daily operation at every level through the practice of "Ask why five times." It is not so difficult to come up with a reason why you do a certain thing. However, when you are asked again and again for the basis of the reason you came up with, it becomes inevitable to ask the essential reason behind your thought or action. Such essential dialogues led Toyota to synthesize many contradictions and go beyond compromises. For example, cost and quality, which used to be considered contradictory conditions, are no longer contradictions at Toyota. By pursuing the essence of quality and cost, Toyota created a new type of manufacturing system that made it possible to lower costs by raising quality.

At Honda, contradictions are dialectically solved through asking three levels of questions. The first level, called level A, is about specifications. For example, there are many contradictions to solve, such as fuel efficiency and power, or safety and speed, in order to decide on the specifications of an engine. Engineers at Honda try to solve such contradictions not by finding the best balance or a compromise between contradicting conditions, but by asking a question at one level higher. The second level, called level A0, is a question about concepts. Engineers go back to the concept of the engine of the car, and then decide on the specifications that are necessary to realize the concept. If the contradictions cannot be solved with the A0 questions, then the third level, called level A00, is asked. It is an existential question: "Why or for what do you do it?" The reason why Honda has to make that particular car, or why

Honda should exist to start with, is questioned at the A00 level. "What is your A00?" is the question asked in the daily operation at Honda.

Such questions seem to be philosophical and to have little to do with business. However, deciding on specifications without thinking the essence of "for what do we do it" just leads to an optimal choice among existing options. To have a new solution that goes beyond the contradictions, one needs to answer the existential question in order to pursue the essence, based on one's own value system and that of the organization.

A dialogue is also an effective method to articulate tacit knowledge into explicit knowledge (externalization), and to systemize explicit knowledge, to deepen it, and to create new knowledge (combination). It also lays a foundation to synthesize knowledge held by organization members, since existential contexts such as deep thoughts or emotions are shared by organization members through engaging in dialogue.

Practice: Synthesis of Action

Practice lays a foundation for sharing tacit knowledge (socialization) through shared experience. Practice is also an effective way to embody explicit knowledge by reconnecting it to a particular context in order to convert it into tacit knowledge (internalization).

Contradictions that cannot be solved through objective analysis alone can be solved by synthesizing subjective views and intuitions that have accumulated through practice. For that, one needs to discard preconceived notions in order to observe and experience the reality as it is. For example, when Suntory developed its new sports drink, DAKARA, the members of the development team discarded their first concept, "sports drink to give one more push for working men," which was created by logical analysis of the existing market. Instead, they went out to observe how such drinks are consumed. After thorough observation, they found that sports drinks are taken by tired people who need "healing" rather than "one more push." The finding led to a new concept, "a drink that you can depend on to protect you when things are a bit too hard" (Nonaka and Katsumi, 2004).

Concepts and hypotheses created out of such observation and experience are converted into reality through dialogue and practice. Practice here does not just mean action. Influenced by Dewey's concept of pragmatism, Schön (1983) emphasized the importance of "reflection in action," which requires one to think hard about the essential meaning of his or her action and its outcome, so as to revise his or her action. In the case of Seven-Eleven Japan, it is not enough to use sales data to check whether a hypothesis was right or wrong. Employees are encouraged to think thoroughly about why it was right or wrong, so as to formulate more effective hypotheses next time. Such reflection on actions requires objective, logical analysis as well as subjective observation and experience. It requires synthesis of the viewpoints of both insiders and outsiders. Through such dialogues and practices, subjective views are objectified to grow into knowledge.

Ba

One of the most subtle, but important, concepts in knowledge creation is *ba*. The word roughly means "place" in Japanese, and can be difficult to translate. However, many philosophers have discussed the importance of place in human cognition and action. Plato called a place for a genesis of existence *chora*. Aristotle called a place for a thing to physically exist *topos*. Heidegger called a place for human existence *Ort*. To include the concepts of such places but to tether them to knowledge creation, we introduce the concept of *ba*. The importance of *ba* to understanding the dynamics of knowledge creation justifies an extended description of the concept.

Ba is a foundation of knowledge-creating activity. It is the point where dialectical dialogues and practices take place to implement the vision and driving objectives of the firm. Building on the concept that was originally proposed by the Japanese philosopher Kitaro Nishida (1921, 1970), we define *ba* as a shared context in motion, in which knowledge is shared, created, and utilized. As Hayek (1945) states, knowledge is context-specific, and therefore needs a physical context, or situated action (Suchman, 1987), for it to be created. When individuals empathize in a shared context, their individual knowledge is shared so that new knowledge is created.

The essence of *ba* is the contexts and the meanings that are shared and created through *interactions* which occur at a specific time and in a specific space, rather than a space itself. *Ba* also means relationships of those who are at the specific time and in the specific space. *Ba* can emerge in individuals, working groups, project teams, informal circles, temporary meetings, virtual space such as e-mail groups, and the front-line contact with the customer. Participants in *ba* bring their own contexts to share, and create new meanings through interactions, since context is in interactions rather than in one's cognition (Ueno, 2000).

We define *ba* as a shared context *in motion* because it is constantly moving. Through interactions with others and the environment, the contexts of both *ba* and the participants grow. New knowledge is created through such changes in meanings and contexts.

Ba as a shared context means that subjective views are understood and shared in the relationship with others. Modern science is based on the premise that subjectivity cannot be shared with others. Subjectivity, in this view, can exist only in individuals, not collectively among them. Inheriting such a premise, some see knowledge creation as mainly an individual activity. For example, Simon claims that "All learning takes place inside individual human heads" (1991, p. 125), while Grant (1996) claims that knowledge creation is an individual activity and that the primary role of firms is to apply existing knowledge. However, as we have argued, knowledge creation needs subjectivity to be shared and to interact with others' subjectivity. *Ba* supports such sharing and synthesizing of subjectivity. To participate in *ba* means to get involved and transcend one's own limited perspective. Nishida states that the essence of *ba* is "nothingness." This does not mean that nothing exists at *ba*. It means that at *ba*, one exists in the relationship with others, instead of as an atomistic and absolute self. At *ba*, one can be open to others by losing oneself. Through such relationships, one can see oneself in relation to others, and can accept others' views and values, so that subjective views are understood and shared. *Ba* supports such sharing and synthesizing of subjectivity, which is necessary for knowledge to be created.

For knowledge to be created, *ba* must have a permeable boundary so that it can accept necessary contexts. *Ba* also needs participants with multiple viewpoints and backgrounds so that they can bring in various contexts, which are shared through dialogues and practices.

Ba does not necessarily mean one meeting or one project. In the theory of the knowledge-creating firm, a firm can be viewed as an organic configuration of multilayered *ba*. It means that we have to look into not only the formal organizational structure of the firm, but also the meanings that are created at *ba*, and the relationship among them.

A view of an organization as an organic configuration of multilayered *ba* synthesizes the views of an organization as an economic structure and as a meaning-creating process. Such a view helps to solve the paradox of explaining structures suited for both routine and nonroutine tasks (Thompson, 1967). The organizational structure of a firm defines the interactions within the firm in terms of formally defined command and information. However, such interactions are only a part of the interactions that occur within the organization to create knowledge. The meanings emerge and evolve through intersubjectivity and dialectic interactions among organization members and/or between organization members and the environment. An organization, therefore, can be seen partly as an organic network of meanings. While the hierarchies on the objective side determine the objective allocation of resources and formal power, social interaction patterns enable actors to locate and utilize knowledge beyond formally defined information-processing routes.

Since the organic configuration of the *ba* extends beyond the economic boundaries of the firm, the issue of a firm's boundary has a meaning different from the existing theories of the firm. Firm boundaries are frequently determined simply by ownership (Arrow, 1974; Williamson, 1975). However, boundary-setting becomes far more complicated when an organization is viewed as an organic configuration of multilayered *ba*. Knowledge is created through interactions, and interactions cannot be owned even by those who are engaged in them. As a consequence, the subjective "out there" may be vital for the economic performance "in here," and cannot be objectively separated when describing the existence and functioning of an organization.

Knowledge Assets

Knowledge assets arise from the knowledge-creating process through dialogues and practices at *ba*. Unlike other assets, they are intangible, are specific to the firm, and change dynamically. The essence of knowledge assets is that they must be built and used internally in order for full value to be realized, and hence they cannot be readily bought and sold (Teece, 2000).

Knowledge assets are not just the knowledge already created, such as know-how, patents, technologies, or brands, but also include the knowledge to create knowledge, such as the organizational capability to innovate. Although current views on knowledge assets tend to focus on the former because they are easier to measure and deal with, it is the latter that need more attention because they are the source of new knowledge to be created, and therefore a source of the future value of the firm.

Knowledge assets also include the social capital that is shared in the organization. The economic value of a knowledge-creating firm arises through the interactions among knowledge workers, or between knowledge workers and the environment (such as customers, suppliers, or research institutes).

One of the most important knowledge assets for a firm is a firm-specific *kata* (roughly, "pattern" or "way of doing things") of dialogues and practices. Nelson and Winter (1982) emphasize the importance of routines for the firm's evolutionary process. Here, we focus on "creative routines" of *kata*, which make knowledge creation possible by fostering creativity and preserving efficiency. *Kata* is different from a routine in that it contains a continuous self-renewal process. The three steps of *kata*—*shu* (learn), *ha* (break), and *ri* (create)—mean that one learns certain patterns first, then breaks away from them and creates new patterns once the old are totally mastered. Continuous self-renewal is achieved by incorporating a high-quality feedback function that sharpens senses and helps to identify and modify the differences between predicted outcomes and reality (Feldman, 2000). *Kata* works as an archetype with a high degree of freedom because it can be modified on the basis of feedback from the real world.

With such self-renewal functions embedded, *kata* keeps a routine from hindering creativity by preventing such tendencies as overadaptation to a past success (Levitt and March, 1988; Leonard-Barton, 1992). At the same time, it helps an organization to work efficiently by functioning as a routine. A firm with a good *kata* looks into the future but also appreciates past successes as a source of its knowledge.

Environment: Ecosystem of Knowledge

For a knowledge-creating firm, environment is not an abstract world that is a subject of analysis for modern science, but a phenomenological "life world" to live in and experience as a reality (Husserl, 1954). Hence, instead of looking at and analyzing the environment objectively (for instance, as industry structure), managers are thrown into strategic decision-making as a way of life. For example, employees of Seven-Eleven Japan are encouraged to think *as* customers instead of think *for* them. Preconceived notions would prevent them from seeing customers as they are, if they view customers as a subject to analyze. The phenomenological method of "seeing the environment as it is" does not mean accepting it unconditionally. By pursuing the essence of it through dialogues and practices, the environment is interpreted, and knowledge is created out of such interpretations.

The ecosystem of knowledge consists of multilayered *ba*, which exists across organizational boundaries and is continuously evolving. Firms create knowledge by synthesizing their own knowledge and the knowledge embedded in outside players such as customers, suppliers, competitors, or universities. Through interactions with the ecosystem, a firm creates knowledge, and that knowledge changes the ecosystem. The organization and environment should thus be understood to evolve together rather than as separate entities. The constant accumulation and processing of knowledge helps firms to redefine their visions, dialogues, and practices, which in turn impact the environment through new or improved services or products.

Such a dynamic relationship is difficult to grasp with the traditional view of the market and organizations embedded in organizational economics. The existence of firms in the ecosystem of knowledge can no longer be defined by ownership. Boundary-setting based on transaction costs is insufficient to understand and manage the competitive advantage based on knowledge. A knowledge-creating firm needs to manage a multilayered *ba*, which stretches beyond organizational boundaries. At the same time, the firm needs to protect its knowledge assets as sources of competitive advantage. Viewed in this context, the protection of knowledge assets is a complex task.

Knowledge Leadership

What drives a firm as an entity to create knowledge continuously? Schumpeter argued that innovations are brought about by entrepreneurial leaders. However, he considered leadership an activity of elites, and therefore entrepreneurship was viewed as a matter of an individual's disposition (Peukert, 2003).

However, leadership in the knowledge-creating firm is based on more flexible distributed leadership, rather than on leadership as a fixed control mechanism. Since knowledge is created through dynamic interaction, leadership in a knowledge-creating firm requires active commitment from all members of the organization, not just a few elite members. In such firms, the planning and implementation of strategy are integrated instead of being separated in strategic planning departments, as suggested by existing theories of strategy and organization. Dynamic capability requires the entrepreneurship of a maestro, who orchestrates the organizational members (Teece, 2003). For such leadership to be effective, the discipline must be shared by the members. This offers a dynamic chain reaction between the development of strategy and its application.

However, it does not mean that everyone starts creating knowledge immediately. For knowledge leadership to work, the mechanism of middle-up-down is key. In such a process, middle managers break down the vision or driving objective into concrete concepts or plans, build *ba*, and lead dialogues and practices. They create tipping points in small-world networks (Gladwell, 2000; Watts, 2003).

Leadership is related to power. However, power here does not necessarily mean formal power, which stems from hierarchical position. Knowledge can be a source of power, and therefore can exist outside the hierarchy of the organization. Knowledge as a source of power also means that it is fragile and needs nurturing. In addition, the human attractiveness of a leader, which depends on his or her values and views of the world, often affects the efficiency and effectiveness of the knowledge-creating process more than what kind of legitimate power she or he exercises. Research indicates that effective leaders are capable of synthesizing contradictions through understanding that contradictory ideas are a part of life. They energize the emotional and spiritual resources of the organization.

Leadership plays various roles in the knowledge-creating process, such as providing vision; developing and promoting the sharing of knowledge assets; creating, energizing, and connecting *ba*; and enabling and promoting the continuous spiral of knowledge creation. Knowledge vision determining the collective ideal mission and domain is rooted in the essential question "For what do we exist?" Knowledge visions materialize as a set of shared beliefs about how to act and interact to attain some determined idealized future state, giving the firm a focus on the knowledge to be created that goes beyond the existing boundaries of the products, the organizational structure, and the markets. The possibilities of attaining a future mode of organizational practice are manifested at each organizational level by answering the question "What can we do?" (Heidegger, 1962). Through personal aspirations and collective sense-making, leaders develop a mental image of a possible and desirable future state of the organization in order to choose a direction.

It is not enough for a leader to set a vision and a driving objective to foster the organizational knowledge-creating process. If it remains just as a written slogan, such a vision or driving objective does not work. Both of them have to be accepted and shared by organization members. For that, leaders have to facilitate constant dialogues and practices to "evangelize" the knowledge vision and driving objectives throughout the organization.

It is essential that leaders also build, maintain, and connect *ba*. *Ba* can be built intentionally or created spontaneously. Leaders can facilitate *ba* by providing physical space such as meeting rooms, cyberspace such as a computer network, or mental space such as common goals, and promote interactions among participants in such a space. Forming a task force is a typical example of the intentional building of *ba*. To build *ba*, leaders have to choose the right mix of people to participate. It is also important for managers to find and utilize spontaneously formed *ba*. Hence, leaders have to read the situation in terms of how members of the organization are interacting with each other and with outside environments in order to quickly capture the naturally emerging *ba*, as well as to form *ba* effectively.

However, building and finding *ba* is an insufficient basis for a firm to manage the dynamic knowledge-creating process. *Ba* should be "energized" to give energy and quality to the SECI process. For that, leaders have to supply necessary conditions such as autonomy, creative chaos, redundancy, requisite variety, love, care, trust, safety, and commitment.

Further, various *ba* are connected with each other to form a greater *ba*. For that, leaders have to facilitate the interactions among *ba*, and among the participants, based on the knowledge vision. In many cases, the relationships among *ba* are not predetermined. Which *ba* should be connected in which way is often unclear. Therefore, leaders have to read the situation to connect various *ba* as the relationships among them unfold.

Ba needs a definite boundary so that a meaningful shared context can emerge. Therefore, leaders should protect *ba* from outside contexts so that it can develop its own context, especially when *ba* is trying to create the kind of knowledge that is not part of the organization's current norm. At the same time, the boundary of *ba* should be open so that it can be connected with other *ba*. It is often difficult for participants to see and accept the need to bring in contexts different from the one shared in *ba*. It is an important task for a leader who is outside *ba* to find and build the connection among various *ba*. Legitimate power can be effectively used to protect the boundary (cocooning), yet keep the boundary open.

Conclusion

The theory of the knowledge-creating firm views a firm as an entity to actively create knowledge by synthesizing contradictions. Unlike other theories of the firm, our theory of the knowledge-creating firm explains the differences among firms not as a result of market failure but as a result of goals and strategy.

- We argue that building the theory of the knowledge-creating firm needs an epistemological and ontological discussion, instead of relying on an analytical approach. Instead of treating knowledge as objective and static "truth," this chapter argues that knowledge is created through the dynamic interaction between subjectivity and objectivity. Knowledge emerges through the subjectivity of context-embedded actors, and is objectified through the social process of knowledge validation. Instead of treating issues such as contexts, values, ideals, and power as "noise" to cloud the facts, we contend that we cannot avoid dealing with such subjectivity if we want to capture the dynamic aspect of the knowledge-creating process. Thinking is not detached reflection, but is a part of humans' view of the world. And knowledge is not just about thinking. It is created through the synthesis of thinking and the interaction of individuals within and beyond the organizational boundaries. The knowledge so created forms a new praxis for interaction, and it shapes the base for new existence through the knowledge creation spiral.

- We propose a framework to capture such a dynamic process of knowledge creation, with the concepts of knowledge vision, driving objectives, dialogues, practices, *ba*, knowledge assets, and environment to deal with the issues of contexts, values, ideals, and power. Since knowledge emerges out of subjective views of the world, it probably cannot be reached by the one and only absolute "truth." The knowledge-creating process is idealistic, since knowledge is created through social justification, which relentlessly pursues a truth that may never be reached. We can say that the theory of knowledge creation is based on an idealistic pragmatism which synthesizes the rational pursuit of appropriate ends, the appropriateness of which is determined by ideals (Rescher, 1987).

- We recognize that this chapter is weighted toward theory that may seem unimportant to managerial readers. But we believe that an understanding of the underlying concepts will give managers a better grasp of the powerful tool of knowledge creation in their organizations. Thus, we repeat our suggestion that readers return to this chapter when they have read later chapters, and reread it. It should be clearer then how it fits into the book's subject.

Acknowledgment

This chapter is adapted from the article "The Theory of the Knowledge-creating Firm: Subjectivity, Objectivity, and Synthesis," by the present authors, that appeared in *Industrial and Corporate Change* 14 (2005): 419–436.

References

Arrow, K. J. (1974). *The Limits of Organization*. New York: Norton.

Chandler, A. D., Jr. (1977). *The Visible Hand: The Managerial Revolution in American Business*. Cambridge, Mass.: Belknap Press of Harvard University Press.

Collins, J. C. (2001). *Good to Great: Why Some Companies Make the Leap...and Others Don't*. New York: HarperBusiness.

Drucker, P. F. (1993). *Post-Capitalist Society*. London: Butterworth Heinemann.

Feldman, M. (2000). "Organizational Routines as a Source of Continuous Change." *Organizational Science* 11(6): 611–629.

Flyvbjerg, B. (2001). *Making Social Science Matter: Why Social Science Fails and How It Can Succeed Again*. Translated by Steven Sampson. Cambridge: Cambridge University Press.

Gladwell, M. M. (2000). *The Tipping Point: How Little Things Can Make a Big Difference*. Boston: Little, Brown.

Grant, R. M. (1996). "Toward a Knowledge-based Theory of the Firm." *Strategic Management Journal* 17 (Winter Special): 109–122.

Hayek, F. A. (1945). "The Use of Knowledge in Society." *American Economic Review* 35, 519–530.

Heidegger, M. (1927/1962). *Being and Time*. Translated by J. Macquarrie and E. Robinson. Oxford: Blackwell.

Husserl, E. (1954/1970). *The Crisis of European Sciences and Transcendental Phenomenology*. Translated by D. Carr. Evanston, Ill.: Northwestern University Press.

Leonard-Barton, D. (1992). "Core Capabilities and Core Rigidities: A Paradox in Managing New Product Development." *Strategic Management Journal* 13(5): 363–380.

Levitt, B., and March, J. G. (1988). "Organizational Learning." *Annual Review of Sociology* 14: 319–340.

Maister, D. H. (2000). *True Professionalism: The Courage to Care About Your People, Your Clients, and Your Career*. Carmichael, Calif.: Touchstone Books.

Merleau-Ponty, M. (1962). *Phenomenology of Perception*. Translated by C. Smith. London: Routledge.

Mogi, K. (2003). *Ishiki towa Nanika—Watashi wo Keiseisuru Nou* (What Is Consciousness: The Brain That Forms Me). Tokyo: Chikuma Shobou.

Nelson, R. (1991). "Why Do Firms Differ, and How Does It Matter?" *Strategic Management Journal* 12: 61–74.

Nelson, R., and Winter, S. (1982). *An Evolutionary Theory of Economic Change*. Cambridge, Mass.: Belknap Press of Harvard University Press.

Nisbett, R. E. (2003). *The Geography of Thought: How Asians and Westerners Think Differently...and Why*. New York: Free Press.

Nishida, K. (1921/1990). *An Inquiry into the Good*. Translated by M. Abe and C. Ives. New Haven, Conn.: Yale University Press.

———. (1970). *Fundamental Problems of Philosophy: The World of Action and the Dialectical World*. Tokyo: Sophia University Press.

Nonaka, I. (1991). "The Knowledge-Creating Company." *Harvard Business Review,* November–December, 96–104.

———. (1994). "A Dynamic Theory of Organizational Knowledge Creation." *Organizational Science* 5(1): 14–37.

Nonaka, I., and Katsumi, A. (2004). *Innovation no Honshitsu* (The Essence of Innovation). Tokyo: Nikkei.

Nonaka, I., Sasaki, K., and Senoo, D. (2004), "Jizokuteki Seichou Kigyou no Sikou, Koudou Youshiki: Risouteki Pragmatism no Tankyuu" (The Thinking and Action Pattern of Sustainable Growth Firms: Pursuing Idealistic Pragmatism). *Think!,* Winter, pp. 92–101.

Nonaka, I., and Takeuchi, H. (1995). *The Knowledge-Creating Company: How Japanese Companies Create the Dynamics of Innovation.* New York: Oxford University Press.

Nonaka, I., and Toyama, R. (2002). "Firm as a Dialectic Being: Toward the Dynamic Theory of the Firm." *Industrial and Corporate Change* 11: 995–1109.

———. (2003). "The Knowledge-Creating Theory Revisited: Knowledge Creation as a Synthesizing Process." *Knowledge Management Research & Practice* 1(1): 2–10.

Nonaka, I., Toyama, R., and Konno, N. (2000). "SECI, Ba and Leadership: A Unified Model of Dynamic Knowledge Creation." *Long Range Planning* 33: 1–31.

Peukert, H. (2003). "The Missing Chapter in Schumpeter's *The Theory of Economic Development.*" In J. Backhaus, ed., *Joseph Alois Schumpeter: Entrepreneurship, Style, and Vision,* pp. 221–231. Boston: Kluwer Academic.

Rescher, N. (1987). *Ethical Idealism: An Inquiry into the Nature and Function of Ideals.* London: University of California Press.

Rescher, N. (2003). *Rationality in Pragmatic Perspective.* Lewiston, N.Y.: Edwin Mellen Press.

Rorty, R. (1979). *Philosophy and the Mirror of Nature.* Princeton, N.J.: Princeton University Press.

Schön, D. A. (1983). *The Reflective Practitioner: How Professionals Think in Action.* New York: Basic Books.

Simon, H. A. (1945). *Administrative Behavior.* New York: Macmillan.

———. (1991). "Bounded Rationality and Organizational Learning." *Organization Science* 2: 125–134.

Suchman, L. A. (1987). *Plans and Situated Actions: The Problem of Human–Machine Communication.* New York: Cambridge University Press.

Teece, D. J. (2000). *Managing Intellectual Capital.* New York: Oxford University Press.

———. (2003). "Explicating Dynamic Capabilities: Asset Selection, Coordination, and Entrepreneurship in Strategic Management Theory." Working paper.

Thompson, J. D. (1967). *Organizations in Action.* New York: McGraw-Hill.

Ueno, N. (2000). *Interaction.* Tokyo: Daishukan Shoin.

Watts, D. J. (2003). *Six Degrees: The Science of a Connected Age.* New York: Norton.

Williamson, O. E. (1975). *Markets and Hierarchies.* New York: Free Press.

2

Knowledge in Organizational Settings

How Organizations Generate, Disseminate, and
Use Knowledge for Their Competitive Advantage

LAURENCE PRUSAK AND LEIGH WEISS

The early years of the knowledge management field spanned the period of approximately 1992 through 1998. During this time, an increasing number of organizations began to recognize knowledge (as opposed to information and data) as a crucial source of competitive advantage and as a factor that somehow could be managed. As knowledge became more the locus of employees' work, questions were raised about how it could be managed more effectively for organizational gain, and knowledge became more and more the actual output of the organization. We will look first at those factors which led knowledge management to gain legitimization, and then turn to the early trends and lessons from this first phase.

The timing was ripe for knowledge management to gain attention in the early 1990s. Knowledge-oriented technologies such as Lotus Notes, the World Wide Web, and a variety of vendor-introduced collaboration tools were catching on. These technologies had capabilities beyond earlier ones, which were better suited to managing data in structured formats. In addition, the forces of economic globalization, which spread employees and products around the world, required a means to spread knowledge globally.

Legitimization

Knowledge management gained credence early on through the legitimization that comes from publications by thought leaders and through focusing on those practitioners who experimented with knowledge management pilots and programs. In 1990 Tom Davenport and Larry Prusak had launched Ernst & Young's Center for Business Innovation. By 1994 they offered the first public conference on knowledge management, at a time when few people knew what the term meant. By 2000, there were more than fifty knowledge management conferences offered globally in that one year alone. In the intervening years, three groups gave the subject its early credentials through case studies, books, articles, and conferences: business practitioners and journalists, academics, and other institutions such as the American Productivity and Quality Center and the Conference Board.

Publishing

Tom Peters's *Liberation Management* (1992) introduced the world to a group of people at McKinsey, especially Brook Manville, who were creating a knowledge management capability. Tom Stewart introduced *Fortune* magazine readers to knowledge management and intellectual capital in a 1991 article. Stewart (1991) revealed projects under way among knowledge management practitioners, and later wrote two books on the subject (1997 and 2001). These practitioners were partly responsible for carrying the movement forward.

Academics also played an important role in making the subject grow. Japanese professors Ikujiro Nonaka and Hirotaka Takeuchi wrote about the use of knowledge by Asian companies in their well-known 1995 book, *The Knowledge-Creating Company*. Dorothy Leonard-Barton, a professor at Harvard Business School, wrote on related subjects from a U.S. perspective in her 1995 book, *Wellsprings of Knowledge*. Her description of Chaparral Steel was one of the earliest case studies showing how an entire company reinvented itself around knowledge. In 1998, Tom Davenport and Larry Prusak published *Working Knowledge*, sharing lessons from knowledge management practices in more than fifty firms. By the end of the 1990s, articles on knowledge management were proliferating in *Harvard Business Review*, *Sloan Management Review*, and *California Management Review*, as well as in more academic journals. The subject was also taught in undergraduate, MBA, and executive education courses. There are even several Ph.D. programs in this area.

Several other institutions were legitimizing forces behind knowledge management. The American Productivity and Quality Center (APQC), led by Carla O'Dell, established multicompany research projects, annual conferences, and publishing projects that raised awareness, especially on the topic of best practices. The Conference Board conducted knowledge management studies and organized an annual conference that is still held.

Practitioner Programs

Many of the publications and conference proceedings were based on actual examples of knowledge management initiatives in organizations. They described how knowledge management interventions led to successful outcomes (though the outcomes were by no means always successful, and our own estimation is that perhaps as many as half of the knowledge management projects failed in some respect or did not achiever their stated goals). Among these efforts were Steve Denning's successes at the World Bank. Denning's approach was based on telling stories about how knowledge projects actually worked and succeeded, rather than relying solely on analytics. His approach is documented in *The Springboard* (2000).

Strategy, Content, and Culture

Several themes characterize organizations' early knowledge management initiatives. They both shed light on where the field has been and establish a foundation for where the greatest future opportunities lie. We will briefly examine the link between knowledge and strategy, content, and organizational culture.

Strategy

Many of the organizations that undertook knowledge management did so in a vacuum, often independent of the company's overarching strategic objectives. While there was growing recognition that knowledge was a source of competitive advantage, knowledge management programs typically were not closely linked to strategy. Often the people who held the newly created chief knowledge officer (CKO) role were not connected to individuals with responsibility for planning and the company's strategic vision. Instead, CKOs oversaw knowledge initiatives that were designed to achieve often fuzzy objectives, such as improving knowledge-sharing or making knowledge more accessible. Many of these initiatives were not primarily about knowledge at all, but were about technology and building systems.

Few recognized that these systems might be effective pipelines, but did not guarantee that knowledge would be created, codified, or shared. The failures of many early efforts highlighted the complexity of knowledge management and the need to go beyond technological systems. As many discovered, and as Wanda Orlikowski's research showed, making Lotus Notes available did little to change a knowledge-hoarding culture into a knowledge-sharing one.

In general, efforts to better manage knowledge followed an unguided approach and a belief that more knowledge-sharing, facilitated by technology, would be better. Sometimes these efforts worked, but more often they were ineffective. Repositories were created that had either too little content or too much content of questionable quality and relevance. A main reason for these shortcomings was that few people asked *what* knowledge was most important to the organization's or division's or unit's strategy, and thus should be codified and shared, and who should be sharing with whom. Efforts that were effective tended to focus more on improving operational process efficiency by attempting to better codify and disseminate practices across multiple locations.

As companies tried to learn how to implement knowledge management initiatives, they often lifted an initiative lock, stock, and barrel from another organization into their own. In many ways first-generation knowledge management was characterized by a "one size fits all" approach that ignored context and placed scant emphasis on the crucial connection between knowledge, and strategy and culture. Not surprisingly, many efforts did not realize the initial hopes of how better knowledge management could help companies gain competitive advantages.

Content

The focus of many early knowledge management initiatives was on documents and codified knowledge. Many companies began technology initiatives to "capture" huge amounts of information on what the company knew. This resulted in giant repositories that resembled overgrown gardens in desperate need of weeding and pruning. Technology was a major enabler of documentation and even replaced the documents themselves as the locus of attention. The content got lost in the shuffle because all content was treated as equal while companies counted the number of documents in their technology systems rather than focusing on which knowledge was most valuable and should be documented.

One of the defining characteristics of first-generation documentation efforts was that people were not thinking about documents in context. In many instances, companies contributed thousands and thousands of PowerPoint decks, process reports, and project summaries to repositories. For many users, however, these documents lacked the context that would make them valuable. Additionally, little attention was paid to the relationship among documents, so knowledge seekers had no idea how a particular document fit into a larger body of experience.

A related shortcoming of the focus on documentation was that the documents typically reflected the thinking of one individual at one time and in one situation. Anyone who has recently worked in organizations knows that much of the valuable work is accomplished by teams or groups. Often the friction and energy between people in brainstorming or problem-solving discussions leads to the creation of new knowledge in the group. Yet there was little recognition that knowledge resided in these teams or groups, and that it would be important to find ways to reflect, store, and share group knowledge. Incentives, too, were mostly oriented toward individuals.

One final characteristic of the content developed and deployed was that it was typically presented in lists. There were lists of documents in the form of search results, lists of experts from nascent "Yellow Pages" that attempted to track expertise, and lists of knowledge resources for someone new to a company. An important shortcoming of the list format is that it fails to show the dynamic and complex web of relationships between different knowledge sources or to make rich sense of them. Lists, in short, are very difficult to navigate. This constraint foreshadows an interesting development, discussed in the next section, about new ways of making knowledge visible to enable better decision-making.

Culture

Surprisingly, many accounts of first-generation knowledge management initiatives do not even mention incentives as an important aspect of organizational culture. There was an implicit assumption that knowledge would be codified and shared if the right mechanisms were put in place. Many organizations relied on rhetoric to encourage knowledge-sharing. Alternatively, they instituted "empty," often ridiculous incentives, such as giving Dove ice cream bars to people who downloaded documents from databases.

Some organizations recognized that creating a knowledge-sharing culture required more than building a sophisticated technology system or handing out meaningless rewards. Those which did, such as some of the professional service firms—especially management consulting companies and leading investment banks—built the behaviors they wanted to encourage into performance review, advancement, and remuneration processes. They created incentives that really did matter to employees, since knowledge was so obviously critical to their performance.

Consistent with the emphasis on documents and technology, little emphasis was placed on the social aspects of the culture, such as trust and relational capital, that we now know have a considerable effect on knowledge management. People share knowledge and go out of their way for others with whom they share common ground. They are helpful when the culture rewards being recognized as knowledgeable by others, not when the culture reinforces a "knowledge is power" or knowledge-hoarding attitude.

Though knowledge management grew considerably during this first phase, it faced a number of challenges. One was that many people—especially many IT vendors and some consultants—conflated the use of knowledge-related technologies with successful knowledge management initiatives. Another problem was scope "creep." Knowledge management began to encompass an increasingly broad set of issues from best practices to organizational learning, document management, technology transfer, talent management, and other tangentially related ideas. The challenge going forward is to build on the early successes while identifying ways to address the shortcomings.

Knowledge Management from a Knowledge Worker's Perspective

We believe that a discussion about knowledge in organizations would be incomplete without commenting on the subject from a knowledge worker's perspective, though this lens is infrequently used. More often, knowledge management is approached from an organizational level of analysis, often without regard for the end user. Early knowledge management technology systems were developed by engineers, IT designers, and librarians with little understanding of how people would actually use these systems.

Looking at emerging trends from a knowledge worker's perspective, we see two main themes. First, greater emphasis on the importance of social networks, new search technologies, and improved approaches to expertise location are making it easier for knowledge workers to find what and whom they need and to establish relationships. Second, increased attention to the importance of adding context to content and the role of group (as opposed to individual) knowledge are making it easier for knowledge workers to apply knowledge more effectively. These forces are leading to greater knowledge worker productivity and better outcomes for organizations.

Finding Experts and Documents and Building Relationships

As people become more aware of the value of knowledge for organizations and for themselves, more emphasis is being placed on networking and reciprocity. The Web has refocused attention on the value of social networks, and *Business 2.0* named social networking "technology of the year" in 2003. Recent research suggests that social networks influence knowledge workers' success and productivity. Rob Cross (Cross, Davenport, and Cantrell, 2003), a faculty member at the University of Virginia, has done research showing that higher performers in organizations have larger social networks. These individuals employ three tactics that make them successful and help them build mutually beneficial connections over time: establishing personal connections that go beyond business relationships, responding to people quickly and keeping commitments, and giving in order to receive. Ron Burt (1992), a well-known network researcher, has shown how managers create and use more ideas when their networks are more dense. Findings by Marshall van Alstyne (Van

Alstyne and Bulkley, 2004), a professor at the University of Michigan, in his research on executive recruiting firms show that recruiters who have larger social networks and more e-mail traffic are more successful.

Technology improvements, especially search capabilities, make it easier for employees to quickly determine relevance and quality when searching for knowledge that could help them in their jobs. Amazon.com, the number-one online retailer of books, DVDs and videos, is an excellent example of how effective these capabilities can be. It provides multiple ways for shoppers to search for what they want. Search criteria include subject, publication date, and format (e.g., hardcover, paperback, audiotape, large print). Shoppers can also search based on Amazon user ratings or determine whether the book is a best-seller.

Imagine if corporate search tools were as highly functional. More often, search results deliver bland lists of documents requiring knowledge workers to scan long lists or open multiple documents to determine which ones are most relevant for their purposes. But this need not be the case. Provision of tools and categorizations to help assess relevance and quality can save users significant time evaluating knowledge and finding what and whom they need, as Michael Idinopolus and Lee Kempler describe in the *McKinsey Quarterly* (2003).

Applying Knowledge

In addition to making it easier for people to network and build relationships, and find documents and experts, organizations are becoming increasingly focused on making it easier for knowledge workers to apply what they know. One general approach is to add context to content. The unhappy reality is that in most organizations, documents are presented in an isolated fashion. There is not sufficient context to enable knowledge workers to make connections between related documents, thereby identifying other material that might be useful or make the document itself meaningful. In this second instance, knowledge workers are required to make their own judgments and assessments about the author's approach, thinking, and key take-aways.

A relatively simple way organizations are addressing this issue, and overcoming a failing of early knowledge management efforts, is through the use of video, audio, and additional explanatory text. Some companies add author notes to Power Point presentations so people who use the material understand more about what the author might have shared in a verbal presentation—such as approaches that did not work or why a particular methodology for data collection was used. Organizations such as the World Bank and others are using video to debrief project leaders, allowing others to see and hear rich details about a project.

The ever-increasing focus on groups and practices is another way organizations are making it easier for knowledge workers to apply what they know. Microsoft's new Share Point software, which is all about making work groups, not individuals, more productive, is in no small way illustrative of this theme. The role of context is important here, as well, because groups that work together often develop shared norms, approaches, and ways of understanding and making sense of their activities, whether the group is a consulting team solving a client's problem or scientists working on the latest drug discovery project. This shared sense of context makes it easier for people to apply what they have learned and share new insights with the group.

As organizations pay more attention to knowledge workers' productivity and as new technologies, processes, and business models light the way to productivity increases, we are likely to see knowledge management looked at more often from an individual knowledge worker's point of view.

Strategic Knowledge Management from an Organizational Perspective

Where is knowledge management headed, from an organization's perspective? It is, of course, difficult to generalize about such a large movement that involves many activities ranging from efficiency tools to knowledge strategies to structures that would make innovation more likely. However, we feel that the activities currently being undertaken can, by and large, be grouped into two buckets—lowering the transaction costs associated with creating, sharing, and applying knowledge, and developing improved strategies to support these activities.

Lowering Knowledge Transaction Costs

The subject of transaction costs has been written about at length by economists such as Ronald Coase, Oliver Williamson, and others, but little attention has been paid to knowledge transaction costs in particular. These knowledge transaction costs might include searching for experts or codified knowledge, qualifying and synthesizing knowledge, and adapting it for work. Organizations can increase knowledge workers' productivity by lowering these specific knowledge transaction costs as well as lowering their costs altogether. A recent research report by IDC estimated that an organization employing one thousand knowledge workers might easily waste over $6 million per year because users fail to find existing knowledge they need, waste time searching for nonexistent knowledge, and re-create knowledge that is available but could not be located. One effect of the growth in knowledge management software has been the proliferation of content repositories across organizations. In the first decade of the twenty-first century, 70 percent of large organizations with more than ten thousand employees have more than one hundred separate content repositories, making it nearly impossible for employees to easily find the knowledge they need.

Clearly, reducing the "drags" on knowledge can significantly help an organization. The sources of these "drags" or transaction costs include

- Physical constraints: lack of proximity, making it difficult to find or talk to the right people
- Technical constraints: lack of effective tools for searching or collaborating, thus slowing a transaction
- Social/political constraints: a rigid hierarchy or ineffective incentives lead to difficulty accessing the right people or documents or getting people to help
- Psychological/situational constraints: difficulty translating knowledge from one context to another or absorbing the knowledge
- Trust-based constraints: lack of a trust-based culture, which slows transactions.

Organizations are taking steps to mitigate as many of these constraints as efficiently as they can. . There are often spillover effects, such as when actions to improve physical proximity also affect trust. There is growing evidence that organizations are taking the issue of physical proximity to heart. Novartis, for example, is considering building a knowledge campus, which would encourage workers to share knowledge either intentionally or serendipitously. Another example of a space designed to facilitate knowledge creation and sharing is the new office for Fuji Xerox in Tokyo. Its physical spaces are all designed to overcome or reduce physical constraints on knowledge transactions.

We will now turn to social and political transaction costs. This type of drag is often found in an organization where "knowledge is power" is the dominant philosophy. Often, the organizational incentives are misaligned with the goals of more effective knowledge-sharing. Organizations are more focused on managing knowledge than on managing knowledgeable employees. Some organizations, especially the leading investment banks and management consulting firms, build knowledge creation and knowledge-sharing into performance reviews, compensation decisions, and promotion criteria.

With the growing recognition that knowledge resides in groups as much as in individuals, some organizations are beginning to shift incentives from individuals to groups or teams. IBM changed incentives for knowledge creation and sharing in this way. One of the authors witnessed a change in behavior. When Lou Gerstner took over as CEO of IBM, he tied significant bonuses to division and group, as well as individual, performance. Knowledge-sharing was explicitly acknowledged as a key behavior for managers to evaluate. Thus, some organizations are addressing the need for appropriate incentives, an issue that was largely overlooked in first-generation knowledge management.

Lack of trust can significantly slow knowledge transactions. It can lead to added transaction costs linked to verifying knowledge, searching out additional knowledge if an employee feels he or she has not been given the full "scoop," and, as important, can be a morale breaker. Creating a trust-based organization is not done overnight, but several of the issues we have discussed can help make headway. Recognizing that knowledge resides in groups and encouraging collaboration where appropriate can help. Some organizations, such as UPS, Mars Candy, and SAS, are placing more emphasis on social capital and supporting relevant social networks.

Improving Connections Between Strategy and Knowledge Management

In knowledge management's early days, knowledge management activities were only loosely connected—if they were connected at all—to an organization's overall strategic objectives. More often, knowledge management was an end in itself and was approached with the goal of sharing more knowledge among more people. Today, organizations are more often designing knowledge strategies to support overarching priorities. For instance, pharmaceutical companies are focused on enabling faster and more comprehensive access to the vast array of inputs important to the drug development process as they try to increase speed to market and reduce research and development costs. Some global professional services firms are recognizing the need to better integrate industry, functional, and geographic experience to serve increasingly specialized client needs. As organizations focus more on how knowledge management activities can support their strategies, they are learning from the successes and failures of other organizations, and have moved beyond the "one size fits all" approach that characterized the early years of the field. A second strategic theme revolves around the need organizations have not only to share knowledge internally but also to share knowledge with partner organizations. For many years, the ease of doing this has been technologically constrained by systems that make it difficult for an external partner to access databases of organizations. While these types of restrictions prevent unauthorized access, they can hinder collaboration when it is legitimate and desired. The life sciences industry is one good example because of the need for pharmaceutical companies to work with many partners at different research and commercial stages. Partner organizations likely include universities, where related research is being undertaken, and hospitals, where patient trials

are conducted. The ability to easily and effectively collaborate with partner organizations is clearly critical to an organization's competitive advantage.

As we look to how organizations are managing knowledge to improve their
competitive position, we believe we will see continuing and novel efforts to
identify and reduce knowledge transaction costs and tighten the link between
strategic decisions and knowledge management activities.

The Future

Management ideas reach a point in their trajectories where typically one of
three outcomes occurs. The ideas become embedded in practice. They go away
or fail to gain traction. Or they hobble along in a marginal way.

The quality movement is a good example of the first outcome, where we see
quality processes, such as quality assurance departments, embedded in practice. There is already some evidence that this is occurring in knowledge management, where "smart systems" assemble collective knowledge and make
it available to employees—for example, the databases used by call center
agents and claims processing techniques used by insurance companies.
However, it is also possible that knowledge management as we currently
understand it will fade in influence, perhaps because of missed chances or,
more likely, because organizations have already spent too much on technology
systems, believing those were the solutions to their knowledge challenges.

For the long term, we believe a focus on knowledge and learning is the
most essential issue for any organization. We may see the merging of learning, which has traditionally been HR-based, and knowledge management,
which has been rooted more in IT and strategy. Certainly many others assert
that knowledge and learning are mainstays of organizational performance.
Among the most recent to advocate this view is a Columbia University economics professor, Joseph Stiglitz. He has argued that the appropriation of
global ideas and the ability to search, filter, and socialize knowledge are the
most important tasks for global organizations today. Take it from a Nobel
Prize winner: this issue is here to stay.

References

Burt, R. S. (1992). *Structural Holes: The Social Structure of Competition*. Cambridge,
    Mass.: Harvard University Press.
Cohen, D., and Prusak, L. (2001). *In Good Company: How Social Capital Makes
    Organizations Work*. Boston: Harvard Business School Press.
Cross, R., Davenport, T., and Cantrell, S. (2003). "The Social Side of Perfor-
    mance." *Sloan Management Review* 44: 20–23.

Davenport, T., and Prusak, L. (1998). *Working Knowledge: How Organizations Manage What They Know.* Boston: Harvard Business School Press.

Davenport, T., and Prusak, L. (2003). *What's the Big Idea? Creating and Capitalizing on the Best Management Thinking.* Boston: Harvard Business School Press.

Denning, S. (2000). *The Springboard: How Storytelling Ignites Action in Knowledge-Era Organizations.* New York: Butterworth Heinemann.

Dixon, N. (2000). *Common Knowledge: How Companies Thrive by Sharing What They Know.* Boston: Harvard Business School Press.

Drucker, P. (1995). *Managing in a Time of Great Change.* New York: Truman Talley Books/Plume.

Foote, N., Matson, E., Weiss, L., and Wenger, E. (2002). "Leveraging Group Knowledge for High Performance Decision Making." *Organizational Dynamics.*

Indinopolus, M. and Kempler, L. (2003). "Do You Know Who Your Experts Are?" *McKinsey Quarterly,* No. 4, pp. 60–69.

Leonard-Barton, D. (1995). *Wellsprings of Knowledge: Building and Sustaining the Sources of Innovation.* Boston: Harvard Business School Press.

Nonaka, I., and Takeuchi, H. (1995). *The Knowledge-Creating Company: How Japanese Companies Create the Dynamics of Innovation.* New York: Oxford University Press.

Peters, T. (1992). *Liberation Management: Necessary Disorganization for the Nanosecond Nineties.* New York: Ballantine Books.

Polanyi, M. (1967). *The Tacit Dimension.* London: Routledge and Kegan Paul.

Polanyi, M. (1969). *Knowing and Being.* Chicago: University of Chicago Press.

Prusak, L. (2001). "Where Did Knowledge Management Come From?" *IBM Systems Journal* 40, (4): 1002–1007.

Stewart, T. A. (1991). "Brainpower: How Intellectual Capital is Becoming America's Most Important Asset." *Fortune,* June 3, 1991.

Stewart, T. A. (1997). *Intellectual Capital: The New Wealth of Organizations.* New York: Doubleday.

Stewart, T. A. (2001). *The Wealth of Knowledge: Intellectual Capital and the 21st Century Organization.* New York: Doubleday.

Van Alstyne, M., and Bulkley, N. (2004). "Why Information Should Influence Productivity." In M. Castells, ed., *The Network Society: A Cross-Cultural Perspective.* Edward Elgar.

3

Knowledge Creation and Transfer

From Teams to the Whole Organization

BETTINA BÜCHEL

Knowledge creation is at the heart of innovation and developing a competitive advantage, and it is a key concern for managers in the business world. Yet, the creation and transfer of knowledge are managerial tasks that remain challenging. The difficulties of managing these processes are due to the tacit nature of knowledge and the inability to understand knowledge because it is frequently tied to a particular context. These factors are especially pronounced when knowledge has to move beyond the boundaries of clearly identified units or functions. Nevertheless, many firms have been able to solve these problems, and it is now possible to learn from teams that have successfully created and transferred knowledge within an organization.

The Challenge of Knowledge Creation and Transfer Within New Product Development Teams

One organizational area where the problematic nature of knowledge creation and transfer is particularly evident is in new product development, since knowledge is developed within the team and has to move across the team to multiple functions in order for new products to be brought to market. Both the creation and the transfer of knowledge are key to a company's success, especially in light of the increasing pressure to deliver growth expectations. Achieving the projected growth rate requires the members of the often multifunctional teams to become exceptional knowledge managers. The team's mandate is to combine facts and ideas to create the product and organizational capabilities that the team then needs to act on. The team not only has to create new knowledge but also to transfer that new knowledge to others—in the organization or outside—for execution. Knowledge creation and transfer are therefore the core responsibilities of product development teams. To understand how successful teams transfer knowledge, it is important to examine the process in more detail.

New product development includes all activities needed to conceive, design, produce, and deliver a product to the market, including solving a steady stream of problems. This requires, on the one hand, generating ideas and, on the other hand, collectively implementing the ideas generated. Consequently, new product development teams need to overcome the apparent contradiction between creative and collective action.

New product development efforts require structures and processes that facilitate both creative action and collective action. To help foster creative action, organizations frequently implement principles such as decentralized decision-making and sharing information across hierarchical divisions. To facilitate collective action, multifunctional teams integrate dispersed knowledge by using plans and schedules to direct the creative processes toward commonly established goals. New product development teams, like high-performing organizations, require both elements (Eisenhardt, 1989) in order to support innovation. The key question is how new product development teams connect the knowledge flow inside and outside of the team to accomplish their innovation goal.

Managing the Knowledge Flow Inside and Outside the Product Development Team

Efficient knowledge flow in product development teams frequently requires overcoming problems at two levels: those affecting the team and those affecting the relationship between the team and other functions inside and outside the organization (Dougherty and Hardy, 1996). At the team level, problems include positioning the product in the market, understanding new markets, and forming multifunctional teams. When team-level problems are resolved, innovation still does not always occur (Dougherty and Hardy, 1996). The second level of problems affects the interface of the team with the rest of the organization—functions such as marketing, production, or supply chain—and with outside constituents.

At the team–organization interface, managing relations with functions such as production or marketing and sales has been shown to play a crucial role in successfully launching a new product. At the interface between the team and external constituents, there is a need to incorporate customer and supplier input in order to develop a product that responds to the demands of the customer. It is only when problems at the team level and between the team and other stakeholders—both inside and outside the organization—are resolved in multiple stages of innovation that new businesses based on new product introductions can develop (Dougherty and Hardy, 1996).

Theories of knowledge creation and transfer developed by major contributors to the field show that if new product development teams are able to create "dense" knowledge networks within the team and build bridges between different organizational and outside stakeholders (Nonaka and Takeuchi, 1995), they will be more successful in creating new businesses. Density is a measure of cohesion and shows the closeness of relations between people. Dense team networks foster shared understanding that leads to the creation of knowledge within the team, which is necessary to mobilize innovative action and help establish communication channels across the team that lead to the implementation of innovative ideas.

The Social Capital Perspective

To understand what it takes to design the organizational capabilities necessary to develop new business ideas, the knowledge flow in product development teams is best approached through the lens of social capital. Social capital is the value that results from the intangible resources found in personal relationships. People can draw upon these relationships to help them achieve an outcome they value. Individuals, teams, and organizations all can have social capital, but here we will focus on a team's internal and external social capital.

The key question is: What is social capital based on? The quick answer is that social capital is based on the nature of social networks. But what are social networks? When someone new to a product development team wants to find out the lines of authority and responsibility within the team, and the link between the team and the organization, that person most frequently looks at a traditional organization chart. The chart shows individuals in the form of boxes with names and titles that are linked to each other. Yet, when a new team member asks questions such as "Whom do I go to in order to find out about the company's product development process?" or "How do we work with customers in order to get new products to market?," the picture drawn will show a "network" of relationships that has evolved among people in the boxes: a social network.

There are two key measures of social networks that can be derived from using social network analysis. One of the key extensively used social network measures is network density. As mentioned earlier, network density is a measure of cohesion, and shows the closeness of relations between network members. For instance, relations between friends are dense or part of a "close-knit network," whereas relations between colleagues are frequently weak or part of a "loose-knit network" Figure 3.1 shows a team consisting of six members (circles) and thirteen organizational stakeholders (rhombus). The team's network is tightly knit—if the number of ties between team members in relation to all possible ties is high—while the organizational stakeholders are loosely knit, and thus are less directly linked. If everybody were connected to everybody else on a team, the density would be 1. Tightly knit networks can exist for a number of different purposes, such as advice network, business opportunity network, or resource network. Depending on the purpose, the density may vary.

Although density of the links among team members and between the team and organizational stakeholders gives one indication of overall communication activity, it does not describe which team members have power to influence others. In the language of social network terminology, a person's degree of centrality is a second measure, which shows whether that person is in

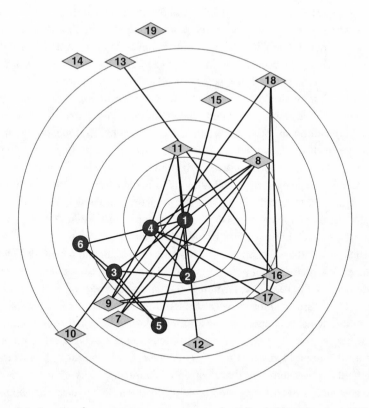

Figure 3.1 A network perspective on a new product development team and its stakeholders.

a broker's position between two subsets of members, and therefore can be used to provide needed knowledge for one of the subsets. Such a unique "bridging" role can be played by linking team members to the knowledge of organizational stakeholders (e.g., team member 1 in figure 3.1) or to knowledge expertise outside the organization.

By tapping into the social capital of particular individuals, cross-functional team members gain access to a broader knowledge base, which serves as a basis for combining facts and ideas to generate new knowledge, and they transfer this new knowledge to others. The key to realizing the value of social capital lies in understanding the social relations between individuals and the resources embedded within these relations. There are two lines of thought on how the two elements—density (i.e., closely knit) and centrality (i.e., individuals in bridging roles to external contacts)—affect performance.

External Contacts

Research, not surprisingly, has shown that networks consisting of individuals in bridging roles are beneficial to innovation. Individuals in these roles connect networks; in the new product development context, they link the team and organizational stakeholders. They can be beneficial to innovation, since they have the ability to broker the flow of information between people, and to control the projects that bring people together from different parts of a wider network. An individual who brokers the flow of information between others in a network has access to more and scarcer information sources, and by using these information sources, can bridge across functions. An individual without these connections is in a weaker position, since he or she has less influence over the information flow. For a team, a greater number of external contacts by individuals in bridging roles will allow it to benefit from a larger knowledge base. These contacts will allow the team to incorporate new information from outside the team. A large number of external contacts increases a team's social capital and has a positive effect on its performance.

The role of external contacts is to challenge the team and potentially lead its members to revise assumptions in light of new information. External constituents play the role of performance evaluators and provide feedback to the team. They can be internal organizational stakeholders or customers. The potential downside of opening a team's boundaries is the loss of cohesion and group satisfaction. The external emphasis leads a team to be loosely connected and unable to pull together the different perspectives brought by its members. Often this is overcome by the creation of dense networks by a leader who actively pushes for greater team-building in order to increase the links between team members.

Dense Networks

As external contacts improve performance, tight or closely knit networks allow team members to have quick access to trusted information from within that will facilitate collective action. Within dense networks, trust and norms are more easily established, and in turn facilitate action toward a common goal. Norms do not exist in many social structures because those structures lack cohesion. The presence of norms of trust and reciprocity ensures the flow of resources and information and minimizes uncertainty within the team, leading to enhanced performance (Pfeffer and Salancik, 1978).

The value of closed networks lies in the ability of the team to access information or resources and mobilize them, and in a generally higher level of satisfaction among members of the network (Lin, Cook, and Burt, 2001). Teams characterized by a closed network have the opportunity to tap into knowledge that can be exchanged only when norms of reciprocity have been established. Individuals on the team then become motivated to provide their expertise to the team, in the expectation that they will benefit in the future. As a result of norms of reciprocity, the team develops higher levels of cohesion and therefore requires fewer management controls.

Putting the Two Views Together

More recently, the two different views have been united by incorporating the inside and outside perspectives of team relations. It has been shown that performance is highest when the density within the team is high and the team has access to many external contacts (Burt, 2001; see figure 3.2).

Yet this perspective needs to be qualified by looking at the "dark side of networks" (Lifschitz, 2003). Closed networks are often relatively small, robust, stable social structures within organizations. As network members are increasingly exposed to each other, there is a greater likelihood that their beliefs, assumptions, and attitudes will grow more similar, thereby leading to a convergence of views. As these networks age, inertia (Hannan and Freeman, 1984) and social embeddedness (Granovetter, 1985) gradually stabilize the social structure.

This means that in older and more mature groups, actors are more likely to stick to old habits, continuing the same relations with their colleagues even when these individuals no longer provide the necessary resources. Since these groups can rely on trust and the smooth mechanisms of cooperation, they are more likely to ignore more profitable alternative contacts outside the group. They therefore become more rigid and more embedded over time, to the point of being too embedded. The group members' strong support for each other and

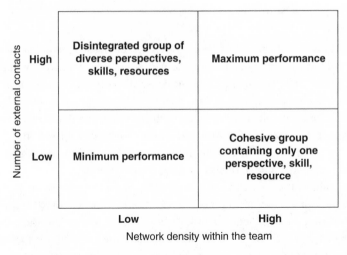

Figure 3.2 Performance effect of network density and external contacts.

the potential blocking of new information result in diminished innovation and a decreased focus on the environment.

In sum, it is wrong to take the proposal that closed networks mean high performance (Burt, 2001) without some caution. This relationship needs to be modified in light of the evidence pointing to the dark side of closed networks. Teams may end up walking a tightrope between being too externally focused and being overly cohesive—establishing internally dense communication networks at the expense of external contacts. Internal loyalties to the team may lead to groupthink or an "us vs. them" attitude, and therefore inhibit the team's ability to establish new external contacts. Essentially, a curvilinear, inverted-U–shaped relationship (see figure 3.3) between network density and team effectiveness is predicted with age—and therefore growing stability (Lifschitz, 2003) as a mediating factor.

Between Early Stage and Maturity

Figure 3.3 graphically represents the hazards facing teams over time. In the early stages of a team's existence, because roles and relationships between team members are not clearly defined and there is a fair degree of turnover as the necessary resources to perform the task are assembled, norms are hard to establish. This situation is similar to the hazard of the "liability of newness," in which a disproportionately large number of younger entities fail in the early stages of establishment. With time and a more stable team composition, and with frequent exchanges between team members facilitated by higher network density, a team's performance will improve.

Between the early stage and maturity, the team has the opportunity to build a frame of reference, trust, and reciprocity leading to smooth cooperation. Ties between team members become more reliable and denser, thereby facilitating the transfer of knowledge. It is at this stage, in particular, that the greatest level of knowledge flow will take place, resulting in the diffusion of innovations across multiple functions. In summary, between the early and mature stages of team formation, the value of greater network density increases regardless of the number of external contacts.

Between Maturity and Becoming Too Embedded

At some point, however, the effectiveness of network density ceases. A threshold is reached where the countervailing forces dominate, and increasing density of a new product development team leads to deteriorating performance. As the team stabilizes and develops norms of trust and reciprocity, the ability to incorporate new ideas from the outside decreases, leading to lower performance. The team's strong internal ties are therefore beneficial only in limited circumstances, after which they become a liability. Thus a very close-knit team is hampered by its inability to accept negative information, and thereby challenge existing assumptions. Over time, the team develops rules and routines that limit its ability to deviate from preconceived courses of action and move to innovative actions.

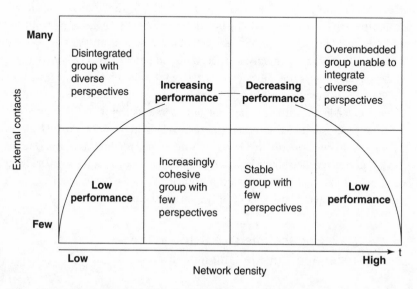

Figure 3.3 The inverted U-curve relationship between network density and performance. *Source*: Adapted from Burt (2001).

In sum, teams need to be aware that closed networks do not always produce benefits. They can produce both benefits and costs. Only an appreciation of both benefits and costs will allow managers to take action to enhance the performance of teams.

The Value of External Contacts

Despite the advice of many business books on teams that emphasize the importance of team-building, there is a downside to being extensively inward-focused because teams may be lower performers in the long run. Due to the potential disadvantage of a dense network, it is crucial for a team to maintain a balance between its internal focus and its external one. Teams with external clients may find that developing externally focused roles is as important as developing internal process skills, if not more so. The key argument for maintaining external contacts is that external constituents allow assumptions to be challenged and provide feedback to the team, thereby ensuring that the team does not fall into the trap of groupthink.

The external perspective can assist a team's knowledge creation and transfer in two ways. First, knowledge creation is facilitated through relationships with the external environment because team members hear about what is important from people they know, are alerted to potentially useful knowledge and information by people they trust, and interpret the meaning of the information based on the value that they attribute to the sources. Through access to many external contacts, team members tap into multiple sources of information and knowledge, and this can facilitate the creation of knowledge within the team by combining individual stocks of knowledge with outside information. Although the internal stock of knowledge is an asset, it needs to be updated regularly with outside information in order to avoid a convergence of views, which does not allow for alternative information to be integrated.

Second, to execute decisions, (new product development) teams require links to outside constituents that not only serve as input to the knowledge creation process but also serve as channels to help implementation. Access to customers that will eventually test a newly developed product is as important as having access to information about the product needs of customers. Drawing on a team's external contacts plays a critical role, since team members with direct connections to customers will help bring the product to market.

Managing the Interface Between the Team and Outside Contacts

Since a closed team is likely to develop specific internal communication mechanisms over time, there is a need to keep the communication channels at the boundary between the team and the outside open. Communication interfaces with the outside are key. Interfacing devices or tools, such as shared electronic repositories, standardized forms and methods, and visualized maps allow the team to bridge differences in interpretation and to integrate new information from the outside. Particularly when a new product development team has created a working business model, knowledge may become embedded in practice. Outsiders may no longer understand the specific functioning of the team, and therefore maps that visualize the mode of operation help bridge this gap.

In order for outsiders to understand the internal mode of operation, team members may have to be assigned specific roles for contacts with external constituents—while some individuals in the team remain in contact with customers, others are in contact with suppliers or competitors. Essentially, the team needs to establish clear communication channels to external contacts in order to ensure the flow of knowledge from outside into the team.

Depending on the type of external contact, the communication technology needed to support the team will vary. If a team's external contacts need to work extensively with the team, then work-sharing software can be used. Technology that supports the ability for everyone to work on the same documents (e.g., online whiteboarding) will facilitate the development and maintenance of these external networks. If the external network can be managed through one person, then simple use of e-mail, with one team member coordinating the flow with each contact, is probably sufficient.

In order for the team to remain open to outside information, the team leader plays a crucial role. Openly confronting information that runs counter to current assumptions rather than avoiding this information is key. This entails the leader's ability to deal with "unwanted" information or "bad news," especially when a junior team member receives information that challenges the team. The team leader needs to have the skills and to understand the right timing to deal with potential conflicts.

The team leader could, for instance, use team 360° feedback instruments to provide input to the team. This feedback will help the team understand their current focus of activities: internal versus external. Based on this feedback, the leader can reorient the team toward building stronger cohesion internally or focusing more on external constituents.

While the importance of building a strong team has been widely recognized, I argue that not only the internal team-building activities require leadership attention; so do the contacts to the outside. Only by managing both the internal and the external interactions can a new product development team successfully create and transfer knowledge that will produce new products in the market.

Decision to Invest in Knowledge Creation and Transfer in Other Business Functions

While product development is key, since it is at the heart of innovation and creating a competitive advantage, and requires investment in knowledge creation within and across different functions, it is not the only functional area in which knowledge creation and transfer take place within an organization. The idea of capturing and transferring knowledge learned from project teams in various functional areas is one that managers find extremely attractive, since the lessons learned could improve quality or save time and money in other functions. The overriding difficulty with transferring lessons learned and captured in databases is that the knowledge is not always understood, or is questioned by the user because the lessons are connected to the social processes of their creation: conversations, interactions, reflections. Effective knowledge transfer implies meetings and frequent interaction between people, and therefore the outcome must be worth the time invested (Dixon, 2004). As a result, it must be asked in which cases and for which projects knowledge transfer should actually be undertaken. To judge whether transferring knowledge across different business functions is worth the cost, consider two dimensions: the monetary or strategic significance of the functional or cross-functional team's work, and the applicability of lessons learned to the potential user's context. Figure 3.4 shows that, in contexts where the team's output embodies high strategic value, and this can be re-applied—for instance, in the next negotiations of a strategic alliance—then the transfer of knowledge to "other individuals" is clearly most significant.

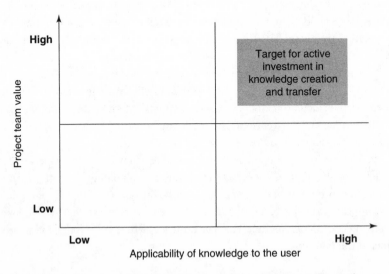

Figure 3.4 A decision to actively invest in knowledge creation and transfer.

The return on investment to actively manage the creation and transfer of knowledge is highest when the output of the functional team's work is of high strategic or monetary value, and when potential users can easily apply the lessons learned within their own context. While the output and learnings of a new product development team within an organization under growth pressures is largely beneficial to the entire organization, the transfer of the output of a public relations team's work may not be considered worth the investment at all times. A potential consequence of investing in active knowledge transfer could be wasted time and disillusionment on the part of the "giving" or "receiving" team. Therefore, the investment of time (which is probably the biggest investment) in sharing the actions, decisions, costs, and outcomes on the part of all involved has to be balanced against the potential value to both the sending and the receiving individuals or teams. If knowledge is to be created and transferred across business functions, a cost-benefit evaluation has to be conducted. Once the investment is considered to be worthwhile, actively managing the team's network internally and externally is the key to successful knowledge creation and transfer.

References

Burt, R. (1992). *Structural Holes: The Social Structure of Competition*. Cambridge, Mass.: Harvard University Press. Examines the role of networks consisting of individuals with external contacts.

Burt, R. (2001). "Structural Holes Versus Network Closure as Social Capital." In Lin N., Cook K., and Burt R., eds., *Social Capital: Theory and Research*, pp. 31–56. New York: Aldine de Gruyter. Looks at the performance effects of dense networks and external contacts of networks.

Dixon, Nancy. (2004). "Does Your Organization Have an Asking Problem?" *Knowledge Management Review*, May/June, pp. 18–23. Shows a step-by-step process to capture and reuse project knowledge.

Dougherty, D., and Hardy, C. (1966). "Sustained Product Innovation in Large, Mature Organizations: Overcoming Innovation-to-Organization Problems." *Academy of Management Journal* 39: 1120–1154. Examines the problems associated with sustained product innovation in firms that average ninety-six years of age and have annual revenues of $9.4 billion. Innovation was thwarted by the companies' inability to connect new products with organizational resources.

Eisenhardt, K. (1989). "Making Fast Strategic Decisions in High-Velocity Environments." *Academy of Management Journal* 14: 532–551. Presents information on a study that explored the speed of strategic decision-making in the high-velocity microcomputer industry.

Granovetter, M. (1973). "The Strength of Weak Ties." *American Journal of Sociology* 78: 1360–1380. Examines the role of ties within a group and their effect on performance.

Granovetter, M. (1985). "Economic Action and Social Structure: The Problem of Embeddedness." *American Journal of Sociology* 91: 481–510. Investigates the extent to which economic action is embedded in structures of social relations.

Hannan, M., and Freeman, J. (1984). "Structural Inertia and Organizational Change." *American Sociological Review* 49: 149–164. Proposes that rates of strategic change vary systemically with age.

Kogut, B., and Zander, U. (1992). "Knowledge of the Firm, Combinative Capabilities, and the Replication of Technology." *Organization Science* 3: 383–398. Focuses on a study that argued the importance of sharing and transferring the knowledge of individuals and groups within an organization.

Lifschitz, E. (2003). "The Dark Side of Networks: Age, Stability and Effectiveness of Cohesive Groups of Organizations." Working paper. Examines the disadvantages of cohesive groups.

Lin, N., Cook, K., and Burt, R., eds. (2001). *Social Capital: Theory and Research.* New York: Aldine de Gruyter, Shows a variety of approaches to social capital, from a theoretical perspective, in a variety of settings.

Nonaka, I., and Takeuchi, H. (1995). *The Knowledge-Creating Company: How Japanese Companies Create the Dynamics of Innovation.* New York: Oxford University Press. Addresses the question of why Japanese firms are successful in innovation and contends that the creation and use of new knowledge requires two types of organizational knowledge: explicit knowledge, contained in procedures and manuals, and tacit knowledge, learned by experience.

Pfeffer, J., and Salancik, G. (1978). *The External Control of Organizations: A Resource Dependence Perspective.* New York: Harper & Row.

4

Knowledge Transfer Within Organizations

DOROTHY LEONARD

When Is Knowledge Transfer Critical?

The need to transfer knowledge from one function, one group, or one brain to another is omnipresent in organizations. In most situations, the transfer is two-way. However, at different times each party can be either the source of knowledge or its receiver, even when the exchange can be characterized as knowledge-sharing. Moreover, there are at least two typical situations in which knowledge transfer is predominantly one-way: when managers are required to increase operational efficiencies and when managers need to counter knowledge loss. Transferring experience and expertise is also of paramount importance in new product/process/service development, where the exchange is at least two-way, for in this third situation the role of knowledge source and receiver shifts back and forth among a number of parties during the creative process.

Reuse of Knowledge

Leveraging knowledge assets through reuse is essential in several different situations. Perhaps the most obvious case is that of physically dispersed operations which must duplicate production processes for competitive, quality, or regulatory reasons. Intel's "copy exactly" philosophy for building semiconductor plants is an example. Local plants must duplicate every detail of the model plant. No change to any specification of a plant can be made without approval of a central corporate committee. Franchises such as McDonald's face a similar knowledge transfer challenge, since they must replicate locally the products and processes of the original business. The strategy of replication requires that the central business first identify what Nelson Winter and Gabriel Szulanski (2000) call the "arrow core": all the information a local franchise needs about valued business attributes and their creation in order to succeed. Businesses that successfully replicate must discover these core knowledge assets (i.e., extract the generic principles and processes from a morass of highly situational and possibly context-dependent knowledge), become proficient at identifying promising replicators, and then transfer the requisite knowledge to their sites.

But companies need not be following a replication strategy in order to profit from knowledge reuse. Buckman Labs constitutes a well-known example of a business that used rapid internal knowledge transfer to outbid competitors. In the 1990s, Buckman set up a worldwide computerized knowledge network through which employees anywhere in the world could seek company expertise to serve local customers. Bob Buckman attributed much of the 250 percent sales growth over a decade, and the almost 35 percent of sales that came from products less than five years old, to this capability (Fulmer, 1999). Consulting companies similarly leverage knowledge that their employees have produced in far-flung offices, so that they can work faster and without costly reinvention. Nonprofit organizations such as the World Bank have greatly increased their ability to respond quickly to local needs by accessing existing know-how in different countries. For example, in 2002 the Bank sent thirty senior leaders from the Africa region on a two-week, five-country tour to see some best practices in transportation and export. It has conducted similar exercises on topics such as rural health care. People learn well from peers whose life and work situations are similar to their own. For that reason, the World Bank has encouraged the growth of more than one hundred "thematic groups" (i.e., networks of peers who share knowledge and learn together, although most of their communications are in cyberspace, rather than in person).

Countering Knowledge Loss

Because of media coverage and events in their own organizations, managers at the opening of the twenty-first century are aware that the Western world anticipates a wave of retirements. The baby boomers will be heading out the door, taking with them, in heads and hands, the accumulated experience and expertise of three or four decades. As organizations anticipate the consequent loss of knowledge, managers are confronted with the necessity to identify critical capabilities and think ahead to how managerial and technical expertise can be transferred to subsequent generations of workers. Knowledge loss is a serious threat to innovative capability, to growth, and to efficiency (DeLong, 2004). Moreover, potential loss of knowledge is particularly critical at various times in an organization's history; DeLong cites an example at DuPont when the engineer who helped invent high-pressure compressors for running big polyethylene reactors was the only person with the knowledge essential to getting them back online when they exhibited the usual problems of a new technology. DuPont was thus hostage to the knowledge in one person's head. It is not an unfamiliar story. Managers often express fears about what would happen if a particular person was "hit by a bus" (the preferred stereotypical, if unlikely, scenario).

Creative Fusion

It is difficult to think of a product or service today that does not require some level of cooperation and contribution by multiple knowledge sources. From futons to photovoltaic cells, from estate planning to environmental assessment, a bevy of specialists are involved. Within organizations, the sources of needed know-how and expertise are often separated functionally, physically, and cognitively; but, as discussed in detail elsewhere, such diverse perspectives are essential for creativity (Leonard and Swap, 1999). The creative fusion that occurs when different mental worlds collide and then coalesce around an innovation requires knowledge transfer of a type different from the reuse described above. In collaboration, the task is to share enough knowledge at the intersections of different parts of the organization so that people can understand each other and build on each other's ideas. Each of the parties involved may take the role of knowledge source or knowledge receiver at different points during the collaboration. For example, the chemical engineer Robert Langer joined forces with the noted surgeon and cancer researcher Judah Folkman to test Folkman's theory that cancerous tumors could be killed by inhibiting the proteins that recruit blood supplies feeding the tumors' growth. Each man had specialized knowledge to contribute. Langer invented tiny plastic capsules that entrapped the proteins long enough to study them for the first time and verify Folkman's theory.

Each of the three situations described above poses somewhat different opportunities, but most of the barriers to transfer, the challenges inherent in the nature of knowledge, and the mechanisms and managerial levers available to stimulate transfer remain constant.

Barriers to Knowledge Transfer

Managing knowledge is challenging in no small part because the term itself (and hence the concept) encompasses such diverse content. Knowledge differs from information and data (see glossary) but may include elements of both. Managers considering the transfer of knowledge will find themselves dealing with facts (know-what), cause-and-effect relationships (know-why), skill-based processes (know-how), and interpersonal networks (know-who). Knowledge always contains tacit dimensions (i.e., unarticulated aspects embedded in people's brains or physical reflexes) that cannot be fully transferred.

Not only, as the famous saying goes, do we know more than we can say, but the obverse is also true: we say more than we know. That is, people are often unable to explain how they do something, but attribute their skill to "intuition." Or, in other situations, they articulate clear reasons for a decision or act—when irrefutable evidence suggests that their actions were motivated by their unconscious mind for an entirely different reason. (See Nisbett and Wilson, 1977, for a review of the psychological evidence behind this statement.) If the knowledge underlying action is not easily accessed by its possessor, how much more difficult it is to transmit that knowledge to others!

These tacit dimensions of knowledge contribute to what we can call the "stickiness" of much knowledge (i.e., the difficulty of separating it from its source). However, there are other reasons why some types of knowledge are particularly sticky. Some knowledge is extremely context-specific. Skilled workers in a factory produce high-quality output with certain machinery, but when operators are separated from familiar machines, both may underperform. The operator in such situations has learned exactly where to position the dials or how to adjust for seasonal humidity in the plant. Another operator with equal experience, but who has been working on a different machine, cannot produce the same results.

Knowledge can also be culturally sticky. Procedures, routines, and assumptions that are commonplace in one culture may be inappropriate, insensitive, or ineffective in another. While this observation applies most obviously to the transfer of knowledge across national and ethnic boundaries in multinational corporations, similar difficulties obtain in working across functions. One of the classic dilemmas for managers in manufacturing firms is how to get design engineers to comprehend the mind-set of manufacturing, marketing personnel to understand engineering, and everyone to share enough knowledge about the customers' needs and desires to converge on a profitable, high-quality product concept. As discussed below, merely talking about these different perspectives is rarely enough to construct a fully shared knowledge base.

Knowledge can also exist in two extreme forms, both of which inhibit transfer: knowledge that is so rigidly codified that it cannot be subjected to even slight adaptation by a receiver, and therefore may be rejected outright (e.g., a set of highly detailed and specific rules for conducting quality circle meetings), or, more commonly, knowledge that is vague, unstructured, ill-organized, and consequently ambiguous (e.g., collections of anecdotes about a new virus that accumulate to only a primitive understanding of cause and effect). In a study of best practices in eight companies, Gabriel Szulanski (1996) found that causal ambiguity (inadequate understanding of the reasons for the success or failure of a practice) was one of the three most important barriers to the internal transfer of a best practice.

Finally, the size and nature of the gap in knowledge between source and receiver can discourage easy knowledge sharing. In the human brain, information received is transformed into some approximation of knowledge when the incoming stimuli hook up to something we have in our memory—a related incident, image, framework or action that helps us make sense of the new experience. We need such *receptors* in order to comprehend new information. As an example of how this works, consider the following question: *What three-dimensional avatar would you like in the next MUD you enter?* To someone who is not a "gamer" (i.e., one who plays a lot of electronic games), the question is almost unintelligible. Gamers know how to represent themselves in cyberspace as a three-dimensional object or personality (an avatar) while they play in a multi-user domain (MUD). Even when the terms are explained, however, a nongamer will not know what criteria to use in selecting an avatar or what it is like to enter an environment shaped by other users. Someone who has not played such games lacks the receptors to process the query intelligently. Similarly, when an expert tries to transfer his or her knowledge to a relative novice, communication can be difficult. The expert may become frustrated with having to stop and explain every term and assumption—or, worse, may be *incapable* of translating jargon and expertise into terms and examples that are accessible to the novice. Therefore, lack of receptors in the target receiver impedes knowledge transfer.

What Aids Transfer?

Two obvious factors help the transfer of knowledge. First is the degree to which it is explicit (i.e., accessible in some articulated form, be it verbal, visual, physical, or text) (see Zander and Kogut, 1995). Explicit knowledge can be packaged and sent around the world in seconds. It can be archived for retrieval. It can be sorted, cataloged, translated, and abstracted. Of course, by the time it has been so structured, it may consist less of knowledge than of information. (See glossary for the distinction between the two words.) (See also Brown and Duguid, 2000.)

The second factor is the physical proximity of the knowledge source and the receiver. Decades ago, writing before the advent of e-mail, Thomas Allen (1977) discovered that communication among colleagues fell off drastically past about ninety yards of separation. Today, while it is true that people will e-mail people only a few offices away, it is also true that knowledge flows over the partitions separating colleagues in the typical rabbit warren of cubicles. Researchers at the Institute for Research on Learning documented with video a practice they called "storking," the habit of cubicle dwellers to stick their heads above the partitions to locate people with whom they wished to communicate or exchange documents.

One of the reasons that physical proximity helps knowledge transfer is that knowledge is most credible when it comes from a trusted source, and working or living with someone provides some basis for establishing trust (or distrust, of course). The basis of trust may be personal (I know and like this person) or professional (I know this person, and she has a good track record in this domain). It may also be based on institutional credibility (He comes from a very respected company) or credentials (She has a Ph.D. in material science)—and this credibility of course does not require personal acquaintance. (See Cohen and Prusak, 2001, for a detailed discussion of trust.)

It also helps if the source is conveying knowledge about a situation akin to the one to which the knowledge will be applied. That is, the knowledge is less sticky if the intended recipient shares some of the culture and context of the source. It is much easier and more efficient to transfer knowledge among people who speak the same technical (or national) language, share some tacit knowledge, and have similar job pressures and incentives. One of the great advantages of *communities of practice* (where people in similar roles, jobs, or functions exchange ideas and learn together) is that people are learning from, and with, peers. Wenger, McDermott, and Snyder (2002) describe how Shell Oil created networks of people sharing a common discipline or interest. One such network of geologists, reservoir engineers, petrophysicists, and other geoscientists interested in a type of geological formations called turbidite structures, called themselves the Turbodudes. These leading experts on the topic meet weekly to talk about technical problems they have experienced, and potential solutions.

Knowledge transfer implies that during a given exchange, one individual or group will at some point know more than the other. (As noted at the beginning of the chapter, knowledge transfer is almost never exclusively one-way; the source in one context may well be the receiver in another—even between the same people or groups.) The reception and use of the knowledge being transferred during a given instance depends upon the intent of both parties—one to teach or inform thoughtfully, and one to learn actively. These intents are shaped not only by personality and ability, but also by the organizational environment in which both parties operate. Managers bear much responsibility for creating an atmosphere in which knowledge-sharing is not only possible, but expected and rewarded. Think of the difference between two organizations: one in which promotions are based solely on demonstrated expertise and contacts in an individual's selected industry, and one in which promotion is not possible until the manager or technician has successfully educated someone enough to take his or her place. Or consider an organization in which training, research, and travel are always the first budget items to be cut, versus one in which a clear criterion for hiring is the desire to learn and in which the business strategy is to out-innovate the competition.

Obviously, it would be easier for an individual to transfer his or her knowledge to another in the second of each pair.

Even if a source is motivated to transfer knowledge and a receiver is eager to receive that imparted wisdom, both parties need to analyze the knowledge gap and the relative need for the recipient to develop receptors. In an ideal situation, the intended recipient of knowledge is somewhat involved even while the knowledge is being created, and therefore has highly developed receptors and some shared knowledge. If this is impossible, the recipient should at least have some say in *how* the knowledge is to be transferred.

Modes of Transfer

Research on learning has shown that people learn better and retain knowledge longer when their brains are actively engaged. This seems like an obvious statement, but why are so many organizational and personal resources expended on preparation and delivery of lectures, PowerPoint slide presentations, guidelines, and codified best practices, and relatively less on apprenticeships and knowledge-sharing communities? You have heard the old adage that a lecture is a form of learning in which the notes of the teacher are transferred to the notes of the student—without passing through the brains of either. Yet our need for speed and efficiency leads us to settle for whatever knowledge is conveyed through such means.

The more the knowledge content to be conveyed can be captured in explicit form, the more effective the modes of transfer featured at the bottom of the arrow in figure 4.1. Lectures, presentations, and directives create receptors in

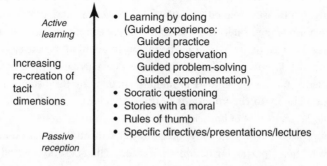

Figure 4.1 Modes of knowledge transfer. *Source*: Reprinted with permission of Harvard Business School Press. From *Deep Smarts* by Dorothy Leonard and Walter Swap. Boston, 2005. Copyright © 2005 by the Harvard Business School Publishing Corporation. All rights reserved.

the brain, or provide knowledge to the extent that receptors already exist. However, the more tacit dimensions that knowledge has, the less likely it is that we can transfer significant amounts from one person or group to another through passive learning techniques. Let us consider why that is.

Rules of thumb ("Location is key" in real estate; "Keep in mind the difference between urgent and important" in management) are useful shorthand for directing action and decision-making. However, there are always exceptions to rules of thumb, and only highly experienced individuals will be able to sort out those (perhaps rare) times when a rule of thumb does not apply. Therefore, the knowledge provided by such rules is very partial. For example, in recent research conducted by the author, young entrepreneurs were given the mantra "focus, focus, focus" by their experienced advisers—good advice for almost any undertaking. However, the entrepreneurs' advisers also on occasion suggested trying out more than one market at a time, so as to learn which niche might be of most value to the business proposition. That is, focus was important most of the time, but there were exceptions when a more diffused approach was wise.

In recent years, stories have come back into vogue as a way of conveying especially context-rich knowledge. Stories have an inherent advantage over other kinds of verbal and text communication because the love of narrative is built into human DNA. When Steve Denning, program director of knowledge management for the World Bank, was trying to convince his colleagues to take seriously the CEO's desire to shift the Bank from a loan institution to a knowledge-leveraging and -sharing organization, he found his most powerful persuasive technique was storytelling (Denning, 2000). When he told stories about the need for knowledge in various countries, and about the huge benefits derived from sharing knowledge across national boundaries, listeners were able to move beyond their skepticism of a "knowledge bank" to a concrete understanding of how such an organization would function. Stories are powerful conveyors of knowledge because they are vivid, engaging, entertaining, and easily related to personal experience. Research shows that they are more memorable than lectures or presentations, are given more weight, and are more likely to guide behavior. In addition, because of the rich contextual details encoded in stories, they are ideal carriers of tacit dimensions of knowledge (although what is ultimately encoded by the listener may not correspond closely to the intentions of the storyteller).

Would-be recipients of knowledge become much more active in their own learning processes when they are forced to think through and articulate *why* they are taking a particular action or decision. The Socratic method, which forces this kind of reflection, is used in many formal teaching environments (e.g., the Harvard Business School) as a way to stimulate active learning. And one of the key techniques used by gurus in the quality movement is the "five whys." Why is the process under examination not working? When that is answered, the follow-up question is "Why?" After five such successive probes, the examiner often reaches past symptoms to identify the root cause of the problem. And the person responding to each increasingly deeper "why" learns about his or her own assumptions in the process. The Socratic method engages the mind of the recipient of the knowledge in an extremely rapid process of sorting through possible responses to the open-ended question. At its best, such questioning causes the respondent to pose hypotheses mentally and reject them. This mental exercise, research in cognitive psychology has shown, results in more knowledge being retained in long-term memory than would be the case if answers to the question were provided, or even hinted at (Leonard and Swap, 2005).

When knowledge is largely tacit (i.e., expertise and know-how gained through experience), it cannot be readily transferred from an expert individual or group to relative novices through any of the methods discussed above. That is, lectures, stories, and even Socratic questioning create receptors in the mind: frameworks and mental models. And these are extremely useful as mental scaffolding on which to build. But many of the tacit dimensions of knowledge simply cannot be transformed directly into explicit knowledge through communication between the person who has built them up over years of experience in a given knowledge domain, and the person who wishes to gain such knowledge. Rather, Leonard and Swap (2005) argue, such wisdom has to be *re-created* in the mind of the receiver.

Guided Experience

That re-creation can occur naturally, without help, as the relative novice gains experience. However, the process can be sped up, and conducted more efficiently and effectively, with an expert guide. The "sink or swim" method of re-creating knowledge (e.g., by sending an individual into a new situation or a new role) undoubtedly has some advantages, in that the novice will not be encumbered by history, but an experienced guide can focus the newcomer's attention on the areas of knowledge and types of experience that will be useful. At least three types of guided experience help to build the tacit dimensions of knowledge that are so difficult to transfer directly: (1) practice, (2) observation, and (3) problem-solving. As discussed below, each of these forms of guided experience involves a coach or teacher who has superior knowledge and wishes to transfer that to a protégé or a group of relative novices.

Guided Practice

In sports such as golf or tennis, practice is obviously key to performance, and even professionals hire coaches to give them continuous feedback on various aspects of their game. In management, we sometimes overlook the expertise that grows through practice: hiring, motivating, firing people; conducting meetings and cutting deals; buying and selling businesses; managing new product development. The graybeards of business have years of experience and much tacit knowledge about such processes. However, managers do not always recognize the need to provide their direct reports with opportunities to practice—with feedback. And too many times, feedback is provided only periodically, through formal channels of performance reviews. Or, worse, feedback is given exclusively in extreme forms: criticism without constructive suggestions for improvement or unmitigated praise, which is equally unhelpful. If Tiger Woods's coach provided feedback only at one of these extremes, how could the golf prodigy progress? So *guided* practice is one way of re-creating some of the tacit dimensions of knowledge held in the head of the coach.

Guided Observation

The most familiar form of guided observation is shadowing someone to learn what she does by watching her in action. Shadowing a master to learn is as old as the human race; and, in fact, parents in the animal kingdom teach their offspring this way as well. However, in today's extremely rushed environment, we often fail to employ this simple mode of knowledge transfer. It sounds inefficient—sending two people to do one job. But if a session of observation is planned, and followed by a debriefing, it is an investment in avoiding problems and in teaching know-how that is impossible to convey otherwise. Know-how is often deeply contextual and situational (Brown and Duguid, 2000). Therefore an expert will not be able to abstract and synthesize for a protégé all that needs to be known, separate from the situations that activate the expert's knowledge. A highly respected and successful consultant was once asked how he had learned his trade. He explained that he had an expert mentor, who invited him to many meetings where his role was to sit at the back of the room and observe. After the meetings, he and his coach would discuss what had occurred, including observations about people's relationships, body language, negotiation tactics, and verbal interactions.

Guided Problem-Solving

Guided problem-solving may involve some observation, but the purpose is qualitatively different and requires much more active engagement from the protégé. The coach may already know the answer to the problem, or may experience the same uncertainty about the solution as the protégé. The major advantage of working on the problem jointly is that the protégé can learn *how to approach* the problem.

In a recently observed engineering situation, a highly experienced design engineer, whose expertise was especially valued, was asked to "train" a younger colleague in the kind of systems thinking for which the older man was renowned. The senior engineer knew that one of his skills was the ability to bring multiple perspectives to any design, including not only engineering knowledge about each and every component (software and hardware) in the complex system the company manufactured, but also an understanding of how the system was to be produced. Therefore, his mode of knowledge transfer was to take his protégé down to the assembly line and have him work on problems with a test engineer for a number of months. The senior engineer joined many of these sessions. While the protégé gained specific knowledge about component parts, the more important know-how transferred was the ability to look at the whole system, see how the interfaces worked, and understand how different functional priorities led to certain design flaws. The protégé also gained respect for the knowledge held in the heads of people working on the assembly line—a critical piece of tacit knowledge that would enable him to listen and learn more than fellow design engineers who never ventured down to the manufacturing floor.

What Is Success?

There are many ways to define the success of knowledge transfer. Some would argue that if the knowledge transferred is employed at all, the transfer is successful. Others would say that knowledge needs to be internalized, that is, emotionally and cognitively accepted as part of the receiving group's or individual's intellectual assets. Either way, one needs to recognize that rarely, if ever, does knowledge transferred equate to knowledge replicated. Knowledge has to be useful in the context into which it is transferred. Even McDonald's, that famous example of the replication strategy in use, produces *tiki masala* burgers in India!

References

Allen, T. (1977). *Managing the Flow of Technology: Technology Transfer and the Dissemination of Technological Information Within the R&D Organization.* Cambridge, Mass.: MIT Press.

Bransford, J. D., Brown, A. L., and Cocking, R. R., eds. (2000). *How People Learn: Brain, Mind, Experience, and School.* Washington, D.C.: National Academy Press. This is an excellent compendium of research on learning, albeit much more focused on children and K through 12 than on adults.

Brown, J. S., and Duguid, P. (2000). *The Social Life of Information.* Boston: Harvard Business School Press. Especially thoughtful treatise that challenges much contemporary hype about information technology.

Cohen, D., and Prusak, L. (2001). *In Good Company: How Social Capital Makes Organizations Work*. Boston: Harvard Business School Press.

DeLong, D. (2004). *Lost Knowledge: Confronting the Threat of an Aging Workforce*. New York: Oxford University Press. This is an excellent source about the potential for knowledge loss—how to analyze areas of loss and respond to loss.

Denning, S. (2000). *The Springboard: How Storytelling Ignites Action in Knowledge Era Organizations*. Boston: Butterworth-Heinemann.

Fulmer, W. E. (1999). *Buckman Laboratories (A)*. Harvard Business School case 9-800-160.

Leonard, D., and Swap, W. (1999). *When Sparks Fly: Igniting Creativity in Groups*. Boston: Harvard Business School Press.

Leonard, D., and Swap, W. (2005). *Deep Smarts: How to Cultivate and Transfer Essential Business Wisdom*. Boston: Harvard Business School Press. Describes how experience-based, practical knowledge develops, and the ways in which it can and cannot be transferred. Includes discussion of the hazards and limits of this type of expertise, as well as ways to manage it.

Nisbett, R. E., and DeCamp Wilson, T. (1977). "Telling More Than We Can Know: Verbal Reports on Mental Processes." *Psychological Review* 84(3): 231–259. Heavily academic but fascinating review of experimental psychological research on the gap between reported motivation for action and the actual reasons, as demonstrated by rigorously observed and measured behavior. Read it only if you have a high tolerance for academic language and processes.

Schacter, D. L. (2001). *The Seven Sins of Memory: How the Mind Forgets and Remembers*. Boston: Houghton Mifflin. Very accessible book by a highly respected researcher in the field.

Schank, R. C. (1990). *Tell Me a Story: A New Look at Real and Artificial Memory*. New York: Scribner's. Written by one of the strongest proponents of narrative.

Szulanski, G. (1996). "Exploring Internal Stickiness: Impediments to the Transfer of Best Practice Within the Firm. *Strategic Management Journal*. 17(Winter Special Issue). 27–43.

Wenger, E., McDermott, R., and Snyder, W. M. (2002). *Cultivating Communities of Practice: A Guide to Managing Knowledge*. Boston: Harvard Business School Press. Written for managers, as a guide to setting up and managing communities of practice. Includes many examples and descriptions of the stages such communities go through.

Winter, N., and Szulanski G. (2000). "Replication as Strategy." *Organization Science* 12 (6): 730–743.

Zander, U., and Kogut, B. (1995). "Knowledge and the Speed of the Transfer and Imitation of Organizational Capabilities: An Empirical Test." *Organizational Science* 6(1): 76–92.

5

Bringing the Outside In

*Learning and Knowledge Management
Through External Networks*

MARTHA MAZNEVSKI AND NICHOLAS ATHANASSIOU

M ost knowledge management initiatives focus on getting knowledge moving around inside a firm—sharing best practices, creating knowledge directories, acquiring leading edge technology, and so forth (Kostova, Athanassiou, and Berdrow, 2004). Although the outside environment is accepted as a source of knowledge, few companies think about how to manage their external knowledge resources strategically, to create value beyond an immediate and specific piece of knowledge or information. In this chapter, we address the issue of bringing the outside in—managing external networks of relationships to increase their knowledge-related value for the firm.

Of course, in today's increasingly interdependent economy, the notion of "external" versus "internal" is less clear than it was in the past. Is a long-term, sole supplier of a key component internal or external? A newly acquired company? A newly divested company? A temporary employee? A member of the board of directors who is CEO of another firm? For this chapter, we define "internal" as belonging to the firm as a legal entity, and "external" as outside of that entity.

In spite of the fuzzy boundary, distinguishing between inside and outside is important in knowledge management for two reasons (Almeida, Anupama, and Grant, 2003). First, the scope and breadth of knowledge available from outside sources is generally much greater than that available from inside sources. This scope offers a lot of potential, but also makes it difficult to focus and identify the most valuable knowledge. Managers must develop scanning and screening mechanisms to find and access valuable knowledge efficiently.

Second, methods for managing and influencing knowledge flows across the boundary of the firm are much more limited than are methods for managing knowledge flows within the boundaries of the firm. For example, a firm can set up a knowledge-sharing database on the company intranet and a compensation system that encourages knowledge-sharing within the firm. However, such "command and control" mechanisms are impractical when trying to bring outside knowledge in. Cross-boundary knowledge flows depend much more on informal influence and other persuasion mechanisms, which are inherently difficult to routinize and control.

Firms can best manage external knowledge—bring the outside in—by leveraging relationships with stakeholders in specific ways. Rather than creating separate knowledge management systems, managers should use networks of relationships they are building for other purposes to improve the knowledge flows across the firm's boundaries. Relationships with customers, suppliers, advisers, and competitors can all bring in valuable knowledge far beyond what is normally exchanged in the narrow business transaction. To avoid limiting their vision to like-thinking groups, managers must also identify and tap into other networks of potential knowledge, such as universities or related industry associations. The keys to tapping into external knowledge resources are recognizing these networks' potential as knowledge conduits and leveraging them in new ways. Such networks of relationships, which can be leveraged to access knowledge and get things done, are the source of a firm's social capital (Lin, 1999).

In the next section we review the notion that important knowledge travels best through personal relationships, describing the types of social capital most important for external knowledge management. We then describe types of relationships that can be leveraged for knowledge management and show how these relationships are already in place or can be built by fostering "normal" business activities. Finally, we outline some challenges associated with bringing the outside in and provide some suggestions for overcoming those challenges.

Knowledge Is Personal: Networks and Social Capital

When I want to know what the government is considering in terms of new legislation for our industry, I call my friend who's a journalist covering the political scene. She knows a lot more than she can print. The sources aren't completely clear or the story's not ready or sometimes the paper's just not interested. She's worked that scene for long enough that she knows all the influence games, and she can predict which legislation will get connected to which concessions elsewhere. Her predictions aren't always 100 percent accurate, of course, but I can always count on her to give me an important heads-up. If I wait to read it in the paper, it's already too late for us to act on it.

(country manager, chemical multinational)

When I sense a shift in one of our customer's buying habits or one of our suppliers says they've got new technology coming, I call up my buddy at the competition and invite him out for a beer. He calls me whenever he hears something. We never share the *really* sensitive information from our companies, but we talk about trends we're seeing and what's happening in the market, and in between goals in the football or hockey games we develop a better picture of what we're doing. It helps us both out.

(sales manager, manufacturing components)

When I moved to this company from the competition, I had to stop talking to all the people from my old company about business. But I built strong relationships with all my distributors while I was there, and now they tell me exactly what my old colleagues are doing and how I can beat them in my new role. They tell me things I could find out eventually in other ways myself, but getting the information from my distributors is faster and lets me act on it much more quickly.

(brand manager, fast-moving consumer goods)

Personal Relationships Carry Valuable Knowledge

It has long been said, "It's not *what* you know that counts, it's *who* you know." This may be an oversimplification, but there is certainly some truth to it. Why are personal relationships so important for knowledge management? Because *who* you know has an important influence on *what* you know, for three important reasons.

First, quite simply, relationships allow us to know where a source of external knowledge may lie. Someone you know may control the knowledge, or may know someone else who does. In either case, your established network links allow potential access to this knowledge.

Second, relationships are the most important conduits of tacit knowledge (Polanyi, 1962; Tsoukas, 2003).[1] Explicit knowledge is knowledge that can be codified, for example, in a manual, a patent, a description, or a set of instructions. It is sometimes called "know *what*." Tacit knowledge is the contextually based, interdependent, and noncodified knowledge that must be built in its own context. Tacit knowledge, or "know *how*," puts explicit knowledge to work.

Although explicit knowledge travels easily from one person to the next, tacit knowledge is much more difficult to share. The most effective way of sharing it is through deep dialogue that comes with personal relationships (Nohria and Eccles, 1992). When two people have a personal relationship, they are more likely to contact one another when a situation is uncertain. Then, they develop a shared context for getting knowledge from information. They discuss how to interpret facts, which facts are important, and why they are important. When they share information, they ask questions, provide examples, and make predictions about implications. This dialogue increases tacit knowledge for each of them. In the examples above, the chemical firm's country manager and the components sales manager had access to explicit information about their industries. But this was not enough. The chemical firm's manager used dialogue to draw on the reporter's tacit knowledge, and the components manager and his competitor used dialogue over a beer to make sense of their experiences together and build a better picture of what was happening.

Third, relationships can provide access to explicit knowledge that is important but not public. In the third example above, the brand manager used the relationships she built up with distributors to get explicit knowledge about what competitors were doing in the highly competitive fast-moving consumer goods (FMCG) industry. When response time is critical, early access even to explicit knowledge can provide a key advantage. Personal relationships can facilitate that access.

Social Capital: What Kinds of Assets in Relationships?

Relationships are important for many aspects of business performance, and different types of relationships help with different business elements. To sort out all these relationships, it is useful to draw on the notion of *social capital*, the set of assets in networks of personal relationships that can be valuable to achieve specific objectives (Adler and Kwon, 2002; Lin, 1999). Like other assets, building social capital requires investing, and the payoff may be immediate or long-term. Social capital can be more or less accessible and convertible to a useful purpose. Furthermore, one must "use it or lose it." Using it can increase it, and not using it can decrease it. Unlike other assets, though, social capital exists entirely in a relationship between parties. One person cannot own social capital by himself or herself; it exists only as a result of a link between people. If one party breaks the link, the social capital disappears. Five properties of social capital are important for knowledge management. We will outline these properties here, then expand on their application to external knowledge management in the next section.

First, some relationships in a network are *strong*, while others are *weak*. Strong relationships are multilayered and complex, and are usually strengthened over time, while weak relationships are more single-dimensional relationships or simple "contacts." Strong relationships are built with the kind of interaction necessary for the establishment of shared tacit knowledge, and are thus deeper knowledge carriers. Strong relationships are characterized by trust—the willingness to have someone take a risk on your behalf or the willingness to take a risk on someone else's behalf. They are also necessary, therefore, for early access to explicit knowledge. Weak relationships can include relationships through association, for example, belonging to the same alumni network or professional association. These relationships are helpful for scanning new environments and for accessing innovative ideas (Granovetter, 1973).

Second, relationships in a network are more or less *flexible*. Some relationships can provide value only in a narrow way. For example, under new legislation, an external auditor should provide services and advice only if they are directly related to the audit. Other relationships are more flexible and can provide value in a broader way. For instance, by being active in a professional association, a consultant may increase his or her access to knowledge about potential clients, new tools and techniques, and colleagues to collaborate with on large projects (Burt, 2000). A relationship may be flexible because one or both parties in the relationship have many areas of knowledge or expertise. It may also be flexible if the relationship is deep and multidimensional, and one or both parties are willing to learn things to share with the other. In general, the more flexible a relationship is, the better it is for knowledge flows.

Third, some relationships are more *transferable* than others. A relationship is transferable if it can be "given" to someone else. Take the brand manager in the example above. If an associate in her company can go to her distributors and get the same information, drawing on the strong relationship that already exists, then her relationship with the distributors is transferable. Usually, weak relationships can be transferred only as weak relationships, and people are often quite easy about transferring these relationships: "Hi, I'm Hans. I met Artur last week, and he told me he'd met you at a conference the week before, and you might be able to help me . . . ." People are often reluctant to transfer strong relationships unless they are certain that the new contact is worthy of the relationship. This is particularly true in collective cultures such as Japan, the Middle East, and Latin America, where the establishment of a strong relationship comes after much time and trust-building effort. In general, the more transferable a relationship is, the more value it provides to a firm for knowledge purposes.

Fourth, some relationships have more *power* than others. Power is access to resources that are both important and scarce. In the knowledge context, a powerful relationship is one that provides access to knowledge which can offer an enduring competitive advantage to the business. Strong relationships can often be powerful because they may provide access to deep tacit knowledge. Weak relationships can be powerful if they provide unique knowledge or access to certain types of knowledge that is more important to one party than it is to the other.

Fifth, some relationships are more *satisfying* to the people in the relationship than others. Satisfaction is the fulfillment of a need, either business or personal. Social capital is maintained and grows through reciprocal actions and mutual usefulness. The relationship link can be nurtured and kept intact only if both parties' needs and objectives are satisfied. Interestingly, these mutual objectives can be asymmetric. For example, in a relationship between a senior manager and a junior colleague, the junior manager may need to access knowledge that helps to achieve a business objective, while the senior colleague may be satisfied by mentoring an interesting, up-and-coming executive. In general, the more satisfying the relationship is to the parties involved, the more value it will provide in terms of knowledge flows.

To summarize, knowledge flows through networks of relationships, creating stocks of social capital. As a general principle, external relationships that have the appropriate strength, flexibility, and transferability, and are powerful and satisfying, will provide better knowledge for the firm. Relationships without these characteristics may provide helpful scanning and filters for explicit knowledge, but the value of tacit knowledge is generally realized only through relationships with these characteristics.

Managers Are Natural Network Builders: Change the Mind-set, Not the Action

In the previous section, we illustrated how managers' networks of personal relationships—their social capital—create flows of external knowledge to the firm (Athanassiou and Nigh, 2002). You might expect that our advice would be to build external networks that increase knowledge flows. But in our experience, this would not be wise advice. As discussed in several chapters in this book, knowledge is not an end in itself in most business relationships, nor can we expect it to be. Knowledge is an essential intermediary product in a firm's quest for better business performance. Our recommendation is that managers should learn to think differently about the networks of social capital they are *always* building and working with, and to leverage these networks for long-term knowledge flows and learning, not just for immediate business needs.

Table 5.1 shows four categories of relationships that managers build. Relationships may be part of a narrow net or a wide net. A narrow net includes relationships that have a direct and immediate—one-step—link with the company, either vertically through a value chain relationship or horizontally because they are part of the same industry. A wide net goes beyond these immediate company-related links. A network may be built around a specific purpose or mandate, such as improving year-end sales or developing a new product for a customer. Or it may be built around a very broad purpose, such as improving performance, given long-term trends in the global economy. Each of the four categories of relationships has its own purpose and characteristics, differing in strength, flexibility, and transferability (power and satisfaction

Table 5.1. Four Categories of External Social Capital for Knowledge Management

	Narrow Net (One Step from Company)	Wide Net (Two or More Steps from Company)
Specific Mandate	Value Chain Relationships *Examples*: Customers, suppliers, consultants	Consortia Relationships *Examples*: Boards of Directors, Chambers of Commerce, Consortium events for specific interest.
	For best knowledge management: Strong and flexible	*For best knowledge management*: Portfolio of strong and weak, transferable.
Broad Mandate	Industry Interest Relationships *Examples*: Trade shows, professional associations, lobby associations *For best knowledge management*: Weak and flexible, some strong	Global Interest Relationships *Examples*: Open conferences and executive programs, charity events, World Economic Forum *For best knowledge management*: Weak and transferable, some strong

should always be as high as possible). With strategic thinking and action, each type of relationship can be leveraged for greater knowledge flows.

Value Chain Relationships

Whenever a salesperson meets with a customer, a purchasing agent meets with a supplier, or a consultant meets with a client, a value chain relationship is being built. These relationships form the normal, day-to-day existence of all the firm's boundary spanners, and the importance of these relationships for the business has long been recognized. In our experiences, the value chain network is both the most extensive external network and the least utilized network for knowledge purposes. Most managers who build value chain relationships are under severe pressure to produce specific results and achieve certain goals; they see these relationships—legitimately—as a means to a very specific end. Their relationships remain weak, and they do not take advantage of the relationships' potential flexibility.

Weak value chain relationships can be used to scan and filter external knowledge. Something important to your firm's customer or supplier is also important to your firm, so a customer or supplier is a good filter for relevant information. Getting this information requires building a relationship that is flexible, that is, it encompasses knowledge beyond the immediate transaction. In a highly successful accounting firm, managers and partners talked with clients about many aspects of their business, not just the service being provided. This way, the accounting firm got a sense of the important issues for its clients, and anticipated needs for new services it could provide.

Strong value chain relationships provide the social capital needed to share tacit knowledge and access nonpublic explicit knowledge. In the professional services firm, discussions with clients provided early hints of potential acquisitions, divestments, or shifting business models. These early hints helped the firm line up resources and develop expertise, which created long-term business value—for the client in question, for other clients, and for the firm. Value chain relationships that are strong and flexible provide more than a transaction: they also provide powerful knowledge about a broad range of business issues.

Industry Interest Relationships

Companies often ally with other companies in their own industry to promote and present the interests of the industry as a whole, even while competing. In the course of these alliances, people build relationships with their counterparts in other companies, and with stakeholders who have an interest in the industry. Such relationships may be built in trade associations and trade shows, professional associations and related conferences, lobbying groups, and sometimes around specific stakeholder interests. These relationships can create social capital for knowledge management in two ways. First, weak relationships help scan and screen the environment for relevant information and knowledge. When sharing ideas and concerns about the industry as a whole, people in the network bring in points of view and information that others may not have considered or heard about. Second, the face-to-face interaction at trade shows, conferences, and other events includes intensive dialogue, which develops shared tacit knowledge around the information. When strong relationships are built, they provide scanning, screening, and sense-making mechanisms long after such an event. In the manufacturing components example above, the two salespeople from competing firms met at a trade show and spent evenings together once the show was closed to the public.

Industry interest relationships are often underacknowledged as conduits of knowledge, and are not used to their potential. In most conversations among people within a firm, these industry relationships are referred to only indirectly, as if they were not quite legitimate. This is not surprising—if a manager is learning something through a relationship with a competitor, there is the strong possibility that the manager is giving information to the competitor as well. Because of the sensitive nature of these relationships, they are often kept at a weak level, with neither party willing to take the risks that would lead to deeper trust. These weak relationships—such as contacts through lobbying or industry groups—can provide good scanning and screening mechanisms, and should be developed explicitly for this purpose.

But it is worth building at least a few strong relationships with other players in the industry. Relationships are extremely powerful if they are characterized by the kind of trust that can create tacit knowledge and provide access to nonpublic explicit knowledge among competitors. In these rare relationships, both parties acknowledge that they can build value together, both parties keep their conversations confidential from other competitors, and both parties respect the need to hold back some information. The relationships tend to be flexible but, because of their sensitive nature, are not transferable.

Consortia Relationships

Sometimes members of companies build relationships with people in other companies that are *not* in the same industry, in to accomplish something specific together. One example is when companies from different industries align themselves to accomplish a joint general objective, such as chambers of commerce to promote economic development in a geographic area. Relationships built through company-level consortia tend to be weak, and helpful for scanning and screening information. To enhance knowledge flows, these contacts are best if they are transferable. In South America, a new regional president of an automotive firm met his counterpart from a construction materials company at a local chamber of commerce meeting, and discovered that they shared a need for highly skilled labor. They transferred their relationship to their human resource directors, who developed a strong relationship and shared experiences. Eventually the two companies developed joint relationships with local institutes of higher education to promote apprenticeship programs.

Another example is boards of directors, where high level representatives of one company sit on the board of another company in a different industry, sometimes without any direct value chain or ownership links. Individual-level consortia relationships like this are usually strong. Although the use of consortia relationships is heavily regulated in the interest of fair competition, there is no doubt that tacit knowledge is developed and shared in these relationships, with the potential to help all the firms involved. The knowledge is dispersed most completely if the relationships are transferable from the board members to other members of their firm.

Global Interest Relationships

A fourth category of social capital is built when people from different companies meet and work together on very broad issues that may have little *direct* impact on their businesses. These are the relationships built at charity events, open executive education programs at business schools, and events such as the World Economic Forum. Typically, global interest relationships are weak, and provide most value for scanning and screening. For better knowledge management, they should also be transferable. In our experiences teaching executive education, where awareness of knowledge management is often heightened, we frequently observe conversations during which business cards are exchanged with the intention to pass the card on to a colleague for follow-up: "My purchasing managers would really be interested in talking with your salespeople about that product line...."

Building a few strong relationships through global interest networks provides another dimension of knowledge. We often hear executives say that they learn most from their strong relationships in this category. These are the people who can provide a completely different perspective on business and value; they can help us question assumptions and put ideas into perspective. These relationships are often the source of innovation and new ideas. They may not provide in-depth knowledge about a manager's own industry or value chain relationships, but they can certainly help develop a broader understanding of the global system in which the manager's company is embedded.

Leveraging the Social Capital

Managers continually build networks of external social capital, but in most firms the knowledge aspect of these relationships is impoverished. Parties to the relationship often see their connection in a very limited way: they focus on the immediate transaction, event, or relationship. They tend not to take the opportunity to develop a flow of related knowledge, or to transfer the knowledge or relationship to others in their own firm whom it would benefit. In other words, managers tend not to leverage strength, flexibility, or transferability of their relationships to increase their power in knowledge management. The relationships and relationship-building opportunities are there—with a different mind-set, they can create more value.

Challenges of Bringing the Outside In

Building and using relationships for knowledge does not come naturally to most managers, nor do organizations naturally engage in supporting flows of knowledge across their boundaries. Here we address the three most important challenges specific to knowledge management and networks of social capital outside the firm.

From the Outside, Individual Equals Firm

In the eyes of an outsider, an individual represents his or her firm. Outsiders see members of the firm as having something in common. For example, people outside tend to assume that when they tell one person from a firm something (e.g., a customer tells a salesperson), the knowledge will likely be diffused throughout the company.

This perception has its dangers. For example, one poor relationship between an employee and someone outside the firm can ruin the knowledge flow for others in the firm, and new social capital is difficult to build on the ruins of the old. There is also the danger that the perception is wrong—the boundary spanner may not follow through and transfer the information internally, and expectations of the outsider may not be met. Worse, the outsider may conclude that the firm has ineffective internal communications and inappropriate power relationships.

On the other hand, the perception can also be leveraged to the firm's advantage. The firm may be able to transfer contacts more readily than it assumes. One manufacturing company we know recently instituted a customer visit program. Every manager in the company must visit a customer once a year, at the customer's site, for intensive information-gathering. At first the sales managers were apprehensive about transferring their social capital to previously faceless internal managers, and these internal managers were worried about leveraging other people's networks. Soon, all learned that the customers were very pleased to use this transfer and expand their networks within the company. Many relationships—both weak and strong—were developed, and resulted in innovations and more valuable products. This broadening of the firm's external network created a firm-level social capital that endures beyond any manager's tenure and assures the flow of knowledge.

In some cases a firm may want to hire someone with established valuable contacts. Hiring an investment banker, a consultant, or an IT professional may result in the transfer of contacts from the individual's previous experience to the new firm.

Finally, managers can leverage their external contacts to create more flexibility in a relationship. When a purchaser is visiting a supplier, she may "drop by" the research and development part of the company, and introduce herself as a link to the research and development department in her own company.

Find the Right Context

One of the most difficult challenges in bringing knowledge from the outside in is seeing its relevance in the first place. Knowledge is valuable because of its relationship to a particular context (Doz, Santos, and Williamson, 2001). In order to bring it inside, the boundary spanner must identify the link between the knowledge and its context, separate the two, and anticipate the value of the recontextualization, or putting the knowledge back in the context of his own firm (Brannen, Liker, and Fruin, 1999). For example, two product managers from different consumer goods firms may go to a packaging trade show. Together they may attend a supplier demonstration of a new type of plastic that is tear-resistant and provides a strong barrier to light even when it is very thin. One, unable to recontextualize the knowledge, may conclude that light barriers are not important to her product's quality, and move on. The other, re-contextualizing the knowledge, may realize that with light barriers in the packaging there are new possibilities in product innovation. He may begin a conversation with the supplier that leads to redefining product characteristics, eventually incorporating light barriers or possibly other innovative charac-teristics in packaging designs his company is developing.

Boundary spanners, in particular, must excel at recontextualizing. The skill is developed through experience and dialogue with coaches, leaders, and peers, trying out ideas, and experimenting with different configurations. Al-though it is an individual skill, it is developed through strong relationships internal and external to the company as tacit knowledge develops. To develop the ability to recontextualize and gain value from external knowledge man-agement, managers must leverage their *internal* networks of social capital not only for straight transfer of knowledge, but also for dialogue about knowledge that may not seem immediately relevant.

Giving Something Back

As discussed earlier, social capital is built through relationships that are sat-isfying to both the parties involved. If an external relationship is to be used as a conduit for knowledge flows, it is most likely that knowledge must flow two ways, at least in the long term. This challenge requires addressing which knowledge from inside the firm can be shared without compromising the firm's performance or the relationship's power.

Some categories of knowledge-sharing are covered by law in many countries (e.g., patient-doctor, lawyer-client, banker-client). Others are cov-ered by employment contracts, confidentiality agreements, and noncompete clauses. Most companies have policies about which information is confidential and which can be shared. In reality, although they may never share specific sales figures or chemical formulas, people tend to share information about their firms with people they trust not to use the information against them or their firm. It is helpful to remember that if a firm believes its competitive value comes from its ability to execute based on tacit knowledge, then sharing explicit knowledge creates goodwill and does not endanger the firm's perfor-mance. For this reason, employees should all have a strong sense of which explicit knowledge really does create strategic value for the firm, and which, under certain circumstances, may be shared.

The dilemma of giving something back is one that each company must address. Our main goal here is to raise the issue and encourage firms to acknowledge that increasing knowledge flows from the outside in usually involves participating more widely in two-way flows.

The three main challenges that are specific to managing knowledge external to the firm—the link between individuals and the firm, recontextualizing knowledge, and giving something back—are also relevant to knowledge flows within the firm. However, in relationships that bridge outside the company, they are both especially difficult and especially influential. Getting value from external knowledge management requires addressing these challenges carefully.

Conclusion

The dilemma with valuing knowledge, and therefore assessing the costs and benefits of knowledge-enhancing activities, is that "We don't know what we don't know."

- The value of knowledge is often a *potential*, something that *could have happened* or something we *could have done differently*. But we cannot compare it with what actually happened. The value of external knowledge is especially elusive. It is difficult, therefore, for any manager to prioritize developing relationships for the eventual transfer and building of knowledge that *might* create value.
- We described here why networks of external relationships must be built to generate powerful social capital for the firm's knowledge. In today's complex, interdependent, dynamic global economy, people constantly interact with colleagues from other firms. We have therefore focused on how managers' natural networking activities can be leveraged to serve knowledge activities. Taking a little extra time and effort to develop relationships beyond the narrow and specific mandate of a business transaction can pay off enormously in knowledge flow.

Notes

1. Other chapters in this book explore the nature of explicit and tacit knowledge in more depth. Here we simply summarize the definitions and implications, and we refer readers to other chapters for more on the nature of knowledge.

References

Adler, P., and Kwon S-W. (2002). "Social Capital: Prospects for a New Concept." *Academy of Management Review* 27(1): 17–40.

Almeida, P., Anupama, P., and Grant, R. M. (2003). "Innovation and Knowledge Management: Scanning, Sourcing and Integration." In M. Easterby-Smith and M. A. Lyles, eds., *Blackwell Handbook of Organizational Learning and Knowledge Management*. Oxford: Blackwell.

Athanassiou, N., and Nigh, D. (2002). "The Impact of the Top Management Team's International Business Experience on the Firm's Internationalization: Social Networks at Work." *Management International Review*, 42(2): 157–181.

Barney, J. (1991). "Firm Resources and Sustained Competitive Advantage." *Journal of Management* 17(1): 99–120.

Brannen, M. Y., Liker, J., and Fruin, M. (1999). "Recontextualization and Factory-to-Factory Knowledge Transfer from Japan to the United States." In J. Liker, M. Fruin, and P. Adler, eds., *Remade in America: Transplanting and Transforming Japanese Production Systems*. New York: Oxford University Press.

Burt, R. S. (2000). "The Network Structure of Social Capital." In R. I. Sutton, ed., *Research in Organizational Behavior*. Greenwich, Conn: JAI Press.

Doz, Y., Santos, J., and Williamson, P. (2001). *From Global to Metanational: How Companies Win in the Knowledge Economy*. Boston: Harvard Business School Press.

Granovetter, M. (1973). "The Strength of Weak Ties." *American Journal of Sociology* 78: 1360–1380.

Kostova, T., Athanassiou, N., and Berdrow, I. (2004). "Managing Knowledge in Global Organizations." In H. W. Lane, M. L. Maznevski, M. E. Mendenhall, and J. M. McNett, eds., *The Blackwell Handbook of Global Management: A Guide to Managing Complexity*. Oxford: Blackwell.

Lin, N. 1999. "Building a Network Theory of Social Capital." *Connections* 22(1): 28–51.

Nohria, N., and Eccles, R. G. (1992). "Face-to-face: Making Network Organizations Work." In N. Nohria and R. G. Eccles, eds., *Networks and Organizations: Structure, Form, and Action*. Boston: Harvard Business School Press.

Polanyi, M. (1958). *Personal Knowledge: Towards a Postcritical Philosophy*. Chicago: University of Chicago Press.

Tsoukas, H. (2003). "Do We Really Understand Tacit Knowledge?" In M. Easterby-Smith and M. A. Lyles, eds., *The Blackwell Handbook of Organizational Learning and Knowledge Management*. Oxford: Blackwell.

Wernerfelt, B. (1984). "A Resource-Based View of the Firm." *Strategic Management Journal*, 5(5): 171–180.

6

Enabling Knowledge-Based
Competence of a Corporation

KAZUO ICHIJO

The Role of Enablers in Knowledge
Creation and Management

In the current knowledge-based economy, individual and organizational knowledge and brainpower have replaced physical assets as the critical assets in the corporate world (Winter, 1987). Therefore, the success of a company in the twenty-first century will be determined by the extent to which an organization's members can develop their intellectual capabilities through knowledge creation. In the present economy, knowledge constitutes the competitive advantage of a corporation (Doz, Santos, and Williamson, 2001). Companies should hire, develop, and retain excellent managers who generate and accumulate knowledge. Attracting smart, talented people and raising their level of intellectual capabilities will be a core competence in the new millennium (Eisenhardt and Santos, 2002).

Successful knowledge creation and management requires, above all, conditions that enable the processes of creation and management. The enabling of knowledge *creation* has been explored in an earlier work (Von Krogh, Ichijo, and Nonaka, 2000). In this chapter I will describe the role of enablers in knowledge creation and expand the concept of enablers to the management of existing knowledge.

While companies encourage their employees to create new knowledge, however, at the same time they should facilitate effective, efficient, and fast sharing of knowledge developed by managers across geographical and functional business boundaries. In other words, to win in the current competitive environment, companies should be very good at knowledge management (Barlett and Ghosal, 1998). Here I define knowledge management more holistically than is generally accepted. My definition includes four important activities for managing knowledge-based competence of a corporation: creating knowledge, sharing knowledge, protecting knowledge, and discarding (obsolete) knowledge. And, as described below, these activities should be based on conditions enabling them to occur consistently and systematically.

Above all, companies should be knowledge-creating, seeking to create new knowledge well ahead of their competitors. After companies successfully create new knowledge, it must be shared among the organization's members across regions, businesses, and functions. Protection of knowledge is protecting assets from competitors by means such as intellectual property laws and hiding corporate knowledge in a "black box"—for example, intentionally avoiding the articulation of tacit knowledge unique to the corporation (Chakravarthy, McEvily, Doz, and Rau, 2003). Companies also should determine whether unique corporate knowledge is outdated. If it is, the firm must discard that existing knowledge and promote creation of new knowledge. Otherwise, companies may not be able to adapt to a changing environment because of the core rigidities of obsolete knowledge (Leonard-Barton, 1995). Finally, it should be kept in mind that maintenance of enabling conditions for knowledge-related activities is indispensable, as will be described in detail later. Figure 6.1 shows this conceptual framework for strategic management of knowledge.

In the age of increasing globalization, knowledge management constitutes a core competence. This is especially the case for companies that operate across geographical boundaries. Firms increasingly distribute tasks over an

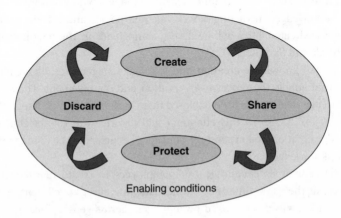

Figure 6.1 Strategic management of knowledge-based competence of a firm.

expanding geographic, sociopolitical, demographic, and cultural area. However, while it is easy to say "sharing knowledge across regions, businesses, and functions," or to discuss the knowledge-based economy in general terms, the human processes involved—creativity, conversation, judgment, teaching, and learning—are difficult to quantify.

Enabling Knowledge Management Within Organizations

Knowledge in an organization is a construction of reality by means of managers' perceptions rather than true in any abstract or universal way. The creation of knowledge is not simply a compilation of facts but a uniquely human process, one that cannot be reduced or easily replicated. It can involve feelings and belief systems that may not be conscious even for managers who create the knowledge. Therefore, knowledge in an organization is both explicit and tacit, and because of this tacit aspect, it is not so easy to share knowledge, especially across functional, business, and regional boundaries. Recognizing the value of tacit knowledge and figuring out how to use it is the key challenge in sharing knowledge across geographical regions, one that requires extended conversations and good personal relationships—knowledge-enabling on a global scale.

As described in the previous chapters in this book, knowledge in an organization is dynamic, relational, and based on human action; it depends on the situation and people involved rather than on absolute truth or hard facts. Therefore, effective management of knowledge—that is, creating, sharing, protecting, and discarding knowledge—depends on an enabling context. An enabling context is a shared space that fosters emerging relationships; in it, managers share their tacit and explicit knowledge with their colleagues. Such an organizational context can be physical, virtual, mental, or—more likely—all three. Managers can share their knowledge face-to-face or on the Internet. In other words, the enabling context for knowledge management requires a physical or virtual place and good social relationships among the people involved. In order to share personal knowledge, individuals must rely on others to listen to and react to their ideas. Constructive and helpful relations enable people to share their insights and freely discuss their concerns. Good social relationships purge a process of distrust, fear, and dissatisfaction, and allow an organization's members to feel safe enough to explore the unknown territories of new markets, new customers, new products, and new manufacturing technologies. The essential thing for managers to remember is that all knowledge, as opposed to information or data, depends on an enabling context and good social relationships.

Five Knowledge Enablers

Companies can generate an enabling context for knowledge management by using five knowledge enablers: (1) instilling a knowledge vision, (2) managing conversations, (3) mobilizing knowledge activists, (4) creating the right context, and (5) globalizing local knowledge (Von Krogh et al., 2000).

Instilling a Knowledge Vision

Instilling a knowledge vision emphasizes the necessity for moving from the mechanics of business strategy to creating an overall vision of knowledge in the organization. It implies communicating an organization's vision until the organization's members begin to move to execute that vision. When managers instill an effective knowledge vision, an organization's members will have a better understanding of the organization's core values or justification criteria for knowledge management. The justification criteria and core values at excellent companies do not change, whereas strategies and operational practices will change according to the changing environment (Collins, 2001).

In 1998, Katsuhiko Machida, the new president of Sharp Corporation, one of the leading consumer electronics companies, announced his aim of upgrading all bulky cathode-ray tube television sets sold in the domestic market to flat-screen LCD sets by 2005. The concept of LCD televisions was very strategic, given Sharp's long-term commitment to developing LCD technologies. It was literally Sharp's "knowledge vision" (Von Krogh et al., 2000), since Sharp has been active in the development of LCDs for nearly thirty years.[1] Sharp's competitors responded cynically to this bold strategy. Many industry experts estimated that it would be later than 2005 before LCD television sets would be standard in the market, due to technological and manufacturing difficulties. For example, Sony, the market leader at that time, stuck to cathode-ray tube television sets, the Trinitrons. Sharp soon took the steps necessary to carry out the knowledge vision. When facing problems or decision-making, the firm would simply refer to Machida's statement: "Replacing all the televisions sold with the LCD televisions by 2005." People at Sharp praised the simple, rigid effects of the knowledge vision. It strongly outlined how they should act. Within five years, Sharp became the number-one manufacturer of LCD television sets worldwide, outperforming Sony. Through its knowledge vision, Sharp gained a competitive advantage on a new business frontier.

Knowledge vision indicates the justification criteria for knowledge creation. As described in the previous chapters, knowledge is defined as justified true belief. Therefore, unique corporate justification criteria for knowledge creation must be clearly articulated and shared among the organization's members. These criteria indicate vision for knowledge creation. They are guiding principles, and indicate to an organization's members in which area knowledge creation or innovation should be pursued, and what competence of a corporation should be utilized to accomplish innovation. At the same time, knowledge creation should clearly indicate what corporate knowledge must be discarded because it is obsolete. Discarding obsolete knowledge is very difficult, especially in successful companies. Therefore, it will not occur without strong leadership. Knowledge vision also indicates guidelines for knowledge-sharing. An organization's members should have a clear idea of what knowledge must be shared and with whom specific knowledge must be shared across functions, businesses, and regions.

Quite often, justification criteria for knowledge management are not sufficiently shared across geographical, functional, and business boundaries. They may be shared within the boundaries of a nation in which a firm's headquarters are located. In a technology-oriented company, justification criteria may be shared within R&D or manufacturing functions, but not within sales and marketing functions. In sales- and marketing-oriented companies, justification criteria may be shared within sales and marketing functions, but not within R&D and manufacturing functions. Even when justification criteria are shared, they may be shared tacitly. However, as long as they are tacitly shared, there remains room for misunderstandings and confusion about knowledge management. Therefore, justification criteria must be articulated so that an organization's members can have a clear and consistent understanding of them. Whether knowledge vision is instilled or not depends on the organization's capabilities for managing conversation.

Managing Conversations

The second enabler, managing conversations, facilitates communication among an organization's members. The essence of an organization's activities resides in communication: communication among its members and communication with people outside the organization—for example, suppliers, stakeholders, and customers. Therefore, determining how to facilitate communication with regard to an organization's activities—for example, using a common language, clarifying and avoiding any misunderstandings and misinterpretations, encouraging active communication among an organization's members, and creating an appropriate context for communication—is a key enabler for creation and sharing of knowledge.

In contemporary business settings, conversations are still an arena (or modern-day agora) for creating and sharing social knowledge. For one thing, they help coordinate individual actions and insights. Outlining a new strategy, crafting a knowledge vision, and justifying beliefs about the success of a new product all require talking to other people. For another, conversations function as a mirror for participants. When group members find individual behavior unacceptable, they will mirror their reaction through body language, corrective comments, and so forth. Just as the ideas being discussed evolve, so do the rules for conducting conversations. Good conversation requires the right pacing and etiquette to achieve the kind of mutual insights discussed above. However, conversational skills often seem to be a lost art in current management circles. Conversations in business settings are often fraught with hidden agendas, issue-selling, unquestioned advocacy, domineering attitudes, and intimidation. Despite their importance for long-term business success, conversational skills are not part of management training in business education. Military metaphors and old-fashioned assumptions about competition still hold sway: to talk is to fight. Using brute force, the conventional wisdom goes, managers enter the battlefield to win, leaving colleagues bewildered, confused, and battered, hoping they will never have to confront the winner again.

However, the most natural and commonplace of human activities—conversations—often end up in the background of managerial discussions about knowledge. It is quite ironic that while executives and knowledge officers persist in focusing on expensive information technology systems, quantifiable databases, and measurement tools, one of the best means for sharing and creating knowledge already exists within their companies. We cannot emphasize enough the important part that conversations play. Good conversations are the cradle of social knowledge in any organization. Through extended discussions, which can encompass personal flights of fancy as well as careful expositions of ideas, individual knowledge is turned into themes available for others. Each participant can explore new ideas and reflect on other people's viewpoints. And the exchange of ideas, viewpoints, and beliefs that conversations entail allows for the first and most essential step of knowledge creation: sharing tacit knowledge within a microcommunity.

According to the former vice chairman of Toyota, Mr. Iwao Isomura, Toyota's core competence is communication. Communication at Toyota should enable the thorough understanding of what is informed among employees at Toyota, one of the leading automotive companies in the world. This kind of communication should generate mutual understanding and trust among the workers. As a result, coordinated actions will occur immediately. In order to facilitate this thorough communication, Toyota intentionally uses an informal organization in which important corporate information is shared with its employees. This information organization may be an association for Toyota-sponsored cultural or sports activities, or an association of managers who obtained their posts in the same year. In these casual settings, important information about current challenges facing Toyota is frequently shared. The participants raise questions and present their opinions regarding the provided information more freely than in a formal setting. Therefore, these informal meetings at Toyota are defined as the context for communication. In this way, thorough understanding of the important corporate information is obtained by the participants. Since Toyota employees have become well acquainted with the current challenges facing the firm through the informal organizations, they can act quickly when the initiatives to deal with these challenges are announced by top management.

In formal organizations or meetings, communication is defined as a key organizational activity at Toyota. Managers should be key enablers for good communication in the teams they lead. For that purpose, they are asked to use practical tools for enabling active communication among their team members. Tools such as "5 whys" (managers repeat "why?" five times so that their team members can identify root causes of problems they have found) and *genchi genbutsu* (going to the source to find the facts needed to make correct decisions, build consensus, and achieve goals, in the shortest time, on the spot) are provided to improve their abilities to enable good communication among their team members. If they are not good enablers of good communication, they cannot be managers at Toyota.

Mobilizing Knowledge Activists

Toyota articulated the Toyota Way in 2001 to let its associates all over the world share its unique justification criteria for knowledge management. The Toyota Way is a set of common values, beliefs, and business methods for all the firm's associates to use to support and guide the continuing evolution of its operations (Liker, 2004). In the past, the content of the Toyota Way was tacitly shared. Toyota did not make any intentional effort to articulate that material. When most of Toyota's business was in Japan, this system of knowledge management worked well. At that time, most of Toyota's managers were Japanese. Therefore, it was not difficult for Toyota managers to share the information tacitly.

However, Toyota has gradually developed its overseas business, especially since the mid-1980s, when it began to start production in the United States. Facing this new situation, in order to let Toyota associates share justification criteria for knowledge management, Toyota introduced the "coordinator" system in every business function, including production, research and development, and human resources. Coordinators, who were Japanese, were sent to overseas operations to teach their counterparts Toyota's way of doing business face-to-face. At that time, this kind of face-to-face sharing could work because Toyota's overseas business was not so large. It could be time-consuming and cost-inefficient, but in order to produce a deeper understanding of Toyota's unique justification criteria, the coordinator system was seen as effective.

Toyota's coordinators are what we call knowledge activists. The third enabler, mobilizing knowledge activists, discusses what active organizational change agents can do to spark creation and sharing of knowledge. Knowledge activism has six purposes: (1) initiating and focusing creation and sharing of knowledge; (2) reducing the time and cost necessary for creation and sharing of knowledge; (3) leveraging knowledge creation initiatives throughout the corporation; (4) improving the conditions of those engaged in creation and sharing of knowledge by relating their activities to the company's bigger picture; (5) preparing participants in knowledge creation for new tasks in which their knowledge is needed; and (6) examining whether unique corporate knowledge needs modification in different regions and analyzing whether unique corporate knowledge has become obsolete.

In other words, knowledge activists are the knowledge proselytizers of the company, spreading the message to everyone. It is not necessarily a job for one senior manager, although visionary executives have certainly played this role. Middle managers may be knowledge activists, as Toyota's coordinator system shows. Managers at all levels of a company are much better at motivating workers, getting people to talk to each other, and coordinating the often disparate efforts of creative professionals than virtual networks or other forms of computerized communication. On the flip side, the increasing importance of innovation for competition indicates that knowledge activism is not just the responsibility of managers at the front line. Top management of a company can work as knowledge activists, especially when creation and sharing of knowledge is a crucial agenda for that company. Top management should have a face-to-face session with associates all over the world to present justification criteria for knowledge creation and sharing, as well as unique corporate knowledge that should be used for innovation.

Creating the Right Context

One of the challenges for Sharp's LCD TV development was developing an advanced color display that is appropriate for LCD television. In the past, LCD was used mainly for PC monitors. A different color coordination for television sets had to be arranged. For that purpose, a joint project team of the LCD group, which held the knowledge of high-resolution color display, and the television development group, with expertise in the television screen color control, was formed. Engineers from the television development group in Tochigi, in eastern Japan, spontaneously joined the LCD development group based in Tenri, in western Japan. Amazingly, this cross-divisional activity occurred relatively smoothly. In general, companies have strong functional and divisional boundaries that make cross-functional and cross-divisional activities difficult. In contrast, at Sharp, such coordination was not new and difficult; it had had "emergency project teams,"[2] cross-functional task forces for strategically important products, since 1977. The organization believed it was natural to work beyond individual divisions. Such a tacit culture has been deeply rooted in the corporation, and was not easy for competitors to duplicate (Reber, 1993). Machida has always praised the advantage of this tacit culture. He believes that the rapid development and production of LCD TVs were due to this "emergency project team" tradition. The strength of an organization is built upon the tacit knowledge brought by the organization's historical activities (Winter, 1987).

The fourth enabler, creating the right context, examines the close connections among organizational structure, strategy, and knowledge-enabling. In the development of LCD televisions, a new cross-divisional context was speedily created for enabling knowledge creation in the new LCD TV business. As Alfred Chandler, Jr., contends, "Structure follows strategy." Organizations must have structures that facilitate creation and sharing of knowledge. By postulating the fourth enabler, the importance of the structural enabling context for knowledge creation is emphasized. Creating the right context involves organizational structures that foster solid relationships and effective collaboration. Given the interdisciplinary character of knowledge in the postmodern era, organizational structures that enable conditions for knowledge creation should be those which facilitate cross-functional, cross-business unit, cross-region activities. In order to support such activities, a strong commitment from top management to knowledge creation and knowledge-sharing initiatives is indispensable (Teece, 2001).

As knowledge and innovation become more central to competitive success, it is no surprise that many executives have grown dissatisfied with traditional organizational structures. Since the mid-1980s, corporations have begun transforming themselves through a variety of alternatives. Just a quick sampling includes cross-functional product development projects (Nonaka and Takeuchi, 1995); reengineering efforts that replace functional organizational arrangements with process-based ones (Hammer and Champy, 1993); virtual corporations that pursue interorganizational activities beyond traditional corporate boundaries (Goldman, Nagel, and Preiss, 1995); and the urgent project team of Sharp, a hypertext organization that crosses small business unit lines (Nonaka and Takeuchi, 1995). The organizational behaviorist Dan Denison (1997) summarizes the recent development of such arrangements as an effort to devise new structural forms that offer an unprecedented level of flexibility and adaptability. In other words, traditional organizational charts, with their rigid hierarchies and vertical integration, can no longer coordinate business activities in a world where boundaries are fuzzy, relationships are ever more complex, and the competitive environment is in constant flux.

Every company must grapple with unique business, cultural, and interpersonal conditions; even if a cross-divisional unit, for instance, can help a firm risk resources on the creation of new knowledge, this kind of arrangement may not work for companies in other businesses or with different strategies. The key is to structure an organization so that creation and sharing of knowledge throughout proceeds more effectively, more efficiently, and faster, dismantling as many individual and organizational barriers as possible. In fact, the whole process of knowledge creation and sharing depends on sensitive and aware managers who encourage a social setting in which good social relationships among organizational members emerge and, as a result, knowledge continues to grow and knowledge-sharing is continuously facilitated. Because an enabling context that is a good fit for a company's strategy and business provides a foundation for all knowledge creation and sharing, this fourth enabler influences how tacit knowledge is shared across functions, businesses, and regions; the creation of concepts; and the resulting prototypes that are built. New knowledge can be created interorganizationally, as the recent growth of virtual corporations and strategic alliances indicates. Therefore, where knowledge creation and sharing is concerned, organizational structures should reinforce tacit-explicit knowledge interaction across many different boundaries.

Globalizing Local Knowledge

Finally, the fifth enabler, globalizing local knowledge, considers the complicated issue of global knowledge dissemination. It almost goes without saying that many midsize and large firms are no longer contained within national borders. Companies continue to globalize their operations for several compelling reasons. By locating manufacturing operations where factory costs are low, firms can gain a cost advantage over competitors. By working closely with advanced and demanding customers in some countries, firms can acquire valuable information for future product development, thereby gaining a differentiation advantage. By setting up business operations abroad, companies can focus on growing foreign markets. And by locating R&D facilities in a country with a well-developed educational and scientific tradition, they gain access to new expertise, technologies, and product concepts. Sometimes executives may choose a foreign location to exploit a business opportunity with a local partner. At other times, locating business operations abroad can be driven by the need to attract the best managerial talent.

Whatever the motive, companies increasingly distribute tasks over an expanding geographic, sociopolitical, demographic, and cultural area. In this age of globalization, it is crucial for the competitive advantage of a corporation operating globally that knowledge created in a certain local unit is disseminated to other local units effectively, efficiently, and quickly. Sharing knowledge globally constitutes competitive advantage for a corporation. Given the necessity for satisfying the unique local needs, disseminated knowledge should not be used immediately, without any concerns for local uniqueness or for accommodation and necessary modifications. However, by globalizing local knowledge, corporations will be able to reduce time and cost for knowledge creation initiatives.

Globalizing local knowledge is, indeed, a major challenge; it is one of the most important responsibilities of the corporate headquarters manager and those local managers who must cooperate in order to make it happen. Thus, executives need to address a number of issues: How should knowledge be globalized? Can knowledge be transferred like any other commodity? Can knowledge be packaged? Who maintains control of knowledge in the new location? Tensions are unavoidable with regard to these issues. All these tensions, however, can be resolved through relationships among people working in different regions. Building enabling infrastructure is critically important to facilitate globalizing local knowledge. In other words, this fifth enabler does not work effectively without the other four. Social networks, mobility, and experiences shared among people working in different regions will overcome the tensions accompanying globalizing local knowledge. We could say that in the current global economy, which requires global knowledge-sharing, relationships are social capital. Building relationships is a critical leadership competence.

Conclusion: Leadership Development as a Crucial Enabler for Knowledge Management

- Excellent global companies spend a tremendous amount of time and energy nurturing the competency of relationship-building in leaders. The practical initiative for enabling knowledge management is developing leaders with the required knowledge by means of action learning. In recent years, the concept of action learning has caught on at many companies. As an initiative to develop leaders who show strong commitment to knowledge management, action learning is the best way to establish an enabling context for creating and sharing knowledge, as well as good social relationships among business leaders. Therefore, excellent companies such as General Electric, Toyota, and Nokia have been using action learning for developing leaders with high relation-building competencies (Tichy and Cardwell, 2002).

- In action learning, a cross-functional and cross-regional task force is formed. As a member of this task force, a high potential leader of a global corporation tackles actual business issues. By having action learning opportunities with global colleagues, such a leader nurtures cross-business and cross-functional friendships that can last a lifetime. Since creating and sharing knowledge is a foundation of the competitive advantage of a global firm, it is very important that high potential leaders recognize the importance of increasing the knowledge asset of a corporation by means of action learning. They must experience the value, difficulty, excitement, and enablers of knowledge management through their own experiences. Focus should be on the tacit aspect of knowledge and creating enabling infrastructure for facilitating knowledge management across geographical regions and business functions.

- Current top leaders should also be involved in action learning. Without the engagement of senior leaders, and the resulting interaction between senior leaders as teachers and would-be senior leaders as students, action learning remains ineffective. In effective action learning, the teaching cannot be one-way from top management. It cannot be assigned to outside experts. It cannot be based on pure theoretical exercises. The process of teaching must be interactive. Top management leaders sit down face-to-face with the students to hear the results of action learning. They provide feedback so that junior leaders can obtain a deeper understanding of a company. And senior managers will be able to learn from would-be leaders as students. Therefore, teaching and learning must be based on real business situations and issues that engage students and give them the opportunity to make a difference while they are learning. Through their action-learning work, students can teach their senior managers that there is room for improvement in business operations.

- Senior leaders also talk about their own experiences, from which students can learn the history, core competencies, and justification criteria for knowledge management in their company. A better understanding of core competencies of a company and justification criteria for knowledge creation will be obtained through face-to-face conversation in this shared context. The outcome of action learning is shared experience and social networks. In other words, an enabling context for knowledge creation and sharing will emerge from action learning.

- Although this may seem obvious, few companies to date have made relationships a priority. They may discuss their commitment to a "caring" workplace in a mission statement, but most do not practice what they preach, often because the language of caring, relating, and enabling sounds so foreign in a business context. No one can deny that the contemporary global arena is more competitive than ever. But, ironically, a company may need to flip some of that cutthroat attitude on its head in order to remain competitive over the long haul. Knowledge workers cannot be bullied into creativity or information-sharing; and the traditional forms of compensation and organizational hierarchy do not sufficiently motivate people to develop the strong relationships required for knowledge creation on a continuing basis. The core of action learning is taking leadership development out of the classrooms, and the interactive teaching and learning by top management leaders and high potential leaders constitutes the key of action learning.

- Knowledge-enabling involves a mix of deliberate decisions and going with the flow. Although managers can certainly influence the process, they may need to reassess their own work style and social interactions. But there *is* a payoff—long-term growth, sustainable competitive advantage, and the kind of culture of innovation that can ensure a company's future—and we propose specific approaches to what may seem to be a thorny, complicated task.

• The real point is that while you may be able to manage related organizational processes, such as community-building and knowledge exchange, you cannot enable knowledge management by command-and-control approaches. Those who try to control knowledge management do so at their peril, often putting up barriers or tumbling into the pitfalls.

Notes

1. The first LCD calculator, EL-805, was sold in 1973.
2. Sharp has developed many hit products via the emergency project team, by assigning firmwide key issues that need immediate and cross-sectional efforts.

References

Bartlett, C., and Ghoshal, S. (1998). *Managing Across Borders: The Transnational Solution.* Boston: Harvard Business School Press.

Chakravarthy, B., McEvily, S., Doz, Y., and Rau, D. (2003). "Knowledge Management and Competitive Advantage." In M. Easterby-Smith and M. A. Lyles, eds., *The Blackwell Handbook of Organizational Learning and Knowledge Management.* Oxford: Blackwell.

Collins, J. (2001). *Good to Great: Why Some Companies Make the Leap. . . and Others Don't.* New York: HarperBusiness.

Denison, D. (1997). "Toward a Process-Based Theory of Organizational Design: Can Organizations Be Designed Around Value Chains and Networks?" *Advances in Strategic Management* 14: 1–44.

Doz, Y., Santos, J., and Williamson, P. (2001). *From Global to Metanational: How Companies Win in the Knowledge Economy.* Boston: Harvard Business School Press.

Eisenhardt, K. M., and Santos, F. (2002). "Knowledge-Based View: A Theory of Strategy." In A. Pettigrew, H. Thomas, and R. Whittington, eds., *Handbook of Strategy and Management.* London: Sage.

Goldman, S. L., Nagel, R. N., and Preiss, K. (1995). *Agile Competitors and Virtual Organization: Strategies for Enriching the Customer.* New York: Van Nostrand Reinhold.

Hammer, M., and Champy, J. (1993). *Reengineering the Corporation: A Manifesto for Business Revolution.* New York: HarperBusiness.

Leonard-Barton, D. (1995). *Wellsprings of Knowledge: Building and Sustaining the Sources of Innovation.* Boston: Harvard Business School Press.

Liker, J. (2004). *The Toyota Way: 14 Management Principles from the World's Greatest Manufacturer*. New York: McGraw-Hill.

Nonaka, I., and Takeuchi, H. (1995). *The Knowledge-Creating Company: How Japanese Companies Create the Dynamics of Innovation*. New York: Oxford University Press.

Teece, D. J. (2001). "Strategies for Managing Knowledge Assets: The Role of Firm Structure and Industrial Context." In I. Nonaka and D. J. Teece, eds., *Managing Industrial Knowledge Creation, Transfer, and Utilization*. London: Sage.

Tichy, N. M., and Cardwell, N. (2002). *Cycle of Leadership: How Great Leaders Teach Their Companies to Win*. New York: HarperBusiness.

Von Krogh, G., Ichijo, K., and Nonaka, I. (2000). *Enabling Knowledge Creation: How to Unlock the Mystery of Tacit Knowledge and Release the Power of Innovation*. New York: Oxford University Press.

Winter, S. G. (1987). "Knowledge and Competence as Strategic Assets." In D. Teece, ed., *The Competitive Challenge: Strategies for Industrial Innovation and Renewal*. New York: Harper & Row.

7

Information Technologies for Knowledge Management

THOMAS H. DAVENPORT

Information technology (IT) has been perhaps the single most important intervention in managing knowledge, at both the individual and the organizational levels, over the past couple of decades. It is highly unlikely that we would even be talking about knowledge management if a variety of new technologies were not available. The advent of personal computers, personal productivity software, personal digital assistants, mobile technologies, group discussion systems, document-sharing systems, web portals, and so forth has transformed the knowledge landscape. Knowledge workers can now create, share, and use information and knowledge almost anywhere and at any time. It is safe to assume that few knowledge workers would give up their technologies.

Still, it is not necessarily safe to assume that these technologies have always enhanced knowledge workers' productivity or effectiveness. We know that we have spent a lot on new technologies, and we know that productivity overall in the economy has risen. But we know very little about how knowledge workers actually use these technologies, and how their jobs have been affected. Most organizations did not do a good job of measuring and managing the benefits of knowledge management, which is one reason why the concept has suffered. There are obvious benefits, such as the ability to reuse stored knowledge, or the ability to locate and access experts. But there are obvious problems as well—lack of reliability of the technology, too much time spent fussing with technologies and functions, the proliferation of low-quality knowledge, and so forth.

Information technology to support knowledge workers can operate at two different levels. In this chapter I will describe both technologies that operate at the organizational level, supporting large numbers of workers, and technology that supports information and knowledge management for individual workers and small groups. I will also describe some technologies that support information and knowledge management together. In the early days of knowledge management, organizations primarily employed a set of knowledge management applications that were separate from those used to manage data and information, and the distinctions between these forms of content were important (Davenport, 1997). Today, however, many knowledge management applications also contain data and information. The emphasis is on providing tools that enable "one-stop shopping" for all forms of content by the user.

The Application That Fits the Role

If knowledge workers have different types of jobs, it is obviously not appropriate to use the same technologies for all knowledge management environments (Davenport, 2005). A matrix I have often used to characterize different types of knowledge work is useful in thinking about the types of technologies that apply to knowledge management (figure 7.1).[1] In the "transaction model," for work that has relatively low amounts of collaboration and judgment, the most appropriate technologies are those which automate structured transactions. A call center system that brings calls and the relevant information and knowledge to the worker would be an example of this type of system.

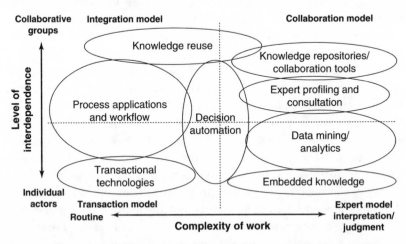

Figure 7.1 Organizational technologies for different types of knowledge work. *Source:* Reprinted by permission of Harvard Business School Press. From *Thinking for a Living* by Thomas H. Davenport. Boston, 2005. Copyright © 2005 by the Harvard Business School Publishing Corporation. All rights reserved.

British Telecommunications' AdvisorSpace system for its call center advisers, described later in this chapter, would be an example of such a system.

As the degree of collaboration moves up into the "integration model," applications that structure the process and the flow of the work begin to make sense. In a new product development environment, for example, lower-level engineers might have their work structured by a "product life cycle management" system that keeps track of designs, components, and approvals for a major product design. Also within the integration cell would be systems for knowledge reuse—again, for example, in a new product development environment, where computer-aided design drawings might be reused. Reuse can also stretch into the "collaboration" environment, where an attorney, for example, might reuse a legal brief (Markus, 2001). Decision automation, which I will describe later in some detail, is suited for job roles with a middle level of structure and expertise, such as insurance underwriting. The lower-level jobs in such roles can be automated, but experts are still necessary to build and refine the system.

In the "expert model" the goal is generally to find some means of having a computer mediate the expert's work. If that is possible, then it is feasible to think about embedding knowledge into the flow of the work process, as I will describe in a health care application later in this chapter. Experts may also benefit from data-mining and decision analytic applications for jobs involving quantitative data.

In the "collaboration model," work involves small groups and is usually iterative and unstructured (Lipnack and Stamps, 2000). The only types of tools that typically work in such environments are knowledge repositories and collaboration aids, which are used voluntarily. There could possibly be systems involving embedded knowledge, but these would be more difficult to develop and use in a highly collaborative work process. I will have more to say about many of these technologies later.

A Brief History of Technologies for Organizational Knowledge Management

Artificial Intelligence and Expert Systems

An idea that originated in the 1970s, and reached its fullest flowering in the 1980s, was the combination of "artificial intelligence" and "expert systems." This technology was supposed to eliminate or reduce the need for knowledge workers by extracting their knowledge and having a computer make important decisions or judgments.

This was an important idea, and organizations are still attempting to accomplish it. But at least in the first set of attempts, automating knowledge-based decision-making did not work out very well (Gill, 1995). A number of expert systems were developed, but the pioneers in the area encountered numerous problems that included the following:

- The knowledge intended for the system was difficult to extract from the expert's brain.
- The knowledge in a system generally needed to change more rapidly than the system designers anticipated, and such change was difficult and expensive.
- The best systems proved to be those which augmented human experts, rather than replacing them—which lowered the potential economic returns from expert systems.

Knowledge Repositories

†The first largely successful generation of organizational technology for knowledge work was known as "knowledge management" (Davenport and Prusak, 1998). This technology began to appear in the mid-1990s with the availability of Lotus Notes and later the Web, and became quite popular until the general retrenchment of information technology in the early 2000s. Knowledge management generally involved the creation of repositories—essentially databases—of knowledge. Organizations stored almost every imaginable variety of knowledge in repositories, including best practices, competitive intelligence, expert biographies, observations about customers, learnings from experience, and so forth. The most knowledge-intensive industries, including professional services, pharmaceuticals, and R&D functions within manufacturing, were all characterized by extensive development of knowledge management repositories.

But even this technology had its problems. It was expected that knowledge workers could consult these repositories to find or contribute knowledge in their spare time. The problem, of course, was that knowledge workers rarely had much spare time; attention was the primary constraint (Davenport and Beck, 2001). As firms became increasingly lean and work processes became increasingly engineered, it became impractical to consult or contribute to knowledge repositories—particularly as some repositories became large and unwieldy. Companies also found it difficult to persuade employees to contribute knowledge to repositories or to access them before making decisions or taking actions—though certain conditions made the repositories more likely to be consulted (Hansen and Haas, 2001). As economic conditions became more difficult and repositories became less valuable in the early years of the new century, knowledge management retreated in many firms.

However, repositories should not be dismissed entirely. There are circumstances in which they are probably the only feasible approach to supplying knowledge workers with the knowledge they need to do their jobs. If a knowledge worker's job process is highly unstructured and collaborative; if it is very difficult to determine in advance what knowledge and information will be needed by a particular worker or job occupant; and if there is no technological application that can mediate the worker's job, then repositories may be the only alternative. This is the case, for example, with the "integration" category of work described in figure 7.1. Jobs such as consulting or investment banking, for example, meet all the criteria described above. It is almost inconceivable that there would be an "investment banker's workstation" that would guide a banker through all the steps of the job, supplying information and knowledge as required. In any case, no one has yet built such a system for investment banking, although such tools for similar jobs have been envisioned, and in some cases narrower tools have actually been implemented (Eccles and Gladstone, 1991). Citibank, for example, developed the Citibank Derivative System to assist traders in designing derivative-based financial products to offer to customers. However, broader jobs remain largely unstructured and unmediated by technology. Therefore, firms that want their knowledge workers to be able to access knowledge will have to free up employee time to enable seeking and sharing knowledge in repositories.

Integrating Knowledge into the Job

What is the alternative to repositories as a knowledge management tool? One answer is to embed knowledge into the flow of the job process itself—the "embedded knowledge" applications recommended in figure 7.1 for expert knowledge workers. Under such an approach, knowledge workers do not have to seek out knowledge; it is delivered to them at the time of need. In fact, "integrating knowledge management into business processes" was selected as the most important issue of knowledge management in a 2002 survey of experts and practitioners.[2]

Are organizations flocking, then, to embed knowledge into the work processes of their knowledge workers? No, unfortunately—it is quite difficult to do this. There are a few good examples, however. One of my favorites comes from Partners HealthCare, a group of Harvard-affiliated hospitals in Boston. Some other health care institutions are pursuing the same technology, but the Partners approach was both early and very well executed (Davenport and Glaser, 2002).

While there are several ways to bake knowledge into knowledge work, the most promising approach is to embed it into the technology that knowledge workers use to do their jobs, which Partners has done for physicians. When knowledge supports the primary technology-enabled transactions used in day-to-day work, it is no longer a "separate" activity requiring slack time and the motivation to seek knowledge.

There are various ways to bring knowledge to physicians in the course of their work, and Partners HealthCare employs several of them. Knowledge is embedded throughout the information systems used by its physicians. When a doctor prescribes a drug, orders a test, refers a patient to another physician, or even calls up the patient's medical record, logic modules and a knowledge base are invoked to potentially intervene in the care process. The system may suggest that referrals are incorrect or unnecessary. Calling up a medical record may lead to a recommendation that certain follow-up tests or recommendations are desirable.

At the heart of the Partners approach, however, is a computerized physician order entry system with trusted knowledge built in. The system may inform the physician that the patient is taking a drug that interacts with the drug being prescribed, or that the drug prescribed is not effective or economical for the indicated disease. In the case of test orders, it may note that the test is not generally useful in addressing the disease or symptoms identified, or that the test has already been performed on the patient sufficient times to indicate a diagnosis or treatment. All of this information is integrated, and leverages a common database of patient clinical information and a common logic engine.

The order entry system is key to the delivery of quality medical care because ordering is where physicians execute their decisions about patient care; it is the moment when knowledge is most valuable. Such order entry systems may also be useful for efficiency, and for added safety in avoiding misinterpretation of poorly written orders. But the primary value is surely the ability to insert knowledge into the process. And the value is significant; the Partners system was responsible for a 55 percent reduction in adverse drug events.

It is not easy to develop such a system—either technically or managerially. Partners developed most of the system itself. There are few off-the-shelf packages for knowledge-intensive business processes that would allow individuals and organizations to embed their own knowledge into systems. Partners needed to create a complex information and technology infrastructure that pulls together the knowledge base and logic modules with an integrated patient record system, a clinical decision support system, the event management system for alerts, the intranet portal, and several other system capabilities. Other leading hospitals have some or all of these capabilities, but Partners' real-time knowledge approaches are certainly at the leading edge.

Performance Support

The idea of baking knowledge into work is new from the standpoint of knowledge management. However, it is not new from the perspective of organizational learning approaches. Well over a decade ago, for example, leading thinkers in the learning and training fields began to notice that training given substantially before a task was performed was not effective in improving performance of the task (Gery, 1991). They argued for just-in-time learning provided through electronic technologies—a vision that is remarkably similar to the just-in-time provision of knowledge at Partners. Supplying learning objects at the point of need is hardly different from supplying knowledge objects in the same fashion.

Gery and her colleagues, who advocated what has come to be known as "performance support," were correct, if ahead of their time. They were confident that the concept would penetrate industries during the next few years, and change the way work and learning are performed in organizations. Unfortunately, however, all too few of these integrated work and learning environments have been implemented. Certainly there were some technological barriers to performance support, but even more problematic have been issues of economic justification, lack of understanding and sponsorship, and resistance from traditionally minded trainers. When performance support does flourish, however, it is likely to look very much like knowledge management that is embedded within work processes.

Role-Specific Portals

The Partners example and performance support technology illustrate how powerful it can be to build customized IT applications with knowledge baked in. But there is another approach to delivering knowledge to knowledge workers that is halfway between a knowledge management repository and a customized application: the role-specific portal. A portal is a Web-based information delivery application that provides a range of information and knowledge on one site (Firestone, 2003). A role-specific portal narrows that range by attempting to provide only that information and knowledge which is required for a particular role or job. Like a repository, it requires that the user search for the information, but it limits the scope so that the search is not difficult.

The information and knowledge accessible to the worker in a role-specific portal may be a mixture of transactional information, textual knowledge, multimedia educational content, and links to sites created by the user. The screen should provide all the information and knowledge necessary to do the job, and no more—otherwise the search would take too much time. Not all of the information on the portal need be unique, but views of commonly available information should be specific to the job.

A great example of such a role-based approach is at the global telecommunications firm British Telecommunications. The role on which BT has focused considerable effort is the "customer contact" worker, of which there are twelve thousand at the company. While this is an example of a "transaction" knowledge work process, the focus for these workers was less on increased productivity (typically measured in call-handling times), and more on improved customer service through better availability of relevant information and knowledge. BT implemented a new role-specific portal, BT AdvisorSpace, within its customer contact centers. BT's goal is to make all needed information and knowledge available in real time, while the customer is on the phone. One of the key design criteria for AdvisorSpace was to create "an interface or 'portal' that focuses on delivering the information and functionality the Advisor requires, as opposed to forcing the Advisor to find the content via help files, intranet sites, and paper documents." Eventually the goal is to bring the relevant information to the screen automatically, based on the context of the current customer transaction (i.e., to move more in the direction of the Partners order entry system). The new system has already led to an increase of several points in the percentage of customers feeling that their adviser was helpful and knowledgeable (it is at 97 percent now). The advisers' confidence in the information they use is up by 23 percent. There have also been improvements in call-handling times. The BT example illustrates what an organization can accomplish when it focuses its efforts and information resources on a particular role.

Like Partners, BT focused its efforts on a single job. It is not possible to transform every knowledge work role at once. Organizations need either to select a role that is critical to its mission (physicians at Partners, for example), or very numerous and expensive (call center representatives at BT).

Automating Decisions

The early dream of expert systems and artificial intelligence is now coming of age in systems that embed knowledge—in the form of both synthesized data and explicitly articulated rules—into automated decision-making applications. With today's lean organizations, few knowledge workers have the time to transform data into knowledge themselves through business intelligence techniques. Instead, many organizations are beginning to ask systems to make the decisions for them (Davenport and Harris, 2005). Automated decision-making systems are penetrating a wide variety of industries and applications, and are taking over previously human decisions at least up to the middle management level. As shown in figure 7.1 above, they also tend to be appropriate for middling levels of expertise and collaboration. With this approach, organizations can speed decision-making, and lower the requirements for highly educated and expensive decision-makers. This is not a new idea—it first took hold, for example, in "yield management" systems in airlines that made automated pricing decisions in the early 1980s—but the applications for the idea are expanding significantly. Sometimes called "in-line" or "embedded" decision support, the concept might be described as the intersection of decision support and artificial intelligence, or the "industrialization" of decision support.

After yield management, automated decision-making became pervasive in the financial services industry, and is still most common there. An increasing amount of information in financial services is available online, which makes it possible to integrate and analyze the information in more or less real time.

In investment banking, these systems and online information are behind the rise of program trading of equities, currencies, and other financial assets. For most consumers, the primary impact of automated decision-making is in the realm of credit approval. Credit scores, such as those from Fair Isaac and Co. (known as the FICO score), are used to extend or deny credit to individuals applying for mortgages, credit cards, telecommunications accounts, and other forms of debt. Housing valuation information is also increasingly available online, which is making online mortgage and home equity loans possible in near-real time.

For example, Lending Tree, a marketplace of lenders for mortgages and other types of loans, uses automated decision-making technology to decide which lenders might be best suited to offer any specific consumer a mortgage. Using seventeen criteria, four banks are selected on the basis of the likelihood they will close on a loan. Then the banks use either their own automated decision-making technology, or software licensed from Lending Tree, to make an immediate decision (within five minutes) on whether to offer a mortgage to the consumer and at what rate and terms to do so. Lending Tree guarantees that the consumer will receive all offers in one business day, but they typically come within minutes. Not only is the process much more efficient than that used by the typical mortgage broker, but Lending Tree has learned that the consumer is 10 percent more likely to accept a loan when it is offered immediately.

In financial services, automated decision-making is being used for a broader variety of applications than just credit decisions. Citibank, for example, uses the technology for automated dispute resolution of credit card accounts. Mortgage banks have created automated systems to calculate nonstandard loan terms; a schoolteacher, for example, could get a loan that is repaid only during the school year. Most large life insurance companies use the technology to underwrite most policies, and some are beginning to employ it for small-business insurance as well. Other firms have begun to use it to manage compliance to the mix of an investment portfolio. IBM Credit is employing an automated system to assess the risk of its entire credit portfolio.

In consumer credit and collections decision-making, several firms—most notably in the telecommunications industry—are beginning to use automated decision tools to move beyond binary decisions. With more complex decision criteria, a cell phone company could decide, for example, that a customer with dubious credit is worthy of a pay-in-advance account, if not a regular credit account. Similarly, a customer who misses a single payment but has an otherwise good credit history should be treated differently than a customer with a history of difficult collections.

Now automated decision-making is penetrating a wide variety of other industries. Some of the U.S. Middle Atlantic-area utilities that avoided the electrical blackout of the summer of 2003 claim that they were able to avert the problem through automated decision-making. An industrial equipment manufacturer is using the technology to determine the tax implications of various equipment contracts, and to calculate bills for maintenance. In insurance, automated decision systems are being employed to process claims and underwrite policies. In health care, they are being used to determine treatment approaches and reimbursement levels.

In travel and transportation, where yield management once helped large U.S. airlines such as American fend off less technically sophisticated discount airlines such as People Express, automated pricing systems have become pervasive (no longer conferring advantage on the financially hurting large carriers). The same tools are now being used in the pricing of hotel rooms and rental cars. Automated pricing is also being employed for other types of products and services, including computers and electronics (at Dell Computer, for example), books (on Amazon), new car promotional offers (Ford), and even apartment rents.

Often these automated decisions are made within the context of a broader business process that is itself automated. "Decision engines" or "business rule engines" for automated decision-making are increasingly being embedded within business process management (BPM) technology that orchestrates the entire work flow for a business process. Some observers call this process "smart BPM." If a bank, for example, were using the technology for credit card dispute resolution, it not only could manage the process from cardholder to bank to merchant and back again, but also embed automated decision-making about how much and when to bill the customer.

Of course, these systems and processes can still involve some human review—either of all decisions or a sampling of them. In many of them, particularly difficult cases are kicked out of the automated system to a human expert, and experts are also needed to help build automated decision systems and refine the rules they use. But the same constraints of time and expertise that limited decision support's rise will probably mean that few humans will be looking over the shoulders of automated decision systems. This will undoubtedly lead to considerable changes in how organizations view knowledge-intensive activities, and in the labor market for analysts and midlevel managers. Thus far, automated decision-making has been largely invisible to the public, but it may lead to a quiet revolution in organizations and societies. It also is not without risk: automating poor decision processes can quickly get a firm in trouble, and managers may not recognize the problem until there are substantial losses.

Other Types of Knowledge Management Software

In addition to embedding knowledge in work processes, performance support, and automated decision-making, there are various IT applications that are intended to improve knowledge workers' performance. These fall into a few specific categories, however, and are unlikely to be applicable to a broad range of knowledge workers' performance issues.

Role-Specific Software

One category is role-specific software for knowledge workers. These applications support a particular role that cuts across several different industries. Call center workers, for example, have at their disposal a broad range of technologies, which are likely to have been chosen and implemented by others, not the workers themselves. This is just one aspect of low-discretion, transaction-oriented work: there is little discretion about what tools to use in performing the job. Most call center agents, for example, do not have access to e-mail and the Internet from their office computers.

The applications for call centers include customer relationship management software, tools for scripting conversations with customers, knowledge tools for solving customer problems, and tools for capturing customer feedback. The goal of these applications is typically to increase the volume of calls that a call center agent can handle, and somewhat less often to increase the quality of service provided to the customer. Some organizations want to go even further and eliminate humans altogether from call centers; hence the rise of "interactive voice response" and other customer self-service technologies.

At the other extreme of role-specific technologies are tools for scientists in pharmaceutical, medical equipment, chemicals and petrochemicals, and environmental firms. Such tools as electronic lab notebooks (not necessarily notebook computers, but software for capturing the results of laboratory experiments) and laboratory information management systems have been available for many years, but the high-discretion workers who use them have generally been given latitude as to whether and how the applications are used. If a scientist wanted to use a paper lab notebook, this was largely tolerated. The information and knowledge gathered were viewed as the scientist's personal property, so it did not matter in what format it was gathered—at least if the scientist was generally productive.

More recently, however, companies have begun to insist that these tools be used in a consistent fashion. As laboratory documents become legal documents, and as laboratory information and knowledge become more critical to R&D and regulatory processes, firms are discovering that they cannot leave the use of laboratory applications to the scientist's discretion. Infinity Pharmaceuticals, for example, a Cambridge, Massachusetts, drug development start-up that employs new approaches to chemistry and genetic screening, mandates that its scientists use electronic lab notebooks, and that they make their information available to everyone in the company. These tools, along with other scientific and analytical applications, have been combined into the

InfiNet Knowledge Platform, which is intended to provide a broad knowledge capture and knowledge-sharing capability for the company and its research partners. As the importance of scientific productivity and knowledge-sharing increases in this type of firm, we are likely to see more mandated use of the previously voluntary solutions.

Experimental Software

Other technologies are more experimental, and not yet of clear value to increase knowledge workers' performance. However, they offer the promise of enabling new functions and applications for knowledge workers.

Social networking software is one such category. The technology offers to enhance the function of social networks both within and across organizations (Cross and Parker, 2004). Certainly these tools remind us that knowledge workers' performance is not only an individual effort; ideas and their execution derive from people working together. However, if it is difficult to measure and understand the performance of individual workers, it is even more difficult to determine how well social networks are performing overall. We are a long way from knowing how to assess the productivity of networks and the value that networking technologies bring to them.

There are other forms of "socialware"—software that supports social relationships—that some view as important to the future of knowledge work. Academics have studied this category for years, including technologies for finding people sharing common interests, for enabling a virtual conversation or discussion, or for group decision support and decision-making. Most such activities have proven stubbornly resistant to any sort of automation, although occasionally a technology gets broader visibility and acceptance.

One example is web logging, or "blogging," which is a means for individuals to record their opinions for others to access. Partisans of blogging argue that there are many potential business applications of the technology (Ives and Watlington, 2005; Suitt, 2003). But I believe that the business value of blogging has yet to be demonstrated. I know of no organization in which the benefits of blogging have ever been measured. Perhaps the biggest problem for blogging is the time it takes to write and read blogs. If anything, this tool has detracted from productivity, not increased it. I am all for freedom of expression and self-publishing, but we should not confuse the phenomenon with increased knowledge workers' performance.

What Should Organizations Do?

Organizations need to strike a balance with new technologies for knowledge workers. They need to experiment and tinker with new technologies, and learn what their potential benefits might be for enhancing performance. But if they are to be used for business, a hard-nosed attitude should be adopted fairly quickly. What is the value? How should any improved performance be measured? Is the payoff equal to the cost—not just in hardware and software, but also in the time required to learn, tinker with, and fix the technology? Ultimately, any evaluation of knowledge worker technologies will require close observation of how the technology fits into the context of the job. Learning and using new technologies is labor-intensive, and understanding their value and performance payoff is even more so.

All of the technologies discussed thus far have been at the organizational level, for organizational processes and objectives. But there is another world of technology and performance applications that operates at the individual knowledge worker level.

Personal Information and Knowledge Management

Most applications to improve performance in business are at the organizational or process level, but it does not have to be that way. We can also improve individual capabilities, and improve organizational knowledge management, through the aggregated behaviors of individuals. Ultimately, knowledge workers' performance comes down to the behaviors of individual knowledge workers. If we improve their individual abilities to create, acquire, process, and use knowledge, we are likely to improve the performance of the processes they work on and the organizations they work for. Most technologies for this purpose also support personal information management, so I will refer in this section to personal information and knowledge management technologies.

Personal information and knowledge management was one of several research projects addressed in 2003 by the Information Work Productivity Institute (IWPI) (www.iwproductivity.org). The IWPI is a consortium of technology firms founded to carry out research and educational initiatives in the areas of understanding, measuring, and enhancing information work productivity, and the role of information technology as an enabler of productivity. The IWPI project on personal information and knowledge management was one of three research projects carried out with the goal of better understanding specific issues and processes in information work productivity.

The companies (Accenture, Microsoft, and Xerox, to be specific) and researchers[3] participating in this project all felt that personal information and knowledge management had strong potential for becoming a major topic addressed by businesses in the near future. One compelling reason for this was that knowledge workers spent large amounts of time (more than three hours per day in our data) messaging, creating documents, searching for information and knowledge, and other information-intensive activities.

Despite this large time commitment, thus far knowledge workers have been mostly left to their own devices, so to speak, with little help from their organizations in how to perform key information and knowledge tasks effectively and efficiently. And those devices, or the technologies used for personal information and knowledge, have been largely separate and unintegrated. Thus far our desktop PCs, laptops, wire-line and cell phones, PDAs, handheld communicators, and other assorted technologies—not to mention the paper-based tools many individuals still employ—have been largely unconnected. At the same time, few individuals can be said to be well-educated and well-informed on how to use the tools to perform their jobs in an optimum fashion.

Working with these devices to manage personal, work-related information and knowledge, however, is increasingly what people do within organizations. It is not hard to believe that with better technology, better education, and better management, the key tasks that knowledge workers perform within organizations could be done with greater speed and quality, and at lower cost.

Knowledge Manager Findings

In the IWPI study we interviewed knowledge or information managers in twenty-one companies about their approaches to personal technologies. Knowledge managers showed considerable variation in their orientation to personal information and knowledge management, with some companies already treating it as an important issue worthy of considerable attention, some on the road to that status, and some unaware—in roughly equal proportions. I suspect that the adoption of the idea will mirror that of other business and management innovations, and a focus on personal information and knowledge management will eventually spread and become much more pervasive. But there is much to learn from organizations that are addressing the issue today.

Companies Already There

The leading-edge companies—found in the information- and knowledge-intensive information technology, pharmaceutical, and financial services industries—exhibited a variety of traits suggesting that they were focused on personal information issues (see figure 7.2 for a graphic display of the orientations to these issues). Some were already dealing with personal information management by means of specific initiatives to address productivity through the use of technology. Cisco Systems had begun, for example, a "Change the Way We Work" initiative for employees, which involved a recommended set of technologies, education in how to use them, and a set of recommended behavior changes for optimum information- processing effectiveness. Capital One, the financial services firm, had a broad initiative under way to improve individual-level productivity with technology. Other companies in this

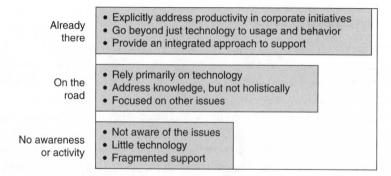

Already there	• Explicitly address productivity in corporate initiatives • Go beyond just technology to usage and behavior • Provide an integrated approach to support
On the road	• Rely primarily on technology • Address knowledge, but not holistically • Focused on other issues
No awareness or activity	• Not aware of the issues • Little technology • Fragmented support

Figure 7.2 Company orientations to personal information and knowledge management. *Source:* Reprinted by permission of Harvard Business School Press. From *Thinking for a Living* by Thomas H. Davenport. Boston, 2005. Copyright © 2005 by the Harvard Business School Publishing Corporation. All rights reserved.

category had similar programs under way, either for all employees or for a particular subset.

One of the earliest adopters of these approaches is Intel, which has created an eWorkforce initiative composed of three previously separate groups addressing knowledge management, collaboration, and personal productivity. The eWorkforce group has determined that better use of these technologies is a pressing problem for Intel, since its workers are aggressive users and spend large amounts of time doing so. Sixty-three percent of Intel employees participate in more than three teams; 62 percent routinely collaborate with people from different sites or regions; 40 percent regularly work with people who use different collaboration technologies and tools; and more than half work with people who use different work processes. The group supports knowledge workers' use of PCs, laptops, cell phones, and PDAs, and is developing integrated solutions for "generic" knowledge work processes—tasks such as arranging and conducting an asynchronous meeting (participants contribute at different times) or managing a project.

These organizations were making heavy use of emerging technologies, such as instant messaging, PDAs and handheld communicators, and shared document repositories. However, their focus was not just on technology, but also on its use and the human issues behind the success or failure of technologies. The companies were generally making some attempt to change users' behaviors and cultures—the informatics and knowledge management organization within Novartis's research group, for example, had created a "global head of knowledge culture." Others were using technology itself to guide the changes in behavior. The support groups for individual users at these firms, like Intel's, did not specialize in a particular technology, but had a holistic focus.

Companies on the Road

Other companies we interviewed were facing challenges with personal information and knowledge and were aware of them, but had not yet formulated a holistic response. I view them as being on the road to a focus on personal information and knowledge management. They were using some of the same emerging technologies as the leading-edge organizations, but the usage was less monitored and managed. There was a strong orientation to technology products as a means of dealing with personal information ("Our major project is changing from Lotus Notes to Microsoft Outlook"), but less of a focus on the use of those tools. There was generally no holistic support group for personal knowledge, but in several cases a community was beginning to emerge across the relevant functions. In several cases, some major technology or business issue seemed to be preventing a focus on individual productivity, but discussion of productivity at a broader level was taking place within the company.

Not Yet Aware

A third group of companies was somewhat interested in the topic (or they presumably would not have taken the time to participate in an interview), but had not really identified it as important enough to address with any seriousness. Some of these organizations were primarily focused on other issues—economic survival, for example. But they did not generally recognize individual productivity as a corporate issue. They had no formal group to support even the basics of knowledge management or individual information use. What support they did provide to individual users was very fragmented by technology type. Little training or education was offered to users, and what was offered was product-specific. These organizations made little use of emerging technologies for personal information and knowledge; several specifically banned instant messaging, for example. Several stated apologetically that "we know we should be doing more in this area, but there is just too much else going on," or made similar remarks.

Information User Findings

Just as the information manager survey showed that companies vary widely in their approaches to personal information and knowledge management, so our Web survey of just over five hundred information and knowledge users revealed a high degree of variance with regard to these issues. In this survey our intent was to discover the behaviors and attitudes of typical users of information technology at work, with particular emphasis on messaging and knowledge distribution technologies. These activities are obviously of importance to individuals and firms, since the average person spent more than three hours on them each day—and it is likely that this number will only increase over time.

There is also no doubt that some people—about 20 percent on each of several questions in the survey—saw a substantial problem with their personal information and knowledge management. This fraction of individuals felt overwhelmed by their information flow, saw too much use of e-mail in their organizations, and viewed e-mail and other technologies as hindering rather than helping their productivity. On each of these issues the remaining 80 percent saw no real problem, although there were considerable differences in how much information they received and the media they used. Overall, few respondents would give up their messaging technologies, but some were frustrated with them.

Many, however, are not sure what to think about this overall topic, and clearly have not given it much thought. When asked what they can do to improve their information environments, many respondents clearly did not know, or had very facile responses, such as ending "spam." The large number of uninformed responses suggests that most individuals have not thought very much about this issue—and that they have probably underinvested in their own personal information and knowledge environments—which other researchers have suggested (Davis and Naumann, 1997).

The survey also asked respondents to what degree their organizations helped them manage their personal information and knowledge environments. Forty-one percent said that they received little or no help from their organization in managing personal information and knowledge; only 3 percent felt that their organization had totally mastered the problem of personal information and knowledge management. This confirmed my expectation that most organizations have a long way to go before they have dealt fully with this set of issues. However, individuals may feel that they are doing all they can, and since they are not getting much help from their organization, in the absence of any direction or contrary evidence they may feel they are doing fine.

Masters of Personal Information and Knowledge Management

I worked with another researcher, Dave Clarke at the American Red Cross, to interview ten individuals who claim that they are highly effective in managing their personal information and knowledge environments. This may not seem like a large number, but I have generally found that less than 1 percent of the audiences to whom I speak on this topic—even among corporate information and knowledge managers—identify themselves in this category.

The ten individuals had a variety of jobs: a fund-raiser for a private school, the administrator for the board of directors of an automobile company, a venture capitalist, a consultant/researcher in a large firm, an independent consultant, a technology manager for a nonprofit organization, a director of member services for a nonprofit research organization, a knowledge manager, an editor, and a professor.

These highly proficient personal information and knowledge managers were not all alike, but they had some things in common. Several of their common attributes are described below:

- *They invested effort in organizing information and knowledge.* One went to the office every Sunday for a couple of hours to prioritize his "to do" lists and organize his files. The venture capitalist had to participate in a large number of conference calls, and he used them to organize his files and folders.

- *They were not missionaries.* When people came to them for help, they provided it, but most did not feel sufficiently capable to broadly advertise their skills. There was one exception to this principle, however: an individual who constantly proselytized about the virtues of better information and knowledge management within his office. Some people found this tiresome, and his supervisor felt strongly that it was "a waste of time." Shortly afterward, he left the organization.

- *They got help.* They did not attend a lot of courses, but they read manuals and called on support people for help. One individual asked a database manager to explain to him the structure of the key databases in the organization, so that he could access information more easily.

- *They used assistants—to some degree.* These individuals relied on their assistants to schedule and confirm meetings, make travel arrangements, and handle some communications. Yet the informationally proficient seemed reluctant to turn everything over to their assistants. None of this group, for example, relied on an assistant to read and answer e-mails; a few utilized their assistants to help with some voice mails.

- *They were not doctrinaire about paper versus electronic approaches.* Though several of the people said they were trying to reduce the role of paper in their lives, nobody was fully electronic.

- *They decided what information and knowledge was most important to them, and organized it particularly well.* The professor had online folders for every article or book he had written, and had a special program for capturing and organizing citations. The venture capitalist had an Excel spreadsheet that summarized the financial situations of all the companies he was involved with. The board administrator had Notes files for every issue that came before the board.

- *They used lists.* Most were not slavish about it, but there was general agreement that lists can be freeing, as David Allen has suggested (Allen, 2003). These individuals kept lists of appointments, things to do, contacts, books to read, and so forth. Some used electronic lists and some used paper.

- *They adapted the use of tools and approaches to the work situation at a given time.* A researcher in a consulting firm had always believed that instant messaging was a waste of her time and attention. Her primary job was to conduct research and create research reports, and even though instant messaging (IM) was becoming a culturally important aspect of her firm, she resisted its use. However, she moved to Prague for six months, and during that time was working on a project with several consultants that required close collaboration and less solitary concentration. She adopted IM and used it very heavily during that period. She felt it was extremely useful not only in doing the collaborative task, but also for reminding people that she was around and available, even though geographically distant.

Consistent with the data from the corporate and individual surveys I reported on earlier in this chapter, most of these people did not get a lot of help from their organization. None of their companies or organizations had made personal information and knowledge management a general priority. None had any holistic interventions available to make people more effective at managing personal information and knowledge. Though there are coaches available to help with this sort of thing,[4] none of the participants in this little survey had ever availed themselves of such coaching. For the most part, they figured it out on their own.

Conclusions

- I believe that the area of personal information and knowledge management is poised to take off. Companies and individual employees are beginning to focus on it, new technologies are increasingly being introduced to address it, and the business case for improving personal productivity is becoming increasingly clear.

- But this is obviously a field in transition, with considerable variation in awareness and behavior. Some companies and individuals are clearly wrestling with the issue and taking action on it. Several companies have specific initiatives to improve the ways their employees manage their information and knowledge. And a good proportion of individuals are concerned about the effect of technology, information, and knowledge on their personal productivity and effectiveness, and are taking active steps to manage personal information and knowledge so they do not become overwhelmed.

- A second group sees the problem, but is not taking concerted action. It is probably only a matter of time before they begin to respond. At the corporate or organizational level, this would mean going beyond a focus on technology products for personal information and knowledge management, and addressing how people use them. It would also mean uniting previously fragmented approaches to supporting individual-level technology and information users. At the individual level, it would mean investing personal time and energy in improving one's own information environment, and seeking help both inside and outside the organization.

- A third group of organizations and individuals clearly does not get it yet. These companies and government agencies, and individual users, do not have personal information and knowledge management on their radar screens, so they are not likely to do anything about the problem anytime soon. The organizations with this attitude may be composed of many individuals who do not care about the issue, and hence do not put any pressure on their companies. Perhaps when consultants and vendors and authors begin to address the issue, they will start moving on it.

- Of course, personal approaches to improving information and knowledge management are only one solution to the problem of knowledge workers' performance. Organizational applications are equally critical, and they will not be supplanted by personal tools. The successful organization will adopt a variety of technologies after determining what kinds of knowledge work they want to support, and what the specific needs of their knowledge workers are.

Notes

1. I believe it was Jeanne Harris, my former colleague at Accenture, who first employed a version of this matrix of technologies, though I have modified it from previous versions.

2. 2002 Delphi study by Humboldt University in Berlin.

3. In addition to me, the researchers on the project included Meredith Vey of Accenture (who did all of the statistical analysis of the user survey), Carla O'Dell of the American Productivity and Quality Center, Mary Lee Kennedy and Susan Conway of Microsoft, and Dan Holtshouse of Xerox.

4. Kevin Lynn of California is such a coach. See htpp://www.officecoach.com.

Bibliography

Allen, D. (2003). *Getting Things Done: The Art of Stress-free Productivity*. New York: Penguin.

Cross, R., and Parker, A. (2004). *The Hidden Power of Social Networks: Understanding How Work Really Gets Done in Organizations*. Boston: Harvard Business School Press.

Davenport, T. H. (1997). *Information Ecology: Mastering the Information and Knowledge Environment*. New York: Oxford University Press.

Davenport, T. H. (2005). *Thinking for a Living: How to Get Better Performance and Results from Knowledge Workers.* Boston: Harvard Business School Press.

Davenport, T. H., and Beck, J. C. (2001). *The Attention Economy: Understanding the New Currency of Business.* Boston: Harvard Business School Press.

Davenport, T. H., and Glaser, J. (2002). "Just in Time Delivery Comes to Knowledge Management." *Harvard Business Review,* July, pp. 107–111.

Davenport, T. H., and Harris, J. G. (2005). "Automated Decision-making Comes of Age." *Sloan Management Review,* Summer, 83–89.

Davenport, T. H., and Prusak, L. (1998). *Working Knowledge: How Organizations Manage What They Know.* Boston: Harvard Business School Press.

Davis, G., and Naumann, J. D. (1997). *Personal Productivity with Information Technology.* New York: McGraw-Hill.

Eccles, R. G., and Gladstone. J. (1991). "KPMG Peat Marwick: The Shadow Partner." Harvard Business School, case 492002.

Firestone, J. M. (2003). *Enterprise Information Portals and Knowledge Management.* Boston: Butterworth-Heinemann.

Gery, G. (1991). *Electronic Performance Support Systems: How and Why to Remake the Workplace Through the Strategic Application of Technology.* Cambridge, Mass.: Ziff Institute.

Gill, T. G. (1995). "Early Expert Systems: Where Are They Now?" *MIS Quarterly* 19(1): 51–81.

Hansen, M. T., and Haas, M. R. (2001). "Competing for Attention in Knowledge Markets: Electronic Document Dissemination in a Management Consulting Company." *Administrative Science Quarterly* 46(1): 1–29.

Ives, W., and Watlington. A. (2005. *Business Blogs: A Practical Guide.* Available online at http://www.businessblogguide.com.

Lipnack, J., and Stamps, J. (2000). *Virtual Teams: People Working Across Boundaries with Technology,* 2nd ed. New York: Wiley.

Markus, M. L. (2001). "Towards a Theory of Knowledge Reuse." *Journal of Management Information Systems* 18(1): 57–94.

Suitt, H. (2003). "A Blogger in Their Midst." *Harvard Business Review,* September, pp. 30–40.

PART II

FUNCTIONAL APPLICATIONS OF KNOWLEDGE
CREATION AND MANAGEMENT

8

The Strategic Management of Knowledge

KAZUO ICHIJO

In the current knowledge-based economy, individual and organizational knowledge, as well as brainpower, have replaced physical assets as critical resources in the corporate world (Drucker, 1993). Therefore, the success of a company in the twenty-first century will be determined by the extent to which leaders can develop their intellectual capabilities through activities for enhancing them. In addition, knowledge created by these leaders should be used effectively and efficiently in the organization. It must also be protected. In today's economy, knowledge and its strategic management constitute a competitive advantage of corporations (Eisenhardt and Santos, 2001). Therefore, a new strategic framework is required to manage the knowledge-based competence of a corporation.

Companies should hire, develop, and retain excellent managers who accumulate knowledge assets. Attracting smart, talented people, raising their intellectual capabilities, and retaining them as long as possible will be a core competence in the new millennium. At the same time, companies should encourage such proficient managers to share the knowledge they develop across geographical and functional business boundaries in an effective, efficient, and fast manner. In addition, companies should create polices that protect knowledge from being imitated by competitors or flowing into external markets. Finally, present knowledge may be obsolete. If it is, companies should recognize this, and not rely on it. Thus, to win in the current competitive environment, companies must be able to manage knowledge strategically. Management of knowledge should also constitute a core competence. This is especially the case for companies doing business across national borders. However, very few firms succeed in their initiative to increase their knowledge assets.

In this age of stiff global competition and rapid technological changes, the way firms manage their knowledge drives key competing factors. In the most advanced industrial areas, with constant technological changes facing them, manufacturers need not only to develop new technologies but also to focus on protecting their original expertise from competitors (Doz, Santos, and Williamson, 2001). Furthermore, when a manufacturer becomes a leader in introducing new technologies, it risks facing destructive technologies that aim to damage its advantage (Christensen, 1997). Managers nowadays have to work relentlessly to prevent their original technologies from becoming obsolete. Decision-making issues concerning the knowledge-based competence of a corporation are becoming broader and more diverse.

In this chapter, I highlight the importance of a holistic and strategic management of the knowledge-based competence of a corporation. That is, a new strategic framework for managing that competence. It is based on four key activities: creation, sharing and utilization, protection, and discarding of knowledge. These activities do not occur consistently without an infrastructure that consistently enables them (Von Krogh, Ichijo, and Nonaka, 2000).

A Need for a New Strategic Framework

For managers, the importance of knowledge in organizations—and the whole knowledge management movement—turns on the practical use of knowledge in a business setting. Talking about the power of tacit knowledge or long-term competitive advantage does no good if the knowledge-based competence of a corporation is not part of a strategic framework. Knowledge, new or otherwise, always adds an element of uncertainty. Yet creating new knowledge—and, perhaps more important, effectively using and protecting the knowledge that already exists in an organization—has now become a core element of business strategy.

In a company that views its competitive advantage in terms of knowledge, the responsibility of management is twofold. The first responsibility managers have is to unleash the potential represented by an organization's knowledge into value-creating actions. That is, they need to identify what the organization knows and in what form it knows it, and to make tacit knowledge accessible and usable. In fact, the business community has begun to accept the knowledge challenge. Pioneering companies such as Sharp and Oracle are charting the progress and use of their intellectual assets, connecting a vision of what knowledge they will need in the future with specific actions and objectives.

The second managerial responsibility is related to a company's competitive situation. Some consultants and organizational researchers suggest that the value of management to a company, and hence executive compensation, should depend on the extent to which managers are able to generate and exploit assets such as knowledge more effectively than their counterparts at competing companies.[1] This means that managers either need to ensure the creation of unique knowledge that can be unleashed in value-creating activity, or to establish better use of public knowledge that is generally available to the company and its competitors.

In the following section, a new strategic framework will be presented from the viewpoint of the knowledge-based competence of a corporation. This framework breaks down the potential of knowledge creation into two basic strategies: *survival strategies*, in which companies focus on existing knowledge to maintain their current level of success and performance, and *advancement strategies*, which emphasize the importance of innovation. We then look at how executives can strike a balance between the two, and the business conditions that might influence them to opt for one or the other. The main point here, however, is that advancement strategies are necessary for knowledge-creating companies. The chapter closes with the story of Sharp, which has been continuously pursuing advancement strategies.

A New Strategic Framework

Although it is a business truism that knowledge yields competitive advantage,[2] not all knowledge has strategic value. Therefore, it is imperative that managers use a practical framework to assess the role of knowledge in relation to strategy. In general, I suggest that the ultimate goal of all knowledge-related activity is to ensure above-average industry profitability for a company, in both the short term and the long term. This is a bold proposition, however, since many advocates of the knowledge movement tend to take a fairly operational view. In practice, the "knowledge issue" tends to become the responsibility of human resources, information technology groups, or corporate R&D; sometimes it is only part of isolated knowledge-management initiatives located deep within various business units. In addition, most theorists, with a few notable exceptions, pay little attention to an overall strategic view.[3]

As a consequence, top management rarely focuses on the strategic role of knowledge or the importance of knowledge-creation initiatives. One possible remedy is to reframe how knowledge is viewed by senior executives and other company strategists. Rather than seeing it as an unknown quantity vaguely connected to creativity, absolutely necessary but impossible to objectify, it can be considered a resource tied to specific actions and business results. The framework shown in table 8.1 highlights the strategic role of knowledge and corresponding knowledge processes. In the following sections, we examine each component separately.

Table 8.1. A Strategic Framework for Knowledge

Strategy	Competitive Advantage	Sources of Competitive Advantage	Role of Knowledge	Important Knowledge Activities	Result
Survival	Current profitability	Economies of scale	Valuable, difficult to imitate, difficult to substitute	Knowledge-sharing	Profitability higher than average of the industry
	Not implemented by competitors	Economies of scope	Exclusively held or public	Knowledge protection	
	Those who try cannot replicate original advantages	Product/service differentiation	Ability to transfer may matter more than content		
Advancement	Future profitability	Potential economies of scale	New knowledge for process/product innovation	Knowledge creation	Future profitability higher than average of the industry
	Not implemented by competitors	Potential economies of scope	Transferable new knowledge	Knowledge protection	
	Those who try cannot replicate original advantages	Potential product/service differentiation		Knowledge-discarding	

Survival and Advancement Strategies

Von Krogh, Roos, and Slocum (1994) describe essentially two types of strategies: survival and advancement. Survival strategies secure current company profitability. This kind of strategy emphasizes current strengths and minimizes current weaknesses in the resources and knowledge base of the company; the aim is to take advantage of existing business opportunities and neutralize threats in the environment (Andrew, 1971). When conceiving of survival strategies, management counts on a fairly clear image of a known business environment.[4] Survival strategies aim at mastery of the company's current business environment. They allow for reducing the bargaining power of existing suppliers and customers; are based on successful product market positioning compared with competitors; and meet the expectations held by various stakeholders in the firm, such as society, the local community, employees, and the government. Survival strategies also make the entry of new competitors unattractive, through experience effects and/or economies of scope, and prepare the company for possible substitutes for their products (Porter, 1990; Fahey and Narayanan, 1986).

Advancement strategies secure future profitability. They build on future strengths and attempt to minimize future weaknesses in the resources and knowledge base of the company; their aim is to take advantage of future business opportunities and neutralize future threats in the environment. When conceiving of advancement strategies, management's experience and understanding of the business environment are of limited use. Creative approaches to strategizing are called for instead, in which new images of the company and its business environment must be considered. Advancement strategies are typical of emerging industries such as information technology, financial services, telecommunications, and digital electronics. The roles of various players and the corresponding bargaining power and product market positioning are in continual transition (Levenhagen, Porac, and Thomas, 1993; Hamel and Prahalad, 1994).

In developing advancement strategies, the experience of senior managers may count less than creative, intuitive, and insightful images drawn from the middle or junior management ranks (Hamel, 1996). Advancement strategies should allow the company to see new aspects of the business environment in order to build up the firm's mastery of its future environment. They outline how the company can gain influence in the evolution of the industry in order to increase future bargaining power over potential suppliers and customers. Such influence might, for example, be achieved by hiring creative researchers, forming strategic alliances with research institutions, developing technological standards, or building strong links with future suppliers and customers. Advancement strategies alert managers to potential competitors and how they are likely to react to the company's initiatives, and they emphasize new product concepts and services, as well as better product market positioning compared with competitors. They also indicate how to meet the future expectations of the firm's stakeholders.

Overall, a careful balance between advancement and survival strategies will allow a company to prepare for vanishing industry boundaries, rapid transition in the industry, the rapid devaluing of existing knowledge and competences, and the obsolescence of existing products and services. But because managers tend to prefer "actionable information" (Mintzberg, 1975), such as the kind that allows them to outmaneuver a difficult competitor in an existing market segment, survival strategies generally win the day in strategic conversations (Von Krogh and Roos, 1996b). This imbalance may push management into a myopic and rigid view of industries and markets. Survival and advancement strategies both provide distinct competitive advantages, draw on particular sources of competitive advantage, put distinct demands on knowledge, and are associated with particular knowledge processes. Therefore, the proper balance between them is essential, and both require equal managerial attention, a point I will return to later.

Competitive Advantage

A company that achieves superior business performance compared with its competitors is said to have a competitive advantage.[5] Under the commonly accepted definition, a firm implements a value-creating (survival) strategy not being implemented by current or future competitors. For example, an aluminum producer might have lower factor costs because it owns power plants while its competitors have to buy electricity on the open market. This competitive advantage may be more or less durable, allowing the company to enjoy superior performance over a longer period of time.

A sustainable competitive advantage is one in which the company implements a value-creating strategy that remains unique, despite attempts at imitation by current and future competitors (Barney, 1991). Competitors of the aluminum company might try to replicate its value-creating strategy by setting up their own power plants, but high initial investments prevent them from achieving the same cost level. Note, however, that few, if any, competitive advantages last forever. New knowledge, technologies, and products will at some point erode the competitive potential of existing knowledge, technologies, and products. Knowledge that currently is strategically important for a company may be obsolete. Sony has been suffering a declining share in the global television market. The reason is that Sony has stuck to its obsolete Trinitron knowledge and did not move fast to create new knowledge about LCD and plasma television. Many companies continue to implement their current value-creating survival strategies, but their managers must think ahead to secure future performance through advancement strategies.

Sources of Competitive Advantage

Competitive advantages derive from low process costs—through economies of scale, scope, and factor costs, and/or product or service differentiation (the result of a unique product quality or product features that customers value); a unique geographical position; or unique skills and service offerings (Porter, 1990; Rummelt, 1980).[6] Survival strategies exploit current sources of competitive advantage: lower manufacturing costs than those of competitors due to more experience; lower quality costs because of a close collaboration with suppliers; shared R&D investments for a large set of products; shared services among various business units; ownership of patents, copyrights, trade secrets, or unique product designs. Advancement strategies explore future sources of competitive advantage: new low-cost manufacturing processes; new products and services with unique features; leveraging gained from existing businesses to create new businesses.

Strategic Role of Knowledge

The role knowledge plays is different for survival and advancement strategies, and by making this distinction managers can begin to grasp why tacit knowledge has so much potential—it is often underdeveloped or actively ignored in traditional strategic models—for knowledge creation. In a business context, knowledge can be separated into two broad categories: unique knowledge held exclusively by the firm and public knowledge held by competitors. For unique knowledge to be a source of sustainable competitive advantages, it has to satisfy three criteria: it must be valuable, difficult for competitors to imitate, and difficult to substitute (Barney, 1991).

Unique firm knowledge is valuable if it can successfully be applied to value-creating tasks (competence) and if it can be used to capitalize on existing business opportunities. Since competitors, in developing their own survival strategies, are likely to benchmark themselves against the industry leader to bring their performance up to that firm's level, knowledge must also be difficult to imitate. In order to make it difficult to imitate, companies should devise and execute initiatives for protecting knowledge. What first comes to mind in this regard is knowledge in the form of patents. Interestingly, the only processes or products that can be patented are based on explicit knowledge. Filing a patent is a time-consuming and costly process, but more important for the strategic role of knowledge, patent rights are difficult to enforce. An ever increasing number of patent engineers complain that manufacturers at distant locations—especially in developing countries—eagerly imitate their technologies. In some instances, patents can be circumvented by making incremental alterations in the basic technology, thereby enhancing the value of a final product for the customer.

Tacit social or individual knowledge, however, is typically more difficult to imitate than explicit knowledge captured in documents and manuals. Either the knowledge is actually impossible to replicate, or the imitation process is so costly that it deprives the imitator of the cost parity it set out to achieve. In 1980, a U.S. government study showed that Japanese manufacturers, on average, had a competitive cost advantage of $2,200 per subcompact car manufactured, which was primarily based on better inventory control, personnel management, and quality control.[7] This created a strong effort by Ford, General Motors, and Chrysler to tap the manufacturing knowledge of Japanese automotive companies. Numerous fact-finding missions were undertaken, several consulting assignments were initiated, and numerous books were written, but the source of the cost advantage proved tremendously difficult to imitate.

In fact, much of the knowledge in Japanese car manufacturing remains tacit (Spear and Bowen, 1999); it is tied to personal relations, shared habits, and intuition, all of which are not easily documented. For example, quality problems in supplies are resolved by intense face-to-face interactions with supplier representatives, not just by exchanging manufacturing procedures, or transferring engineering documents and product specifications. This is possible because of the close physical proximity of suppliers and manufacturers. The average distance of suppliers from Toyota, for instance, is thirty miles; as a consequence, the company clocks 10,635 person-days of face-to-face contact with its suppliers. This is difficult for Toyota's American counterparts to match. General Motors, for example, is located an average distance of 427 miles from its suppliers, and the resulting face-to-face contacts with them amount to 1,107 person-days (Dyer, 1996). Moreover, better personnel management involves job rotation programs and on-the-job training, which are either poorly documented at Japanese companies or difficult for an external observer to comprehend. Even in terms of inventory management, tacit knowledge plays an important role. Suppliers to Japanese car manufacturers are invited to share tacit manufacturing knowledge by working as guests during a company's manufacturing process, especially at the initial stages.

Tacit knowledge at such companies has another essential dimension: it is social, not just individual. It is deeply embedded in the social capital of a corporation. Although it may be hard to document such knowledge in a manual or a computer program, it is shared by all relevant organization members, as well as other stakeholders, such as suppliers. The competitive advantage of Japanese car companies, based as it is on tacit social knowledge, allows for a better understanding of how supplied parts affect final product quality, especially when the bottlenecks are located in the manufacturing process, the storage conditions for and use of supplied parts, just-in-time manufacturing schedules, and so on. Suppliers are also integrated into the improvement of the manufacturing process itself, continuously creating new knowledge that is difficult, if not impossible, for competitors to imitate.

It is not appropriate, however, to overemphasize the merit of tacit unique corporate knowledge. It indeed has potential disadvantages. As long as it remains tacit, it takes time and requires considerable effort to share it across functions, businesses, and geographical regions. For example, Toyota, the best automotive company in the world in terms of its market capitalization, sends its Japanese coordinators to Toyota's overseas operations so that its local affiliates can share unique tacit corporate knowledge developed in Japan face-to-face, as is done in Toyota's Japanese plants. The coordinator system has worked very well, and as a result, Toyota is growing fast outside Japan. This fast growth, however, has made it very difficult for Toyota to continue to use the coordinator system. Toyota cannot send enough coordinators to communicate the firm's unique knowledge. In addition, Toyota wants to grow fast when people show a growing interest in its energy-efficient hybrid engines. The face-to-face coordinator system has constrained potential growth.

Facing this challenge, Toyota announced the Toyota Way 2001. With the geographic expansion of Toyota's businesses and the widening of its business domain, people with diverse perceptions have come to be part of its global team. While recognizing the importance of diversity, Toyota has also realized an urgent need to clearly articulate and implement a set of common values, beliefs, and business methods, some of which are tacit and shared face-to-face, to support and guide the continuing evolution of its global operations. These approaches to work, which had been implicit in Toyota's corporate tradition, were compiled into a brochure that was distributed worldwide. Despite its effort, Toyota believes that some of its tacit unique knowledge will not be articulated. Due to the nature of knowledge, it is impossible to articulate corporate knowledge completely. Certain knowledge will remain tacit, a point that is very important to protect its competitive advantage. Companies must be careful about what is articulated and what is not. Toyota's experience teaches us that a company may have to change its strategy as it grows its business globally.

Finally, in order for knowledge to be a source of sustainable competitive advantage, it must be difficult for competitors to achieve the same level of costs or differentiation by substituting it for other knowledge. Efficiency in current operations, as well as innovation, can be enhanced by transferring and leveraging unique individual and social knowledge, and by sharing investments and costs across products, markets, and businesses. Some tacit knowledge can almost never be substituted because of what is called the "hegemonic effect": one or a group of companies (A) with the only source of tacit knowledge engages in knowledge-sharing with another company (B) based on expected returns; when those returns are satisfactory for A, future transactions with other companies (C) to achieve similar returns are avoided. This typically happens when suppliers work closely with customers, tapping their tacit knowledge in order to provide future solutions to customers' problems. Once a company has successfully shared tacit knowledge with a given supplier, however, it is unlikely to continue such exchanges with other firms.

Given that a firm's unique knowledge often adds such value, can public knowledge ever allow a company to achieve a sustainable competitive advantage? Based on the above discussion, the answer would seem to be no. Typically, public knowledge is the technical sort shared in research reports, engineering drawings, conference publications, textbooks, consulting manuals, and classrooms; often it represents general technical solutions that are freely available on the market. It is predominantly social explicit knowledge or individual tacit knowledge with the potential to become social knowledge in easily documented forms. Some public knowledge is of a narrative kind,[8] in which managers tell, hear, and retell stories about the industry, their competitors, the company, and themselves. Narrative knowledge often takes the form of "Did you hear that company A tested the new XC 3400 machine, with excellent results?" In this way, narratives give substance and life to technical knowledge, and may catch the interest of the listener enough for him or her to investigate further.

While public knowledge may not be as obvious a source of competitive advantage as unique knowledge, I propose that the process matters more than the content; in other words, what the company eventually does with its knowledge in terms of applying it to value-creating tasks matters more than the public availability of that content. The ability to transfer generic knowledge to various areas of a business may play a key role in a company's success, and the process itself may be unique, valuable, difficult to imitate, and difficult to substitute. Public knowledge shared across organizational units in different products, markets, or businesses can improve innovation and ultimately secure the sources of competitive advantage. For example, Buckman Laboratories, a U.S.-based producer of specialty chemicals, built an electronic communications system to encourage relationships among its employees and to allow for the effective transfer of knowledge, both public and unique, throughout its worldwide network of companies. Buckman's success lies more in the commitment of employees to using the electronic means of communication than in the sophistication of the system. In fact, the information technology itself can be imitated. But re-creating Buckman's culture of communication, in which the organization's members actively use the system to solve their local problems, is a very difficult task.[9]

Core Knowledge Activities for Strategic Management of Knowledge-based Competence of a Corporation

In the past, discussions about strategic management of knowledge assets of a corporation tended to focus on creation and sharing activities for managing the knowledge-based competence of a corporation. However, in order to execute the advancement and survival strategies, a more holistic view of them is required. Holistic knowledge management consists of four main activities: *creating, sharing, protecting,* and *discarding.*

First, companies should be knowledge-creating, trying to generate new knowledge well ahead of competitors (Nonaka and Takeuchi, 1995). After new knowledge has been created within a company, this knowledge has to be shared among organizational members across regions, businesses, and functions. Protection is literally about protecting knowledge assets from competitors. Preventing knowledge from being imitated is all about activities that increase complexity, tacitness, and specialty of products or services. Furthermore, companies should reflect on whether their knowledge is outdated. In some cases, it may be necessary to discard the existing knowledge and promote creation of new knowledge.

It should be kept in mind that the maintenance of enabling conditions is indispensable for facilitating these activities. Sharing a mission and vision throughout an organization, a unique strategy to attain them, an organizational culture that promotes knowledge creation and sharing, and leadership to initiate building up strong competitiveness are considered to be the necessary enabling conditions. Such activities, building blocks of knowledge management, need not only to coexist but also to be linked with each other. In short, it is very important to make them influence each other in order to allow knowledge assets to reach their full potential.

Survival and advancement strategies result in these four key knowledge activities. Knowledge creation constitutes a core of advancement strategy. However, in order to create new knowledge, a company has to discard obsolete knowledge. Newly created knowledge must be protected from being imitated by competitors. Retaining excellent managers who created new knowledge, so that knowledge outflow will not occur, is also an important activity of knowledge protection. While there are elements of knowledge-sharing for advancement strategies, the predominant process is one of discarding obsolete knowledge and creating new knowledge for future sustainable competitive advantage.

Knowledge protection is also a very important survival strategy along with knowledge-sharing. In executing this strategy, once knowledge is at hand, its effective utilization and protection critical are to sustain competitive advantage. Although there are elements of knowledge-discarding and knowledge creation in survival strategies, the focus is on rapid and effective knowledge-sharing across the business.

Balancing Survival and Advancement Strategies

Despite the value of unique knowledge, current managerial practice is dominated by survival thinking and the formulation of survival strategies. Few managers seem to have the courage to think beyond existing knowledge, resources, customers, suppliers, and competitors. The knowledge that executives use for strategizing is therefore limited to two scales—the company and the industry—and it is honed by identifying and utilizing current sources of competitive advantage. Perhaps this preoccupation with survival can be attributed to the difficulty of thinking in the future tense; admittedly, it is much harder to generate knowledge about something that *could* exist than about something that already exists. And managerial horizons are predominantly influenced by the immediate needs of stakeholders: shareholders want their returns now, customers want excellent service now, employees want their salaries today, and so on.

There are many reasons why individual managers opt for business survival over advancement; few of the reasons are rational, but they are based on solid fears, anxieties, and threats to self-image. Some managers fall prey to immediate needs and cannot see beyond the short term. Others just do not have time to develop advancement strategies. Some of these managers may well understand the importance of advancement strategies, but hope that the negative effects of emphasizing survival will not surface until they have left the company. Yet others find that thinking about the future, developing advancement strategies, and creating new knowledge have high associated risks.

In a stable environment, of course, a firm can thrive with a survival strategy. If unique knowledge continues to be a source of competitive advantage, still difficult to imitate or substitute, such knowledge will allow a company to maintain its hold on unique products and services, geographical positioning, low manufacturing costs, high yield on marketing expenses, and so forth. But if the environment of the firm changes, or if the firm itself undergoes major changes—such as a major loss of executive or professional talent—a preoccupation with current survival will endanger its future (March, 1991). Changes demand the creation of new sources of competitive advantage; the firm's executives must conceive of and implement advancement strategies not simultaneously being implemented by current *and* future competitors; and the benefits of these strategies must resist attempts at imitation.

Strategic management concerns the formulation and implementation of strategies, and ultimately determines the areas in which a company will do business and to what extent it will be successful in competing in those areas. Because strategy formulation is about resource allocation for maintaining current competitive advantages and developing new ones, this is the first place to restore the balance between advancement and survival. Some managers start with survival and advancement on a personal level. The senior vice president of strategic planning in an international telecommunications group, for instance, may spend one day a week in solitude in order to allow for personal advancement that can be transferred to the firm. Some management teams spend a portion of their time on team development, using "boundary-breaking" sessions in which team members must present unconventional ideas about how the industry or competitive environment could develop. Other management teams have structured their strategy formulation around survival and advancement, setting short- and long-term strategic horizons.

During such sessions, asking a number of questions can be helpful in order to achieve the right balance for a given company. Among them are the following.

Survival Strategies

1. How do we need to change our survival strategy in order to retain or improve our profit levels?
2. Who are the current and possible future competitors that are beginning to implement similar survival strategies?
3. What are our current sources of competitive advantages, and how do we need to improve these in order to sustain our competitive advantages over time?
4. How do we retain the value and uniqueness of the company's knowledge while securing it against possible imitation attempts and substitution by competitors? How do we transfer unique and public knowledge across our various products, markets, businesses, and organizational units more effectively than competitors?

Advancement Strategies

1. What should our advancement strategy be in order to secure future profit levels?
2. Who are the possible competitors that could implement similar advancement strategies?
3. What should be our future sources of competitive advantage, and how could these be made sustainable?
4. How do we create new knowledge that can become a source of sustainable competitive advantages? What should this knowledge encompass? How do we make this knowledge difficult to imitate and substitute at the outset of the creation process—in other words, *how can we use tacit knowledge to our advantage?* How do we transfer new knowledge across products, markets, businesses, and organizational units?

When you begin asking such questions, keep some ground rules in mind. First, in developing advancement strategies, a management team needs to go through a process of envisioning future knowledge, not just future business.

A second ground rule for strategizing is to recognize that there are no natural authorities on the future. Senior managers attain their positions through experience, but this experience is firmly grounded in the history of the company, past knowledge, current competence and assets, the past competitive dynamics of the industry, and past stakeholder expectations. Because much of their wisdom may be based on past experience, top managers are not always the most in tune with future business needs. When formulating the future knowledge needs of a company, then, many voices should be heard. A broad perspective on potential changes will increase a management team's awareness of possible courses of action. Do not hesitate to broaden your management team with young participants who have unconventional ideas. Diversity of team membership is very useful for managers to change their perceptions about customers, competitors, and their company itself.

Third, the formulation of advancement strategies requires scaling. At the outset, the management team might talk about knowledge in broad categories, in order to generate a more complete perspective on possible advancement strategies. These broad categories, in turn, can guide increasingly fine distinction-making. For example, the management team of a computer manufacturer might start by identifying knowledge associated with five broad generations of computing: mainframe computing, personal computing, servers, mobile computing, and ubiquitous computing.[10] Then, for each generation, finer distinctions can be made. For ubiquitous computing, such distinctions might comprise "private computing" versus "public computing." Private computing could be broken down into "intelligent homes," "intelligent consumer products," and "intelligent communication devices."

Fourth, and perhaps most important, strategic conversations are an asset to the company. Strategic conversations represent the cradle of the future in the purest sense. Records of conversations should be kept, and time should be allocated to reflect collectively on the conversations themselves. What insights did they generate? In which areas should the company seek more knowledge, and where is further fact-finding necessary? Why were certain ideas abandoned for others? Did all participants have a say in the process? Was participation sufficiently broad in the first place? These questions are raised during strategic conversations.

Incidentally, conversations are very useful to strengthen unique corporate capabilities that are required to execute advancement strategies. For example, conversations are core elements and are the most important activities in Toyota's every function. Toyota managers are encouraged to frequently raise open-ended questions to their subordinates so that they will improve problem-solving skills. High problem-solving skills are required of Toyota employees because they are the essence of doing *kaizen* (continuous improvement), Toyota's competitive advantage. In effective and efficient problem-solving, problems to be solved must be identified by comparing ideal situations and current situations. After the problems are thus identified, the root causes of the problems are found and effective countermeasures are taken against the root causes. Therefore, Toyota employees are routinely trained in problem-solving skills through conversations with their bosses, in on-the-job training. When a problem is identified, Toyota managers repeatedly ask their subordinates "why?" This "why?" will be repeated until the subordinates identify the root causes of the problem. "Why?" is repeated at least five times, and therefore this way of strengthening problem-solving capabilities through conversations is called "5 Whys."

In general, escaping the trap of the past is essential for the formulation of successful advancement strategies. The challenge for managers is to strike a balance between survival and advancement thinking in daily practice—that is, to honor the past but keep one's eyes on the future. But in too many business organizations, even if new ideas are given lip service, advancement strategies are neglected. In doing so, such organizations often undercut knowledge creation or are unable to grasp its competitive potential. Companies should pay more attention to advancement strategies and allocate sufficient resources to them. In order to have a better understanding of the strategic importance of advancement strategies, the example of Sharp is very instructive.

Sharp: Growth Through Advancement Strategies

Companies facing stiff competition should develop holistic views of knowledge management. A case in point is Sharp and its "black box" knowledge asset, which makes the company's unique knowledge difficult to imitate. This is done by using a combination of factors such as product customization, complexity, and intellectual property protection. Sharp has made this the keystone of its corporate strategy.

Sharp is one of the best-performing electronics manufacturers in Japan. In fiscal year 2004 (ended March 2005), consolidated sales reached 2.53 trillion yen (12 percent greater than in fiscal 2003), operating profit was 150 billion yen (up 23 percent), and net income was 75 billion yen (up 24 percent). While other Japanese electronics firms have been struggling with falling sales, Sharp's performance has been outstanding.

This success was mainly brought about by LCD devices and related products. For example, in 2002 Sharp was the first firm in the world to introduce mobile phones with cameras. Creation of this market was possible because of Sharp's development of the necessary components.

Head-to-Head Competition in Asia

Sharp has become a leading global electronics manufacturer by cultivating new frontiers using its LCD technologies. LCDs were developed by Radio Corporation of America (RCA) in 1963, and in 1968 RCA made the first LCD panel. However, due to manufacturing difficulties, RCA and other U.S. companies gave up commercialization of LCDs.

Sharp, on the other hand, identified growth opportunities in the business and took the lead in exploiting LCD technologies for innovative products. The first was a small calculator with a black-and-white LCD, introduced in 1973. PDAs (personal digital assistants) and camcorders followed. Sharp's strategy was to continuously and relentlessly improve LCD technology in order to produce new LCD product markets. As a result, Sharp become the industrial leader.

Developing ever larger LCD panels posed a technological challenge. In 1988, Sharp succeeded in building a 14.4-inch LCD panel for PCs. In the 1990s, LCDs gradually began to replace CRTs (cathode ray tubes) as PC monitors. As a result, Taiwanese LCD manufacturers emerged as strong competitors. Many U.S. PC makers outsource manufacturing to companies in Taiwan, so firms such as Unipac Optoelectronics were established to produce LCDs. One of their competitive advantages was being able to collaborate with leading PC makers such as IBM. This meant they could produce appropriate monitors with shorter delays and at a much cheaper cost.

Taiwanese firms simply purchased the same production equipment being sold to Sharp and other Japanese LCD manufacturers. They were especially competitive in producing smaller panels for PC displays. In contrast, Japanese firms were more interested in bigger panels so that they could produce monitors much more efficiently. The leading Taiwanese LCD manufacturers, Unipac and ADT (Acer Display Technology), merged in 2001 and became AU Optronics (AUO).

Korean competitors include Samsung Electronics and LG Electronics. Samsung is a particularly challenging competitor. The company was left with a huge debt burden following the 1997 Korean financial crisis, a crash in memory chip prices, and a $700 million write-off related to the takeover of AST Technologies, a U.S. maker of PCs. Samsung Group chairman Lee Kun-Hee, the son of the Group's founder and its head since 1987, brought in a new CEO, Yun Jong, in 1996. They saw a turnaround opportunity in the shift from analog to digital, and undertook a radical transformation of Samsung. Speed and intelligence would be key success factors in the new digitized electronics industry. Samsung rationalized its operations, selling businesses considered non-core for $2 billion. This, together with other job cuts, reduced employment by 24,000.

To gain profitability, Samsung focused exclusively on fast-growing digital products and devices such as LCDs, plasma displays, cell phones, digital cameras, and flash memories. Competing through speed in new product development, manufacturing launches, and economies of scale was to be its winning strategy. (For more on the company's remake, see *Business Week* (June 16, 2003).[11]

Samsung has become a fast mover in the LCD business, but it had always lagged Sharp in LCD panel launches. However, it surprised the public by bringing the fifth generation of LCD panels (LCD panel generations relate to their size; the fifth was 1100×1250 mm) to market in mid-2003, well ahead of Sharp.

Sharp's Strategy for the LCD Business

Although it has faced tougher competition from companies such as AUO, Samsung, and LG Electronics, Sharp has not changed its strategy: always be a technological leader. In 2002, Sharp developed continuous grain (CG) silicon liquid crystals. It was the first technology to create and control crystal particles that could be made into thin layers and attached to glass. This meant a simple glass board could be transformed into an LCD panel or television screen. Moreover, it had the capability of storing TV programs by operating semi-conductor memories inside. CG silicon has the advantage of providing a clearer display compared with other LCDs. Moreover, it is possible to arrange the display and related devices on the same glass board. Each product can be conveniently customized according to customers' needs. The technology is being used in a number of Sharp products, and panels are sold to others, including competitors producing camera cell phones.

However, the development was not shared even within Sharp before its release to the market. Sharp has filed for only a few patents related to CG silicon. This is very different from the usual practice in the industry. For a long time, Sharp had been famous for filing the largest number of LCD-related patents. Now, it emphasizes "black boxed know-how and technologies" to maintain competitiveness. The shift reflects realization that filing patents means revealing the essence of the technology to competitors.

One consequence of the shift was having created equipment for manu-facturing CG silicon inside the company. With this move, *the stickiness of knowledge* concerning the technology was expected to improve (1988). When equipment was purchased from outside, Sharp customized it beyond recognition.

Black box knowledge requires continuous management attention to dis-semination of knowledge within the company. Sharp faced a complicated chain of decisions.

1. Further development of CG silicon as a result of knowledge creation;
2. Customizability of final products (such as avoiding the imitation of a product by potential competitors);
3. Accelerated structuring of the production process;
4. Shaping the skills of mass production and managerial techniques.

The third and fourth decisions aimed at delaying competitor catch-up. The steps taken were strategically very effective. Only with the implementation and continuation of tightly related strategic plans could Sharp expect to remain the leader in the LCD market for mobile-sized devices—that is, screens used on mobile phones and personal digital assistants (PDAs), such as its own Zaurus (called Wizard in the United States).

In the 1990s Sharp saw the importance of the niche market—mobile-sized LCDs that can be used for such products as PDAs and mobile phones—when all the other manufacturers were focused on larger sizes. Sharp's strategic choice may have been a result of a unique corporate policy of "achieving the top in a one-of-a-kind industry." Adding to such niche positioning, the fact that mobile LCDs were often customized helped prevent products from being commoditized.

Uniqueness of knowledge is one of the effective factors that prevent technology imitations (Chakravarthy, McEvily, Doz, and Rau, 2003). This extra layer of competitive shield, brought by niche positioning and customizability, completely eliminated followers. However, in order to sustain advantage, Sharp must first utilize the knowledge created to develop innovative products and protect it effectively. The combination of strategic positioning and strategic management of knowledge-based competence of a firm is crucially important for Sharp in gaining and sustaining its competitive advantage.

The development of CG silicon shows that layers of interrelated knowledge-based activities protect corporate knowledge assets. Sharp is now trying to change the rules of competition in the large-LCD market by applying the same line of attack. The next section looks at the case of LCD televisions in more detail, in order to formulate a valid hypothesis concerning knowledge-based management.

Knowledge Vision and Innovation in the Television Market

Sharp is known for pioneering revolutionary LCD televisions, and is one of the leading players in this market. In 2004 it had a 34 percent global share, selling nearly 1.5 million sets. The share in Japan was almost 50 percent (755,000 sets), and outside Japan it was almost 27 percent ((726,000 sets). In the four years beginning in January 2001, when it introduced the Aquos series, Sharp accounted for 36 percent (5 million) of the 14 million LCD sets sold in the world.

In 1998 Katsuhiko Machida, Sharp's president, announced his vision of selling only LCD sets in the Japanese market by 2005. This was only two months after he assumed the helm. Machida had long been concerned about the future of Sharp's televisions. At the time, aggressive Korean competitors were affecting the market. Although Sharp started production of fourteen-inch CRT sets in 1953, original equipment manufacturers had supplied the CRTs, and the company had continued to rely on outside sources, many of them competitors in the finished-set market.

Machida, having served as general manager of television products, foresaw the approaching loss of corporate negotiation power if sales of TVs, the most prestigious electronics product line at the time, started to plunge. Thus, the new vision was aimed at gaining and sustaining competitive advantage in the global electronics industry. To that end, Machida was willing to discard the company's knowledge of how to produce CRT TV sets. This was a bold decision. Although Sharp did not produce the CRTs, it had developed considerable knowledge regarding CRT TV sets, including manufacturing processes and color coordination technologies.

At the same time, Sharp had been active in development of LCDs for nearly thirty years, and had introduced the first calculator with an LCD in 1973. Still, including television in its long-term commitment to developing LCD technologies was significant. It was an aspect of Sharp's knowledge vision, because the company has always pursued innovation as an electronics company.

The vision statement was a surprise. At that time, the general belief was that tube TV sets would be the mainstream for quite a while longer. Technically, it was not easy to expand the size of an LCD panel, which made the vision a risky bet. Sony, Sharp's strongest competitor in TVs, was not willing to discard its knowledge of producing traditional CRTs, given its success with its Trinitron monitors.

Machida's knowledge-based vision statement was not a forecast. It described his strong intention to gain and sustain competitive advantage in the LCD TV market. It was an instance of pure originality. Shigemitsu Mizushima, then development manager of the LCD television project, was among those astounded by the announcement. Now general manager of the display technology development group, Mizushima did not know of the new vision until it was publicly announced. At the time, he did not have enough confidence in making LCD panels through 100 percent internal production. Nevertheless, he was assigned to lead the product development team.

Previous products with LCDs, such as personal computer monitors, were designed for viewing from the front. Televisions required a broader viewing angle. This led the team to develop a customized LCD, the Advanced Super View. Color display was another major issue. A joint project team from the LCD group, which had knowledge of high-resolution color display, and the television group, with expertise in television screen color control, was formed. Engineers from the television group in Tochigi, north of Tokyo, spontaneously joined the LCD group, which was based in Tenri, near Osaka.

Japanese companies generally have strong functional and divisional boundaries that make cross-functional and cross-divisional activities difficult. In contrast, for Sharp, such coordination was neither new nor difficult: it had been using "urgent project teams"—cross-functional task forces—since 1977. The teams had developed a number of hit products. Thus, the organization believed it was natural to work beyond one's own division. Such a culture was deeply rooted and was not easy for competitors to duplicate (Reber, 1993). Machida has always praised the advantage of this tacit culture. He believed the rapid process of development and production was due to this "urgent project team" tradition. The strength of the organization was built on the tacit knowledge brought about by historical organizational experience (Winter, 1987).

In 2005 Sharp purchased Fujitsu's LCD panel operations. These had been unprofitable, and Fujitsu was looking to exit the business. Sharp also acquired ownership of some technology it previously had paid to license.

Spiral Process and "Black Box" Knowledge

Working toward the knowledge vision led the organization to further success. Sharp's market share in all kinds of televisions improved from 11.5 percent in 1998 to 20.0 percent in 2003. In 2002, Sharp's LCD television revenue surpassed that of tube televisions.

The company invested 100 billion yen in a new plant with the latest equipment in Kameyama, in Mie prefecture between Osaka and Nagoya. All processes, from production of LCD panels to assembly of LCD TVs, are housed in the plant, which started operations in January 2004. The plant produces sixth-generation panels, which are 1500 x 1800 mm. That is large enough to make eight thirty-inch LCD TVs. The plant can produce some 100,000 panels each month. The machine used in panel production is so large that, at first, it seemed impossible to find a road on which to transport it to the plant. The Kameyama plant was a strategic initiative for Sharp, and was intended to change the rules of the LCD business. Panel size had been the key factor, with companies focusing on enlarging them. By aiming at optimization of devices and products, with the Kameyama plant project Sharp took the lead in terms of efficiency. Thus, Sharp leaped directly from fourth- to sixth-generation panels. To do this, project members reviewed technologies and processes, and changed them radically. By combining the production of mother glass and the assembly of TVs in one place, Sharp was able to achieve both high speed and cost effectiveness. This exemplifies what is called the "spiral effect." Although the circuits in LCD panels and TVs are different, concentrating the production site enhanced integration.

The Kameyama plant physically created the context of innovation (knowledge creation), in which organization members share tacit and explicit knowledge with each other through dialogue, thus facilitating cross-divisional and cross-functional coordination. The LCD technology and TV development departments had been located far apart. However, top management thought collaboration between the two was crucial in developing new LCD TVs faster, more effectively, and efficiently. Experience with ad hoc "urgent project teams" allowed cross-divisional and cross-functional coordination on a permanently institutionalized level in Kameyama.

One Kameyama-based engineer in LCD technology development commented, "It is so exciting to see the process of LCD TV development . . . on the spot. I am so happy to see new LCDs I had developed . . . assembled into TV sets just in front of me" (interview by author, January 15, 2004). As this shows, the social relationship among engineers in the two departments has improved. This is an important part of the context for knowledge creation, as well as a key enabler for knowledge creation.

An innovative mix of novel LCD development and manufacturing technology with TV production technology also created an important barrier of complexity. This protects Sharp from being imitated. As the value chain premise indicates, the more different activities are linked, the higher the value that can be created. Increased complexity makes technology difficult to copy (Simon, 1962).

When plans for Kameyama were announced in 2002, production was expected to start in May 2004. However, rapid growth of the LCD television market led to accelerated actions: productions began in January 2004. Sharp had launched another plant in Mie, where it tested various activities, in June 2003. The experience gained was incorporated into the Kameyama plant, and the plant is now called the "knowledge-integrated building." In January 2005, Sharp announced plans to build a 150 billion yen plant adjacent to the existing one in Kameyama that would build eighth-generation panels (2160 × 2400 mm) to be used in forty-inch and fifty-inch TV sets. It is expected to open in October 2006.

Conclusion

In order to cultivate a new business frontier, companies should gain and maintain competitive advantage. To gain competitive advantage, taking the lead in developing new technologies, and producing innovative products and services using these technologies, are critically important. In other words, knowledge creation *does* matter. Knowledge creation is the core knowledge activity for executing advancement strategies.

- In order to avoid the catch-up by competitors, companies should be good at utilizing new technology for various business opportunities, as well as protecting them from imitation. Therefore, knowledge-sharing and knowledge protection are important in sustaining competitive advantage. The importance of these two aspects of knowledge creation cannot be emphasized too much, especially for companies that execute survival strategies.

- It is important to emphasize that any technology will ultimately become obsolete. Companies that have been leading the industry by developing core technologies, tend to be especially late in developing and using new technologies that may replace the existing ones. Therefore, in order to accomplish sustainable growth, thus avoiding the innovator's dilemma, companies should not be afraid to discard obsolete knowledge. The success of execution of advancement strategies will be strongly influenced by whether companies can discard obsolete knowledge.

- To catch new business opportunities before any other competitor, and to keep that advantage for long, it is indispensable to protect and defend knowledge that leads to innovation. Asserting knowledge ownership by acquiring patents is not enough. Management of knowledge assets has to go further than simple technology management. Knowledge creation is a product of human activities. Therefore, companies should not forget the importance of retaining excellent knowledge workers by enhancing social capital within their organizations.

- The time has come to realize holistic strategic management of the knowledge-based competence of a corporation, and gain sustainable competitiveness. Those who intend to gain and sustain in the rapidly moving environment must pay more attention to the importance of creating, sharing, protecting, and discarding knowledge, and facilitate these activities consistently. All four activities are important for companies to consistently improve their intellectual assets.

Acknowledgments

This is the revised version of chapter 5 of *Enabling Knowledge Creation: How to Unlock the Mystery of Tacit Knowledge and Release the Power of Innovation*, by Georg von Krogh, Kazuo Ichijo, and Ikujiro Nonaka (New York: Oxford University Press, 2000). The significant revision was made on the concept of four core knowledge activities.

Notes

1. For more on this discussion, see Harris and Helfat (1997); Castanias and Helfat (1991).

2. See, for example, Kalthoff, Nonaka, and Ueno (1997); Nonaka and Von Krogh (1999).

3. Although Davenport and Prusak (1997) do an excellent job of identifying knowledge management approaches, their discussions related to strategy are quite rudimentary. One exception to the rule is the special issue of *Strategic Management Journal*, "Knowledge and the Firm" 17 (December 1996), as well as the special

issue of *International Business Review*, "Knowledge in Organizations, Knowledge Transfer, and Cooperative Strategies" 3, no. 4 (1994).

4. According to Prahalad and Bettis (1986), management holds a "dominant logic" that to a large extent is historically influenced. Historical conceptions of resources and the environment are embedded in rigid cognitive structures. The dominant logic is particularly manifest when making resource allocation decisions within the corporate portfolio. See also Bettis and Prahalad (1995), as well as Von Krogh and Roos (1996a).

5. Although there are several ways to measure company performance, profitability is one of the key measures in the literature on strategy. For more on this, see, for example, Banker, Chang, and Majumdar (1996).

6. I choose to talk of "cost and/or differentiation" rather than just one or the other. There are several grounds for such claims, some residing in empirical studies of successful companies, such as IKEA and Swatch, and others in theoretical arguments. For more on this, see, for example, Hamel and Prahalad (1994).

7. See documents from the Grace Commission (1980–1984).

8. For more on "narrative knowledge," see Lyotard (1984).

9. This example is based on Knowledge Inc. (1997) and a 1997 presentation by Buckman Laboratories.

10. Mark Weiser, "The Computer for the Twenty-first Century." *Scientific American*, September 1991, pp. 94–10.

11. "The Samsung Way." *Business Week*, June 16, 2003, pp. 46–53.

References

Andrew, K. (1971). *The Concept of Corporate Strategy*. Homewood, Ill.: Dow Jones-Irwin.

Banker, R. D., Chang, H.-H., and Majumdar, S. K. (1996). "A Framework for Analyzing Changes in Strategic Performance." *Strategic Management Journal* 17 (9): 693–713.

Barney, J. B. (1991). "Firm Resources and Sustained Competitive Advantage." *Journal of Management* 17(1): 99–120.

Bettis, R., and Prahalad, C. K. (1995). The Dominant Logic: Retrospective and Extension. *Strategic Management Journal* 16 (1): 5–14.

Castanias, R. P., and Helfat, C. E. (1991). "Managerial Resources and Rents." *Journal of Management* 17 (1): 155–171.

Chakravarthy, B., McEvily, S., Doz, Y., and Rau, D. (2003). "Knowledge Management and Competitive Advantage." In M. Easterby-Smith and M. A. Lyles, eds., *The Blackwell Handbook of Organizational Learning and Knowledge Management*, pp. 205–323. Oxford: Blackwell.

Christensen, C. (1997). *Innovator's Dilemma: When New Technologies Cause Great Firms to Fail*. Boston: Harvard Business School Press.

Davenport, T., and Prusak, L. (1997). *Working knowledge: How Organizations Manage What They Know*. Boston: Harvard Business School Press.

Doz, Y. L., Santos, J. F. P., and Williamson, P. J. (2001). *From Global to Metanational: How Companies Win in the Knowledge Economy*. Boston: Harvard Business School Press.

Drucker, P. F. (1993). *Post-Capitalist Society*. New York: HarperBusiness.

Dyer, J. H. (1996). "Specialized Supplier Networks as a Source of Competitive Advantage: Evidence from the Auto Industry." *Strategic Management Journal* 17(4): 271–293.

Eisenhardt, K. M., and Santos, J. F. (2001). "Knowledge-Based View: A New Theory of Strategy." In A. M. Pettigrew, T. Howard, and R. Whittington, eds., *Handbook of Strategy and Management*. London: Sage.

Fahey, L., and Narayanan, V. K. (1986). *Macroenvironemtal Analysis for Strategic Management*. St. Paul, Minn.: West.

Grace Commission. (1980–1984). *Documents from the Grace Commission: President's Private Sector Survey on Cost Control*.

Hamel, G. (1996). "Strategy as Revolution." *Harvard Business Review*, July/August: 69–71.

Hamel, G., and Prahalad, C. K. (1994). *Competing for the Future*. Boston: Harvard Business School Press.

Harris, D., and Helfat, C. E. (1997). "Specificity of CEO Human Capital and Compensation." *Strategic Management Journal* 18 (11): 895–920.

Kalthoff, O., Nonaka, I., and Ueno, P. (1997). *The Light and the Shadow*. Oxford: Capstone.

"Knowledge and the Firm." *Strategic Management Journal* 17 (December, 1996).[A] Special issue.

"Knowledge in Organizations, Knowledge Transfer, and Cooperative Strategies." (1994). *International Business Review* 3 (4). [B]Special issue.

Levenhagen, M., Porac, J. F., and Thomas, H. (1993). "The Formation of Emergent Markets: Strategic Investigations in the Software Industry." In P. Lorange, B.Chakravarthy, and J. Roos, eds., *Implementing Strategic Processes*. Oxford: Blackwell Business.

Lyotard, J. F. (1984). *The Postmodern Condition: A Report on Knowledge*. Translated by Geogg Bennington and Brian Massumi. Minneapolis: University of Minnesota Press.

March, J. G. (1991). "Exploration and Exploitation in Organizational Learning." *Organization Science* 2 (1): 71–85.

Mintzberg, H. (1975). "The Manager's Job: Folklore and Fact." *Harvard Business Review*, July–August: 49–61.

Nonaka, I., and Takeuchi, H. (1995). *The Knowledge-Creating Company: How Japanese Companies Create the Dynamics of Innovation*. New York: Oxford University Press.

Nonaka, I., and von Krogh, G. (1999). Wissens-Hysterie. *Managermagazin*, April: 164.

Porter, M. E. (1990). *Competitive Strategy: Techniques for Analyzing Industries* New York: Free Press.

Prahalad, C. K., and Bettis, R. A. (1986). "The Dominant Logic: A New Linkage between Diversity and Performance." *Strategic Management Journal* 7 (6): 485–501.

Reber, A. S. (1993). *Implicit Learning and Tacit Knowledge: An Essay on the Cognitive Unconscious.* New York: Oxford University Press.

Rummelt, R. P. (1980). "The Evaluation of Business Strategy." In W. F. Glueck, ed., *Business Policy and Strategic Management,* 3rd ed. New York: McGraw-Hill.

"The Samsung Way." *Business Week,* June 16, 2003: 46–53.

Simon, H. A. (1962). The Architecture of Complexity. *Proceedings of the American Philosophical Society* 106: 467–482.

Spear, S., and Bowen, H. K. (1999). "Decoding the DNA of the Toyota Production System." *Harvard Business Review,* September–October: 97–106.

Von Hippel, E. (1988). *Sources of Innovation.* New York: Oxford University Press.

Von Krogh, G., Ichijo, K., and Nonaka, I. (2000). *Enabling Knowledge Creation: How to Unlock the Mystery of Tacit Knowledge and Release the Power of Innovation.* New York: Oxford University Press.

Von Krogh, G., and Roos, J. (1996a). "A Tale of the Unfinished." *Strategic Management Journal* 17 (9): 729–739. Special issue.

———. 1996b. "The New Language Lab—Parts 1 and 2." *Financial Times* 21 (3): 9–12.

Von Krogh, G., Roos, J., and Slocum, K. (1994). "An Essay on Corporate Epistemology." *Strategic Management Journal* 15: 53–72. Special issue.

Winter, S. G. (1987). "Knowledge and Competence as Strategic Assets." In D. Teece, ed., *The Competitive Challenge: Strategies for Industrial Innovation and Renewal.* New York: Harper & Row.

9

Market Research in Product Development

DOROTHY LEONARD

The greatest challenge in product and service innovation is to match what customers will buy to what the organization can produce. Usually the knowledge requisite to accomplish that task resides in two different contexts: that of the users and that of the organization's developers. It falls to marketing professionals to blend the experience base of the user with the experience base of the creators. Marketers must absorb enough of the customers' worldview and experience to envision value-adding products and services—especially those which the customers themselves cannot describe—and to use that vision to guide the development of the innovation. Since the early twentieth century, marketing research has developed a highly sophisticated set of tools focused on that task of discovery. The advent of computers has allowed the splintering of huge amounts of data on customer preferences and behaviors into ever more atomized clusters that can be targeted with specialized offerings. Companies can collect information and data about relatively small population segments, say, stay-at-home mothers with two or more children or Hispanic middle school art teachers.

However, even such highly sophisticated, statistics-based research has limits in guiding development of new products or services. It is far easier to deliver information and data about market segments than knowledge about what customers really need, what they are thinking, or what unconscious motives are driving their behavior. In the sections below, I first discuss some of the limits of traditional market research and then describe various nontraditional modes of research that offer insights into the customers' minds—insights that are sometimes unavailable to the customers themselves. In focusing on nontraditional techniques, I do not intend to deny the utility of market research as generally practiced. Rather, I seek to highlight less used but powerful ways of digging deeper into the customer's psyche. I suggest that the tools described below provide critical knowledge based more on deep-seated beliefs and actual behavior than on customers' statements about their desires and intents.

Limits of Inquiry

One of the most venerable tools of the marketer is the large sample survey, conducted over the telephone, through the mail, or by e-mail. Everyone knows the frustration of answering a telephone survey (usually at dinnertime). Even while you are selecting the answer (1 to 5) that best represents your opinion, your mind is busy with caveats and exceptions. Often you do not think the survey poses the right questions or allows you to express your real feelings about the topic. When you hang up the phone, you wonder what possible use can be made of the partial answers you were forced to give to (as you see it) peripheral questions about the topic. Certainly, data and even information can be derived when your responses are combined with hundreds of others. But you are not sure that the survey has produced real knowledge about your preferences and needs because of the way the questions were framed and necessarily bounded by the medium.

Focus groups have some advantages over surveys, especially for assessing human factors and the ease of using a product. However, they are often not good guides for developing and testing new product and service ideas, for a number of reasons (Zaltman, 2003). Usually, the groups are so large that an average participant has ten to twelve minutes to speak, which is time enough to garner relatively superficial reactions and opinions—but not enough time to delve deeply into that individual's thoughts and experiences. Groups are also subject to the usual biases of group dynamics, including the influence of strong speakers and the lack of enough trust among the strangers drawn together for the session to speak candidly about personal issues.

Personal, one-on-one interviews have many advantages over surveys and focus groups, in that they allow for the interaction so essential to learning a respondent's viewpoint. Unless the interview protocol is so rigid as to prohibit discussion, the person interviewed is free to object to the way a question is worded and to offer details, nuances, and context. Moreover, usually an interview allows more time for reflection and exploration. However, unless the interviewer is extremely skilled in interpreting body language, the conversation still skims along the surface. The data are subject to response bias (the inclination of an interviewee to say what he or she thinks the interrogator wants to hear) and to an interviewee's natural reticence with a nonintimate, that is, the disinclination we all have to discuss personal matters with a stranger, especially if the discussion will embarrass us.

There are a host of other barriers on the road to anticipating customer purchasing behavior, regardless of which tools of inquiry are employed.
There is a well documented, wide chasm between attitude—or even expressed
intent—and behavior, between the mouth and the money (Fishbein and
Ajzen, 1975). For a variety of reasons, people often do not buy the services
and products that they enthusiastically endorsed in theory.

All of us find it difficult to foretell whether or how we will use a product or
service that has no direct analogy in our experience. In fact, people often try
to use a new product as they did its most closely analogous predecessor, for
example, ignoring the automatic wrap-around feature of a computer to type a
"carriage return" at the end of each keyboarded line. Moreover, customers
tend to focus on their current needs and desires, about which they are articulate, but have trouble predicting what they will require three years hence.

Analysis from market research is especially difficult to interpret, and can even
mislead when the product, process, or service is radical—new to the world. Many
radically new products or technologies require the coevolution of complementary services to reach their potential. Think of how many alterations were required of the food industry before we began to use microwave ovens as they
were originally intended—to cook whole dinners. And what of the World Wide
Web until there were browsers and search engines? Only those individuals who
understand the theoretical capabilities of a new technology can envision future
uses. So if you had been asked in the early 1990s how you intended to use the
Internet, it is unlikely that you could have foreseen "Googling" long-lost high
school friends, or prospective employees and in-laws. There was little in your prior
experience to lead you to imagine conducting such activities from your desk.

Perhaps the most daunting gap between expressed preferences and actual
behavior results from the inaccessibility of many of the brain's operations to
its owner. We are simply unaware of our own processing of stimuli, and we
are therefore unable to accurately inform anyone (including ourselves) about
what we really want and need. The value of some products and services is
based on largely intangible attributes. True, market research is sophisticated
enough to query people about preferences in sound (e.g., the distinctive, well-
known, and legally protected sound of a Harley Davidson motorcycle motor)
and smell (e.g., the scent of leather in a new Nissan Infinity). However, understanding why some people like a movie, or prefer one financial adviser over
another, is more difficult. Products or services that evoke deeply based emotions about such issues as trust, beauty, or honesty can be difficult to design
and deliver. The service producer cannot simply ask the customer how to
create the attributes that will elicit the desired emotional response.

The less familiar the product category is, the more difficult that inquiry
becomes. One reason that motorcycle fans can talk knowledgeably about the
sounds of motors and car owners' noses can differentiate among the scents of
different leathers is that these products have been around for decades. As noted

above, people are less able to express opinions about unfamiliar product possibilities—and that lack is exacerbated when the potential products have many intangible characteristics. In fact, inquiry can mislead, as the customers will try to express explicitly needs that are in fact implicit, buried in the tacit dimensions of knowledge. Psychological research has revealed that people pressed to explain their choices or decisions based on unconscious reasoning will give explanations that are clearly unrelated to their actual behavior. For example, customers asked to select a type of stockings will overwhelmingly select those placed in a certain physical relationship to the rest of the choices. But when asked *why* they chose the brand they did, they will never state that reason. They will cite price, or color, or other attributes (Nisbett and Wilson, 1977).

In short, people will readily tell researchers what they think the questioners want to hear, will blithely predict behaviors that they will never undertake or falsely explain those which they do, but cannot describe needs they do not know they have and will not tell researchers about ones that embarrass them. For all these reasons, even the most skilled inquiries face barriers in anticipating consumers' purchasing behavior.

Knowledge from Nontraditional Market Research

A number of nontraditional research techniques attempt to break these barriers and provide real knowledge—not just information or data. In the following examples, I discuss how to get into the mind of the ultimate user of a product or service. All of the techniques discussed are more qualitative than quantitative (although all have proven, quantifiable benefits in product and service design and delivery), and differ significantly from those which rely upon large samples of the population. They all involve small numbers of respondents, and sometimes such individuals are selected precisely because they are *not* representative of a general populace but have particularly valuable experience and knowledge. These nontraditional methods dig deep rather than explore broadly. Findings are often counterintuitive. However, all these types of market research are better tools for *generating* new product and service ideas than they are for *testing* those ideas. All the following nontraditional market research techniques require follow-up with traditional prototyping and testing to be sure that the ideas generated appeal to a broad enough customer base to warrant the investment in their development.

Lead User Research

Lead user research collects information about both needs and solutions from users at the leading edges of the target market, as well as from customers in other markets who face similar problems, but in a more extreme form. The methodology originated from the academic research of Professor Eric von Hippel at the Massachusetts Institute of Technology's Sloan School of Management. Von Hippel found that, contrary to most apparent assumptions, in many cases users, rather than manufacturers, were the initial developers of innovations that proved to be commercially significant new products and processes (von Hippel, 1988). Further study revealed that the innovation was concentrated among "lead users" of those products and services. Lead users have two characteristics: (1) they are motivated to innovate because they can benefit from a solution to their needs and (2) they have those needs earlier than most others in the target market.

Manufacturers have little incentive to serve such a population, since their greatest profits will accrue from a larger market than the one represented by these initial needy users. Lead users cannot wait; they innovate on their own. They are therefore excellent harbingers of future trends. The market research approach that has evolved from von Hippel's work includes a "pyramid" networking exercise to get to lead users at the very forefront of knowledge about important trends. The researchers ask lead users in a given field to identify people even more expert than themselves; each informant provides contacts, and therefore contributes to an overall knowledge map of lead users in a particular domain. Lead users may also identify lead users in other markets who face even more extreme challenges. These users provide information that researchers shape into preliminary product, service, and strategy ideas that can be further refined into feasible business opportunities (von Hippel, 2005).

Because lead users have already analyzed their own needs and even produced solutions themselves, they have valuable knowledge about market trends in advance of any that research among current, typical users could provide. That is, the innovations that lead users produce embody knowledge which would likely be inaccessible to producers through traditional market research. At 3M, a company renowned for innovation, researchers conducted an experiment to determine if products identified through the lead user research were more likely to be breakthrough innovations than those identified through traditional market research methods. Their findings showed that the lead user process indeed outperformed the usual methods on this criterion. For example, lead users identified a new approach to the prevention of infections associated with surgery. Instead of the usual generic methods, lead users identified a portfolio of patient-specific measures based on each patient's individual biological susceptibilities. This innovation was successfully and profitably brought to market (Lilien, Morrison, Searls, Sonnack, and von Hippel, 2002).

The lead user research methodology depends upon the ability of the users to articulate their needs, through explicit responses to interviews and/or through solutions that they themselves have created. Thus, the knowledge garnered through lead user research is accessible to the researchers either through explicit knowledge transfer from expert users, or through knowledge embodied in prototype products or processes. But what about knowledge that is so tacit, so deeply buried in consciousness or difficult to explain, that users or customers cannot readily convey it to researchers and developers? We look next at techniques designed to address that problem.

Metaphors and Consensus Mapping

Building on an understanding of how the unconscious mind works, Gerald Zaltman (2003) has developed a metaphor elicitation technique for exploring people's largely unconscious feelings about a product or experience. Zaltman explains, "Metaphors do not exist as words in memory, but as networks of abstract understandings that constitute part of our mental imagery... [M]etaphors are the primary means by which companies and consumers engage one another's attention and imagination" (Zaltman, 2003, pp. 89, 92). For example, Chevrolet truck managers took advantage of a number of mental associations when they designed one of their most successful advertisements with the tag "like a rock." Such a metaphor is relatively obvious, but Zaltman also searches for what he calls "core" metaphors, which are deep, tacit, and even unconscious. Core metaphors are useful to generate ideas for new products or the positioning of existing ones. Understanding core metaphors is also helpful in strengthening a company's brand and image.

Research in the Mind of the Market Laboratory at Harvard Business School honed the metaphor elicitation technique, which involved getting people to find photographs or drawings that conveyed their feelings about a given company or product, and then interviewing those informants at length to understand their choice of imagery. The researchers then built a "consensus map" of shared constructs and their interaction in a network from a number of these individual interviews. So, for example, a financial services firm found, to its surprise, that one customer who had closed his account with it described the company with a picture of Mount Everest—strong, lasting, but unyielding and unchanging. A consensus map constructed for this firm from a number of such metaphor elicitation exercises showed that patronage, dignity, responsiveness, hospitality, moral character, honesty, and dependability were linked in the minds of the consumers. Each of these words had depths of underlying meaning, and the connections among them elicited from informants suggested some needed changes in customer interfaces with the company. The firm decided to work on strengthening clients' association of dignity and dependability, and subsequent evaluations showed that this linkage had value both internally for employees and externally in contrast to competitors (see Zaltman, 2003, chaps. 6 and 7).

Ethnography and Empathic Design

Another set of techniques designed to uncover the tacit dimensions of customers' knowledge focuses on observable behavior, followed by interviews or debriefing. Techniques originally developed for use in anthropological research have found their way into marketing and new product development in the form of *empathic design*, which is a process of developing such deep empathy for another's point of view that you can use that perspective to stimulate novel design concepts (Leonard and Swap, 1999, pp. 82–88). The more deeply a researcher can get into the mind-set, the perspective, of a prospective or actual user, the more valuable is the knowledge thus generated. There are a number of ways of gaining this perspective: the product, process, or service designer can take the role of anthropologist and observe behavior; the designer can provide ways for the user to observe and document his or her own behavior; or the designer can become a user of the targeted product or service.

Developer/Designer as Observer

In recent years, one fourth of the graduates of anthropology programs in the United States has gone to work for corporations. Why? Because they have been trained in research methods that are particularly powerful in uncovering unarticulated user needs. Anthropologists and ethnographers use in-depth observation of people in their native habitats to understand the significance of behaviors (both ritualistic and routine), artifacts, and symbols. Looking through the ethnographer's lens at any civilization focuses the attention on the unspoken, the taken-for-granted, the context in which decisions are made—including purchase decisions.

Such observation is valuable, of course, when language or custom makes inquiry difficult. For example, anthropologists working for Motorola in Azerbaijan discovered that cell phone customers looked at the bar codes underneath the batteries to determine where a phone was manufactured, in the belief that production in the United States was the best guarantee of quality (Weise, 1999).

But anthropological techniques can be just as useful in very familiar settings. One of the most famous instances of observation changing the course of product development was a study in 1979 by anthropology graduate student Lucy Suchman at the Xerox Palo Alto Research Center, where such innovations as the graphical user interface and the computer mouse originated. Suchman worked in the intelligent systems laboratory, where researchers were trying to make copiers easier to use by building in artificial intelligence. She produced an unintentionally hilarious film of two of the brainiest Xerox scientists trying to figure out how to copy some documents, thereby underlining the need for simplicity in use. Thereafter, all Xerox machines had a simple "copy" button to use for uncomplicated jobs.

Many design firms have since hired social scientists, particularly ones trained in ethnography, to observe and document people's actual, as opposed to reported, behavior. For example, Silicon Valley–based IDEO was asked by Advanced Cardiovascular Systems to redesign a medical instrument used by technicians during balloon angioplasty procedures for heart patients. The balloon is guided through the femoral artery in a patient's leg up into an obstructed coronary artery, where it is inflated to stretch the artery and compress plaque blocking the blood flow. IDEO was told the new design, like the old one, had to allow for one-handed use. But observations in operating rooms revealed that no one had hands big enough to do that, and that almost everyone used both hands. By changing the design to accommodate two-handed use, the designers were able to add many improvements, including greater ease in inflating and deflating the balloon, more control and precision, better pressure gauge visibility, and elimination of a ratcheting noise that was particularly frightening to the patients (Kelley and Littman, 2001). Similarly, the design firm GVO changed the way that SC Johnson Professional (SCJP) worked after the designers spent three months researching SCJP janitorial services in eleven countries, twenty-five cities, and seventy facilities. The largest discoveries were (1) that SCJP's historical segmentation of customers into industry-based categories (e.g., fast-food versus schools) no longer made any sense and (2) that cleaning had evolved from a centralized, station-based process into a nomadic activity. The commercial cleaners needed easily transportable tools and systems. From that insight was born the J-Fill dispensing system, a handheld mobile set of dispensers and cleaning concentrates that reduced cleaning times and mistakes in diluting the concentrates.

Observation can also identify opportunities for new products because people reveal unrecognized emotional or psychological needs through their behavior. For example, GVO helped Kimberly-Clark design a very successful new diaper line after in-home visits showed that parents were embarrassed that their toddlers still needed diapers. As a step toward "grown-up" clothes, Kimberly-Clark produced Huggies Pull-Ups, which both kept the children dry and also satisfied the parents' ego requirements. Kimberly-Clark continues to profit handsomely from this product line.

In the physical world, the researcher shadows subjects, taking notes, pictures, or videos to document behavior. The equivalent activity in cyberspace is following mouse tracks (i.e., observing how a cyber denizen moves from Web site to Web site, what icons he or she clicks on, and what he or she decides to purchase. In 1999, a little fifty-person, no-revenue company named Alexa Internet that sought to keep track of absolutely everything on the Internet was sold to Amazon.com for $250 million. The reason? Alexa's huge databases made it possible to search out buying and Web-surfing patterns.

Collabrys, a Silicon Valley venture, started out as an online publisher, providing e-publications to individuals. However, after a few years, company leaders found that the company had built tremendous value from its ability to derive psychographic profiling and lifestyle segmentation from people's responses to the publications; with suitable privacy protection in place, the company could then provide those data to clients in a variety of industries.

Such ethnographic research, whether conducted in the real world or in cyberspace, does not stop with the initial observation and documentation of behavior. In fact, the observations are useful only if they are followed by significant attention to analysis and the derivation of meaningful patterns from the sea of observations. The analysis is best conducted by multifunctional groups, so that diverse knowledge bases are focused on the data. Such diversity enables creative abrasion—intellectual disagreements that help a group identify assumptions and avoid premature convergence on a particular solution (Leonard and Swap, 1999). And if creative abrasion is well managed, that is, if debate is encouraged but also is closed down at some point to enable progress, the result is creative fusion—the combination of different perspectives that leads to innovative products and services.

User as Observer

It is even possible to get users to document their own behavior, and report it to product developers. Design firms that employ empathic design techniques often provide their subjects with disposable cameras, or even loaned video cameras, so that the informants can document their own environment and behavior. The advantage of having the user do his or her own observation is that there is relatively little researcher influence on the focus or method of documentation. Presumably, therefore, the data gathered are closer to real behavior. So, for example, designers researching potential products for teenagers might inhibit behavior if they were physically present. However, of course, the users who do the documenting introduce their own biases into the selection of behaviors and surroundings to film. Nevertheless, keen ethnographers can look at the films and identify rituals, symbols, and patterns of interaction that are so commonplace to the participants that they are invisible.

Developer/Designer as User

Designers or developers can also learn much about the unarticulated needs of users by becoming temporary users themselves. One of the most famous product and industrial designers, Henry Dreyfuss, was noted for trying everything that he could. Obviously, he could not participate in surgery or other activities that required professional qualifications, but he drove tractors, washed dishes, ran a locomotive, spread manure, operated sewing machines—anything that constituted an everyday activity. He thereby created his own experience-based knowledge about what worked and what did not. It was this kind of visceral understanding of the user perspective that Lucy Suchman stimulated in the copier designers at the Xerox PARC, when she had highly trained scientists try to use a Xerox machine. The great advantage of such exercises is that knowledge about user needs is melded with knowledge about how to design and develop a superior product—in one brain.

User as Developer/Designer

The same advantage obtains when a user designs the product or service that he or she wants. The first roll-on suitcase was developed by a Northwest Airlines pilot who was tired of carrying his luggage. Superior snowshoes were designed by a man who was forced by circumstances to use a pair of highly unwieldy ones, and knew he could develop better ones. Oxo kitchen utensils, with their soft, easily grasped handles, were designed by a husband who saw his wife struggle in cooking because she had difficulty holding the usual potato peelers and knives with her arthritic hands.

"Cool hunting" is a process of seeking out people who have already innovated—the same principle underlying lead user research—but these are usually fashion leaders rather than lead users of technology. So, for example, DeeDee Gordon, a cool hunter barely out of her teens, predicted a craze in sandals for Converse. She had been in Los Angeles, where she saw white teenage girls dressing like Mexican gangsters in outfits that included shower sandals. When Converse brought out a thick-soled sneaker-sandal, it was a huge hit (Gladwell, 1997). California is a hotbed of such user-led innovations, both for clothes and for cars, which are often tortured into nearly impossible creations with bodies way out of proportion to their huge wheels, and customized decorations.

Perhaps the ultimate in such user innovation is direct, intentional participation in design, encouraged by producers who give customers the tools to create their own products. Participatory design has recently seen a revival through the development of what Thomke and von Hippel (2002) call "tool kits for customer innovation." GE Plastics has long helped customers use their basic polymers, but now it has Web-based tools that customers can access. Bush Boake Allen (BBA), a global supplier of specialty flavors, has built a tool kit that enables client companies such as Nestle to develop their own flavors—which BBA then produces. Users who know what they want, but would have difficulty articulating that need to BBA, can now go to an Internet-based tool with a large database of flavor profiles, select and mix the profiles, send that information to an automated machine, and get a sample manufactured within minutes. The customer can then taste the sample, adjust the design, and try again. As Thomke and Von Hippel point out, producing such tools is not that easy. A tool set must enable users to complete a series of design cycles and trials, must be user-friendly, must have high quality and tested libraries of components, and, finally, must provide information about the capabilities and limitations of the large-scale production process that will be used to manufacture the product.

A Final Caution (Caveat Lector)

- Any research technique can be misused or directed toward undesirable ends. The tools and techniques described above are less well understood, and for the most part are less direct, than the usual market research techniques. When the objective is to understand the customers' minds even better than they do, one should be aware that there is a certain "big brother" flavor to the endeavor. However, such caveats are true of many searches for knowledge. Knowledge exists in the realm of experience and behavior more than in opinion or the spoken word. Marketers who wish to satisfy true needs—including unarticulated and even unrecognized ones—must experiment with tools and techniques that are rarely taught in marketing courses.

References

Fishbein, M., and Ajzen, I. (1975). *Belief, Attitude, Intention, and Behavior: An Introduction to Theory and Research.* Reading, Mass.: Addison-Wesley. This seminal work is still authoritative on the topic.

Gladwell, M. (1997). "The Coolhunt." *The New Yorker,* March 17: 78–88.

Kelley, T., and Littman, J. (2001). *The Art of Innovation: Lessons in Creativity from IDEO, America's Leading Design Firm.* New York: Currency/Doubleday. Description of the development processes in the leading design firm in the United States.

Leonard, D., and Swap, W. (1999). *When Sparks Fly: Igniting Creativity in Groups.* Boston: Harvard Business School Press. Easy-to-read guide for managers interested in enhancing the creativity of any group. The authors debunk myths about leading creativity, and provide insights and practical tips for increasing organizational innovativeness. Based on research.

Lilien, G. L., Morrison, P. D., Searls, K., Sonnack, M., and von Hippel, E. (2002). "Performance Assessment of the Lead User Idea Generation Process." *Management Science,* 48 (8): 1042–1059. An empirical test of the lead user methodology at 3M.

Nisbett, R., and DeCamp Wilson, T. (1977). "Telling More Than We Can Know: Verbal Reports on Mental Processes." *Psychological Review*, 84 (3): 231–259.

Thomke, S., and von Hippel, E. (2002). "Customers as Innovators: A New Way to Create Value." *Harvard Business Review*, April, product #9640. Practical guide to helping customers become innovators.

Von Hippel, E. (1988). *The Sources of Innovation*. New York: Oxford University Press. The original report on this line of research.

Von Hippel, E. (2005). *Distributed Innovation: Hacking the Manufacturer Bottleneck*. Cambridge, Mass.: MIT Press. Brings the reader up to date with the latest research on leader user methods and branches into a discussion of open source software as a user-dominated innovation.

Weise, E.(1999). "Anthropologists Adapt Technology to World's Cultures." *USA Today*, May 26: 4D. A contemporary look, in the popular press, at this kind of work.

Zaltman, G. (2003). *How Customers Think: Essential Insights into the Mind of the Market*. Boston: Harvard Business School Press. Excellent and accessible explanation of many of the unconscious influences on consumer decisions, along with a description of Zaltman's techniques for uncovering those influences.

10

Human Resources Management and Knowledge Creation

MARGIT OSTERLOH

P eter Drucker stated that less than one fifth of the workforce nowadays consists of blue-collar workers doing manual work, while white-collar workers doing knowledge work make up two fifths of the workforce. Yet, when it comes to our understanding of a knowledge worker's productivity, we are "in the year 2000 roughly where we were in the year 1900 in terms of productivity of the manual worker" (Drucker, 1999, p. 83). If companies could enhance productivity of knowledge workers in the twenty-first century as much as they did that of manual workers in the twentieth century, the payoffs would be astronomical.

This chapter will describe new ways of managing the human resources function in organizations of knowledge workers and how this can enable knowledge creation. To understand the task of introducing new human resource policies in knowledge worker organizations, it is important to see how human resources management is still shaped to a large extent by ideas on how to manage *manual work*. In order to gain new insights on how to enhance the productivity of knowledge workers as dramatically as was the case with manual workers in the past, it is necessary to start by asking what are the main similarities and what are the main differences between traditional manual work and knowledge work in firms.

Similarities Between Manual and Knowledge Teamwork

Basically, all work inside firms—whether traditional work or knowledge work—is teamwork. The word "team" indicates that the employees are interdependent. Together, team members can produce a higher output than the sum of the separate outputs of each team member working independently. This is just as true for manual workers jointly lifting cargo into a truck as it is for knowledge workers jointly designing a new software product. A team or a firm thus creates what is commonly known as synergy. The more effort exerted by one person, the more productive other members of the team become. Creating synergies is precisely what makes it advantageous to organize people in firms instead of depending wholly on market transactions (Simon, 1991).

At the same time, creating synergies constitutes what is sometimes called a collective good. A collective good is a good that can be used by people who have not contributed their share to its production. This is the case in team production. When a product or service (a "good") is produced by a team effort, it is often impossible to know which members contributed to it and which did not. It is hard to determine what input each person has contributed to the joint output. Some team members get a free ride at the expense of others. The possibility of free riders on a team can result in poor performance. While most team members would no doubt prefer to contribute their share to the team's task, the suspicion that some may not can inhibit their contribution. Thus the purpose of the team—its potential to produce more than the members could individually—is not achieved. This problem is sometimes called a "social dilemma." It characterizes situations in which the actions of rational and self-interested individuals lead to situations of collective irrationality in which everyone is worse off. A "tragedy of the commons" (Hardin, 1968) may arise, which exemplifies the true meaning of a tragedy: each team member is fully aware of the situation and realizes that his or her action leads to a negative outcome, and "every team member would prefer a team in which no one, not even himself, shirked" (Alchian and Demsetz, 1972, p. 790). Individuals would be happy to enjoy that good at the cost of their individual contribution, if there were a guarantee that everyone else would contribute his or her share. However, one rational but selfish person is unable to solve such a dilemma on his or her own. If all or most of the team members free ride, the collective good will not be achieved, or at least will be undersupplied. Synergies will not be created. This is the reason why solving social dilemmas is at the heart of human resources management in firms (G. J. Miller, 1992).

The traditional manual work solution to social dilemmas was to give supervisors the right to punish shirking. This is exactly what Frederick Taylor and Henry Ford preached. Owners or managers could oversee production workers and assess their individual productivity. A strictly horizontal and vertical division of labor—making it clear what each worker's job was—made supervision work. It enabled owners, managers, or engineers to control the inputs and measure the outputs of employees. Supervision includes all human resources tasks, particularly selection, instruction, observation of individual effort, sanctioning and rewarding, as well as adjusting the terms of measuring the productivity of individual workers. Does this traditional solution to solve social dilemmas work when manual work is replaced by knowledge work?

Differences Between Manual and Knowledge Teamwork

Most work is no longer manual, but knowledge, teamwork. Teams are the fundamental learning units in modern organizations, and there is increasing recognition that collective work in teams is the most efficient way of creating knowledge. Therefore, it is vital to understand the differences in obstacles to overcoming social dilemmas in knowledge teams from those in manual teams. There are three main differences.

First, in contrast to manual teamwork, pure knowledge teamwork raises productivity of the team only if different knowledge is dispersed among different people (Hayek, 1945). If all knowledge workers in teams have the same knowledge, one person could do the whole job almost entirely alone. This difference between knowledge teamwork and manual teamwork becomes quite clear if you compare a team of workers lifting cargo into a truck with a team of fashion designers. Fashion designers do creative work and need to integrate diverse knowledge about, for example, production processes, the garment, CAD software, and marketing. If the team leader knows and learns what his or her subordinates know and learn, then he or she can create the design. If the leader does not know what subordinates know, then he or she can neither monitor whether subordinates have chosen the most productive activities nor whether they shirk. The only thing that can be done is to evaluate whether certain professional standards are met. If the outputs are marketable products or modularized tasks, the leader can use and benchmark the team's output without understanding how the good was produced, just as certain software can be used without knowing how it works. But this does not help to prevent shirking by individual team members producing new software or new fashion designs. If the team's output is not measurable, the situation is even worse. An example is knowledge created within the fashion design team. To evaluate such knowledge, the supervisor must be an expert. But if this is the case, teamwork will not produce much knowledge that exceeds the supervisor's knowledge. As a result, knowledge workers in teams are in a good position to hide their expertise vis-à-vis their superiors (Davenport and Prusak, 1998).

Second, the result of joint knowledge work is at least in part new explicit knowledge that can easily be disseminated and further developed by all members of the firm. This new knowledge is seen as the feedstock of competitive advantage. Nonaka and Takeuchi (1995), in their famous SECI model, clearly illustrated how organizational learning proceeds by integrating more and more tacit and explicit knowledge to become collective explicit knowledge. The access to this knowledge—for example, knowledge that is collected in an electronic database—is unrestricted to members of the firm. It is a firm-specific common good, while individual tacit knowledge is a private good from which free riders can be excluded. If an employee makes individual tacit knowledge explicit, he or she changes a private good into a common good. Why should he or she do that? By making this tacit knowledge explicit, the employee may gain some reputation, but at the same time lose his or her competitive edge. Sharing knowledge with colleagues may negatively affect an employee's ability to outperform them. In addition, supervisors are enabled to monitor the employee more effectively. As a result, selfish knowledge workers in teams not only are in a better position, but they also have an incentive to hide their expertise from their superiors and colleagues.

Third, knowledge workers have much more bargaining power vis-à-vis the owners or managers than manual workers do. They cannot be easily replaced. Consider the example of the team of workers lifting cargo into a truck. These workers can be trained quickly, and their skills can be easily transferred. They can be paid the going wage in a competitive labor market. In contrast, knowledge workers are a critical resource for the firm, because their abilities must be idiosyncratic to enhance the productivity of teams. This goes hand in hand with a changing balance of power between knowledge capital and financial capital (Rajan and Zingales, 2004). Financial capital is crucial in traditional firms to exploit economies of scale of physical work. Today, flourishing financial markets have made financial capital less critical as a source of power. Rather, knowledge capital has become the critical resource. The changes that have taken place are best summed up in the following statistic: in 1929, 70 percent of the top earners derived their income from holdings of capital. In 1998, only 20 percent of their income came from capital and 80 percent from wages and entrepreneurial income (Fogel, 2000, p. 219). In general, knowledge workers have gained considerable power compared with the owners of financial capital. Within firms, this power is dependent on the degree of knowledge specific to each firm. It is true that this kind of knowledge also makes the employee more vulnerable to the employer. If the employer fires the worker, he or she loses not only wages, but also a large amount of human capital that has been built up. But if the employer threatens firing, the employee will "underinvest" in firm-specific knowledge without the employer being able to control this underinvestment efficiently. As a consequence, the competitive advantage of the firm will suffer.

To summarize, to the extent that teamwork contains knowledge work, traditional tools of human resources management built on supervision and control will fail. To raise the productivity of knowledge teams, we have to look for new solutions to solve the inherent social dilemmas.

New Approaches for Human Resources Management of Knowledge Teamwork: Structural or Motivational?

Joint knowledge teamwork is crucial not only to enhance productivity by creating synergies, but also because it is the source of competitive advantages for the firm, which is hard to imitate. Today, there is a growing conviction among companies, researchers, and consultants that joint knowledge work is the most important source of dynamic capabilities, which are unique and hard to imitate or substitute. What new solutions need to be found by human resources management in order for these goals to be fulfilled? How can social dilemmas be overcome and at the same time enhance the sources for sustainable competitive advantage?

The suggestions discussed for solving social dilemmas can be divided into structural and motivational solutions. Structural solutions change the rules of the game to make cooperation more attractive for selfish employees. These approaches are preferred by economists and human resources managers who believe that compensation policy is the most important part of their job. Motivational solutions focus changing preferences of employees. They are preferred by social psychologists or human resources managers who believe that preferences are not given but are plastic. They can be altered by the work content itself as well as by the work environment.

Structural Solutions

Activating the "Shadow of the Future"

The most influential proposal for solving social dilemmas is to extend the shadow of the future by means of long-term, reciprocal relationships (Axelrod, 1984). A win-win situation may arise. However, it is often disregarded that this strategy works only when individuals have information on how the other persons behaved in the past. The more team knowledge is dispersed and tacit, the less this strategy is likely to be applicable.

A selective incentive is a private good (e.g., a bonus) given to individuals as an inducement to contribute to a common good. For instance, all firm members may have access to the electronic database, but only contributors receive a reward. However, selective incentives raise two problems. First, they increase costs, and second, you might subsidize hot air. Take the case of a reward for contributions made to an electronic database. As a result, you might get a high number of contributions with little value. If you count the downloads, the value of the contribution might work. However, it might also happen that the contributors induce their colleagues to downloadtheir contributions. You have become the victim of "the folly of rewarding A while hoping for B"

(Kerr, 1975). This is particularly true for knowledge work. Knowledge work contains some easy-to-measure components (e.g., pages of written text) and some hard-to-measure components (e.g., the importance of the text). Reward systems have to concentrate on few clear-cut criteria. As a consequence, rational employees will focus on the easily measurable components and leave aside the components that are not so easy to measure.

Profit Centers

One frequently discussed structural solution to social dilemmas is to decentralize decision authority into profit centers or modules so that internal market forces can do their work via (transfer) prices. The leaders of the profit centers could then be remunerated according to measurable criteria. However, there are some problems with knowledge work organized as profit centers. First, the leader of a profit center has no incentive to share knowledge voluntarily with other profit centers, because that would be giving away strategic opportunities for free. This is especially true for tacit knowledge. The transfer of tacit knowledge can be less well monitored compared with the transfer of explicit knowledge (Osterloh and Frey, 2000). Second, the sources of hard-to-imitate competitive advantages will be undermined. In order to be able to bargain over (transfer) prices and service-level agreements across the boundaries of profit centers, some tacit knowledge must be made explicit. As a consequence, the knowledge incorporated in the profit centers may become more tradable and imitable (Chesbrough and Teece, 1996).

To summarize, structural solutions might mitigate some problems of joint knowledge work. But the more the knowledge is complex and dispersed among employees, the more structural solutions worsen the problem. In these cases structural solutions must be replaced by motivational solutions.

Motivational Solutions

As Simon (1991, pp. 31–32) stated, "In most organizations, employees contribute much more to goal achievement than the minimum that could be extracted from them by supervisory enforcement." This makes it clear that motivation is a main factor inside of firms. This is true for manual work as well as for knowledge work. A highly motivated workforce keeps costs of supervision and monetary incentives low. But as far as knowledge work is concerned, "management by motivation" (Frey and Osterloh, 2002) not only might save costs, but also might become the most important factor in sustaining a competitive advantage. Since tacit knowledge is the main source of inimitability, and its creation and transfer cannot be monitored and remunerated accordingly, motivation, and in particular, intrinsic motivation, are the keys to dynamic capabilities as a foundation of long-term strategy.

Extrinsic and Intrinsic Motivation

Two kinds of motivation can be distinguished: extrinsic and intrinsic. In reality, pure extrinsic motivation and pure intrinsic motivation are extremes on a continuum.

Extrinsic motivation serves to satisfy indirect needs, such as money. Thus, money is almost always the means to an end—for example, paying for a vacation or buying a car—and not an end in itself. In this instance, a job is simply a tool with which to satisfy one's needs by means of the salary it pays. Structural solutions focus mainly on extrinsic motivation. As discussed, they can mitigate social dilemmas, but cannot solve them when dealing with knowledge work.

Intrinsic motivation works through immediate need satisfaction. An activity is valued for its own sake and is undertaken without any reward except the activity itself (Deci and Ryan, 1985). Intrinsic motivation is fostered by commitment to the work, according to the saying "If you want people motivated to do a good job, give them a good job to do." If employees are motivated intrinsically, then shirking is not a preferable action, because the activity causes a benefit instead of a cost. The social dilemma disappears and a win-win situation arises. There are two kinds of intrinsic motivation: enjoyment-based motivation and prosocial motivation.

Enjoyment-based intrinsic motivation refers to a satisfying flow of activity. Examples are skiing, playing a game, reading a good novel, climbing a mountain, or solving an interesting puzzle. In each case, pleasure is derived from the activity itself and not from compensation. During such activities, people often report a "flow experience" (Csikszentmihalyi, 1975) that makes them lose track of time. The individual acts as a "homo ludens" (Huizinga, 1986), a playful human being. Recently, in one of the most innovative industries—the software industry—this kind of motivation turned out to be crucial. One of the most successful kinds of software is open-source software such as Linux, which has become a serious competitor of Microsoft. It is produced voluntarily as a public good that everybody can download from the Internet. This is done to a large extent without monetary compensation and invocation of private intellectual property rights. Important contributors to open-source software, such as Linus Torvalds, report that they are doing the programming "just for fun" (Torvalds and Diamond, 2001). A "flow experience" is often reported in all kinds of creative work.

Prosocial intrinsic motivation takes the well-being of others into account without expecting a reward. The welfare of the community enters into the preferences of the individuals. A wealth of empirical evidence demonstrates that many people are indeed prepared to contribute to the common good of their company and community (Frey, 1997). Individuals feel better if they have observed group norms such as ethical standards, professional codes of practice, or norms of fairness, reciprocity, or team spirit. Empirical work shows that due to different group norms, substantial differences in shirking exist between branches of a company, despite identical monetary incentives (Ichnio and Maggi, 2000). Two major instances in real life—voluntary rule following and extra-role-behavior—have been discussed, both of which include sacrificing individual interests for the sake of the whole company.

Extra-role Behavior

People are prepared to follow rules and regulations that limit their self-interests without sanctions, as long as they accept their legitimacy (Tyler and Blader, 2000). Employees not only observe rules voluntarily, however, but also exert "organizational citizenship behavior" (Organ and Ryan, 1995). They provide voluntary inputs, going far beyond the duties stipulated in their employment contracts. "Extra-role behavior" is thought of as a "willingness to cooperate." Of particular interest are helping behavior, organizational compliance, and "whistle-blowing" if rules of conduct are violated (e.g., in the recent corporate scandals "whistle-blowers" disclosed malpractices to their bosses and risked being punished or even dismissed).

Laboratory experiments reveal that a large number of people voluntarily contribute to common goods (see the survey by Rabin, 1998). They show that a large number of people are willing to punish unfair behavior at a cost to themselves. It is important to note that these experiments have found that there are considerable variations across different cultures (Henrich, Boyd, Bowles, et al., 2001). This indicates that prosocial motivation is not hardwired. It can be changed by institutional measures. It is the most important task of human resources management to provide such measures.

How to Foster Intrinsic Motivation

It is more difficult to guide intrinsically motivated persons to work according to the particular goals of the firm than to guide persons who work mainly for monetary compensation. First, intrinsic motivation cannot be enforced. It can only be enabled. Second, firms are not interested in enabling some kinds of intrinsic motivation, such as the pleasure of reading a novel during office hours. In contrast, extrinsic rewards can easily focus the motivation of employees on the firm's goal. However, some measures that strengthen extrinsic motivation to induce employees to pursue the firm's goals, weaken intrinsic motivation. The question arises of how human resources management can induce the kind of intrinsic motivation that is required.

Self-determination theory offers an answer (Deci and Ryan, 2000). According to this theory, the preconditions of being intrinsically motivated for a certain job are autonomy, feelings of competence, and social relatedness. Interventions of human resource management must be judged by whether they crowd in (increase) or crowd out (decrease) intrinsic motivation by increasing or decreasing these three preconditions.

Autonomy

Autonomy is the most important precondition for creativity, solving complex problems, and conceptual work (e.g., Amabile, 1998). A well-known example of how to enhance productivity by enlarging autonomy is 3M (Gundling, 2000). 3M is one of the most innovative companies: 30 percent of its sales comes from products new to the market. It has introduced the famous 15 percent rule: 3M employees are allowed to spend 15 percent of their time on individual research or initiatives. At the beginning of each innovation process—in the "doodling phase"—management tends to be absent. In addition, 3M has established a strong culture of camaraderie.

The perception of autonomy decreases if people perceive that their self-determination is reduced when doing an intrinsically interesting activity. They feel that they are not the origins of their behavior. Their attention shifts from the activity to the reward or sanction. The content of the activity loses its importance. This is the case, however, only if the individuals were intrinsically motivated in the first place. Only then can this motivation be undermined. In contrast, in situations where no intrinsic motivation exists in the first place, monetary rewards can increase performance, as in the case of simple manual work on an assembly line. Lazear (1999) provides an empirical example. He found that in a large auto glass company, productivity increased between 20 percent and 36 percent when the firm switched from paying hourly wages to piece rates. Knowledge teamwork is very different from that kind of job.

The crowding-out phenomenon has been firmly established by numerous laboratory and field experiments (for an overview, see Frey and Jegen, 2001). An impressive field experiment showed that monetary rewards can undermine prosocial motivation. Gneezy and Rustichini (2000a) analyzed the behavior of schoolchildren collecting money voluntarily, that is, without monetary compensation (e.g., for cancer research or disabled children). The children reduced their efforts by about 36 percent when they were promised a bonus of 1 percent of the money collected. Their effort to collect for a good cause could be raised when the bonus was increased from 1 percent to 10 percent of the money collected, but they did not reach the initial collection level again. This field experiment shows clearly that there are two countervailing forces affecting behavior: a crowding-out effect of rewards and an effect of motivating the children extrinsically after the intrinsic motivation has been decreased. It also shows that a "hidden cost of rewards" exists. The money collected after a bonus has been offered comes at a high price compared with strengthening intrinsic motivation.

Feelings of Competence

Feelings of competence grow when individuals understand what they are doing and when they feel responsible for the outcome. Researchers have shown that when people are encouraged to feel that they are competent, they make greater contributions to the community (e.g., Kollock, 1998). However, there are two important preconditions.

First, individuals must get positive feedback about the outcome of their contributions that does not eclipse their feelings of autonomy. Feedback on outcomes strengthens intrinsic motivation only if it is perceived as supporting rather than controlling. This condition makes feedback processes one of the most important measures of human resources management, and at the same time makes it the most difficult measure to handle.

On the one hand, feedback about outputs or processes can be supplied by supervisors, team leaders, or peers only if there are measurable outputs, or if there is a sufficient overlap of knowledge between these authors. As I have argued, fulfilling these conditions with knowledge teamwork sometimes comes at a high price. If team leaders are able to control only some easy-to-measure task components, then the "the folly of rewarding A while hoping for B" will arise. Too much overlap of knowledge will decrease the productivity of creating new knowledge. In these cases, human resources management must rely on other tools, in particular giving the employees feedback about having observed professional or social norms.

On the other hand, if it is possible to get efficient feedback from the supervisor, the latter must be very careful not to act in a controlling way. This explains why the crowding-out effect is stronger with monetary rewards than with symbolic rewards, and why the effect is greater with expected rather than with unexpected rewards. Experiments show that if labor contracts are regarded primarily as a "gift exchange" (Akerlof, 1982) rather than as a disciplining tool, employees exert more effort. In a telling experiment, two different settings were compared. In the first setting, the "principals" offered a fixed amount of money and the "agents" chose an effort level. In the second setting, the principals had to make a choice between a fixed wage and a piece rate, and then the agents chose their effort level. In this setting, efforts were higher when fixed wages were offered, compared with when piece rates were offered. Also, in the case of fixed pay, agents mentioned the well-being of the principal significantly more often than in the case of piece rates (Irlenbusch and Sliwka, 2003). The social norm of reciprocity, which worked in the fixed-pay setting, was crowded out in the piece-rate setting. This provides a strong argument for fixed wages whenever intrinsic motivation is crucial.

Second, individuals must believe that their participation is important for the provision of the common good. Then they ask, "What happens if I stop contributing?" When people believe that their actions will have a discernible effect on the value of the common good, they will be more likely to contribute to it. There are two ways to enhance responsibility for the outcome (Cabrera and Cabrera, 2002). One way is to give *informational feedback* whenever other team members have received and used the posted contributions. It is important not to link such information to monetary rewards, in order to avoid the "the folly of rewarding A while hoping for B" and the crowding-out effect. Rather, the rewards should be symbolic. An example would be to honor an employee with an award for helping behavior that is made visible widely. The second way to improve the perceived impact on the value of the common good is by supplying *training* for the providers as well as the recipients of information. People may not get feedback on their contributions for two reasons. They may not know which information is most valuable for others and how they can present it effectively. Or the possible receivers may not be able to use efficient knowledge-sharing systems or electronic databases. In both cases, training can increase responsibility for the collective outcome.

Social Relatedness

Perceived social relatedness is of special importance for prosocial motivation. It raises group identity, which has proven to have a strong impact on the number of contributions to common goods (e.g., Kollock, 1998). Human resources management has a variety of measures to enhance social relatedness and group identification. The more people feel they are treated fairly, the more likely they are to identify with a group. Fairness can be divided into distributive fairness, procedural fairness, and fairness of contributions to a common good.

Distributive Fairness

Distributive fairness concerns whether people believe that outcomes or rewards are allocated in a justified manner. Empirical evidence shows that people are less concerned about what they earn in terms of absolute income, compared with what they earn relative to their close colleagues (Adams, 1963). Different fairness norms exist under different conditions. In settings where performance varies considerably between individuals and is easy to measure, *equity* according to individual outcomes is the prevailing criterion. As already mentioned, individual performance is hard to measure where knowledge work in teams is concerned. In such situations, *equality* is often considered to be fair. In close social settings, such as families or close-knit groups, the norm of *need* is often applied. Elements of need are also found in work settings, for example, when supplements to wages are paid according to the number of children a worker has. In any case, what matters is not fairness in an objective sense, but what employees *perceive* to be a fair distribution. A lot depends on cultural, occupational, and demographic factors, and may vary across industries. Human resources management has to find out empirically which fairness norms prevail in which subsets. Whatever criteria are applied, one can suppose that the exorbitant salaries paid to top managers, as was recently revealed in the media, were perceived as extremely unfair. When superiors feather their own nests, it is no wonder that employees are no longer prepared to contribute to the common good of the firm (e.g., by reporting colleagues whose behavior is not acceptable or by revealing knowledge voluntarily to the community).

Procedural Fairness

While distributive fairness is related to outcomes, procedural fairness is related to the process leading to the outcome. Empirical evidence shows that procedural fairness impacts the willingness to contribute to common goods and to follow rules more than distributive fairness does. This is true even in situations that are not favorable to one's self-interest (Tyler and Blader, 2000). The characteristics that lead to perceived procedural fairness can be summarized as participation, neutrality, and being treated with dignity and respect. *Participation* gives individuals a process control or the use of voice. It has been found that the use of voice is not just dependent on controlling outcomes; people value the opportunity to express their views. As a consequence, in cases of conflict, mediation has proven to be perceived as a fairer procedure than formal trials. Mediation typically provides greater opportunity for participation than formal procedures do. A precondition of *neutrality* is the belief of employees that their superiors do not allow personal advantages to enter their decision-making. In laboratory experiments, it has been shown that sanctions which served the punisher's interests crowded out cooperative behavior, whereas sanctions perceived as prosocially motivated enhanced self-interests (Fehr and Rockenbach, 2003). It follows that supervisors and team leaders, who lay down the rules and regulations, should not be given an incentive to manipulate the corresponding criteria in their favor. In management, the exact opposite took place in recent times: top executives were given the opportunity to manipulate the criteria by which they were evaluated and compensated (Osterloh and Frey, 2004). Under these circumstances, it is difficult to maintain neutrality. Human resources management not only should be committed to rules of neutrality, but also should make this commitment part of written policy. *Being treated with dignity and respect* has proved to be of high importance for organizational citizenship behavior, including helping behavior, altruism, and extra-role behavior (Niehoff and

Moormann, 1993). Note that all three characteristics of procedural fairness (participation, neutrality, and being treated with dignity and respect) are essentially unrelated to outcomes. Therefore, procedural fairness is crucial in situations that might lead to unfortunate results for the employees (e.g., in resolving conflicts or making decisions concerning promotions).

Conditional Cooperation

A third form of fairness is related to contributions to common goods. The more people expect others to contribute to common goods, the more likely they are to do so themselves. They are conditional cooperators. On the other hand, many people are conditional defectors. As a consequence, prosocial intrinsic motivation deteriorates if too many people free ride. No one likes being the only one who contributes to a good cause and thus being a "sucker." This is shown by overwhelming empirical evidence (e.g., Fischbacher, Gächter, and Fehr, 2001). It follows that an employee's inclination to cooperate is undermined if he or she feels that colleagues do not pull their weight, which is often not observable in knowledge teams. Therefore, human resources management should be aware of the importance of protecting the company from malefactors in the workforce and should give prosocial preferences more weight in the selection process. This is important because a higher number of prosocially motivated employees increases conditional cooperation.

Personal Contacts

Communication, or other conditions reducing social distance between persons, increases contribution in public goods activities (Ledyard, 1995; Frey and Bohnet, 1995). Communication has two important effects. First, experiments show that most people, after some minutes of talking to each other, have higher expectations of others' cooperative behavior. If they believe that others do not free ride, their willingness to contribute increases (conditional cooperation). This effect is much stronger when communicating face-to-face than when communicating via the computer. Second, communication provides an opportunity to invite other individuals to cooperate. It has been shown that being personally asked greatly enhances contributions to collective goods. These results might be summarized in such a way that the less the situation approximates to a competitive market, the more prosocial behavior is likely to be observed. The growing role that "communities of practice" and "epistemic communities" play in knowledge-based industries underpins the significance of personal contacts and communication (Orr, 1990; Lave and Wenger, 1991). Many large companies, such as Microsoft, Xerox, and Daimler Benz, have realized that communities based on communication and personal contacts foster not only creativity but also social relatedness and identification within the group.

Instructions

People seem to be inclined to do what they are asked to do, especially when the request comes from someone who is perceived as a legitimate authority. Instructions to cooperate in public-good activities raise the cooperation rate as much as 40 percent (Sally, 1995). In real-life settings, people adhere to rules and accept the decisions of authorities they believe to be legitimate, even if it is not in their self-interest to do so (Tyler, 1990). This is contrary to what economists have taught us. They instruct people that it is clever to behave as a selfish *Homo economicus* rather than risk appearing foolish or naïve. As a result, people behave in a selfish way: economics has to some extent become a self-fulfilling prophecy. Interestingly, most people overestimate the power of self-interest to affect the behavior of others, even when their own behavior is not primarily self-interested (Miller and Ratner, 1998). Human resources management can stop this self-fulfilling prophecy by providing employees with information about existing social norms and social behavior in their company and in their community. In addition, there could be public recognition and (nonmonetary) awards for helpful and caring behavior, as is the case with 3M.

Framing of Socially Appropriate Behavior

People are highly sensitive to signals about socially appropriate behavior. This became evident in an experiment. Players were divided into two groups. Each group played exactly the same game. The first group was told they were going to play "the Wall Street Game." One third of the group cooperated. The second group was told that they were playing "the Community Game." More than two thirds cooperated (Liberman, Samuels, and Ross, 2003). A strong framing effect was also shown in a field study where parents were fined for picking up their children late from a child care center. The fine had an adverse effect: it led to a significantly lower level of punctuality. When the fine was discontinued, punctuality remained at the lower level (Gneezy and Rustichini, 2000b). Fining switched the frame from a prosocial frame to a gain frame. It indicated that in the gain frame, it was socially acceptable for parents to arrive late. A similar affect can be assumed with pay for performance. It signals that doing one's duty without extra pay is not socially appropriate. This signal could become a self-fulfilling prophecy. As a consequence for human resources management, variable pay with knowledge work might be dangerous. Fixed pay, based on fair overall procedural evaluations, avoids framing the team-work into the "Wall Street Game."

Conclusions

Knowledge workers' productivity is the biggest challenge of the twenty-first century, in particular for developed countries. Making knowledge workers more productive and contributing to a sustainable competitive advantage requires profound changes in the thinking of human resources management. What are the main differences between principles of human resources management for manual and knowledge work?

- *Pay for performance has had its day.* As soon as knowledge work prevails in teams, pay for performance loses the status of "management mantra" that it had achieved in recent years. Variable performance pay

  1. crowds out intrinsic motivation, which is needed for efficient knowledge creation in teams when supervision and control fail.
  2. shifts attention from the activity to the reward.
  3. undermines prosocial behavior by providing a frame which tells employees that doing one's duty is not socially appropriate.
  4. hinders the flow of knowledge between individuals and teams because employees are provided with incentives not to give up their competitive edge.
  5. subsidizes hot air with complex tasks by the "folly of rewarding A while hoping for B."
  6. decreases the competitive advantage of knowledge work.

- *Strengthen autonomy, competence, and social relatedness.* Since pay for performance is no longer a remedy to solve social dilemmas in knowledge teamwork, it is important to strengthen feelings of autonomy, competence, and social relatedness. The following measures are of particular importance:

  1. Fixed pay based on overall evaluations that, in the first place, have to be perceived as procedurally fair.
  2. Selection of intrinsically and prosocially motivated employees, to make sure that conditional cooperation works.
  3. Supportive feedback that does not eclipse feelings of autonomy.
  4. Training the providers and the recipients of knowledge to strengthen perceived efficacy.
  5. Providing opportunities for personal contacts and communication.
  6. Giving instructions about appropriate social behavior and avoiding gain frames in favor of normative frames of behavior.

- Some of these proposals clash with conventional wisdom but, based on existing research in economics and psychology, they promise to effectively raise the productivity of knowledge workers. At the same time, they give knowledge work a hard-to-imitate competitive advantage.

Acknowledgments

I am grateful to Bruno Frey and Antoinette Weibel for helpful remarks.

References

Adams, J. S. (1963). "Toward an Understanding of Inequity." *Journal of Abnormal and Social Psychology* 67: 422–463.

Akerlof, G. A. (1982). "Labor Contracts as Partial Gift Exchange." *Quarterly Journal of Economics* 84: 488–500.

Alchian, A. A., and Demsetz, H. (1972). "Production, Information Costs and Economic Organization." *American Economic Review* 62: 777–795.

Amabile, T. M. (1998). "How to Kill Creativity." *Harvard Business Review* September/October: 77–87.

Axelrod, R. (1984). *The Evolution of Cooperation.* New York: Basic Books.

Cabrera, A., and Cabrera, E. F. (2002). "Knowledge-Sharing Dilemmas." *Organization Studies* 23(5): 687–710.

Chesbrough, H. W., & Teece, D. J. (1996). "When Is Virtual Virtuous? Organizing for Innovation." *Harvard Business Review* 74: 65–73.

Csikszentmihalyi, M. (1975). *Beyond Boredom and Anxiety.* San Francisco: Jossey-Bass.

Davenport, T. H., and Prusak, L. (1998). *Working Knowledge: How Organizations Manage What They Know.* Boston: Harvard Business School Press.

Deci, E. L., and Ryan, R. M. (1985). *Intrinsic Motivation and Self-Determination in Human Behavior.* New York: Plenum Press.

Deci, E. L., and Ryan, R. M. (2000). "The 'What' and 'Why' of Goal Pursuits: Human Needs and the Self-Determination of Behavior." *Psychological Inquiry* 11(4): 227–268.

Drucker, P. (1999). "Knowledge Worker Productivity: The Biggest Challenge." *California Management Review* 41: 79–94.

Fehr, E., and Rockenbach, B. (2003). "Detrimental Effects of Sanctions on Human Altruism." *Nature* 422: 137–140.

Fischbacher, U., Gächter, S., and Fehr, E. (2001). "Are People Conditionally Cooperative? Evidence from Public Good Experiments." *Economic Letters* 71: 397–404.

Fogel, R. (2000). *The Fourth Great Awakening and the Future of Egalitarianism.* Chicago: University of Chicago Press.

Frey, B. S. (1997). *Not Just for the Money: An Economic Theory of Personal Motivation.* Brookfield, Vt.: Edward Elgar.

Frey, B. S., and Bohnet, I. (1995). "Institutions Affect Fairness: Experimental Investigations." *Journal of Institutional and Theoretical Economics,* 151(2): 286–303.

Frey, B. S., and Jegen, R. (2001). "Motivation Crowding Theory: A Survey of Empirical Evidence." *Journal of Economic Surveys,* 15(5): 589–611.

Frey, B. S., and Osterloh, M. (2005). "Yes, Managers Should Be Paid Like Bureaucrats." *Journal of Management Inquiry* 14(1): 96–111.

Frey, B. S., and Osterloh, M. (eds.). (2002). *Successful Management by Motivation: Balancing Intrinsic and Extrinsic Incentives*. Berlin and New York: Springer.

Gneezy, U., and Rustichini, A. (2000a). "Pay Enough or Don't Pay At All." *Quarterly Journal of Economics* 115(2): 791–810.

Gneezy, U., and Rustichini, A. (2000b). "A Fine Is a Price." *Journal of Legal Studies* 29: 1–18.

Gundling, E. (2000). *The 3M Way to Innovation: Balancing People and Profit*. Tokyo: Kodansha International.

Hardin, G. (1968). "The Tragedy of the Commons." *Science*, 162: 1243–1248.

Hayek, F. A. (1945). "The Use of Knowledge in Society." *American Economic Review* 35(4): 519–531.

Henrich, J., Boyd, R., Bowles, S., et al. (2001). "In Search of *Homo economicus*: Behavioral Experiments in 15 Small-Scale Societies." *American Economic Review (Papers and Proceedings)* 91: 73–78.

Huizinga, J. (1986). *Homo Ludens*. Boston: Beacon Press.

Ichnio, A., and Maggi, G. (2000). "Work Environment and Individual Background: Explaining Regional Shirking Differentials in a Large Italian Firm." *Quarterly Journal of Economics* 115: 1057–1090.

Irlenbusch, B., and Sliwka, D. (2003). "Incentives, Decision Frames and Motivation Crowding Out: An Experimental Investigation." Working paper, University of Bonn.

Kerr, S. (1975). "On the Folly of Rewarding A while Hoping for B." *Academy of Management Journal* 18: 769–783.

Kollock, P. (1998). "Social Dilemmas: The Anatomy of Cooperation." *Annual Review of Sociology* 24: 183–214.

Lave, J., and Wenger, E. (1991). *Situated Learning: Legitimate Peripheral Participation*. Cambridge: Cambridge University Press.

Lazear, E. (1999). "Personnel Economics: Past Lessons and Future Directions." *Journal of Labor Economics* 17: 199–236.

Ledyard, J. O. (1995). "Public Goods: A Survey of Experimental Research." In J. Kagel and A. E. Roth, eds., *Handbook of Experimental Economics*, pp. 111–194. Princeton, N.J.: Princeton University Press.

Liberman, V., Samuels, S., and Ross, L. (2003). "The Name of the Game: Predictive Power or Reputation vs. Situational Labels in Determining Prisoners' Dilemma Game Moves." Working paper, Department of Psychology, Stanford University.

Miller, D. T., and Ratner, R. K. (1998). "The Disparity Between the Actual and Assumed Power of Self-Interest." *Journal of Personality and Social Psychology* 74: 53–62.

Miller, G. J. (1992). *Managerial Dilemmas: The Political Economy of Hierarchy*. Cambridge: Cambridge University Press.

Niehoff, B. P., and Moorman, R. H. (1993). "Justice as a Mediator of the Relationship between Methods of Monitoring and Organizational Citizenship Behavior." *Academy of Management Journal* 36(3): 527–556.

Nonaka, I., and Takeuchi, H. (1995). *The Knowledge Creating Company: How Japanese Companies Create the Dynamics of Innovation*. Oxford: Oxford University Press.

Organ, D. W., and Ryan, K. (1995). "A Meta-Analytic Review of Attitudinal and Dispositional Predictors of Organizational Citizenship Behavior." *Personnel Psychology* 48: 775–782.

Orr, J. (1996). *Talking About Machines: An Ethnography of a Modern Job.* Ithaca, N.Y.: ILR Press.

Osterloh, M., and Frey, B. S. (2000). "Motivation, Knowledge Transfer, and Organizational Firms." *Organization Science* 11: 538–550.

Osterloh, M., and Frey, B. S. (2004). "Corporate Governance for Crooks: The Case for Corporate Virtue." In A. Grandori, ed., *Corporate Governance and Firm Organization,* pp. 191–211. Oxford: Oxford University Press.

Rabin, M. (1998). "Psychology and Economics." *Journal of Economic Literature* 36: 11–46.

Rajan, R., and Zingales, L. (2004). *Saving Capitalism from the Capitalists.* London: Random House.

Sally, D. (1995). "Conversation and Cooperation in Social Dilemmas: A Meta-Analysis of Experiments from 1958 to 1992." *Rationality & Society* 7: 58–92.

Simon, H.A. (1991). "Organizations and Markets." *Journal of Economic Perspectives* 5: 25–44.

Torvalds, L., and Diamond, D. (2001). *Just for Fun: The Story of an Accidental Revolutionary.* New York: HarperBusiness.

Tyler, T. R. (1990). *Why People Obey the Law.* New Haven, Conn.: Yale University Press.

Tyler, T. R., and Blader, S .L. (2000). *Cooperation in Groups: Procedural Justice, Social Identity, and Behavioral Engagement.* Philadelphia: Psychology Press.

11

Corporate Finance

Intangible Assets' Effect on Shareholders' Value

MAKOTO NAKANO

Despite its growing size, attention, and importance, little academic research has succeeded in empirically identifying the relationship between shareholders' value and intangible assets.[1] There are several classes of intangibles. First, R&D-related capital is created primarily through innovation and discovery. Second, brand equity is created by a combination of marketing strategy and advertising. Third, human capital and organizational capital are also included in intangible assets. Considering their size and effect on financial performance, I focus on R&D-related intangibles in this chapter. The goal of this chapter is to shed light on the relationship between shareholders' value and R&D investment. Empirical analysis will cover countries including the United States, the United Kingdom, Germany, France, Japan, Korea, Taiwan, Hong Kong, and Australia. The pharmaceutical and biotechnology sectors are additionally analyzed because of their science-intensive (knowledge-intensive) characteristics.

As our society has become more knowledge-intensive or science-intensive, many firms have transformed themselves from capital-intensive to knowledge-intensive. Firms use different valuation schemes when they consider R&D projects, and R&D managers frequently ask themselves, or are sometimes asked by their finance department, "Will this R&D project contribute to our financial performance in the future?" Most of the firms are struggling to develop better valuation schemes for their R&D projects. Based on my interviews with several leading Japanese firms, I have found two types of R&D valuation and management schemes. One is technology-oriented, and the other is finance-oriented.

Technology-oriented firms tend to select one technology area, using a top-down strategy. The R&D managers of the selected technology area are then required to present a pro forma financial sheet including key forecasted numbers such as sales, profits, and cash flow. Based on those numbers, a final decision is made by the top managers, who consider the technology and the numbers in synthesis. Technology comes first, and finance follows. In other words, technology is the first hurdle, and finance is the second. In contrast, finance-oriented firms encourage many R&D managers to submit their plan with numbers. The plan has to clear the financial hurdle first. Projects that successfully clear the financial hurdle can be on the top managers' meeting agenda. Here, finance is the first hurdle, and technology is the second. Though the order is reversed, in both cases the financial criteria of the R&D project ultimately have to be evaluated if a private firm is involved. One of the aims of this chapter is to examine the performance of R&D investments financially rather than technologically, especially from the shareholders' point of view.

Although R&D capability has become one of the most important factors for gaining and sustaining competitive advantage in recent years, current accounting rules do not recognize such intangible assets as accounting assets. These rules do not convey relevant and timely information about the innovation process of business enterprises. Investment in intangible items, not only R&D outlays but advertising and employee training outlays as well, are by and large expensed immediately in financial reports. A major reason for not recognizing these assets on balance sheets is concern about whether their values can be estimated reliably. Accounting rules treat all R&D, advertising, and employee training outlays as the current year's expense rather than as investments, even when they are considered as investment inside the firm. According to a thirty-year-old U.S. generally accepted accounting principles (GAAP), which requires the immediate expensing of R&D in financial reporting, "A direct relationship between research and development costs and specific future revenue generally has not been demonstrated, even with the benefit of hindsight" (Financial Accounting Standards Board, 1974). The presumed absence of a relationship between R&D expenditure and subsequent benefits is a major reason for the Financial Accounting Standards Board (FASB) to require the full expensing of R&D outlays in income statements rather than recognize them on balance sheets. However, since the mid-1970s the existence of an association between R&D expenditures and subsequent benefits has ceased to be in doubt. Several empirical investigations (e.g., Lev and Sougiannis, 1996; Chan, Lakonishok, and Sougiannis, 2001) have found an economically meaningful and statistically significant relationship between R&D investment and subsequent benefits. Aboody and Lev (1998) found that the capitalized development costs of software-related firms, where capitalization is permitted when the project passes a technological feasibility test, are accompanied by a statistically significant improved stock price.

In recent years, R&D investments have become as large as traditional capital investments. For example, financial data in fiscal year 2001 demonstrate that Japanese firms invested in R&D programs as much as in capital expenditure. The R&D investment ratio (R&D expenditure divided by capital expenditure) is calculated for firms listed on the Tokyo Stock Exchange, First Section. The mean is 95.0 percent, and the median is 51.4 percent for firms that reported both nonzero R&D expenditure and nonzero capital expenditure. We should look at the median rather than the mean, because there are highly R&D-intensive firms whose R&D investment ratio exceeds 3,000 percent. The median, 51.4 percent, shows that Japanese listed firms, on average, invest in R&D half as much as in capital expenditure. The growing trend of R&D expenditure is one of the most impressive characteristics of the recent economy. Since this ratio is the median among *all* firms, it is clear that R&D-intensive firms would have a higher ratio. In the consumer electronics industry, the R&D investment ratio is 133 percent for Sony, 183 percent for Matsushita, and 85 percent for Sharp. In the pharmaceutical industry, R&D investment far exceeds capital expenditure. The ratio is 224 percent for Takeda, 319 percent for Sankyo, and 218 percent for Eisai. For pharmaceutical companies, the capability to develop new medicine is their most important source of distinctive competitive advantage. In the global merger and acquisition wave in this industry, R&D investment is becoming the most critical value driver and, at the same time, an effective defense against takeovers by competitors.

Let us look at global automobile industry data. Figure 11.1 compares R&D expenditures with traditional capital expenditures of leading automobile

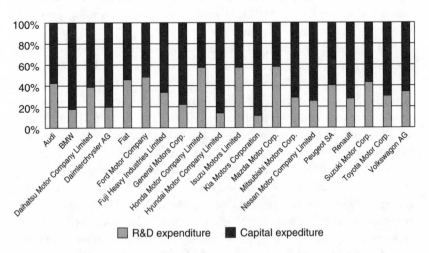

Figure 11.1 R&D investment and capital expenditure: world automobile industry, FY 2003.

companies for fiscal year 2003. Some companies report R&D expenditures that are almost equal to or more than capital expenditures. The average ratio of R&D expenditure divided by capital expenditure is approximately 62 percent. This shows that investment in intangible assets, such as R&D, is important not only for science-based/high-tech companies, but also for manufacturing companies. This means that in recent years, a manufacturing firm's competitive advantage has come to lie in R&D capability.

Nonaka and Teece (2001) argue that more quantitative research is needed in knowledge management. They point out that "An important starting point will be coming up with acceptable operational indices of superior financial performance. Market-based approaches (such as Tobin's Q) are likely to be preferable." In the context of corporate finance and equity valuation using accounting information, the rise in the importance of science-based firms raises the question of whether their stock market values reflect their intangible R&D capital. Although financial analysts and business managers intuitively perceive the importance and existence of intangible assets, this important subject is only infrequently examined in corporate finance and accounting literature. It is pointed out anecdotally that R&D investments have a positive impact on shareholders' value. The relationship between R&D activity and financial performance has been described in the form of detailed case studies, especially in management literature.

The remainder of this chapter investigates the relationship between R&D investment and shareholders' value based on large-sample empirical research, and discusses its application to knowledge management. It is organized in the following manner. First, I describe the relationship among R&D investments, earnings, and shareholders' value. Next, empirical analysis begins by applying simple models to Japanese firms. Following that, I expand the analysis into more countries, including the United States, the United Kingdom, Germany, France, Japan, Korea, Taiwan, Hong Kong, and Australia, in order to check generality. Then I focus on science-based industries such as biotechnology and pharmaceuticals. The summary and conclusion are followed by an appendix in which the technical details of the valuation models are explained.

The Relationship Among R&D Investments, Earnings, and Shareholders' Value

Figure 11.2 presents a conceptual and rather intuitive diagram of the relation among R&D, earnings, and shareholders' value. First of all, current R&D investments undoubtedly reduce current-year earnings under current accounting standards. At the same time, current R&D investments are expected to build the *R&D capability* of the organization, a theme that has been exhaustively

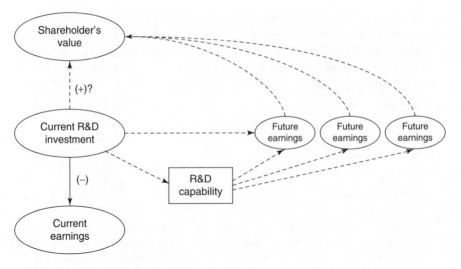

Figure 11.2 R&D value diagram.

analyzed in many management and organization works. Dierickx and Cool (1989) explain it using a bathtub metaphor:

> At any moment in time, the stock of water is indicated by the level of water in the tub; it is the cumulative result of flows of water into the tub (through the tap) and out of it (through a leak). In the example of R&D, the amount of water in the tub represents the stock of know-how at a particular moment in time, whereas current R&D spending is represented by the water flowing through the tap; the fact that know-how depreciates over time is represented by the flow of water leaking through the hole in the tub.

It should be noted that R&D capability is accumulated in the firm through continuous R&D investment. Distinctive competitive advantage can be built through consistent choices about strategic expenditures. Following figure 11.2, accumulated R&D capability can be expected to create future earnings. Based on the residual income model (RIM) or the well-known discounted cash flow model (DCF), all future earnings are discounted and summed up to current stock price. (The details of the valuation model are discussed in the appendix.)

Based on this conjecture, although a direct relationship cannot be observed among these variables, we assume that current R&D investments have indirect, positive impact on shareholders' value via future earnings. This hypothesis seems plausible because business managers invest in uncertain R&D programs in the belief that they will contribute to firm performance and shareholders' value in the near future.

In this chapter, some empirical models are used. Gross profit margin (GPM) and return on equity (ROE) stand for current profitability, which is supposed to have an impact on future profitability. Also, the logarithm of R&D expenditure is the proxy variable for the future value-creating capability of the firm. Although R&D outlays reduce current net income, they are one of the most important factors in gaining and sustaining competitive advantage in the future. Pharmaceutical firms with lower R&D outlays can report a high net income in the current year. But what will happen to the firm in the future? No R&D capability means no new medicine, no profit, and no growth, and eventually will lead to the death of the company. For this reason, it is rational to suppose that R&D outlays are related to future value-creating capability, and boost price-to-book ratio (PBR). Based on these considerations, we use two models, in the next section, for Japanese firms:

$$PBR_i = \alpha + \beta \cdot GPM_i + \gamma \tilde{n} \cdot \log(RD_i) + \varepsilon_i \qquad (1)$$

$$PBR_i = \alpha + \beta \tilde{n} \cdot ROE_i + \gamma \tilde{n} \cdot \log(RD_i) + \varepsilon_i \qquad (2)$$

These models assume that shareholders' value can be explained by a combination of current profitability, which also relates to future profitability, and R&D activity.

R&D Investment and Shareholders' Value: Evidence from Japan

In the recent global merger and acquisition (M&A) wave, the competition of R&D programs is very fierce. Why are there so many M&A deals in the pharmaceutical industry in the United States, the European Union, and Asia? Everyone supposes that there should be economies of scale in R&D. Even if one firm has a higher R&D-to-sales ratio, size is more important than R&D intensity in finding new medicine quickly. That is because the more rapidly "trial and error" is employed, the higher the probability of successful R&D. In order to beat competitors, it appears that the speed of R&D is crucial. This is the reason we see so many megamergers globally. For this reason, in this chapter I use the logarithm of R&D expenditure as the proxy for the size of R&D spending.

As a starting point, I analyze Japanese firms based on simple empirical models in equations (1) and (2). First, using the Nikkei NEEDS (Nikkei Economic Electronic Databank System) database, I collected data of companies listed on the Tokyo Stock Exchange, First Section (TSE1) in fiscal year 2003 whose fiscal year ended in March.[2] Financial institutions were then removed from consideration. To be included in the final sample, firms must have provided both financial data and market price data. These procedures resulted in 844 firms. I used stock price data at the end of March and looked carefully at science-intensive industries such as information and communication, electric machinery, automotive and transport equipment, and chemicals, the four industries that were analyzed.

Table 11.1 presents the results of the analysis. R&D investments are accompanied by a significant stock price increase for most of the industries on both the GPM model and the ROE model. This result strongly suggests that R&D size has a positive impact on shareholders' value. In the electric machinery, automotive and transport equipment, and chemical industries, higher investments in R&D are accompanied by higher shareholders' value. The global competition in new product development is fierce in the electric machinery,

Table 11.1. OLS Regression Results of Japanese Firms in FY2003

Panel A: Dependent variable is price-to-book ratio. Independent variables are gross profit margin and logarithm of R&D expenditure (t-statistics in parentheses). ***, **, and * denote statistical significance at the 1%, 5%, and 10% level, respectively.

	Information & Communication	Electric Machinery	Automotive & Transport Equipment	Chemical	TSE 1
No. Companies	44	125	55	100	844
adj R^2	0.17	0.1	0.19	0.26	0.11
intercept	0.74	0.04	−0.23	−0.38	0.21
t	[2.21]**	[0.11]	[−0.58]	[−1.29]	[1.95]*
GPM	0.01	1.52	2.61	2.32	0.02
t	[2.72]***	[2.98]***	[1.63]	[4.79]***	[7.84]***
log(R&D)	0.07	0.17	0.23	0.23	0.13
t	[0.53]	[1.94]*	[2.09]**	[2.79]***	[4.02]***

Panel B: Dependent variable is price-to-book ratio. Independent variables are return on equity and logarithm of R&D expenditure (t-statistics in parentheses). ***, **, and * denote statistical significance at the 1%, 5%, and 10% level, respectively.

	Information & Communication	Electric Machinery	Automotive & Transport Equipment	Chemical	TSE 1
No. Companies	44	125	55	100	844
adj R^2	0.17	0.02	0.12	0.49	0.04
intercept	0.33	0.4	−0.09	−0.17	0.36
t	[0.89]	[1.14]	[−0.22]	[−0.71]	[3.31]***
ROE	2.78	0.04	−0.05	8.47	−0.01
t	[2.76]***	[0.22]	[−0.42]	[8.16]***	[−0.29]
log(R&D)	0.32	0.19	0.31	0.25	0.21
t	[2.74]***	[2.03]**	[3.01]***	[3.63]***	[6.20]***

and automotive and transport equipment industries. It is plausible that in those industries, higher investments in R&D are accompanied by higher shareholders' value.

Global Evidence

Model and Data

My analysis of Japanese firms shows that higher investments in R&D are accompanied by higher shareholders' value. There still remain, however, two points to verify the findings. First, the sample includes Japanese firms only. It is very important to expand the coverage of analysis to verify the hypothesis. In this section, the analysis will cover the United States, the United Kingdom, Germany, France, Japan, Korea, Taiwan, Hong Kong, and Australia. Second, we need to incorporate other variables in order to verify the results. In the previous section, as a starting point of analysis, I used very simple models that included only profitability and R&D size as independent variables. PBR is, however, affected by many factors other than profitability and R&D activity. Hence, we must control for those potential factors. Stock price is affected by factors such as risk, growth, and financial structure of the firm. In general, as investors use β of stock as a typical proxy for risk, I follow the standard treatment.[3] Capital market participants pay considerable attention to the growth rate of the firm. I use a five-year compounded growth rate of sales as a proxy for the growth of the firm. Last, PBR is largely affected by the financial structure of the firm. Firms with a high debt-to-equity ratio (total debt divided by total equity capital) tend to have high PBR because they have less book value of equity. Hereafter, I incorporate these factors in order to verify the results.

Empirical regression models to be used are shown as below:

$$PBR_i = \rho_0 + \rho_1 \cdot GPM_i + \rho_2 \cdot \tilde{n}\log(RD_i) + \rho_3 \cdot \beta_i + \rho_4 \cdot \text{Sales growth}_i + \rho_5 \cdot \text{DE ratio}_i + \varepsilon_i \tag{3}$$

$$PBR_i = \rho_0 + \rho_1 \cdot ROE_i + \rho_2 \cdot \tilde{n}\log(RD_i) + \rho_3 \cdot \beta_i + \rho_4 \cdot \text{Sales growth}_i + \rho_5 \cdot \text{DE ratio}_i + \varepsilon_i \tag{4}$$

To compile the sample, I gathered data from the Worldscope database for fiscal year 2003. In the previous section, I analyzed Japanese firms. In order to expand the country coverage, I gathered data for the United States, the United Kingdom, Germany, France, Japan, Korea, Taiwan, Hong Kong, and Australia. For the United States, I collected data by separating the NYSE (New York Stock Exchange) sample from the NASDAQ (National Association of Securities Dealers Automated Quotations) sample because of the different firm characteristics.

The target stock markets are the London Stock Exchange for the United Kingdom, Frankfurt for Germany, Paris for France, Tokyo for Japan, Seoul for Korea, Taipei for Taiwan, Hong Kong for Hong Kong, and Sydney for Australia. For inclusion as a sample firm, we set the upper boundary and the lower boundary for every variable as follows: PBR, between 0 and 50 times; ROE, between −1000 percent and 1000 percent; GPM, between −100 percent and 100 percent; equity β, between −10 and 10; debt-to-equity ratio, between 0 percent and 1000 percent. Firms outside these ranges were excluded as outliers. Firms that reported either zero R&D expenditure or did not report R&D expenditure were excluded as well.

Concerning the GPM-based model (equation (3)), these procedures resulted in a sample of 395 NYSE firms, 624 NASDAQ firms, 218 firms in the United Kingdom, 171 firms in Germany, 89 firms in France, 1,152 firms in Japan, 180 firms in Korea, 103 firms in Taiwan, 28 firms in Hong Kong, and 32 firms in Australia. For model (4), the number of observations is shown in the last column of panel B of table 11.2. It may be surprising that so few firms are included in our sample except for in the United States and Japan. This is due to the fact that many firms do not report R&D expenditure.

Results

Table 11.2 presents the regression results. There are several findings. First, higher investments in R&D are accompanied by higher shareholders' value for the NYSE, United Kingdom, Germany, Japan, Korea, and Taiwan on the GPM-based model (see panel A). Second, panel B demonstrates that higher investments in R&D are accompanied by higher shareholders' value for the NYSE, United Kingdom, Germany, France, Japan, Korea, and Taiwan on the ROE-based model. What we are concerned with here is whether higher R&D investments are accompanied by higher shareholders' value. We can deduce from the data that R&D investments are accompanied by significant stock price increases except for NASDAQ, Hong Kong, and Australia. It is notable that the relationship between R&D investment and shareholders' value is strong in the United Kingdom, Japan, Korea, and Taiwan in both regression models.

In the interpretation, in the case of Hong Kong and Australia, I did not observe meaningful results, possibly due to the small sample size. The original database contained more than 1,500 Australian firms. Most of them, however, did not have R&D expenditure data available. The same is true for Hong Kong. The original database provides more than 1,000 Hong Kong firms, but again, very few firms reported R&D expenditure, which caused the small sample size. With regard to the NASDAQ, the sample size was 624 for the GPM model and 657 for the ROE model, which is large enough to run OLS regression. In both panel A and panel B, R&D investments are not correlated with shareholders' value. We can interpret this result in the following way.

NASDAQ includes various types of companies. Some grow rapidly while recording negative earnings. In fact, the results show that *sales growth* has a positive impact on PBR. Some may have very small book value of equity, and incorporate huge risk. These factors bring diversity and volatility among the sample firms. That is probably the reason why no significant relationship can be observed between PBR and R&D. NASDAQ firms may have a different dynamic structure that the model does not yet capture. Future research should take this into consideration.

It is worth noting that the number of Japanese observations is the largest among the nine countries. This is not due to the fact that the author lives in Japan. Worldscope is one of the leading financial information databases. Japanese firms, however, report R&D expenditure more frequently than others do. It is reasonable to suppose that the positive relationship of R&D size and PBR is outstandingly robust in Japan for the year 2003.

Knowledge-Intensive Industry in FY 2001–2003

As I mentioned at the beginning of the chapter, although accounting standards require firms to fully expense R&D outlays, those outlays generate some of the most precious economic assets in the knowledge society. The impact of R&D activities is much larger in science-based industries than in others. Although I do not show the details of statistics, R&D investment is huge in knowledge-intensive industries such as software, computers, semiconductors, chemicals, communications and technology, pharmaceuticals, and biotechnology. For example, let us look at the ratio of R&D investment versus capital expenditure, which is R&D investment divided by capital expenditure. The median of the ratio is 230 percent for pharmaceuticals and 900 percent for biotechnology in fiscal year 2003. What needs to be emphasized is that biotechnology firms invest in R&D activities nine times as much as in physical assets such as plant, property, and equipment. According to Hand (2001a), "The largest and most important components of a biotech firm's production and investment functions are its R&D expenditure and the discoveries made by the knowledge and skill of its bioscientists and bioengineers." The same is true for pharmaceutical firms. Healy, Myers, and Howe (2002) present the key phases of a pharmaceutical firm's drug discovery and development. They are basic research, pre-clinical testing, phase I clinical trials, phase II clinical trials, phase III clinical trials, FDA filing, and commercial launch. Huge amounts of money are invested in R&D programs throughout each phase. Accordingly, in this section, I would like to focus attention on these two R&D-intensive industries.

Once again, data were gathered from the Worldscope database. Following the Dow Jones industry code, I chose the biotechnology and pharmaceutical

Table 11.2.   OLS Regression Results: International Comparison in FY2003

Panel A: Dependent variable is price-to-book ratio. Independent variables are gross profit margin, logarithm of R&D expenditure, β, sales growth (a five-year compounded growth rate of sales), and DE ratio (total debt divided by total equity capital). *t*-statistics are in parentheses. ***, **, and * denote statistical significance at the 1%, 5%, and 10% level, respectively.

Country	Intercept	GPM	Log (R&D)	β	Sales Growth	DE Ratio	Adj. R^2	No. Companies
NYSE	-0.68 [-1.45]	0.08 [8.70]***	0.46 [2.29]**	-0.22 [-1.10]	-0.02 [-1.76]*	0.01 [9.04]***	0.30	395
NASDAQ	1.27 [2.90]***	0.05 [6.30]***	-0.46 [-1.91]*	0.43 [3.18]***	0.01 [0.13]	0.01 [7.77]***	0.16	624
UK	-3.64 [-3.23]***	0.04 [5.28]***	0.59 [3.38]***	0.10 [0.46]	0.00 [2.68]***	0.01 [4.48]	0.23	218
Germany	0.35 [1.25]	0.03 [5.55]***	0.19 [1.78]*	0.18 [1.23]	0.00 [0.91]	0.00 [3.08]***	0.19	171
France	0.59 [1.49]	0.03 [3.36]***	-0.03 [-0.19]	0.64 [3.58]***	-0.02 [-1.49]	0.00 [1.95]*	0.21	89
Japan	-0.48 [-3.63]***	0.02 [12.29]***	0.12 [6.37]***	-0.01 [-0.17]	0.03 [10.75]***	0.00 [12.34]***	0.31	1152
Korea	0.08 [0.58]	0.01 [1.64]	0.12 [2.65]***	0.16 [2.25]**	0.00 [-0.47]	0.00 [1.12]	0.09	180
Taiwan	0.95 [3.95]***	0.00 [0.31]	0.23 [2.93]***	-0.42 [-3.03]***	0.02 [4.91]***	0.00 [1.94]*	0.38	103
Hong Kong	2.75 [3.12]***	-0.01 [-0.44]	-0.19 [-0.43]	-0.64 [-1.05]	0.02 [1.11]	0.00 [-0.11]	-0.04	28
Australia	0.44 [0.32]	0.03 [1.43]	1.25 [1.50]	-0.26 [-0.37]	0.11 [2.57]**	0.00 [-0.38]	0.15	32

Panel B: Dependent variable is price-to-book ratio. Independent variables are return on equity, logarithm of R&D expenditure, β, sales growth (a five-year compounded growth rate of sales), and DE ratio (total debt divided by total equity capital). t-statistics are in parentheses. ***, **, and * denote statistical significance at the 1%, 5%, and 10% level, respectively

Country	Intercept	GPM	Log (R&D)	β	Sales Growth	DE Ratio	Adj. R^2	No. Companies
NYSE	0.74 [2.00]**	0.06 [12.57]***	0.57 [3.17]***	0.49 [2.47]**	−0.02 [−1.90]*	0.01 [8.45]***	0.40	396
NASDAQ	3.47 [10.49]***	−0.02 [−7.90]***	0.01 [0.03]	0.06 [0.46]	0.01 [3.37]***	0.01 [3.12]***	0.16	657
UK	−2.29 [−1.84]*	0.00 [0.49]	0.59	0.35 [1.38]	0.00 [0.27]	0.01 [3.22]***	0.11	220
Germany	1.32 [5.63]***	0.00 [2.00]**	0.24 [2.08]**	0.19 [1.16]	0.00 [−0.03]	0.00 [2.30]**	0.06	172
France	1.55 [4.51]***	−0.02 [−4.44]***	0.40 [2.56]**	0.13 [0.66]	0.00 [−0.07]	0.00 [−1.37]	0.27	90
Japan	−0.49 [−3.50]***	0.00 [−2.07]**	0.20 [9.80]***	−0.08 [−2.30]**	0.03 [11.67]***	0.00 [9.02]***	0.23	1153
Korea	0.13 [0.94]	0.00 [1.50]	0.14 [3.06]***	0.16 [2.17]**	0.00 [−0.55]	0.00 [1.43]	0.09	180
Taiwan	1.04 [4.67]***	0.00 [−0.51]	0.23 [2.90]***	−0.46 [−3.25]***	0.02 [4.87]***	0.00 [1.11]	0.39	103
Hong Kong	1.73 [2.18]**	0.05 [2.10]**	−0.21 [−0.50]	−0.32 [−0.54]	0.00 [−0.19]	0.00 [0.71]	0.13	28
Australia	3.20 [2.62]**	−0.02 [−0.91]	1.22 [1.66]	−0.61 [−0.77]	0.01 [0.49]	0.00 [−0.58]	0.12	35

industries, which included firms from all over the world. The Worldscope database, which is provided through Thomson Financial, covers more than fifty-five established and emerging markets, and nearly 96 percent of the world's stock market value. It is no exaggeration to say that our sample coverage is wide and global. The period of analysis was from 2001 to 2003. Here, model (3) and model (4) are used to estimate the relationship between R&D and PBR.

Table 11.3 presents the results of OLS regression based on equations (3) and (4). First, for the pharmaceutical industry in panel A (GPM model), higher investments in R&D are accompanied by higher shareholders' value in 2001 and 2002. We see from panel B that higher investments in R&D are accompanied by higher shareholders' value in all three years. It is worth noting that explaining power of the model increased from 18 percent in 2001 to 37 percent in 2002, and 55 percent in 2003. Second, regarding the biotechnology industry, R&D size is positively related to shareholders' value in 2003 in both the GPM model and the ROE model. Although the results are slightly different, we have good grounds for interpreting the results to suggest that higher investments in R&D are accompanied by higher shareholders' value in knowledge-intensive industries in recent years. As Dierickx and Cool (1989) point out, there are "time compression diseconomies" in R&D programs. To build high-quality R&D asset stock, which eventually creates shareholders' value, choosing appropriate time paths of flows is necessary. Although R&D investments are invisible, top managements in knowledge-intensive industries must comprehend this dynamics well.

Findings and Implications

Findings

This chapter sheds light on the relationship between R&D investment and shareholders' value. My analysis began with Japanese firms. Next, I expanded the analysis into more countries, including the United States, the United Kingdom, Germany, France, Japan, Korea, Taiwan, Hong Kong, and Australia, in order to check generality. The following section focuses on typical science-based industries, such as biotechnology and pharmaceuticals. Although the results are slightly different, we have good grounds for interpreting the results to suggest that higher investments in R&D are accompanied by higher shareholders' value. This finding supports the hypothesis shown in figure 11.2 as "R&D value diagram."

There are two issues that need to be resolved before reaching a conclusion. First, the probability of success is quite low in an R&D project.[4] That may raise a question about the relationship mentioned above. Boer (1999) shows that there are several stages in an R&D project: (1) raw ideas, (2) conceptual project, (3) feasibility, (4) development, (5) early commercialization, and (6) commercial success. It is well known that an R&D project is a long-term undertaking, and the probability of success is not high. Only a limited percentage of the projects can survive and achieve commercial success. Nevertheless, knowledge-intensive firms invest large sums of money in R&D programs. The reason is that once an R&D project reaches the final stage, it definitely contributes to financial performance. A new medicine project is a good example. Second, capital market participants cannot access detailed information about the content and process of an R&D activity. Accounting rules do not require firms to disclose the details of R&D activities. In addition, R&D activity is unique and, at the same time, too innovative for capital market participants to know the real price or value.[5]

In spite of these unresolved issues, this chapter demonstrates the following:

- There is a positive and statistically significant correlation between R&D investment and increased shareholder value based on large-sample empirical work.
- This relationship was found in many countries; not only in the United States, but also in Europe and Asia.[6]
- While R&D investments reduce current-year earnings, they build the R&D capability of the organization for the future. Accumulated R&D capability can be expected to create future earnings, which relates to shareholders' value.

Management and Theoretical Implications

Barney (1986) argues that "When different firms have different expectations concerning the future value of a strategy, it will often be possible for some strategizing firms to obtain above-normal returns from acquiring the resources necessary to implement a product market strategy, and then implementing that strategy." Different firms have different expectations concerning the future value of R&D programs. R&D investment strategy is one of the key choices to obtain sustainable abnormal earnings and increase shareholders' value. A unique R&D program is nontradable and nonimitable. Hence, it can be a source of distinctive competitive advantage in the knowledge society. Top management needs to understand it and control R&D projects effectively in order to maximize shareholders' value.

In practice, however, less attention is paid to the profitability of intangible investments. In the case of traditional capital expenditure, profitability is strictly measured by using ROI or ROIC (return on invested capital). In contrast, in the case of intangible investments such as R&D, advertising, and

Table 11.3. OLS Regression Results: Global Knowledge-intensive Industries, 2001–2003

Panel A: Dependent variable is price-to-book ratio. Independent variables are gross profit margin, logarithm of R&D expenditure, β, sales growth (a five-year compounded growth rate of sales), and DE ratio (total debt divided by total equity capital). t-statistics are in parentheses. ***, **, and * denote statistical significance at the 1%, 5%, and 10% level, respectively.

Industry	Intercept	GPM	Log (R&D)	β	Sales Growth	DE Ratio	Adj. R^2	No. Companies
Pharmaceutical 2001	-5.45	0.02	0.88	1.89	0.00	0.00	0.18	108
	[-2.31]**	[2.03]**	[2.86]***	[3.55]***	[0.08]	[0.66]		
Pharmaceutical 2002	-0.76	-0.01	0.24	-1.35	0.03	0.01	0.28	124
	[-0.35]	[-0.47]	[1.77]*	[-3.07]***	[5.44]***	[3.20]***		
Pharmaceutical 2003	-0.55	0.04	-0.07	0.69	0.04	0.03	0.23	147
	[-0.22]	[2.07]**	[-0.19]	[1.24]	[2.36]**	[5.47]***		
Biotechnology 2001	1.68	0.04	-0.12	1.31	0.00	0.04	0.21	59
	[0.25]	[1.67]	[-0.14]	[1.63]	[-0.71]	[3.53]***		
Biotechnology 2002	4.48	0.01	-0.21	-0.66	0.01	0.01	0.13	76
	[1.17]	[0.42]	[-0.38]	[-1.75]	[0.95]	[3.32]***		
Biotechnology 2003	-0.41	-0.01	1.33	0.18	0.00	0.01	0.07	120
	[-0.43]	[-1.03]	[2.81]***	[0.57]	[0.18]	[2.10]**		

Panel B: Dependent variable is price-to-book ratio. Independent variables are return on equity, logarithm of R&D expenditure, β, sales growth (a five-year compounded growth rate of sales), and DE ratio (total debt divided by total equity capital). t-statistics are in parentheses. ***, **, and * denote statistical significance at the 1%, 5%, and 10% level, respectively.

Industry	Intercept	GPM	Log (R&D)	β	Sales Growth	DE Ratio	Adj. R^2	No. Companies
Pharmaceutical 2001	-6.01	0.01	1.09	1.71	0.01	0.00	0.18	114
	[-2.60]**	[2.74]***	[3.81]***	[3.72]***	[1.69]*	[1.27]		
Pharmaceutical 2002	0.34	-0.03	0.44	-1.29	0.01	0.01	0.37	133
	[0.17]	[-5.77]***	[1.78]*	[-3.64]***	[3.27]***	[1.67]*		
Pharmaceutical 2003	-1.77	-0.04	0.60	-0.03	0.02	0.01	0.55	159
	[-0.96]	[-11.14]***	[2.49]**	[-0.07]	[2.34]**	[3.11]***		
Biotechnology 2001	1.19	-0.03	0.32	0.72	0.00	0.02	0.19	72
	[0.18]	[-2.19]**	[0.35]	[1.11]	[-0.28]	[2.38]		
Biotechnology 2002	6.20	-0.02	-0.38	-1.05	0.00	0.01	0.18	94
	[1.50]	[-3.81]***	[-0.68]	[-2.53]**	[0.54]	[1.56]		
Biotechnology 2003	-2.32	-0.01	1.53	0.52	0.00	0.00	0.13	171
	[-3.14]***	[-3.48]***	[2.94]***	[1.35]	[-0.02]	[0.16]		

employee training outlay, we often forget to measure the profitability. It is no exaggeration to say that there is asymmetry in the performance evaluation among tangible and intangible investments. We are prone to hope that R&D outlay may create product development capability, and advertising outlay may be accumulated in the form of brand equity. In other words, business managers are generous toward intangible investments: they undervalue the huge amount of invisible investments due to their intangible characteristics.

In recent years, as I mentioned at the beginning of this chapter, the growing trend to invest in intangible assets has been one of the most impressive characteristics of the economy. However, intangible investment is a *double-edged sword*. On the one hand, it can be a source of competitive advantage in the knowledge society; on the other hand, low-profit intangible investment can destroy firm value when its performance is not adequately measured. In fact, some firms are losing because they invest too much in unprofitable R&D projects and branding activities. Business managers should try to measure the profitability of both tangibles and intangibles effectively. How? My suggestion is to recognize intangible investments as assets *for internal use,* not for financial reporting objectives. First, recognize them as assets in the organization. Second, amortize them for their service life, which varies among industries and kinds of investments. Firms can choose the service life by themselves because it is not for financial reporting, but for strategic use inside the firm. Third, measure the profitability of the intangible investments based on the calculated intangible assets amount. This method may seem too simple, but it is better than no measurement. Without measurement, we can control nothing.

On the theoretical side, the valuation framework of intangibles urgently needs to be developed. DCF is one of the most widespread methods for investment project decision- making and equity valuation. However, the method has some serious disadvantages in practical situations. In the traditional DCF method, both tangible and intangible investments are deducted in the calculation of free cash flow (FCF). In the DCF method, FCF is calculated as follows: FCF = (cash flow from operation) – (capital expenditure). Intangible investments, such as R&D investment, are already deducted in "cash flow from operation." Tangible investments are deducted as capital expenditures. Since both tangible and intangible investments are deducted in the FCF calculation process, in the short term, investments are treated as a loss of value. Long-term forecasting is required to recognize cash inflows from those investment projects. The more the firms invest, the more value is destroyed in the DCF framework. We may make the wrong decision in the growing phase if we rely too much on DCF. Growing firms typically record negative FCF as a result of their huge investment. How can we value these firms in the DCF framework? Some would raise the objection that DCF can incorporate long-term FCF in the form of terminal value or continuing value. It is quite difficult, however, to make a long-term forecast, especially in an uncertain economy. As is widely known, terminal value estimation in the DCF includes serious misevaluation. Are there any other frameworks that overcome these disadvantages? The answer is "yes."

Any investment is treated as value loss in the traditional DCF framework. This creates an overreliance on the continuing value (terminal value) calculation, and causes a great deal of uncertainty. In contrast, the residual income model (RIM) and the economic profit model can incorporate intangible factors as residual income or economic value added. In the RIM framework, equity price equals the sum of book value of equity and the present value of future residual income stream. Residual income is positive when net income exceeds what shareholders expect, which is cost of equity capital. In contrast, residual income is negative when net income is below the cost of equity capital. Although the RIM is simple, it has two advantages. First, capital expenditure is added to book value of equity as a value input. Hence, it is easier to value growing firms by using RIM than by using DCF. Second, RIM can capture the value-creating ability of intangible assets, such as R&D capability, brand equity, and human capital. The information provided in balance sheets about intangible or knowledge-based assets is quite inadequate under current accounting rules. All such investments with long-term benefits are uniformly expensed in income statements, leaving no information on the balance sheet. The balance sheet includes physical and financial assets only. In the RIM, however, intangible asset factors are reflected in the residual income, not in the book value of equity. If knowledge-related assets have a high value-creating capability, then it will be reflected in the high future residual income. In addition, the forecast horizon can be shorter than for DCF analysis. Several empirical investigations in accounting and finance, such as Francis, Olsson, and Oswald (2000) and Penman and Sougiannis (1998), show that RIM valuation performs far better than DDM (discounted dividend model) and DCF valuation models. Francis et al. (2000) found that RIM value estimates are more accurate and explain more of the variation in security prices than DCF or DDM value estimates do.

On the theoretical side, the DDM, DCF, and RIM are all identical. On the empirical side, however, RIM valuation demonstrates a better estimation of performance than the others do. It is remarkable that the RIM incorporates both balance sheet and income statement items with cost of equity, and describes the value of knowledge-based assets and shareholders' value fairly well. PBR reflects the market participant's hope for the firm's future value-creating capability. Much premium is added to a value-creating firm's stock price, which results in a PBR that is greater than 1. In other words, stock price is composed of current net value plus future premium (residual income), and PBR is composed of 1 plus future value-creating capability. The same is true for the economic profit or economic value-added valuation model. It can treat capital expenditure as a value input in the form of "invested capital." Intangible factors are incorporated in the future economic profit parts. These new frameworks, rather than the traditional DCF, should be used for intangibles in order to accurately capture the value-generating capability of the knowledge-intensive firms.

Appendix: Valuation Model

Under the DDM, equity value equals the sum of discounted present values of future expected dividends.

$$V_t = \sum_{i=1}^{\infty} \frac{E(D_{t+i})}{(1+r_E)^i} \tag{5}$$

V: value of equity
r_E: cost of equity capital
$E(\cdot)$: expectation operator
D: dividends

Following theoretical work by Ohlson (1995), if forecasts of earnings, book value of equity, and dividends satisfy a "clean surplus relation" (eq. 6), then current stock price would be equal to the sum of current book value of equity and the present value of expected residual income (eq. 7). Residual income is positive when net income exceeds what shareholders expect, which is cost of equity capital. In contrast, residual income is negative when net income is below the cost of equity capital. Residual income is similar to economic value added (EVA), which is defined as net operating profits after taxes (NOPAT) minus weighted average cost of capital (WACC). Residual income is a net concept, whereas EVA is a gross concept. Hence, in the valuation framework, residual income is related to the value of equity only. On the other hand, EVA is used to calculate the value of the enterprise; value of equity plus value of the debt. In finance, we strictly distinguish value of the firm from value of equity. In the following analysis, attention is focused on the value of equity.

$$B_{t+i} = B_{t+i-1} + X_{t+i} - D_{t+i} \tag{6}$$

B: Book value of the equity
X: Net income

$$V_t = B_t + \sum_{i=1}^{\infty} \frac{E(X_{t+i} - r_E B_{t+i-1})}{(1+r_E)^i} \tag{7}$$

The stock price is composed of the current book value and the present value of the forecasted residual income. Hence, if we indicate residual income as RI, we can rewrite equation (7) as follows:

$$P_0 = B_0 + \sum_{t=1}^{\infty} (1 + r_E)^{-t} E[RI]_t \tag{8}$$

RI: residual income

P: stock price

These equity valuation models, equations (7) and (8), are called residual income models (RIM). The RIM is quite popular both in academics as well as in the portfolio investment strategy practice. For example, Morgan Stanley started to use the RIM globally to do equity valuation in 2004. Penman (2004) closely explains the details of the RIM.

Paraphrasing the RIM, equity price equals the sum of book value of equity and residual income. Dividing both sides of the RIM by book value of equity, we get equation (9).

$$P_0/B_0 = 1 + 1/B_0 \left(\sum_{t=1}^{\infty} (1 + r_E)^{-t} E[RI]_t \right) \tag{9}$$

This equation means that

- Firms that are expected to create positive future residual income have a PBR of more than 1.
- Firms that are expected to create negative residual income will have a PBR of less than 1.
- Firms that are expected to create net income equal to equity cost of capital will have a PBR equal to 1, because residual income is equal to zero.

The first term on the right-hand side of equation (9), 1, is the normal level of PBR. It indicates a competitive economic environment where no firms can earn abnormal earnings. The second term on the right-hand side of the equation means premium over equity cost of capital. In short, the capital market evaluates each firm's value-generating capability over investors' expectations.

Acknowledgments

I am grateful to Kazuo Ichijo and Herbert Addison for their helpful comments and suggestions. Following their suggestions, the valuation models are moved from the body of the chapter to the appendix. Their comments surely made this chapter more approachable for business managers. I thank D. Kubota for her editing. My appreciation also goes to Junko Kamita for her discussion on the pharmaceutical industry. I am grateful for the financial support of New Energy and Industrial Technology Development Organization.

Notes

1. Nakamura (2003) demonstrates that firms in the United States invested approximately $1 trillion in intangible assets in 2000.

2. Fiscal year-end for more than 90 percent of Japanese firms is March.

3. Following the definition of the Worldscope database, $\hat{O}$ is a measure of market risk that shows the relationship between the volatility of the stock and the volatility of the market. This coefficient is based on between twenty-three and thirty-five consecutive month-end price percent changes and their relativity to a local market index.

4. See Healy et al. (2002) for the success probability of drug development programs.

5. See Aboody and Lev (2000) on information asymmetry and R&D activity.

6. This chapter, of course, has limitations. First, we should include relative R&D size in each industry or industry-adjusted R&D investment as another independent variable, because investors compare equity value relatively. Second, what has been demonstrated in this chapter is not a causal relationship but correlation. I believe the causality should be analyzed and described thoroughly in literature with a case-based rather than an empirical approach. Pharmaceutical firms voluntarily disclose the details of R&D activity. Analyzing this information may give us interesting insights. Third, the main stress in this study is on R&D activity. We should also cover other intangibles, such as brand equity, human capital, and organizational capital.

References

Aboody, D., and Lev, B. (1998). "The Value-relevance of Intangibles: The Case of Software Capitalization." *Journal of Accounting Research* 36 (supp.): 161–191.

Aboody, D., and Lev, B. (2000). "Information Asymmetry, R&D, and Insider Gains." *Journal of Finance* 55 (6): 2747–2746.

Association for Investment Management and Research (AIMR). (1993). *Financial Reporting in the 1990s and Beyond.* Charlottesville, Va.: AIMR.

Barney, J. B. (1986). "Strategic Factor Markets: Expectations, Luck, and Business Strategy." *Management Science* 32 (10): 1231–1241.

Boer, P. (1999). *The Valuation of Technology: Business and Financial Issues in R&D.* New York: Wiley.

Chan, L., Lakonishok, J., and Sougiannis, T. (2001). "The Stock Market Valuation of Research and Development Expenditures." *Journal of Finance* 56 (6): 2431–2456.

Dierickx, I., and Cool, K. (1989). "Asset Stock Accumulation and Sustainability of Competitive Advantage." *Management Science* 35 (12): 1504–1511.

Financial Accounting Standards Board (FASB). (1974). *Statement of Financial Accounting Standards*, no. 2, *Accounting for Research and Development Costs*.

Francis, J., Olsson, P., and Oswald, D. R. (2000). "Comparing the Accuracy and Explainability of Dividend, Free Cash Flow, and Abnormal Earnings Equity Value Estimates." *Journal of Accounting Research* 38: 45–70.

Hand, J. (2001). "The Market Valuation of Biotechnology Firms and Biotechnology R&D." Working paper, Kenan-Flagler Business School, University of North Carolina at Chapel Hill.

Healy, P., Myers, S., and Howe, C. (2002). "R&D Accounting and the Tradeoff between Relevance and Objectivity." *Journal of Accounting Research*, 40 (3): 677–710.

Lev, B. (1999). "R&D and Capital Markets." *Journal of Applied Corporate Finance* (Bank of America) 11 (4): 21–35.

Lev, B., and Sougiannis, T. (1996). "The Capitalization, Amortization, and Value-relevance of R&D." *Journal of Accounting and Economics* 21: 107–138.

Nakamura, L. (2003). "A Trillion Dollars a Year in Intangible Investment and the New Economy." In J. R. M. Hand and B. Lev, eds., *Intangible Assets: Values, Measures, and Risks*. New York: Oxford University Press.

Nonaka, I., and Teece, D. (2001). "Research Directions for Knowledge Management." In I. Nonaka and D. Teece, eds., *Managing Industrial Knowledge: Creation, Transfer and Utilization*. London: Sage.

Ohlson, J. (1995). "Earnings, Book Values, and Dividends in Security Valuation." *Contemporary Accounting Research* 11: 661–687.

Penman, S. (2004). *Financial Statement Analysis & Security Valuation*, 2nd ed. New York: McGraw-Hill Irwin.

Penman, S., and Sougiannis, T. (1998). "A Comparison of Dividend, Cash Flow, and Earnings Approaches to Equity Valuation." *Contemporary Accounting Research* 15: 343–383.

12

Perspectives on Research and Development

Organizing and Managing Innovation in a (Global) Knowledge-Based Economy

---

MIE AUGIER AND DAVID J. TEECE

R&D and (the Economics of) Knowledge

There is no doubt that technological innovation is the primary driver of economic growth. While classical economists ranging from Adam Smith to Karl Marx were aware of the importance of technology and knowledge in economic growth, it was probably Schumpeter who brought innovation to center stage. Indeed, according to Joseph Schumpeter, innovation is the engine of the capitalist system: "The fundamental impulse that sets and keeps the capitalist engine in motion comes from the new consumers' goods, the new methods of production or transportation, the new markets, the new forms of industrial organization that capitalist enterprise creates" (Schumpeter, 1942 p. 83). Schumpeter was ignored for decades, while economists modeled firms as employing more capital, labor, and other factors of production to increase output—possibly with technical change as a shift parameter in the production function.

It is now widely recognized, however, that the creation and use of intangible rather than tangible (physical) assets are the keys to wealth creation. As Peter Drucker suggested: "The traditional factors of production—land, labor and capital—have not disappeared. But they have become secondary. Knowledge is becoming the only meaningful resource" (Drucker, 1993, p. 42). Moreover, the business enterprise is the dominant player in the creation and deployment of intangible assets.

Schumpeter's ideas have been developed further in recent years by insightful scholars with eclectic dispositions. These scholars include Paul David, Giovanni Dosi, Chris Freeman, Zvi Griliches, Edwin Mansfield, David Mowery, Richard Nelson, Nathan Rosenberg, Sidney Winter, and occasionally Kenneth Arrow and Robert Solow. Each has taken innovation issues seriously, and they have initiated several streams of research that have built a rich understanding of the economics of technological change. In recent years, business economists and management scholars have added considerably to the understanding of technological change and intellectual capital as well.

Most economists were slow to recognize innovation in their models primarily because they lacked the conceptual and mathematical apparatus to deal with technological change in anything other than the most primitive manner. Moreover, the process of innovation was so poorly understood that there was little consensus on terms, definitions, and basic propositions about innovation. The challenges posed by technological change for economic theory have been recognized since at least Frank Knight (1921). Yet it was not until Teece (1981, 1986), Nelson and Winter (1982), and Nonaka (1995) that issues such as the tacit nature of much technological and organizational knowledge came to be widely recognized, and the ramifications explored.[1] Because of the tacit (i.e., difficult or costly to articulate) nature of know-how, those practicing a technique may be able to do so with great facility, but they may not be able to transfer the skill to others without demonstration and involvement.

The growing recognition of the importance of innovation, knowledge, and intangible assets, and of their tacit nature, and the desire to understand what creates competitive advantages at both the level of the firm and the level of the economy have stimulated many diverse (but not always consistent) streams of research on technological innovation and knowledge management. The intention of this chapter is to review some historical developments in our understanding of the organization of research and development (R&D) and the production of new technology. The chapter concludes by discussing how and where R&D is developed today, and how managers can think about their strategy of creating new knowledge through R&D. Our focus is primarily on the United States.

Organizing Innovation, R&D, and Knowledge Production Activities

At the heart of understanding innovation and R&D is knowledge generation, transfer, protection, and application. Business organizations develop and manage knowledge. They generate and process knowledge, formulate plans and strategies, make decisions, and monitor behavior and experiences; they also transfer and protect know-how.

We may define innovation as the search for and the discovery, development, improvement, adaptation, and commercialization of new processes, new products, and new organizational structures and procedures. Innovation involves uncertainty, risk-taking, probing and reprobing, experimenting, trial and error, and testing. It requires the availability of a labor force with necessary technical skills; economic structures that permit considerable autonomy and encourage entrepreneurship; economic systems that permit and enable a variety of approaches to technological and market opportunities; access to venture capital; good connections within the scientific community (universities) and between users and developers of technology; strong protection of intellectual property; the availability of strategies and structures to enable innovating firms to capture a return from their investment; and, in fragmented industries, the ability to quickly build or access co-specialized assets inside or outside the industry (Teece, 1986, 1993). Innovation is a process where blind alleys and dry holes are frequent; where breakthroughs are often unexpected, and where the innovator will often lose in the marketplace to imitators and fast followers.

The business firm is at the core of the American system of technological innovation (Chandler, 1990). The emergence and growth of (mainly) privately funded organized industrial research and development inside business firms during the twentieth century must rank as one of the most important economic developments in modern American history. Industrial research conducted by and substantially funded by business firms has thus played a key role in American prosperity. It was also key to the outcomes in both world wars, and arguably to the ending of the Cold War. What, then, is the genius behind this system? How did it emerge, how does it work, and how has it changed, particularly since the mid-twentieth century?

Early Developments of Organized R&D

Industrial research and development is the activity in which scientific and engineering knowledge is used to create and bring to market new products, processes, intellectual assets, and services. R&D encompasses several activities that can occur in any order. The industrial R&D laboratory is a key component—but not the only component—of the knowledge-generating engine of the modern corporation.

Consider various types of R&D activity. There is basic research, which is aimed purely at the creation of new scientific and technical knowledge. Its purpose is to advance understanding of phenomena.[2] Its core foundations are usually quite abstract. There is applied research, designed to implement new scientific and technical knowledge, which is work expected to have a practical, but not necessarily a commercial, payoff. While basic research is aimed at new knowledge for its own sake, applied research has practicality and utility as its goal. There is also development in which the new knowledge is embedded in a product or process and is honed for commercial application. Boundaries among these activities are quite fuzzy, and the manner in which they have been organized and linked has changed over time (Teece, 1989). Nevertheless, for almost a century and a half, organized research activities have played an important (though ever changing) role in knowledge generation.

The first organized research laboratory in the United States was established by Thomas Edison in 1876. Others soon followed. In 1886, Arthur D. Little, an applied scientist, started his enterprise, which became a major technical services/consulting organization to other enterprises. Eastman Kodak (1893), B. F. Goodrich (1895), General Electric (1900), Dow (1900), Du Pont (1902), American Telephone & Telegraph (1907), and Goodyear (1909) followed soon thereafter with in-house corporate R&D laboratories. The industrial laboratory constituted a significant departure from an earlier period of U.S. history when innovation was largely the work of independent inventors such as Eli Whitney (the cotton gin and interchangeable parts, especially of guns), Samuel Morse (telegraph), Charles Goodyear (vulcanization of rubber), and Cyrus McCormick (the reaper).

The founding of formal R&D programs and laboratories stemmed in part from competitive threats, which necessitated a more proactive strategy toward innovation. For instance, AT&T at first followed the telegraph industry's practice of relying on the market (individual inventors) for technological innovation. However, the expiration of the major Bell patents and the growth of large numbers of independent telephone companies helped stimulate AT&T to organize Bell Labs. Competition likewise drove George Eastman to establish laboratories at Kodak Park in Rochester, New York, to counteract efforts by German dye and chemical firms to enter into the manufacture of fine chemicals, including photographic chemicals and film.

During the early years of the twentieth century, the number of research labs grew dramatically. By World War I there were perhaps as many as 100 industrial research laboratories in the United States. The number tripled during World War I, and industrial R&D maintained its momentum even during the Great Depression.

The interwar period also saw the industrial research labs produce significant science. In 1927 Clinton Davisson began his work at Bell Labs on electron diffraction that led to his receiving the Nobel Prize in physics in 1937. (Over the years, Bell Labs researchers have been awarded six Nobel Prizes and one Turing Award, and Bell Labs has received almost 30,000 patents; their list of inventions includes the solar cell, the UNIX operating system, and the C and C++ programming languages.) According to Gehani (2003), the creativity and large number of inventions at Bell Labs were to a large extent the result of the nature of the research lab: it was like a university, in that many (but not all) researchers were assigned to projects, rather than specific tasks, and were allowed to use their talent as a university researcher would, but without having to teach (and with a much larger research budget). Other innovative research institutions, such as the RAND Corporation, shared these characteristics. When the funding and the organization of Bell Labs began to change, the intellectual freedom began to disappear.

At Du Pont, Wallace Carothers developed and published the general theory of polymers, and then went on in 1930 to create synthetic rubber and, later, a strong, tough, water-resistant fiber called nylon. These technological breakthroughs were in and of themselves of great importance, but it took time and money to leverage them into marketable products. For instance, it took more than a decade to get from the beginning of research in superpolymers to the production of nylon on a commercial basis.

The Golden Era of "Big Science" (1945–1980)

Building on wartime success, including the Manhattan Project to build the atomic bomb, the era of big science began, fueled by the optimism that well-funded scientists and engineers could produce technological breakthroughs that would benefit the economy and society. University scientists, working with the engineers from corporate America, had produced a string of breakthrough technologies including radar, antibiotics, the digital electronic computer, and atomic energy. The dominant intellectual belief of the immediate postwar period was that science-driven research programs would ensure the development of an endless frontier of new products and processes. The development of the transistor at Bell Labs strengthened this view. Many firms augmented their commitments to industrial R&D. For instance, in 1956 IBM established a research division devoted to world-class basic research.

The background for this was World War II, the first time in American history that large-scale mobilization of scientists and engineers had been achieved. These initiatives included more than scientists and technicians working on the Los Alamos atom bomb project; the MIT Radiation Lab, Vannevar Bush's Office of Scientific Research and Development, and the Secretary of War's panel of expert consultants from science and industry were included as well. After the war, the success of the wartime cooperation among science, the military, and industry brought a new awareness (among scientists as well as industry and the military) of what this type of collaboration could accomplish on important problems (not just national security problems), and it constituted a model of how scientists could continue their work and produce major scientific breakthroughs.

One of the results was the fostering of broadband technology in the United States. In the 1950s, when *Sputnik* had raised doubts about U.S. technological sophistication, the Department of Defense created ARPA (Advanced Research

Project Agency). There was a general interest in the strategic nature of information that raised questions such as how the United States could maintain a national telecom network in case of nuclear war. And how could the government authorities communicate in case of war in general? Wires and switches were vulnerable to attack, so the question was whether a self-healing telecommunications network could be created. Research (most of it done at the RAND Corporation) demonstrated that the traditional telecom system (based on an analog, circuit-based hierarchical network of wires and switching systems) was vulnerable because there was no capacity for rerouting traffic around damaged parts of the network. As a result, ARPA wanted to develop a more flexible and resilient system. A RAND research proposal recommended a network designed to operate with no central authority. The system was assumed to be unreliable all the time and thus was designed to work around any broken parts, thereby transcending its own unreliability. This idea proved to make the U.S. telecommunications infrastructure more efficient—and became known in the 1960s in the packet-switching approach to digital transmission. Specifically, the information was divided into packages (instead of an analog signal), each separately addressed and working through the network on its own; in the end the information was reassembled into the original package. (The route of the information was irrelevant; only the final outcome was important.) Thus, if pieces of the information network were broken down, the packages would still be delivered, traveling through whatever modes in the network survived. The major advantage of the system was that it was considerably more flexible. In the event of a nuclear war, it would make it possible to reroute information around parts of the system that had been eliminated or damaged. The early system—the ARPA net—was taken over by the NSF and eventually privatized, and became the basis of what is now known as the Internet. The same digital-based transmission (packet-switching) also became the platform for the information that accommodated types of communication networks and broadband capabilities that later developed into the telecom networks.

The development of packet-witching also illustrates the development of a new technological paradigm (Dosi, 1982); the transition was accompanied by considerable controversy over whether improvements in the old paradigm would make a new paradigm (packet-switching, in this case) irrelevant. The old circuit system paradigm was so embedded in the researchers' minds that the revolutionary science of packet-switching was met with skepticism. As Vinton Cerf, one of the founders of the Internet, recalled: "The packet-switching network was so counterculture that a lot of people thought it was really stupid. The AT&T guys thought we were all beside ourselves; they didn't think that interactive computing was a move forward at all."

As tensions increased during the Cold War (*Sputnik* being one example), government funding increased considerably. In 1957, government funding of

R&D performed by industry eclipsed the funding provided by the firms themselves. By 1967, however, private funding had taken the lead again. By 1975, industry funding of industry-conducted R&D was twice the federal level, and the ratio was expanding. Government procurement was perhaps even more important to the technological development of certain industries, as it facilitated early investment in production facilities, thus easing the cost of commercialization. The newly emerging electronics industry in particular was able to benefit from the Defense Department's demand for advanced components and products. By 1960, the electronics industry had come to rely on the federal government for 70 percent of its R&D dollars. Perhaps as an unfortunate consequence, the United States ceased to be the leader in consumer electronics as it became preoccupied with the requirements of the U.S. military.

In addition to the realization that scientific talent was needed to work on industrial problems; it became obvious that the scientific problems on the horizon required insights from multiple fields, including the social sciences. The realization that (social) science research could have direct implications for industry, national security, and national welfare was explicitly stated by Warren Weaver (head of the applied mathematics panel of the National Defense Research Council during the war) at a 1947 conference in New York devoted to recruitment for the RAND Corporation. In particular, Weaver painted a picture of the academic landscape as inadequate to measure up to the challenges of the Cold War world:

> Every piece of knowledge we have in sociology and in economics and in political science, everything we know about social psychology, everything we know about propaganda.... Every piece of information of that sort, I say, is a weapon ... since the last war there has been a change in the character of war, a change in the character of the inevitable amalgamation of all the intellectual and material resources of the country which are necessary to maintain our position in peace and to enable us to defend ourselves.... There have also emerged some patterns of working together, particularly among the biological, physical and social sciences, which seem to me to have great promise ... the whole fields of the social sciences and of the physical sciences must be brought more closely together.
>
> (RAND memo D-182)

The Changing Nature of R&D

By the early 1970s, however, business managers were beginning to lose faith in the science-driven view of industrial research and technological innovation, primarily because few blockbuster products emerged (to benefit those who provided the funding) from the research supported during the 1950s, 1960s, and 1970s.[3] As a result of this and other factors, since the mid-70s there has been a marked change in organization and strategy, as both industry and government have come to recognize that the classical form of R&D organization—with centralized research and a science-driven culture—was simply not working well enough, in part because new technology was not getting into new products and processes soon enough, and imitation rates had increased. Foreign competitors, often leveraging technology developed in the United States, began undermining the traditional markets of many U.S. firms.

Many companies were confronted by the paradox of being leaders in R&D and the creation of intangibles but laggards in capturing value from their investments (Teece, 1986). The fruits of much R&D were being appropriated by domestic and foreign competitors; alternatively, too much technology was "trapped" in too many research laboratories.[4] In telecommunications, Bell Labs' contribution to the global economy far outstripped its contribution to AT&T. In the semiconductor industry, Fairchild's large research organization contributed more to the global economy through the spin-off companies it spawned than to its parent. Xerox Corporation's Palo Alto Research Center made stunning contributions to the global economy in the area of the personal computer, local area networks, and the graphical user interface that became the basis of Apple's Macintosh computer (and subsequently Microsoft's Windows operating system). Xerox shareholders benefited, but most of the benefits ended up in the hands of Xerox's competitors and of consumers.

Emergence of the "Distributed" Approach to Industrial R&D

The primary knowledge management problem confronting the U.S. economy by the 1980s and 1990s was not the generation of new knowledge, but its timely, successful, and profitable commercialization. Different modes of organization and different funding priorities were needed because the effectiveness of various mechanisms to capture value had changed, driven by developments in communications, the mobility of scientists and engineers, and shifting global capabilities. A distinctive competence was needed in the business enterprise to allow new knowledge to be diffused throughout the firm and to become embedded in new products that must in turn be introduced into the marketplace quickly and efficiently. New ways of conducting R&D and developing and commercializing new products were needed.

By the 1980s and 1990s, a new model for organizing R&D and new product development had emerged. First, R&D activity came to be decentralized inside large corporations, with the aim of bringing it closer to the users. Intel, the world leader in microprocessors, was spending over $1 billion per year on R&D, but did not have a separate R&D laboratory. Rather, development was conducted in the manufacturing facilities. It did not invest in fundamental research at all, except possibly through its funding of university research.[5] It did, however, participate actively in the development and sharing of new process knowledge through its funding of Sematech.

Second, many companies were looking to the universities for much of their basic or fundamental research, maintaining close associations with the science and engineering departments at the major research universities. Indeed, the percentage of academic research funded by industry grew from 2.7 percent in 1960 to 6.8 percent in 1995. However, strong links between university research and industrial research are limited primarily to electronics (especially semiconductors), chemical products, medicine, and agriculture. For the most part, university researchers are insufficiently versed in the particulars of specific product markets and customer needs to configure products to the needs of the market. Moreover, in many sectors the costs of research equipment are so high that universities simply cannot participate.

Third, corporations have embraced alliance arrangements involving R&D, manufacturing, and marketing in order to get products to market quicker and leverage off complementary assets already in place elsewhere. (It is important to note, however, that outsourcing R&D is a complement to, not a substitute for, in-house R&D.) Outsourcing and codevelopment arrangements had become common by the 1980s and 1990s (e.g., Pratt & Whitney's codevelopment programs for jet engines) as the costs of product development increased, and as the antitrust laws were modified to recognize the benefits of cooperation on R&D and related activities. The National Cooperative Research Act of 1984 and its amendment in 1993 provided greater clarity with respect to the likely positive antitrust treatment of cooperative efforts relating to technological innovation and its commercialization. Cooperation was also facilitated by the emergence of capable potential partners in Europe and Japan.

These developments meant that at the end of the twentieth century, research and development and the creation and exploitation of intangible assets were being conducted in a manner quite different from the early decades of the century. Many corporations had closed their central research laboratories or dramatically scaled back, including Westinghouse, RCA, AT&T, and Unocal, to name just a few. Alliances and cooperative efforts of all kinds were of much greater importance in both developing and commercializing new knowledge. The biotechnology industry in particular has been built around a plethora of important alliances. Henry Chesbrough has referred to this as the "open innovation" model (Chesbrough, 2003).

Relatedly, a transformation in industry structure brought about through venture capital–funded start-ups was well under way. New business enterprises (start-ups) were in part the cause of the decline of research laboratories, but in many ways the start-ups still depended on the organized R&D labs for their birthright. Beginning in the late 1970s, the organized venture capital industry, providing funding for new enterprise development, rose to significance. This was particularly true in industries such as biotech and information services. While venture capital in one form or another had been around for much of the twentieth century—the Rockefellers, Morgans, Mellons, Vanderbilts, Hilmans, and other significant families had been funding entrepreneurs for quite some time—institutional sources of money, including pension funds and university endowments, hitherto had not been significant sources of capital. This changed in the 1970s and 1980s as the funds that were available from institutional sources increased dramatically, along with the professionalism with which "the money" provided helpful guidance to a new breed of entrepreneurs eager to develop and market new products incorporating new technology.

However, the investment time frames of these funds were five to ten years at most. Institutional money, and hence venture capital money, was not interested in funding long-range research. Rather, this new source of capital was interested in supporting technology development and market launches of new products in a manner that would enable an exit for the financial investor as soon as possible.

As a result, venture-funded start-ups have proliferated in many sectors of the U.S. economy. Thus, while in the 1970s Apple Computer significantly "bootstrapped" (although it did take modest venture funding from Arthur Rock and others) itself into the personal computer industry, in the 1980s Compaq Computer and others received much larger infusions of venture capital to get started. In biotechnology, venture funding has also grown to great significance.

However, it is extremely unusual for venture funds to support the efforts of companies making investments in basic research. Rather, venture funding tends to be focused on commercializing intangibles. Venture capitalists are not interested in creating the enabling science. Successful start-ups frequently begin with a product or process concept (and often personnel) that has been "incubated" to some level in a research program of an established firm. Nevertheless, the phenomenon of venture funding is significant, as it is now a very important channel by which intangible assets are employed and new products and processes are brought to market. Practically all of the great names in Silicon Valley—from Apple to Intel, Affymetrix, Silicon Graphics, and many others—used venture funds to get started.

Conclusions

- At least compared with half a century earlier, privately funded research (both corporate and institutional venture capital) had by 2000 become more short-run in its focus and more commercial in its orientation. The era of the great corporate research labs—AT&T, Xerox, GE, and

Westinghouse—was over. International competition and the competition from spin-offs forced that outcome. Research laboratories at AT&T, GE, Exxon, Westinghouse, Xerox, and Unocal were either gone or shadows of their former selves.

- The leakage of technology was such that there was a greater than even chance that one's competitors would benefit as much, if not more, from any research funding. For example, half a century earlier, AT&T could rely on each of the Bell operating companies (BOCs) to pay (by contractual arrangement) a more or less pro rata share of the cost of Bell Labs; but the BOCs were divested in 1984. Their contracts to pay a fixed percent of revenues to support research and development were cancelled in the breakup of AT&T. There was no longer an easy appropriability mechanism in place. Many research laboratories simply had too much difficulty getting the fruits of research into new products fast enough.

- Industry and society are now left with a deep concern—the concern that insufficient resources are being invested in supporting the production of the scientific "seed corn." Perhaps the solution will lie in more collective funding of research. Perhaps industrially relevant basic and applied research in universities can be expanded. The issues are related more to the allocation of resources than to the amount. Clearly, as shown in table 12.1, in the United States the federal government has continued to provide considerable resources to support industrial R&D. But whereas it was more than half of the total in 1960, it was only about 16 percent by 1995. A reallocation of resources from government labs to private and university labs would be one possible avenue to improve productivity and augment prosperity.

- In the regime of "open" or distributed innovation that characterizes the global economy today, knowledge generation occurs in multiple geographic and organizational locations simultaneously. In order to prosper in this environment, business enterprises need to be extremely adept at identifying market and technological opportunities, and at orchestrating new combinations of specialized and cospecialized tangible and intangible assets in a timely manner. This orchestration must take place with respect to both technology development and commercialization. This orchestration capability is what we have called elsewhere a dynamic capability (Teece, Pisano, and Shuen, 1990, 1997; Teece and Pisano, 1997; Teece, 1998, 2006). In the broadest sense, knowledge management is a component— perhaps the core component—of dynamic capabilities, certainly in industries where intangible assets lie at the core of competitive advantage.

Table 12.1.   Industrial R&D Expenditures by Funding
Source: 1953–1998 (Millions of Current Dollars)

Calendar Year*	Total	Federal Govt.[a]	Industry[b]
1953	3,630	1,430	2,200
1954	4,070	1,750	2,320
1955	4,517	2,057	2,460
1956	6,272	2,995	3,277
1957	7,324	3,928	3,396
1958	8,066	4,436	3,630
1959	9,200	5,217	3,983
1960	10,032	5,604	4,428
1961	10,353	5,685	4,668
1962	11,037	6,008	5,029
1963	12,216	6,856	5,360
1964	13,049	7,257	5,792
1965	13,812	7,367	6,445
1966	15,193	7,977	7,216
1967	15,966	7,946	8,020
1968	17,014	8,145	8,869
1969	17,844	7,987	9,857
1970	17,594	7,306	10,288
1971	17,829	7,175	10,654
1972	19,004	7,469	11,535
1973	20,704	7,600	13,104
1974	22,239	7,572	14,667
1975	23,460	7,878	15,582
1976	26,107	8,671	17,436
1977	28,863	9,523	19,340
1978	32,222	10,107	22,115
1979	37,062	11,354	25,708
1980	43,228	12,752	30,476
1981	50,425	14,997	35,428
1982	57,166	17,061	40,105
1983	63,683	19,095	44,588
1984	73,061	21,657	51,404
1985	82,376	25,333	57,043
1986	85,932	26,000	59,932
1987	90,160	28,757	61,403
1988	94,893	28,221	66,672
1989	99,860	26,359	73,501
1990	107,404	25,802	81,602
1991	114,675	24,095	90,580
1992	116,757	22,369	94,388
1993	115,435	20,844	94,591
1994	117,392	20,261	97,131
1995	129,830	21,178	108,652

(continued)

Table 12.1. *(continued)*

Calendar Year*	Total	Federal Govt.[a]	Industry[b]
1996	142,371	21,356	121,015
1997	155,409	21,798	133,611
1998 prelim.	168,922	22,216	146,706

Data are based on annual reports by performers except for the nonprofit sector; R&D expenditures by nonprofit sector performers have been estimated since 1973 on the basis of a survey conducted in that year.

[a]For 1953–1954, expenditures of industry Federally Funded Research and Development Centers (FFRDC) were not separated out from total Federal support to the industrial sector. Thus, the figure for Federal support to industry includes support to FFRDCs for those two years. The same is true for expenditures of nonprofit FFRDCs, which are included in Federal support for nonprofit institutions in 1953–1954.

[b]Industry sources of industry R&D expenditures include all non-Federal sources of industry R&D expenditures.

*These calendar-year expenditure levels are approximations based on fiscal year data.

Source: National Science Foundation, Division of Science Resources Studies (NSF/SRS), National Patterns of R&D Resources (Arlington, Va.: biennial series).

Acknowledgments

We are grateful for the comments of Kazuo Ichijo and Herb Addison, and for conversations with Sid Winter and Giovanni Dosi on the issues discussed in this chapter.

Notes

1. Frank Knight is an often overlooked advocate for the fact that technological change makes economic predictions difficult. As he stated: "The most fundamentally and irretrievably uncertain phases or factors of progress are those which amount essentially to the increase of knowledge as such. This description evidently holds for the improvement of technological processes and the forms of business organization and for the discovery of new natural resources. Here it is a contradiction in terms to speak of anticipation, in an accurate and detailed sense, for to anticipate the advance would be to make it at once" (Knight, 1921, p. 318).

2. Most basic research is of course funded by governments and universities.

3. There were many great commercial successes for which the identities of those who supported the research were different from those who garnered marketplace advantage (Teece, 1986).

4. While this technology frequently diffused worldwide in professional societies, it failed to get into the financial supporters' products and processes.

5. The company set up laboratories close to university campuses, such as the Intel laboratory in downtown Berkeley.

References

Chandler, A. D. (1990). *Scale and Scope: The Dynamics of Industrial Capitalism.* Cambridge, Mass: Belknap Press of Harvard University Press.

Chesbrough, H., and Rosenbloom, R. S. (2002): "The Role of the Business Model in Capturing Value from Innovation: Evidence from Xerox Corporation's Technology." *Industrial and Corporate Change* 11(3): 529–555.

Dosi, G. (1982). "Technological Paradigms and Technological Trajectories: A Suggested Interpretation of the Determinants and Directions of Technical Change." *Research Policy* 11: 147–162.

Dosi, G., Marseli, O., Orsenigo, L., and Salvatore, R. (1995). "Learning, Market Selection and the Evolution of Industrial Structures." *Small Business Economics* 7(6): 411–436.

Dosi, G., Orsenigo, L., and Sylos Labini, M. (2002). "Technology and the Economy." Working paper, University of Pisa.

Drucker, P. (1993) *Post-Capitalist Society.* New York: HarperCollins

Gehani, N. (2003). *Bell Labs: Life in the Crown Jewel.* Summit, N.J.: Silicon Press.

Hounshell, D. A. (1996). "The Evolution of Industrial Research in the United States." In R. S. Rosenbloom and W. J. Spencer, eds., *Engines of Innovation: U.S. Industrial Research at the End of an Era.* Boston: Harvard Business School Press.

Mansfield, E. (1968). *The Economics of Technological Change.* New York: Norton.

Moore, G. E. (1996). "Some Personal Reflections on Research in the Semiconductor Industry." In R. S. Rosenbloom and W. J. Spencer, eds., *Engines of Innovation: U.S. Industrial Research at the End of an Era.* Boston: Harvard Business School Press.

Mowery, D. C. (1981). "The Emergence of Growth of Industrial Research in American Manufacturing, 1899–1945." Ph.D. diss., Stanford University.

Mowery, D. C. (1989). "Collaborative Research and High-temperature Superconductivity." In A. Link and G. Tassey, eds., *Cooperative Research and Development: The Industry-University-Government Relationship.* Boston: Kluwer Academic.

Schumpeter, J. (1942). *Capitalism, Socialism, and Democracy.* New York: Harper and Brothers.

Teece, D. J. (1981). "The Market for Know-how and the Efficient International Transfer of Technology." *The Annals of the Academy of Political and Social Science,* November: 81–96.

Teece, D. J. (1986). "Profiting from Technological Innovation." *Research Policy* 15(6): 285–305.

Teece, D. J. (1990). "Contributions and Impediments of Economic Analysis to the Study of Strategic Management." In J. Frederickson, ed., *Perspectives on Strategic Management.* Grand Rapids, Mich.: Harper Business.

Teece, D. J. (1993). "The Dynamics of Industrial Capitalism: Perspectives on Alfred Chandler's *Scale and Scope* (1990)." *Journal of Economic Literature* 31: 199–225.

Teece, D. J. (1998). "Capturing Value from Knowledge Assets: The New Economy, Market for Know How, and Intangible Assets." *California Management Review* 40(3): 55–79.

Teece, D. J. (2006). "Explicating Dynamic Capabilities." Unpublished working paper.

Teece, D. J., Pisano, G., and Shuen, A. (1997). "Dynamic Capabilities and Strategic Management." *Strategic Management Journal* 18(7): 537–533.

Weaver, W. (1947). "Opening Remarks at the RAND Social Science Conference." RAND memo D-182, Unpublished.

PART III

THE LEADERSHIP CHALLENGE
OF KNOWLEDGE-CREATING COMPANIES

13

Globalizing Local Knowledge
in Global Companies

XAVIER GILBERT

A compelling justification for globalization is that it yields substantial competitive advantages without which companies could no longer survive, such as access to new markets, opening the door to volume-related cost advantages, first-entrant advantages, or market power, to name a few. A business presence in multiple geographical locations also gives a significant advantage that is not always fully exploited: an abundance of insights into fast-evolving global competitive advantages—provided the global firm can leverage the locally developed knowledge.

Companies globalize local knowledge when they leverage their locally developed knowledge, that is, collect and disseminate for use throughout their organizations knowledge developed in their local offices, branches, factories, marketing units, and other activities, no matter where they may be.

Instead, many companies shoehorn their home strategy into new local contexts, expecting the latter to adapt and eventually see the truth. They reinvent the wheel time and again, without ever learning to leverage local feedback. In brief, they ignore the fact that strategic thinking is a learning process which, like any learning process, is significantly enriched by the variety of the contexts within which it takes place.

Local Knowledge Matters

A company pursuing international expansion will generally proceed by deploying its centrally accumulated knowledge and experience in every new location. But even the smartest global strategies are not mere "plug and play" wherever they are applied. A robust strategy is one that has been tested in many different contexts and is continuously enriched with the feedback from these varied contexts. This feedback allows companies to improve their strategy for local execution, and provides local insights that broaden a firm's scope or lead to new strategic developments.

Local insights about local resources—people's capabilities, technological know-how, infrastructure, local opportunities of all kinds—obviously can have a global impact. Local insights about market changes, customer expectations, and competitive offers will also provide numerous data points that should eventually feed into the global strategic road map. They provide a better understanding of what may make the global strategy stumble and, eventually, what will help it work effectively as a firm moves into new markets. They can accelerate international expansion.

It is also important to note that local insights matter equally for purely domestic companies: their local competition is in fact, more often than not, global. The European shirtmakers and "plumbers," among many others, faced with Asian competition, have become painfully aware of this development. They should not see protectionism as a viable alternative to global learning. Most of the obstacles to learning that I will describe in this chapter also exist in these companies that wrongly see themselves as domestic. And the corresponding approaches that I will propose to tap local knowledge are also available to them.

The challenge is not only to legitimate this local knowledge; it is also to redeploy it in such a way that it is put to use globally. Many companies try to centrally document the local knowledge found in their outposts, with the best intentions in the world, but this does not seen to be sufficient to redeploy it globally. I submit that this is because learning processes are poorly understood and, as a result, poorly supported by the organization processes and leadership style in most organizations.

After proposing a model of learning, I will discuss organization mechanisms, specifically organization processes, and the leadership style and organization culture, that help deploy local learning across a global organization.

Constructing Knowledge

It is important to understand how learning takes place in order to come to terms with the potential obstacles to globalizing local knowledge in global organizations. The model of learning I propose describes how individuals cope with a complex, changing context. Business situations are a case in point, never repeating themselves exactly; generalizations are, at best, tentative; and continuous learning from feedback seems to be the only way to proceed, building on and broadening prior experience. In a global context, the learning challenge is bigger. Prior knowledge and experience are even more tentative, making further learning more critical.

Constructivism is a "theory of knowing" (Von Glasersfeld, 1995), a theory of how individuals construct their own knowledge in order to remain fit and effective in their context. Modern constructivism was pioneered by Jean Piaget[1] and has been promoted by several prominent epistemologists, such as Ernst von Glasersfeld and Jerome Brunner, among many others.

The central proposition of constructivism is that knowledge is constructed by the learner in order to maintain an equilibrium with his or her context, rather than passively absorbed from preexisting bodies of knowledge. Business situations are again a case in point; the preexisting bodies of knowledge on international expansion, for example, while providing ideas, have no meaning for the manager who has not yet experienced the feedback of applying them in a variety of contexts. And the experienced manager is aware of how tentative this knowledge remains when moving into new ventures.

Maintaining equilibrium with the context starts with an attempt to apply prior knowledge and experience. Piaget observed that the experiential information received from a new context was first *assimilated*—meaning selectively absorbed, as food is absorbed by the body—by previously built schemes that have been deemed effective by the learner (see, for example Piaget, 1967).

Herbert Simon observed that managers "satisficed" themselves with this "bounded rationality" when addressing complex problems (Simon, 1997). Managers compare a new situation against a previously experienced one, but mostly tend to recognize in it what they have seen before, and not what has no reference to their prior knowledge and experience. They relatively easily see the new situation as similar enough to previously experienced ones, and apply their previously successful schemes to it. Assimilation is a simplifying mechanism that allows managers to provide a response to an apparently familiar situation.

This transfer of knowledge, however, is unlikely to deliver the expected results, which triggers a suspicion that something may have been missed. There is a gap that needs to be filled by looking further for unseen information, with a broader "relevance bandwidth."

This is the next step in regaining an equilibrium with one's context. Piaget describes it as mental *accommodation*, similar to the eye's accommodation to focus on a different distance. In the managers' minds, the now unsuccessful schemes try to accommodate to the initially disregarded elements in the context that may have caused the unsatisfactory outcome. It is the process of accommodation of previously built schemes to hitherto unseen information, in response to an unsatisfactory outcome, that generates new knowledge. Indeed, many managers agree that their failures have been their greatest sources of learning. Accommodation yields inferences that allow the construction of more encompassing mental schemes.[2] Managers endeavor to synthesize and give meaning to prior knowledge and to the new information at the same time, and as a result, the newly synthesized knowledge can have more general applicability and can handle more complex situations.

There are several challenges in evolving from assimilation to accommodation to get in balance with one's context. Admitting a failure is one; failures can be dismissed due to personal pride, or present a risk to be avoided. Another challenge for many individuals is to broaden their relevance bandwidth in order to see what they have not yet seen; many people are quite content with a comfortable, limited scope. Constructing more encompassing overview schemes is also an obstacle; provincialism is, most of the time, preferred to the effort of conceiving new knowledge. Thus, if the emotional stakes of maintaining equilibrium with the context are not perceived as being high enough to overcome these obstacles, there will be no learning. Managers tend not to learn much from situations that they perceive as being of no consequence. But the emotional commitment to learning is not just an ignition mechanism; it is needed at all times and must be maintained through the frustrations of evolving from assimilation to accommodation.

The human brain resorts to three main approaches to evolve from assimilation to accommodation.

Mental rehearsal is reasoning through the inferences that add up to a logical overview scheme. It requires challenging one's own perceptions, entertaining new hypotheses on dimensions of the problem that were perhaps missed, and trying out plausible syntheses. "Insofar as their results can be applied and lead to viable outcomes in practice, thought experiments [mental rehearsals] constitute what is perhaps the most powerful learning procedure in the cognitive domain" (Von Glasersfeld, 1995). But everyone has experienced how painful it can sometime be. This is the reason for satisficing oneself with modest accommodation. Intellectual laziness hides behind intense activity.

Intellectual confrontation occurs when individuals actively or passively exchange information, look for overlaps across each other's schemes (assimilation), and enrich their own schemes with insights from each other (accommodation). There are two sides to intellectual confrontation. Most managers have little difficulty with the first one: trying to convince colleagues of the validity of their own views. This interaction serves as further mental rehearsal; explaining one's (tentative) understanding helps to test its coherence: "I guess what I mean is..." It is the feedback from colleagues that managers often have more difficulty with, as suggested by Argyris (1977), who recommends combining "the skills of advocacy with those of encouraging inquiry and confrontation of whatever is being advocated" as the way to foster new, more robust schemes. Inquiry, soliciting feedback, possibly being confronted with disagreement, and even being proven wrong are naturally perceived as unnecessarily threatening. The unwillingness to get this feedback and to broaden one's scheme accordingly will hide behind forceful advocacy.

Experimenting, to gain more feedback from the context, further broadens the accommodation range and generates more encompassing learning. Without experimenting, there is no learning. In fact, any action should be seen as experimental. Action with the certainty of being right removes any opportunity for correction and improvement, and will prevent any learning. The fear of failure, and its intellectual and personal risks, can also lead to the dismissal of feedback and to paying only lip service to accommodation, attributing failure to outside factors rather than to one's own incomplete schemes. Solid mental rehearsal could help, but "shooting from the hip" prevails, hidden behind routinely blaming others.

The boundaries between mental rehearsal, intellectual confrontation, and experimenting certainly overlap; these approaches support each other to construct knowledge. Some individuals more naturally accommodate through mental rehearsal, while others more naturally do so by discussing, and others by experimenting. But assimilation and accommodation themselves should not be misunderstood as "opposing ways of dealing with the world," subject to individual preferences, as Kolb (1984, pg. 29) proposes. Preferences may apply to the means, but not to the end, which is evolving from assimilation to accommodation, if knowledge is to be constructed.

The constructivist perspective, according to which the purpose of learning is to regain an equilibrium with one's context, when applied to a business context, provides an effective model for strategic thinking. Two observations will underline this point. The first is that this equilibrium-seeking is meant to be dynamic, in the sense that it is meant to shape one's context and master it, beyond merely responding to it. Peter Senge refers to this purpose as the pursuit of "personal mastery," which he sees as one of the five disciplines of organization learning, and as "generative learning," the level of learning that is not only meant to adapt but also, and more critically, to shape the future (Senge, 1990a, 1990b). Such is also the purpose of strategic thinking.

The second observation is that, as we have seen, the context is to a very large extent constituted of others who are also learning. In business organizations, this has a very substantial impact. "Organizational learning is not merely individual learning, yet organizations learn only through the experience and actions of individuals," Argyris and Schön (1978) suggest. Learning accrues when individuals exchange feedback and accommodate to each other's action schemes, constructing and converging toward an overview that is a strategic road map. Across the organization, all who are involved share this learning opportunity, making strategic thinking an interactive learning process. The challenge of global organization learning is to ensure that this interaction is broad enough across the organization for local learning not to stop there, but to trigger further interactive learning across the organization, converging toward global strategic road maps.

Globalizing Local Learning

I propose to tackle the challenge of globalizing local learning by providing organizational support to mental rehearsal, intellectual confrontation, and experimenting. This support will rely on selected organizational processes and, quite importantly, on the leadership style and organization culture of the global company. The first condition, however, is to communicate an emotional commitment to addressing these challenges.

International Expansion Must Matter

Global learning requires a corporate commitment to international growth. This commitment is to be communicated at the rational and emotional levels in order to raise the stakes for managers across the company. People will eventually do what is in their best interest, and if there is no clear organizational commitment to international expansion, there will be no need to learn how to play a role in it. Clear signals that international expansion matters can be provided by some of the organization processes and by the leadership style at different levels.

Organization Processes   International expansion must first be clearly prioritized in the *strategy process*. The rationale for it must be explicit—specifically, what competitive advantages are expected from international growth must be clearly identified: cost advantage, market share and volume, positioning. Specific operating objectives and time frames are also important in reinforcing the importance of international expansion. Indeed, many companies go international without a clear set of strategic objectives, making it difficult for management in different countries, and centrally, to focus on the variables that matter and to learn how to manage them more effectively.

Decision processes, specifically managing the tension between global integration and local responsiveness (Bartlett and Ghoshal, 2002), may often be perceived as a power struggle rather than as managing a learning agenda. When this is the case, the willingness to learn is likely to switch off. Global integration needs continuous feedback from local responsiveness; in other words, local learning is essential for global integration to be sustainably effective. Signaling that the ability to manage this tension is expected as a key managerial competence in a global firm will help maintain a stronger commitment to interactive learning.

Human-resources processes also play an important part in emphasizing the importance of international expansion. Companies that emphasize international career paths as a must for employees to progress also signal the importance of local learning as an input to building global strategic road maps. The best evidence that an international career is not a sidetrack appears when the members of the top management team have all had international experience.

Leadership Style and Organization Culture

Top management's personal commitment to, and involvement in, international expansion is of course essential. Many companies, particularly those with a strong product orientation, tend to "delegate" international matters to their international sales organization, thus indirectly signaling that this is not what really matters. In these companies, local learning is likely to be perceived and treated as parochial and of little consequence for central decision-making. Top management's commitment to international expansion is made visible by its frequent physical presence in local outposts, and its interest in, and knowledge of, the local challenges and of the people facing them.

The presence of different nationalities in the top team also helps to make this commitment to interactive learning more compelling. By contrast, in a company that, because of its very fast international expansion, required a high retention rate of its internationally trained managers, some complained: "Working for this company has been great learning, but it's time to go—we have the wrong nationality to move further up."

Mental Rehearsal Focuses on Building Overview Capabilities Across Local Knowledge

Openness to local feedback is essential to build more encompassing global strategic road maps by comparing the similarities and differences of various local situations, and by inferring which variables matter. These more globally robust strategic road maps will, in turn, help managers to deal more effectively with future local challenges. For example, they will help prioritize the issues to be dealt with, see when information may be missing, and interpret what does not seem to fit. In this process, global knowledge is progressively inferred from local knowledge—a process described by Robert Galvin, the CEO who made Motorola a global company, as expanding by "global inference."

In a global company, the relevance bandwidths are narrow "by construction" and, in theory, the organization should provide many opportunities to have conventional wisdom challenged. Practically, however, there are effective ways to dismiss this feedback: by blaming the locals if one is in the center, or blaming the center if one is in a foreign country. In many companies, local knowledge, particularly on less developed areas, is seen as being of very limited relevance. And similarly, local companies often believe that nothing useful ever comes from the center. Dismissing local feedback may also be the result of fearing the consequences of being proven wrong. The center can always enforce its authority, but this produces no learning for the future. The local learning opportunities remain underexploited.

In an international setting, it is also more difficult to infer global patterns. It is easier to see the world as a disjointed patchwork of complexities, or in a binary way, with areas where there is usable knowledge and areas where there is none. Accommodation remains superficial, and managers will jump to conclusions on the basis of a few local observations, without trying to refer to a wider-scale scheme.

Yet, organization processes, as well as the leadership style and organization culture, can effectively support mental rehearsal focused on building over-views from local feedback.

Organization Processes

Human-resources processes are important in building overview capabilities. Career management, for example, can help managers develop those cap-abilities. In some companies, the "expat" flow goes only one way, taking experts from the center to tell the locals how to do it. This is great learning for these experts, who have a chance to enrich the central perspective with more local feedback. This learning is not always appreciated, however, and some expats are criticized for having "gone native." But the expat flow should really be multidirectional, to support a global learning process. An effective way not only to develop local managers, but also to make their knowledge more globally applicable, is to expose them to different local contexts, not just to send them to the center for training. Bertrand Collomb, when he was CEO of La-farge, a global construction materials company, once said, "At Lafarge, we are not concerned about expats—anyone can be one."

Career management will also help by designing assignment paths through contrasting situations across countries and cultures. Siemens, for example, expects experience in three different countries—as well as in three different products and three different functions—from its high-potential managers. Faster career progression will signal the importance that the company gives to these global overview and think-out capabilities.

The design of the strategic planning process will also help local managers build a broader view of the trade-offs the company is confronted with globally. Top-down strategic planning, with a finished strategy delivered by a central strategic planning department, will do little to help local managers build their local overview capabilities. By contrast, the strategic process of Nokia involves a large number of local managers across the company, through task forces that make proposals on a number of global strategic issues. These proposals are presented and discussed in plenary global meetings where local managers can see the trade-offs being addressed when top management finalizes its choices.

Organization processes designed to support *horizontal coordination* across local units, without necessarily resorting to higher-level referees, can go a long way in helping local managers address the trade-offs at a higher level than their own unit, and think through their implications in different local settings. These processes can apply to sharing resources, serving common customers, or building competence centers, for example.

Leadership Style and Organization Culture

Senior managers can challenge the relevance bandwidth across the organization by pointing out the experience and know-how they have observed in different locations, for example, and suggesting that local managers find out how similar issues are dealt with by their colleagues. Fighting the "not invented here" syndrome—helping people see what works in another location, even though it contradicts their current mental patterns—will help them revisit what they took for granted at home and will help broaden the relevance bandwidth.

Senior management can then play a critical role in coaching local managers to develop overview capabilities. This is done by adopting a style of open questioning, leading the "coachees" through the reasoning of building more encompassing overviews. Asking them to explain their strategic road maps, challenging them with information from different local settings, and pointing to alternative road maps from other local units will provide the kind of mental rehearsal from which both the local "coachee" and the global coach can benefit.

An organization culture that values providing reasons for the decisions made and for the trade-off choices will effectively support the conceptualization of broader global overviews by local managers. The openness in discussing these reasons, agreeing that they may not provide the only perspective, and emphasizing that they may be completed when new compelling local data are presented, after thinking through their meaning and implications, will signal that global overview road maps are serious works-in-process to which all local managers are expected to contribute.

Intellectual Confrontation Leverages the Interaction across Geographical Boundaries

Orchestrating an intellectual debate across units will help globalize local knowledge, with the other parts of the organization benefiting more intensely through a "snowballing" learning process. In this global intellectual confrontation, local managers not only are expected to advocate views but also, and more importantly, to invite feedback from other local managers and from managers with central integrative responsibilities.

This global debate, to build on global knowledge, needs to be varied and multidirectional; it distributes learning and yields further learning opportunities for all those involved in the interaction. There are risks, however, that I will address in this section. One is that advocacy may prevail over inquiry, and another is dispersion and loss of focus.

Organization Processes

The *strategic planning process*, at the same time it contributes to the development of overview capabilities of local managers, provides a forum for intensive debate converging toward a set of strategic priorities. This interaction allows managers from across the company to compare notes, identify where their respective schemes overlap and differ, accommodate to information that they had missed in their own templates, and eventually build more encompassing schemes from a new range of local inputs. Senior management must manage this discussion process to help it converge toward a few, commonly understood, strategic priorities that frame the learning agenda and avoid dispersion. GE's numerous widely attended management meetings, held throughout its strategy cycle, exemplify how this debate can be guided.

Information-sharing processes also contribute to the learning debate among local managers. Global functional workshops, for example, are normal practice in many companies, allowing functional managers to share feedback on their respective approaches. International project teams are increasingly used, not only to resolve specific issues but also as a powerful device to share feedback on possible approaches. Benchmarking processes, internal or external, provide similar benefits. In these information-sharing processes, beyond the exchange of information, the collective learning accrues from advocating approaches, and seeking feedback from the local units that have adopted (possibly adapted), in different contexts, the approaches of others.

Human-resources processes also contribute importantly to an open debate by ensuring that a diversity of national origins and cultures is recruited. This diversity of perspectives ensures the diversity of feedback and a richer intellectual confrontation.

Leadership Style and Organization Culture

Leadership plays an important role in clarifying the learning agenda that ensures a relevant and focused intellectual confrontation. Senior managers in companies that emphasize global interactive learning miss no opportunity to communicate a few global strategic priorities time and again, and to discuss their local implications.

Senior management should also promote an open management style that encourages questioning each other and volunteering information on each other's competitive challenges. In many organizations, local managers will refrain from these activities because they are not part of the culture. The management style can then be described as "hub and spoke," with the senior manager dealing one-on-one with each direct report while the others are silently watching, thinking that the time spent on one colleague will not be spent on them. On the contrary, a fruitful confrontation of ideas characterizes the true global management teams, with every member collectively responsible for, and debating, the global business while still individually accountable for their own decisions.

More generally, the companies that foster the confrontation of ideas have developed a culture of surfacing local challenges and soliciting feedback and advice. As a result, and in spite of the geographical dispersion, problems are surfaced faster and dealt with more effectively. In complex global situations, no one could be expected to have all the answers while several brains can effectively debate a more robust global perspective.

Experimenting Locally and Debriefing Globally to Build More Robust Global Road Maps

Experimenting locally is essential to get feedback on a broader range of variables. As already discussed, this local feedback can have global meaning that enriches the global strategic road map. Orchestrating global experimenting goes one step further; several local experiments are run in parallel, in well selected contexts and with specific control variables, to get more learning insights on a specific strategic priority. The after-action review will identify which variables seem to matter, and when and where they matter, in making these choices, and will allow companies to build more robust global road maps as they move into more local contexts. Lafarge, seeing knowledge as one of its most critical competitive weapons, has used this learning approach to develop and deploy optimal integration strategies across many different local markets.

There is, of course, resistance to local experimenting. The center often prefers to avoid local initiatives, seeing too many business risks in them; locally, perceived personal risks may discourage such initiatives. Experimenting and after-action review need to be supported by specific organization processes and by the leadership style and organization culture.

Organization Processes

Processes for experimenting and for after-action review are generally lacking, and especially when a firm is operating in many geographical locations.

A top-down, centrally imposed methodology is necessary, but is also likely to be easily circumvented. On the other hand, funding of coordinated, multiple local experiments, run by steering committees representing different perspectives, may receive better acceptance. Project transparency and visibility, senior management sponsorship, airtime and stage-light in global meetings, and the positive impact on one's career will help to get local support for a corporate, disciplined experimenting methodology.

The composition of the experiment teams should make the experiment itself, as well as the debriefing, richer; for example, with team members who can ask the "stupid" questions or who can provide insights on unusual dimensions. By including in the team people from different local contexts, this diversity will be enhanced, emotional and local pride issues can be contained, and the roll-out of the findings to further local contexts will be facilitated. This is an approach that Holcim, a global cement and concrete manufacturer, has used to develop and rapidly deploy customer relationship management systems in its Asian markets.

Performance management processes also must support experimenting. More often than not, the standard set of key performance indicators will achieve the exact opposite. The CEO of Nokia, Jorma Ollila, was known to emphasize the need for "well thought-out mistakes" if any learning was to take place. Local managers must be expected to explore territories off the beaten paths in addition to delivering the expected performance.

Leadership Style and Organization Culture

The leadership style must encourage well-thought-out experimenting as an alternative to lengthy discussions of hypothetical schemes. Even a seemingly costly experiment will often be less expensive than ignorance or no action at all; a well-managed experiment can be an attractive, just-in-time, learning option, compared with theoretical, just-in-case, management training.

A climate of transparency is essential to make experimenting an effective learning device. Experimenting cannot be an excuse for manifestations of local pride and independence. The value of local experimenting lies in the ability to compare a range of local results; coordination and synchronization of efforts must be part of the culture. A culture where local managers are well acquainted with working on global projects will help.

A leadership style of open questioning, as opposed to "giving the right answer," will motivate local managers to stretch beyond their comfort zones and lead them to generate new knowledge. Frequent follow-up of these experiments during plenary meetings will keep them within the scope of the global learning agenda and yield further learning in other local units. The supportive-challenging closeness of top management fosters this experimenting climate.

Conclusions

- Globalizing local learning ("outside-in" learning) is not an easy path. It is easier to push out centrally developed knowledge, in an "inside-out" process, and many companies do so with relative success. Their control-heavy organization processes and top-down management styles avoid noncompliance and lack of dispersion, but ignore local learning. Contrary to common belief, outside-in learning offers a more effective path to global convergence.
- The ingredients for successful globalization of local knowledge are not central knowledge-management tools. They are people-based, and rely on outside-in learning among geographically dispersed teams: a strong strategic commitment to international expansion, mental rehearsal focused on global overview perspectives, intellectual confrontation across geographic areas, and globally orchestrated experimenting and debriefing.
- These ingredients are not easy to build up. They require organization processes focused on supporting knowledge construction. But, above all, they require strong learning leadership that is keen to help local managers and heads of central units interactively construct the knowledge that will help them progress successfully in the global corporate context. Steering this outside-in global learning process is the most critical task of the global leader.

Notes

1. Because of Piaget's work on the development of cognitive processes in children, he is often mistakenly thought of as being relevant only for understanding children's learning. His real aim was in fact to arrive at a generalizable model of cognition.

2. "More encompassing schemes" are what Peter Senge refers to as "system thinking" (Senge, 1990a).

References

Argyris, C. (1977). "Double-loop Learning in Organizations." *Harvard Business Review*, September-October: 115–124. The concepts of single-loop and double-loop learning are frequently referred to, but not always understood.

Argyris, C., and Schön, D. A. (1978). *Organizational Learning: A Theory of Action Perspective*, vol. 1. Reading, Mass.: Addison-Wesley.

Bartlett, C. A., and Ghoshal, S. (2000). "Going Global: Lessons from Late Movers." *Harvard Business Review*, March–April: 132–142. A compelling case for outside-in learning.

Bartlett, C. A., and Ghoshal, S. (2002). *Managing Across Borders: The Transnational Solution*, 2nd ed. Boston: Harvard Business School Press. A foundation book on the challenges of the global corporation, introducing the concepts of local responsiveness, global integration, and coordination.

Brunner, J. (1960). *The Process of Education.* Cambridge, Mass.: Harvard University Press. A short but powerful book on learning.

Garvin, D. A. (1993). "Building a Learning Organization." *Harvard Business Review,* July–August: 78–91.

Glasersfeld, E. von. (1995). *Radical Constructivism: A Way of Knowing and Learning.* Washington, D.C.: Falmer Press. A short and clear presentation of the foundations of constructivism, particularly on Piaget's thinking.

Kolb, D. A. (1984). *Experiential Learning: Experience as the Source of Learning and Development.* Englewood Cliffs, N.J.: Prentice-Hall. The theoretical foundations of Kolb's framework, often referred to in the context of management development, have been questioned and challenged, specifically his references to Lewin, Dewey, and Piaget.

Piaget, J. (1967). *La Construction du Réel chez l'Enfant.* Neuchâtel, Switzerland: Delachaux et Niestlé. Piaget was a prolific author, but a difficult one to read. In addition, the translations of his work in English often misinterpreted his thinking.

Senge, P. M. (1990a). *The Fifth Discipline: The Art & Practice of the Learning Organization.* New York: Doubleday/Currency. A well-known book on organization learning; Senge's fifth discipline, found in effective learning organizations, is systems thinking. This is what we meant by "overview schemes/road maps."

Senge, P. M. (1990b). "The Leader's New Work: Building Learning Organizations." *Sloan Management Review* 32 (1): 7–22.

Simon, H. A. (1997). *Administrative Behavior: A Study of Decision-Making Processes in Administrative Organizations,* 4th ed. New York: Free Press.

14

Governance Information in
Knowledge-Based Companies

JAY W. LORSCH

The Scope of the Problem

The issue of the information needed by boards of directors to govern companies that are knowledge-intensive businesses is doubly complex. As in any company, there are problems with keeping the governing body (normally the board of directors) informed. This is always a significant challenge, but in knowledge-intensive companies there is the added fact that the information which directors need in order to govern may be especially difficult for them to obtain and understand. Although these two difficulties are interrelated, I shall describe them separately and then suggest remedies that address their combined effect.

The Information Problems
of Boards of Directors

To be effective in overseeing their company and to make the major decisions that are their responsibilities, directors obviously need to have an adequate understanding of their company—its performance, its relationships to customers and competitors, how its employees are contributing to its performance, and, of course, the company's financial results. In a world in which there is an increasing emphasis on boards consisting of as many independent directors as feasible, achieving such an understanding of the company among the independent directors is often very difficult. I say "as many independent directors as feasible" because the proportion of independent directors that is required and/ or the norm varies from country to country. For example, in the United States, while the requirement (imposed by the Sarbanes-Oxley Act and the Stock Exchange Listing Requirements) is for only a majority of independent directors, the boards of most public companies now are made up entirely of independent directors, except for the CEO and possibly one other member of management. In the United Kingdom, the number of independent directors on any board of an FTSE company is typically less than half the total. In other countries, while there is a growing emphasis on adding independent directors, the proportion of the total number of such directors varies from country to country.

Definitions of what is meant by "independent" vary from jurisdiction to jurisdiction, but at its heart the concept of independence means that these directors have no relationship to the company other than their board seat, and that they have no conflicts of interest between their duty as a director and their other activities. As a practical matter, this definition of independence means that before joining the board, independent directors are quite unlikely to have worked in the industry or profession in which their company operates. Therefore, they join a board without much knowledge about the company or its business. They have to learn as they serve, which is not easy; and gaining a real understanding can take a couple of years, since boards generally meet five to six times a year for a day at a time. Besides starting with this serious knowledge gap, independent directors have a related handicap (which they share with those who are not independent, and may therefore have industry knowledge). The amount of time they can devote to serving on the board of a given company is limited. Not only is limited time spent in meetings, but these directors are usually successful and busy executives and professionals who have limited time to devote to each board both at meetings and between them.

While there is no uniform requirement for the frequency of board meetings or their length, in most countries, boards seem to meet five to six times a year for perhaps a day at a time. Another way to understand the limits of the time that directors can and do devote to each board is to consider the number of hours directors spend annually on each board. According to recent surveys, this varies from country to country but is in the range of 100 to 150 hours per year. Included in these hourly data is not only the time spent in board and committee meetings, but also the time directors spend reviewing information prior to board meetings. Either way one thinks about the matter, directors can and do devote a relatively small amount of time to understanding each company, compared with what they need to know. And let me be clear: companies (large and small) are complex, dynamic creatures. Considering the amount of time the typical director can devote, it is difficult to understand his or her company sufficiently to perform the tasks required. The less prior knowledge directors have about the business, the more problematic this understanding becomes. Further, the interval of weeks and months between meetings complicates their problem. Being busy executives and professionals, members focus on many other matters between the meetings of a particular board.

Therefore, it is not surprising that they lose track of issues between meetings. That they do so is supported by data collected in a survey of over 100 CEOs of companies on all continents (figure 14.1). Over half these CEOs either disagreed that, or were unsure whether, the independent members of their company's board understood the factors that drove the performance of the company's main business. Similarly, an almost equal proportion responded that independent directors did not recall previous discussions (figure 14.2). These problems are, of course, complicated by the fact that companies do not stand still.

All of these circumstances mean that it is difficult for directors to stay informed about their company. In fact, this difficulty is arguably one of the major reasons that boards can and do fail in their duties. While lack of information is most obviously a problem in instances of fraud or sabotage by management, the lack of time and prior knowledge is a persistent difficulty under less extreme circumstances. However, there is another problem for directors: not lack of information but too much information—information overload. Management, which is the primary source of information for the board, in an honest effort to keep the directors informed, too often provides them with a level of detail and complexity the directors cannot digest or comprehend in the time they have available.

Whether it is too little or too much information, the end result is the same. The directors do not know what is going on! And things are even worse, as we shall see, in knowledge-intensive companies.

All CEO responses
(%)

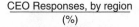

CEO Responses, by region
(%)

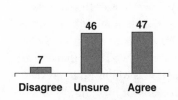

Region	Disagree	Unsure	Agree
North America	4	50	46
Europe	9	42	49
Asia Pacific	7	47	46
Total	7	46	47

Note: The CEOs responded to a 5-point scale where 1 = Strongly Disagree and 5 = Strongly Agree. We have classified 1 and 2 as "disagree" and 4 and 5 as "agree."
Source: BCG HBS Global Survey of 132 CEOs in 2001 (Proposition B1)

Figure 14.1 "NEDs" do understand the factors that drive performance in each of the main businesses. *Source:* Reprinted by permission of Harvard Business School Press. From *Back to the Drawing Board* by Colin B. Cater and Jay W. Lorsch, p. 206. Boston, 2004. Copyright © 2004 by the Harvard Business School Publishing Corporation. All rights reserved.

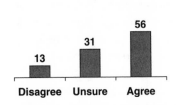

All CEO responses (%)			CEO Responses, by region (%)			

Region	Disagree	Unsure	Agree
North America	20	28	52
Europe	9	31	60
Asia Pacific	10	37	53
Total	13	31	56

Note: The CEOs responded to a 5-point scale where 1 = Strongly Disagree and 5 = Strongly Agree.
We have classified 1 and 2 as "disagree" and 4 and 5 as "agree."
Source: BCG HBS Global Survey of 132 CEOs in 2001 (Proposition B1)

Figure 14.2 "NEDs" recall previous discussions, and management does not have to keep repeating things in subsequent meetings. *Source:* Reprinted by permission of Harvard Business School Press. From *Back to the Drawing Board* by Colin B. Cater and Jay W. Lorsch, p. 206. Boston, 2004. Copyright © 2004 by the Harvard Business School Publishing Corporation. All rights reserved.

Knowledge-Intensive Companies

There are fundamental reasons why these information difficulties, which are embedded in the very nature of knowledge-intensive firms, are exacerbated in these companies. To understand why this is so, we need to be clear about what we mean by a knowledge-intensive company. By the broadest definition, almost every company in the world could be considered knowledge-intensive. This is because most companies use huge amounts of embedded knowledge to develop, produce, and market their products. As important as this knowledge may be to every company's success, I feel it is inappropriate to consider all companies knowledge-intensive. In all companies the board and management should, of course, pay attention to the underlying knowledge that creates products, but at the end of the day their primary focus will be on the revenue and income from selling the products and the reasons for these results, not on the embedded knowledge itself. In essence, in such firms this knowledge is important, but not critical to company success.

Another way to think about the issue is to think of companies as if they were arranged along a continuum of knowledge intensity. At the low end would be companies with simple products or services (e.g., fast-food chains, companies manufacturing and selling glass jars and other containers). At the high end would be companies that sell knowledge (e.g., consulting and law firms, software developers, and biotech research companies). It is these firms for which embedded knowledge is most critical. In fact, it is what they produce and sell. Developing the knowledge is what leads to competition and financial success.

Characteristics of Successful High-Knowledge-Intensity Companies

Companies at this end of the spectrum have characteristics that make them extremely difficult to govern. As Lorsch and Tierney (2002) point out, such companies depend on two key factors for their success: sound relationships with clients (customers), and employees who are highly talented and motivated professionals (stars)

Clients or customers are important for obvious reasons. They pay for the services—they are the source of revenue and profits. What is not so obvious to most observers, and even to those who work in these firms, is why one firm in a profession or an industry is more successful with clients than others are. Clients often have difficulty judging which firm will do a better job for them, for example, as an auditor, on a consulting assignment, or on a legal matter. The reason is that clients really do not have an easy or simple way to judge the quality of the service they are receiving, especially in relation to the other options that might be available. Consequently, clients and potential clients make judgments based almost entirely on the quality of the relationship they have with a firm's professionals and believe they can have in the future.

By "quality of the relationship" I do not mean only an interpersonal liking or attraction that may develop between the service-providing professionals and the client. Of course this can be important—no client wants to work with a professional who is personally irritating. But what matters even more in determining the quality of the relationship, and seems critical for whether the client will purchase the service, is the level of confidence and trust the client has in the knowledge-intensive provider.

When clients are buying knowledge (or expertise, if you prefer), they are paying for a service about which they know very little. That is one reason why they engage the professional. A simple analogy that illustrates my point is the patient-doctor situation. When someone has a medical problem, he or she may understand the symptoms, but is very unlikely to comprehend the causes. The person goes to a physician to get a diagnosis and, hopefully, a cure. If the cure is effective, the person trusts the doctor and is likely to return to him or her for a similar problem in the future, even though there may be no understanding of the physician's "magic." The same is true with clients and knowledge-intensive providers. The client comes to trust the provider if the latter's work solves the problem, even without understanding exactly how it is done. The point related to governance and information is that members of such a knowledge-intensive firm's governing board find it very difficult to understand how clients view their firm. This is especially true because most client relationships are in the hands of outstanding professionals who operate independently and often over a wide geographic area.

Another factor that can affect the success of knowledge-intensive firms is their success in developing and introducing new ideas, services, or products. In this regard there is an important difference between firms that actually develop, produce, and market a product (e.g., pharmaceuticals or software companies) and those which deliver a professional service (e.g., consultants and accountants). In the case of a product company, innovation is obviously the name of the game—the key to success. Each company tries to beat its competitors by introducing a new and better "mouse trap"—and, of course, one that appeals to its customers. Patents are obtained to protect the new product from competitive imitation for as long as possible.

For professional service firms, the advantages of new ideas or services are less evident, and certainly not as enduring. Of course it is great to develop a new idea, such as the investment banker Salomon Brothers' mortgage-backed securities, or the "poison pill" invented by Marty Lipton at the law firm of Wachtell, Lipton, Rosen and Katz, or the concept of brand print (understanding the psychological significance of the product to customers) that was developed by the advertising professionals at Ogilvey & Mather under Charlotte Beer's leadership. The problem is that the advantage of such ideas is short-lived. They cannot be legally protected by patents or copyrights. So if they prove to be attractive to clients, the stars in other firms can develop them and offer them to their clients in a matter of weeks or months. In fact, they usually do! Thus the true advantage of new ideas in these firms is short-lived, and outstanding and alert stars will develop imitations to minimize their impact. In these firms, stars are the key asset—in fact, the only meaningful asset—and new ideas have less salience.

Not surprisingly, outstanding professionals (stars) are the second factor that drives the success of firms which are highly knowledge-intensive. It is these outstanding professionals who attract and retain clients, not just through the reputations that precede them but also by the quality of the work they deliver through their activities and those of their associates.

What makes knowledge-intensive firms so different from other companies is their complete reliance on outstanding professionals. It is not an exaggeration to say that the only meaningful assets these firms have are their stars. New ideas, fancy offices, and sophisticated computer systems matter very little compared with those human assets.

Thus, finding, attracting, and motivating this talent is key to company success. For my purposes here, it is not necessary to go into great detail about how successful firms do all this. Suffice it to say that they accomplish the attraction and motivation of stars by creating internal structures and processes which are internally consistent and together reward the stars for

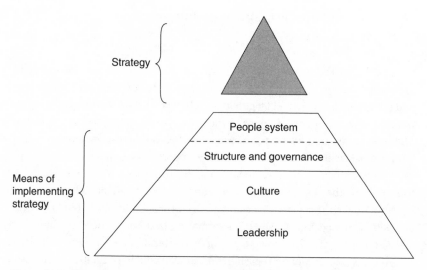

Figure 14.3 Alignment pyramid. *Source:* Reprinted by permission of Harvard Business School Press. From *Aligning the Stars* by Jay W. Lorsch and Thomas J. Tierney, p. 61. Boston, 2002. Copyright © 2002 by the Harvard Business School Publishing Corporation. All rights reserved.

behavior that accomplishes their firm's strategy. Figure 14.3 illustrates how the concept of alignment ties all this together.

It is also important to understand that over time these aligned structures and processes create within each firm a culture that reinforces the alignment among the firm's stars, its organization (structure and process), and its strategy. In essence, the culture is a set of do's and don'ts that tell the stars what behavior is expected of them both inside the firm and when they work with clients. Because so many of the activities of these firms are carried out by independent-minded professionals at client locations far from the home office, the culture becomes critically important. It provides a social mechanism to keep these professionals behaving in a way that is aligned with the firm's strategy.

Making these structures and processes work as intended, and also their original design, is the job of the leaders of the firms. In fact, another unusual characteristic of many knowledge-intensive firms is that their leaders not only take responsibility for managing the firm, but also continue to do professional projects. Furthermore, in many of these firms the leaders are significant owners of the company, either as shareholders or as partners.

All of these characteristics—the emphasis on client relationships built on trust; the importance of aligning stars, organization, and strategy; and the multiple roles played by firm leaders—have an impact on the problems of information and governance that are my focus in this chapter.

Governance of Information-Intensive Organizations

In considering the governance of information-intensive firms, one needs to make a distinction between those which are owned entirely by their employees and those which are owned by public shareholders. I shall start with the latter, because in some respects they raise the most complicated governance issues. This is because a majority of the directors on their boards (at least in the United States) must be independent. As pointed out earlier, this means they are unlikely to be familiar with the company and its business. Further, it is also likely that the time they can devote to their duties as directors will be limited.

What makes these two facts especially problematic for a publicly held company is the peculiarities of the information that boards need to obtain for effective oversight. The problem is not with the financial information that summarizes the company's past performance, which is relatively concise, precise, and easy to obtain. Rather, the difficulty is in understanding the drivers of company performance, which are critically important because you cannot govern a company by looking in the rearview mirror.

As pointed out earlier, one major determinant of success is the perceptions clients have of the company, its professionals, and their work. How much confidence and trust do they have in the firm? This type of information is difficult to obtain in any comprehensive way. It certainly is not likely to be in the firm's database. In fact, the only way to gather it is by surveying client opinion, and this is a process fraught with difficulties. One cannot be sure that clients are saying what they truly feel. Even unhappy clients may find it simpler to say everything is fine, but not continue to use a firm's services. Or clients who are truly unhappy may be the most likely to respond to a survey, thus biasing results in a negative direction. Whichever case turns out to be more likely, the truth about how clients feel about the firm is going to be hard to discern. This is further complicated by the problem of knowing whom in the client organization to ask about the relationship, and whether the person responding is really the most informed person.

Another approach to trying to understand client relationships is to track repeat engagements or sales. Certainly clients who come back for more work must be satisfied. One problem with this approach, though, is that it is never clear why clients do not come back. Is it because they were dissatisfied with prior work? Is it because competitors made a better proposal, either economically and/or in terms of the quality of service offered? Or is it simply because they have not had any further need for the services the firm offers? To answer such questions, one is again driven back to the survey.

Another related difficulty in relying on a measure of repeat work as an indicator of client satisfaction is that there is apt to be a lag time between the completion of one project and the next piece of work. So even if you ignore the other difficulties, such an indicator is going to be late in providing evidence of client satisfaction. In many instances we would have to wait years to know how clients felt about prior work.

Thus, gaining any reliable information about client perceptions of the company and its professionals is a big problem for these firms and their managements. And if management does not understand these relationships, it is obvious the board will not. Directors can and should press management to do post-engagement surveys with clients to gain the best view of client satisfaction. Further, directors themselves may want to reach out to significant clients to get first-hand impressions.

The other factors that drive financial performance are all related to the ability of the firm's stars and the alignment of the organization intended to motivate them. Again, information about these factors is very complex and not easy to accumulate, and therefore is difficult for directors to comprehend.

Some of it, of course, can be gathered systematically; for example, the results of the firm's efforts to recruit new staff. How many people were interviewed? What percentage of them were hired? What were the qualifications of those who accepted offers compared with those who did not? But when the success rate is less than desired, it is hard to identify the reasons. Was it because the firm leaders charged with recruiting were not effective? Or perhaps the firm's reputation on a university campus has deteriorated because of the way past graduates have been treated. Any of these factors are possibilities. How can directors know? They must insist that the firm's management seriously track such matters and share the information with the board.

But many aspects of the functioning of organizations are hard to discern from the boardroom. Take the example of providing sound performance feedback and coaching to young professionals on the way up. A firm may have the best-designed and most sophisticated system for such feedback and learning, but if the firm's leaders are not really engaged in making the system work, nothing is being accomplished. It is hard for directors to understand such matters. They can be provided with books and presentations describing the formal process, but they will still not know whether the younger professionals feel they are getting helpful feedback. Again, the best solution is to insist on seeing surveys of the young professionals' views on how performance reviews are being handled, and perhaps even to meet directly with some of them.

Thus the independent directors have a very difficult role to play in publicly owned knowledge-intensive firms. At first glance, it would seem that the situation might be less difficult in privately (employee) owned companies. At least the board is less likely to contain so many independent members. More members are apt to be owners and firm officers who more probably understand the clients and what is happening in the organization. Or so it would seem. However, even "management directors" will have information problems. While they may be familiar with what is happening in their particular part of the company, they may be no more familiar with other parts than independent directors are, and will have the same information problems the latter do. Further, their involvement in their own part of the firm may make them less objective about what is happening there.

A further problem for private-company boards is caused by the absence of independent directors. A strong argument for independent directors is that they will be objective. It is this objectivity that is lost in the boards of private companies without independent members. Without independent directors, there is also the danger that firm politics will enter into board discussions, further confusing and complicating the interpretation of the information the board is receiving. In essence, directors who are directly involved in the business will tend to interpret any information from the perspective of their particular leadership position in the company. This brings the normal disagreements among firm leaders about how to interpret data into the boardroom. When I say "normal disagreements," am referring to the well-established fact that managers are likely to interpret information from the perspective of their parochial position in the organization. There is nothing sinister in this; it is just what happens in the normal course of organizational events. The problem, though, is that when such biases are carried into the boardroom, it makes it more difficult for members of the company's ultimate governing body to make balanced and objective assessments of their situation. In fact, it damages one underlying reason to have a board of directors in the first place: having a body that is able to take a firmwide perspective by rising above the parochial interests of the operating managers.

Conclusions

In the end, the remedy for the information and knowledge difficulties facing the boards of knowledge-intensive firms is really to do the best they can in a difficult situation. There are two general actions that both new and experienced board members should take:

- Insist on some independent directors in order to provide objectivity and freedom from internal conflicts.
- Gather systematic data about client relationships and about the attitudes of the firm's stars and other employees. Board members should occasionally interact directly with both groups.

Such information may not be perfect, but it is vastly better than trying to govern in total ignorance of these matters.

References

Carter, C. B., and Lorsch, J. W. (2004). *Back to the Drawing Board: Designing Corporate Boards for a Complex World.* Boston: Harvard Business School Press.

DeLong, T., and Nanda, A. (2003). *Professional Services: Text and Cases.* Boston: McGraw-Hill Irwin.

Harvard Business Review on Corporate Governance. (2000). Boston: Harvard Business School Press.

Lorsch, J. W., and Tierney, T. J. (2002). *Aligning the Stars: How to Succeed When Professionals Drive Results.* Boston: Harvard Business School Press.

Maister, D. H. *Managing the Professional Service Firm.* (1993). New York: Maxwell Macmillan International.

15

Enhancing Social Capital for Knowledge Effectiveness

DON COHEN

The networks of informal trust relationships that we call "social capital" provide an essential social infrastructure for knowledge-sharing and the knowledge creation sparked by new combinations of existing knowledge. In this chapter, I describe how several organizations maintain the high levels of social capital that support successful knowledge exchange. The policies, values, and behaviors that sustain and strengthen social capital in those organizations suggest principles of social capital development which other firms can use to enhance their own social capital and improve their knowledge effectiveness.

From the early days of knowledge management, practitioners and commentators have noted that culture is important to successful knowledge-sharing in organizations. Efforts to understand knowledge management disappointments—knowledge repositories that failed to capture or disseminate valuable knowledge, or expertise locators that seldom connected knowledge seekers with experts, as well as the probably rarer instances of knowledge management success—have led to a refinement of that idea: an appreciation of the essential role that social capital plays in knowledge exchange. Knowledge is most readily shared by people who have relationships characterized by trust, some degree of mutual understanding, and generalized reciprocity—the expectation that help will probably be offered as readily as it is requested. In other words, knowledge moves most effectively along existing social pathways, through networks of trust relationships. Although definitions of "social capital" vary in their details, the term refers at heart to this stock of social connections.

John Seely Brown, Paul Duguid, Etienne Wenger, and others implied this connection between knowledge and social capital in their work on communities of practice, noting that knowledge develops and travels most effectively within communities, that is, among people who know and generally trust one another and who, speaking "the same language," can communicate what they know.[1] Cohen and Prusak (2001) discuss the elements and sources of organizational social capital and its benefits, which include better knowledge-sharing and collaboration, greater organizational coherence, and the knowledge retention and savings associated with lower employee turnover.[2]

At United Parcel Service (UPS), for instance, a culture of loyalty and promotion from within has resulted in a managerial turnover rate of less than 2 percent and careers with the company that typically last twenty-five or thirty years or more. The overwhelming majority of senior managers have worked for UPS for more than two decades, and most began their careers as drivers or package handlers. These long and varied tenures create extensive personal networks that span departments, functions, and much of the global geography that the company inhabits. Those networks serve as robust and rich sources of knowledge, advice, and assistance—provided by individuals who have developed their professional knowledge and judgment over decades of work with the company. Individuals who stay in the same job for many years also create useful knowledge. Many UPS drivers have done the same work (some even driving the same routes) for decades, developing rich expertise in their jobs and profound knowledge of their customers.

Thus robust social capital has significant value for organizations, especially those which depend on knowledge-sharing and collaboration. Investing in social capital should be a priority for knowledge-intensive organizations and an essential element of knowledge management projects, but building social capital is not easy.

Social Capital Is Born, Not Made

The problem is that this social phenomenon based on trust and authenticity cannot be manufactured or mandated into existence. No exhortation to employees to trust one another can generate trust. No assigning of employees to "communities" can bring genuine communities into existence. The brief organizational enthusiasm for assembling communities of practice has mainly died away, dampened by disappointing results. The failures had little to do with the knowledge value of communities, which I believe is as great as proponents claim, and everything to do with the impossibility of building a community from scratch by instructing or requiring people to relate to one another. These misguided efforts blur the distinction between a community (a naturally forming social organism characterized by common interest and generalized mutual aid, rather than any particular productive aim) and a team (a mandated work group with a specific productive goal), and end up with neither. Trying to order social capital into existence is as futile as the gloomy Miss Havisham's insistence, in Charles Dickens's *Great Expectations,* that the boy Pip "play!" on command.

Firms can, however, take action to preserve the social capital they have, and to encourage and strengthen trust relationships by nurturing the seeds and tender shoots of social capital that exist in every organization. Successful efforts to engender social capital call for persistence and subtlety, but they are possible.

The good news and the bad news (good for organizations rich in social capital, bad for those deficient in it) is that the best way to build social capital is to have it already. The founders of high-social-capital firms, including UPS, Hewlett-Packard, W. L. Gore and Associates, and Costco, operated from the beginning on principles of equity, cooperation, and trust—key encouragers of social capital. Even when the founders are long gone, those principles are kept alive in part by directly evoking their legacy. UPS managers often refer to founder Jim Casey's values and actions, and the company's annual senior management conference includes a Jim Casey Night that relates his business philosophy to current issues.

More important, though, is the way early behavioral norms propagate themselves, passed from generation to generation of employees as newcomers match their behavior and expectations to the organizational society they join. Experience and experiment amply demonstrate the power of social norms. Groups teach their beliefs and behaviors by example and through stories, and enforce them with reward and punishment, praise and blame, inclusion and ostracism. With rare exceptions, newcomers either adopt those beliefs and behaviors or leave the group. Where trust and cooperation are the norm, the social power of the group encourages and even demands collaboration and knowledge-sharing; trust and trustworthiness are common and expected. Where suspicion, factionalism, or knowledge-hoarding dominates, those norms just as powerfully inhibit the flow of knowledge and undermine at-tempts to increase social capital.

Russell Reynolds, an executive search firm where, according to President and CEO Hobson Brown, Jr., "Everything . . . works because of social capital," provides an example of how group norms—social expectations—and explicit company policies combine to maintain a culture of knowledge-sharing and collaboration.[3] According to one longtime employee, helping is "an ingrained habit." Newcomers describe hearing about the company's cooperative envi-ronment but believing what they hear when they see it in action—for in-stance, recruiters return phone calls from colleagues first and calls from customers second, and meet regularly to describe their current work and share information and advice. People who do not conform to this culture would not succeed in the company, and are seldom hired. Like many high-social-capital organizations, Russell Reynolds hires for cultural fit ("sociability and cooperative spirit," in Brown's words), not just on the basis of impressive résumés. Policies that reflect and reinforce this cooperative culture include the five-call rule, the requirement that a recruiter's first five phone calls relating to a new search must be to people within the firm.

Norms of trust and mutual aid can, of course, erode over time, under the influence of negative behaviors; disruptive events, such as a downturn that results in many layoffs or the arrival of new management with very different values, can cause more acute damage. By the same token, the right new values and behaviors can foster new social capital over time. A look at essential sources of organizational social capital and some high-social-capital firms will provide clues to effective approaches to enhancing social capital and the knowledge flows that depend on it.

W. L. Gore and Associates

W. L. Gore and Associates provides a striking example of a firm designed to foster social capital. For more than fifty years, Gore has developed one chemical compound—polytetrafluoroethylene, the basis of Teflon—into a variety of products, ranging from wiring insulation to GoreTex insulating fabric to artificial blood vessels to guitar strings to dental floss. Continuing innovation over the fifty-plus years of the firm's history has fueled its success and growth. The commitment and creativity responsible for that innovation are built on a social capital foundation, and the company perennially ranks high on "best places to work" lists. Gore invests in social capital mainly in the following ways:

- Providing environments that make it easy for coworkers to communicate directly and form close working relationships
- Demonstrating trust and respect by giving workers autonomy
- Ensuring fairness of recognition and reward.

Employing about six thousand in toto, W. L. Gore limits the population of individual facilities to two hundred because its leaders judge that to be the largest number of people who can know one another well and develop the trust and understanding that effective collaborative knowledge work requires. Most of these facilities are single-story buildings, thus avoiding the physical, and therefore social, separation that multiple floors produce.[4] Rather than increase the size of groups beyond this limit, the firm responds to growth by establishing new units, each with the same considerable degree of autonomy. Second, the company relies on voluntary association much more than formal assignment. In line with founder Bill Gore's dictum, "Leaders have followers," project teams form when a Gore associate convinces others that his or her new idea is worth pursuing. Another company policy that supports autonomy and demonstrates trust authorizes anyone at any level to make decisions, including purchasing decisions, that affect his or her work, provided that decision is not "below the waterline"—that is, so expensive or far-reaching that a poor outcome would sink the unit or the company. Subject to that one constraint, researchers or secretaries can order equipment or take other actions they judge important to their performance without asking permission of bosses or budget minders—a far cry from companies that lower morale, communicate distrust, and slow decision-making by requiring approvals for actions and expenditures both large and small. Gore also strives for reasonable equity of recognition and reward—another social capital builder—with compensation based on peers' judgment of the contribution, as well as profit-sharing and a stock purchase plan (with matching company contribution) available to anyone who has been with the firm at least a year.

Many companies, especially large companies, will not and cannot undertake the radical redesign necessary to copy W. L. Gore's social-capital-friendly environment, but the Gore example suggests essential elements of social capital and some of the steps other organizations can take to strengthen them.

Space and Time to Meet

W. L. Gore, with its small, single-story facilities, offers an especially dramatic example of an organization giving its members opportunities to meet and talk and develop the relationships on which cooperative work depends. Many other organizations design offices and campuses to encourage meetings. Open work spaces, strategically placed cafés and lounges, atriums, main streets, and stairways and escalators (instead of more isolating elevators) are all intended to bring people together. The explicit aim of this investment in workplace design is enhancing knowledge exchange, but that process and the process of building social capital are inextricably linked. People meeting together form relationships that make knowledge exchange possible; knowledge exchange strengthens relationships, making more knowledge exchange and greater trust possible; and so on.

The spaces allow people to see one another and meet; the fact of investment in the spaces signals the organization's belief that informal meetings have value, giving employees "permission" to stop and talk. Or they should signal that belief. Often the signals are mixed. I have visited firms (and suspect many more exist) where the café tables and conversation nooks are always empty; employees keep to their cubicles, eyes fixed on computer screens. In these organizations, the belief persists that real work happens at your desk, and that people chatting in the café probably do not have enough to do. And people overwhelmed with work or looming deadlines do not have much time for conversation.

Time is a rarer commodity than space in most organizations. Management is less likely to invest in giving employees time to breathe than in the pleasant public spaces people would frequent if they had a spare moment or two. Efficiency and productivity trump conversation. Efficiency is essential in business, but when taken to extremes, it is the enemy of social capital, snuffing out opportunities for connection, choosing the speed of e-mail over the time and expense of meeting, cutting off far-ranging and possibly creative discussion to concentrate on getting the job done. Healthy social capital does not require long stretches of time devoted to social chatter. In fact, organizational social capital probably develops best in the course of daily work, provided there is enough room—enough time and an appropriate physical space—for people to exchange the little stories that communicate understanding and values, to work together and watch one another work, to ask for and offer help.[5] And because human relationships of trust and understanding need time to deepen and strengthen, they need those moments of time over time. Repeated brief interaction builds social capital more effectively than one longer connection not reinforced by later association. UPS drivers often build surprisingly close (and valuable) relationships with customers they see only a minute or two at a time because they have that contact every workday for months or years.

Building Trust

Trust is the bedrock of social capital. Without it, cooperative social connections cannot exist. Where distrust prevails, it is almost impossible even to begin to build social capital because the most benign or generous action is greeted with suspicion and given a negative twist. (Think of the difficulty of making progress in political situations where adversaries thoroughly distrust one another.) Thus trust and social capital grow from existing trust, and the first job of the social capital builder is to locate pockets of trust and nurture them. As the section on space and time suggests, a critical element of that cultivation is giving people connected by some degree of trust opportunities to talk and work together to develop more.

Frío Aéreo, a cooperative produce-refrigeration facility at the Lima airport in Peru, provides an example. In a country where trust (of government, of people other than family and close associates) is in short supply, getting potential partners to work together was a lengthy process, the five-year effort of one or two persistent leaders to keep up a conversation among producer/exporters who already knew one another (and had developed some initial trust) until enough of them agreed on the project to be able to launch it. Once that partnership was formed, the joint work the members undertook to organize and run the facility further strengthened the trust that had been built so laboriously. Early in the life of Frío Aéreo, representatives of the partners met to set standards for asparagus, their main export, examining spears one by one in order to arrive at a shared definition of quality. That process of working together to articulate what had been largely tacit and intuitive judgments of quality, and arrive at an unambiguous common standard, increased trust as it shared knowledge.

It also established a precedent for clarity and openness. Openness, or transparency—the widest possible sharing of information about what is happening in an organization and why it is happening—is another important encourager of trust. Secrecy breeds distrust, the suspicion that those keeping secrets are planning something they do not want others to know about; transparency fosters trust, showing that others, and the organization in general, have nothing to hide, and suggesting that "we are all in this to-gether."[6] Frío Aéreo has made openness and objectivity its operating princi-ples, giving members regular reports detailing the quality, temperature, and speed of loading of all produce going through the facility, and engaging staff and members in continual conversations about its processes and procedures. They have created what manager Alvaro Salas describes as "the glass house," a vivid image of organizational transparency. Over time, this open culture and the proven reliability of shared information have disarmed suspicion and in-creased members' willingness to share knowledge. Along with increased trust, the practical result of this knowledge-sharing has been a dramatic increase in average quality and speed, as initially less expert member companies have learned both that the work can be done better and how to do it better.

Sharing information openly is a form of trusting. Trusting, in its various forms, is an important builder of trust. People generally live up (or down) to expectations. Trust them, and they respond by being worthy of trust. Distrust them, and reflect that distrust through close monitoring, locked doors, accu-sations, and strict rules about how and when to do everything, and many will see what they can get away with. At W. L. Gore, trusting is clearly demon-strated by the autonomy granted to every worker. People are trusted to define their own work and to make the decisions that affect it. The vast majority rise to the challenge by being responsible and committed members of the organiza-tion, and they trust those who trust them.

At 3M, high social capital and the trust that characterizes it contribute di-rectly to that company's record of successful innovation. The "15 percent rule," which encourages employees to spend up to 15 percent of their work time on independent projects and is a measure of the organization's trust in its members, has resulted in discoveries and inventions that have become valuable products. Mutual trust among employees and the open sharing of ideas it supports have led to important and profitable innovations. For instance, the Post-It Note came into existence because Dr. Spence Silver shared information about the new kind of adhesive he had invented with many colleagues, including Art Fry, who had been thinking about the value of bookmarks that would not fall out but knew of no technology that could make his idea a reality.

Leaders can foster trust by being trustworthy themselves. "Do as I say, not as I do" works no better in organizations than it does anywhere else. Mission statements that promise integrity, openness, and fairness (as Enron's did) mean nothing when leaders' actions are dishonest and corrupt. Although leaders cannot impose a particular culture on their organizations, their behavior powerfully influences it for good or ill. In addition to modeling trust through their own actions, they can encourage organizational trust by rewarding trustworthy behavior and punishing dishonesty in others. If someone widely recognized as honest, fair, and cooperative receives an important promotion, that sends a powerful signal to others in the organization that trust is alive and well. If a scheming or flattering individual who takes credit for others' work gets that important promotion instead, the opposite message is just as powerfully communicated.

As anyone who has been part of an organization knows, stories of events like these—the admired coworker or the schemer who got promoted—travel through even large organizations with astonishing speed and have immense influence. Along with direct personal experience (which we often turn into stories we tell others), stories of what actually happens shape our understanding of the values of the organization and tell us whether we can trust our leaders and colleagues, and whether they are likely to trust us. Official policies or pronouncements are powerless against stories that tell the truth of experience.

Ensuring Equity

The cooperative relationships that characterize social capital (and knowledge exchange) flourish in equitable environments, where reward and recognition correspond at least roughly to contribution. Glaring disparities between who does the work and who benefits, and insufficient opportunities for talented and hardworking employees to advance, create resentment and destroy social capital. Equity does not mean equality, but gross gaps between the pay of senior executives and "ordinary" workers damage social capital, especially when organizations experience financial difficulties and workers lose jobs, pensions, and insurance while executives walk away with millions or tens of millions of dollars. In thriving companies, the demoralizing effects of the inequity are less acute, though experience suggests a subtler damage: connection and cooperation with one's peers, but alienation from so-called leaders. In many high-social-capital organizations, including UPS, Costco, and Whole Foods, the ratio of the pay of the least and most senior members is smaller than the average for American companies by at least a factor of ten. High-social-capital companies also often have profit-sharing or stock purchase plans that reward people at all levels when the firm does well.

Equitable recognition of good work and opportunities for advancement help build social capital as much as, and probably more than, financial rewards. Trust, commitment, and cooperation (including willingness to share knowledge) require a reasonable assurance that people will get credit for their contributions. There is no surer destroyer of social capital than seeing others appropriate one's ideas without acknowledgment or take sole credit for joint work. An important element of the recognition should be in the form of advancement. Companies rich in social capital often promote from within and strive to be long-term or lifetime employers that are bound by mutual commitment to high-performing employees. Newspaper and journal articles about the death of loyalty and the peripatetic "company of one" exaggerate a partial truth about recent changes in employment, ignoring the continuing existence and importance of loyalty and long careers in many companies, large and small.[7]

As in the case of trust-building, actions speak louder than words when it comes to equity. Calling employees "associates" creates only cynicism if in fact they are underpaid, disrespected, and have no say in what happens in the organization. The people who work at W. L. Gore and those who work at Wal-Mart are called "associates," but the extent to which they genuinely enjoy the partnership that word implies is dramatically different. Gore associates significantly define their own jobs; they make decisions that influence the company's future direction; and they share in its economic success. Most Wal-Mart "associates" have no such autonomy. Their work is strictly defined and controlled by managers; and their low wages make the company more profitable for stockholders.

Building Social Capital Through Analysis

Analysis can help build social capital in organizations in several ways. First, and most obviously, it makes visible the often hidden social networks and communities in organizations, as well as the gaps where productive collaborative relationships could exist but do not. Armed with an accurate picture of elements of its social capital, the firm can nurture those elements with encouragement and modest support, and take care to avoid damage that sometimes occurs when social capital remains invisible (caused, for instance, by moving or firing someone whose role as a communicator or connector has gone unnoticed, or breaking up informal communities through a reorganization). The firm can also work to bridge the gaps the analysis reveals by creating opportunities for meetings and joint work for currently unconnected individuals and groups with mutually valuable knowledge and skills. Second, investment in analysis acts as a signal that, like investment in meeting space, tells people in the organization that social capital matters, that these relationships are valued and encouraged. Analysis often involves people working together, drawing them into conversations about their working relationships that, like other organizational conversations, can help mend or strengthen relationships. Thus, the very process of analysis can help create the social capital it is designed to locate and measure.

Social network analysis (SNA) is probably the most sophisticated social capital tool so far developed, a source of clear, accurate information about networks and relationships. Based on surveys that ask members of organizations or of groups within organizations whom they contact for information and advice, SNA generates maps of social networks that differ from reporting relationships described in organizational charts and from participants' assumptions about who talks to whom. These maps can reveal not only how information and knowledge travel, but also the anatomy of trust relationships, sources of group energy and inertia, and where people go for advice.[8] SNA can contribute to social capital in all three ways described above: by providing specific information about social networks that helps organizations nurture and protect them; by signaling the importance of social capital; and as an occasion for collective activity.

Some organizations regularly measure employee satisfaction with surveys that measure changes and reveal problems related to social capital. UPS carries out an annual Employee Relations Index survey that asks questions about opportunities for advancement, recognition, fairness, and trust, and about managers' openness to new ideas. As is true of social capital analysis, such surveys can influence social capital in multiple ways: by uncovering problems that can then be addressed; by serving as a signal; and by providing opportunities for social-capital-building conversation.

What About Virtual Relationships?

My emphasis on the need for time together to build trust and understanding may seem quaint (or irrelevant) in a world of high-speed global companies, where widely dispersed "virtual" teams are common and employees spend more time communicating via e-mail than they do talking face-to-face with colleagues. Twenty-first-century managers might reasonably ask how, and if, electronic relationships can enhance social capital.

Of course, even in the largest companies with the most sophisticated intranets, videoconferencing facilities, and e-mail systems, people meet in person for the discussions and decisions that matter most: to convince leaders to support projects; to explain or analyze ambiguous information; to demonstrate commitment, trustworthiness, and skill to peers and bosses. My colleague Laurence Prusak conducted an informal survey of businesspeople shuttling between

Boston and New York, asking where they were going and why. About half were traveling to a meeting of their firm, and chose the hassles of travel over the convenience of videoconferencing or teleconferencing because they knew they needed to be there is person to champion their ideas and strengthen important relationships. To a significant extent, social capital depends on being there. Working relationships created and maintained purely via e-mail and other electronic media seldom or never produce robust social capital.[9] Most of the million signals we receive and evaluate to decide whether a new acquaintance is trustworthy do not travel readily via e-mail or even videoconference (although a good video link probably communicates more of the signals than text or voice alone.)[10] Also, electronic media do not lend themselves to the sometimes discursive conversations and joint activities that shape mutual understanding of ambiguous terms and ideas. The Frío Aéreo standard-setting meeting could not have been as successful in setting standards and building trust had it been conducted by videoconference. Potential leaders at W. L. Gore could not win colleagues' commitment to their new ideas via e-mail.

Virtual connections can build social capital, though, as part of a repertoire of connections. Teams and groups that meet in person as part of their formation process can maintain the trust and understanding they develop face-to-face through e-mail and other long-distance communications. Without that ongoing contact, those new relationships would tend to fade away if many months passed before the teams or groups met again, so virtual contacts can strengthen social capital that is rooted in more traditional connections. Communities and teams that periodically meet in person to make decisions or (to use John Seely Brown's term) to "recalibrate" their shared understanding can do most of their work and much of their social-capital maintenance virtually.

Some companies reject even this blend of connections, balking at the expense and inefficiency of travel, or convinced (mistakenly, in my opinion) that electronic media provide all the contact necessary to get work done. Companies frequently reduce or eliminate social-capital-building personal contact just when the commitment and creativity that come with high social capital are most needed—when the firm experiences a downturn that only new ideas and renewed dedication can reverse. The short-term savings that come from this kind of corporate belt-tightening may prop up a company's stock price—but at the cost, I believe, of endangering future capability and long-term success.

A Long-Term Investment, a Near-Term Perspective

That common response to crisis suggests why social capital investment is not more common, especially when, I would argue, it is most needed. Nurturing social capital requires an investment of resources over time to create value over time. Building trust and cooperation is a long-term effort, and it is unlikely to generate dramatic economic benefits in the short run. It is no accident that many of my examples of high-social-capital organizations are privately held (W. L. Gore, SAS, Frío Aéreo, UPS until recently). Publicly traded companies, under extreme market pressure to generate as much profit as possible right now, have difficulty making the investments that will pay off only in the long run. Costco, a high-social-capital, publicly traded company, is devalued by Wall Street (compared with Wal-Mart) despite its remarkable success because, by paying employees high enough wages to earn their commitment, it "fails" to squeeze every dollar of profit out of current sales by lowering costs.

It is probably unfair, however, to blame the paucity of social capital investment entirely on shortsightedness and ruthless efficiency. Culture change is difficult, and skepticism about the possibility of successful cultural transformation may be well founded. In any organization, though, taking a social capital perspective on specific knowledge projects is likely to improve the chances of the project's success and to plant seeds of cultural change. Such a perspective would apply the principles I have described here to the planning and execution of projects: analyzing the social connections of the people involved; providing space and time for conversation among those the project is intended to serve; trusting them to participate in the design and management of their work (which helps to ensure its appropriateness and their commitment).

Conclusions

Efforts to share knowledge and spark innovation in organizations are likely to fail unless they are built on a firm foundation of social capital, the relationships of trust and mutual understanding that make knowledge collaboration possible. Organizations high in social capital tend to have similar supportive policies, behaviors, and values that suggest principles for social capital development. Organizations that hope to maintain and foster social capital would do well to apply those principles—certainly to knowledge projects, where they are likely to spell the difference between success and failure, and perhaps to all organizational activities. The essential elements of social capital creation are the following:

- *Provide space and time* to meet, and opportunities for members of the organization to work closely together so that they can develop mutual understanding and trust.
- *Build trust* by trusting employees and by demonstrating trustworthiness.
- *Ensure equity* of opportunity and reward to foster commitment and cooperation.
- *Analyze existing social networks* to see where valuable relationships should be preserved or strengthened, and to signal the importance of social capital.

Whatever path organizations take to foster social capital, high-social-capital firms will have an important long-term advantage in this era of knowledge economics. I believe that the commitment and knowledge collaboration they enjoy will keep many of them thriving long after most of today's leaner and meaner organizations have lost their luster.

Notes

1. See, for instance, Wenger (1998) and Brown and Duguid (2000).
2. Cohen and Prusak (2001).
3. Saidel and Cohen (2000), p. 10.
4. Morris (1999) is one of several published descriptions of W. L. Gore's workplace design.
5. My observations of social-capital creation in many American settings (see Putnam, Feldstein, and Cohen (2003), who suggest that social capital is usually created by people working together to accomplish some other aim, not for its own sake.
6. Rousseau (1995) says that clearly and fully explaining the circumstances and reasons for staff reductions makes it easier for people to accept even that traumatic event.
7. De Geus (1997) does not use the term "social capital," but his description of promotion from within in long-lived companies touches on the same issues of equity and commitment.
8. Rob Cross has contributed significantly to the increasing subtlety and sophistication of SNA. See Cross and Parker (2004).
9. See Davenport and Pearlson (2004) for examples of the drawback of work at a distance. And at the 1998 Berkeley Forum on Knowledge and the Firm, Ilkka Tumo of Nokia cited studies that found trust is harder to keep alive in electronic networks than through face-to-face contact.
10. British Petroleum found that commitments made via video connection (using their virtual teamwork technology) were honored more often than commitments made by phone or e-mail. See Cohen and Prusak (1996).

References

Brown, J. S., and Duguid, P. (2000). *The Social Life of Information.* Boston: Harvard Business School Press.

Cohen, D., and Prusak, L. (1996). "British Petroleum Virtual Teamwork Program." Case study, Ernst & Young Center for Business Innovation.

Cohen, D., and Prusak, L. (2001). *In Good Company: How Social Capital Makes Organizations Work.* Boston: Harvard Business School Press.

Cross, R., and Parker, A. (2004). *The Hidden Power of Social Networks: Understanding How Work Really Gets Done in Organizations.* Boston: Harvard Business School Press.

Cross, R., Parker, A., and Sasson, L., eds. (2003). *Networks in the Knowledge Economy.* New York: Oxford University Press.

Davenport, T., and Pearlson, K. (1998). "Two Cheers for the Virtual Office." *Sloan Management Review* 39(4): 51–65.

De Geus, A. (1997). *The Living Company: Habits for Survival in a Turbulent Business Environment.* Boston: Harvard Business School Press.

Langdon, M. (1999). *Social Design: The Link between Facility Design, Organization Design, and Corporate Strategy.* White paper, Innovation Labs.

Lesser, E., ed. (2000). *Knowledge and Social Capital: Foundations and Applications.* Boston: Butterworth-Heinemann.

Lesser, E., and Prusak, L., eds. (2004). *Creating Value with Knowledge: Insights from the IBM Institute for Business Value.* New York: Oxford University Press.

Putnam, R., Feldstein, L., and Cohen, D. (2003). *Better Together: Restoring the American Community.* New York: Simon & Schuster.

Rousseau, D. (1995). *Psychological Contracts in Organizations: Understanding Written and Unwritten Agreements.* Thousand Oaks, Calif.: Sage.

Saidel, B., and Cohen, D. (2000). "Russell Reynolds Associates: The Power of Social Capital." *Knowledge Directions* 2 (Spring): 10.

Wenger, E. (1998). *Communities of Practice: Learning, Meaning, and Identity.* New York: Cambridge University Press.

16

Knowledge Management
and Corporate Renewal

BALA CHAKRAVARTHY AND SUE MCEVILY

This chapter is about continuous corporate renewal, in which a firm seeks to improve its operational excellence even as it explores for new markets and competencies. It explains that the process of renewal mirrors that of knowledge management. The corresponding activities are protecting, leveraging, and building knowledge. The chapter describes these activities and illustrates them with three examples: Best Buy (the leading North American retailer of consumer electronics), Pearson (a leading U.K.-based media giant), and Dr. Reddy's (a leading generic drug company based in India).

It then goes on to describe three key executive actions that can help corporate renewal. Each of the three actions—setting a daring vision, making flexible commitments, and balancing organizational power—is illustrated with the help of the three examples.

Corporate transformation is typically viewed as a multistage process (Chakravarthy and Gargiulo, 1998) that follows a sequence of restructuring, revitalization, and renewal (see figure 16.1). Restructuring, also called "simplification" (Baden-Fuller and Stopford, 1994), involves a major downsizing of the organization, a delayering of its structure, and a reengineering of its business processes. However, this in itself is not enough to restore the firm's competitiveness. In addition, the transformation process must help identify new market opportunities and build the firm's core competencies (Hamel and Prahalad, 1994). The focus in this second stage, revitalization, is on growth; the profit threshold has been crossed during restructuring. The third and final stage of the transformation process is renewal, in which the firm seeks to continuously improve its operational excellence, even as it seeks to explore

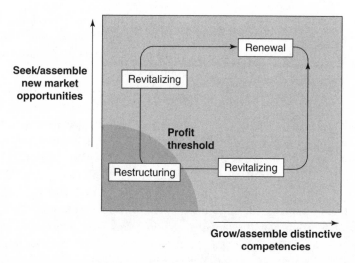

Figure 16.1 A stage model of corporate transformation.

new markets and to renew its competencies—thus embodying aspects of both restructuring and revitalization on an ongoing basis.

As popular as this model of corporate transformation is, we do not have many examples of firms that have progressed successfully through all three stages. One of the primary difficulties has been that organizational behaviors, such as employee empowerment, which are essential to revitalization are suppressed during restructuring (Chakravarthy and Gargiulo, 1998). While restructuring (followed by revitalization) is unavoidable if a firm is teetering on the verge of bankruptcy, the real goal of a top management team must be to avoid such a dramatic decline in performance. It must seek continuous renewal.

Our current research on continuous renewal has brought us close to the inner workings of several leading multinational companies around the world. Let us briefly describe the challenge facing three of these. The first company is Dr. Reddy's Laboratories (Dr. Reddy's), a generic drug company in India. Founded in 1984 by a Ph.D. chemist, in 2001 Dr. Reddy's became the first Asian (excluding Japan) pharmaceutical company to be listed on the New York Stock Exchange. From its modest origins as a pharmaceutical chemicals company, Dr. Reddy's has transformed itself through product diversification, international expansion, and the acquisition of new capabilities. It was recently recognized for its excellence in *Forbes* magazine's list of two hundred small global companies to watch. Instead of resting on its laurels, this $400 million firm is busy transforming itself into a discovery-led pharmaceutical company ready to compete with the Goliaths of its industry (Chakravarthy and Jha, 2003).

The second is Pearson, a leading U.K.-based publishing powerhouse with revenues of over $6 billion in 2003. In 1997 Marjorie Scardino was recruited from *The Economist* to head Pearson. Pearson was then a collection of discrete businesses, including the Tussauds Group (a visitor attractions business) and Mindscape (a consumer software developer). Recent annual earnings growth had averaged 3 percent, and Pearson was frequently mentioned as a breakup candidate. Scardino and her new management team immediately announced that their major goal was to produce annual double-digit earnings growth for the company and to focus only on businesses in which Pearson enjoyed market leadership. By the end of 2000, Scardino had made over £5 billion worth of acquisitions and £2 billion of disposals. In that year Pearson had three main businesses: business information, consumer publishing, and education. Education was the largest sector in terms of sales, followed by the Financial Times (FT) Group and the Penguin Group. Pearson, too, has gone through a metamorphosis, consolidating its businesses and moving its presence up the value chain from content to applications and services (Chakravarthy and Thompson, 2003).

Or take the case of Best Buy. Based in Richfield, Minnesota, it is the largest consumer electronics retailer in North America. Sales were $24.5 billion for the fiscal year ending in 2004. The company has grown its U.S. sales at a 17 percent compound annual rate since 1996, far outpacing the industry, which grew at only 4.9 percent over the same period. In its January 12, 2004, issue, *Forbes* magazine declared Best Buy the Company of the Year. In addition to the consumer electronics category that made up 37 percent of its sales, Best Buy's product mix included home office items (34 percent), entertainment software (23 percent), and appliances (6 percent). Best Buy outpaced other consumer electronics retailers in all these categories. It held the number one spot, with a 16 percent share of the $130 billion North American retail market for electronics and packaged media. Despite its phenomenal success, this industry giant is currently ripping up a very successful business model in order to build an even more successful customer-centered one (Chakravarthy and Bourgeois, 2004).

These companies differ in size, industry, and geographic scope, to name just a few dimensions. And yet they all face a common challenge, described metaphorically as one of changing wheels on a speeding train or erecting a new mast on a sailboat at full clip (Chakravarthy, 2004). Dr. Reddy's Laboratories, Pearson, and Best Buy are each trying to protect and extend their core business because of the short-term performance that it brings, while simultaneously diversifying beyond the core, in terms of both competence platforms and markets served. There is risk here. But staying the course also has its risks. It is this continuous renewal, and not one-time transformation, that is of interest to us. We will limit our attention to how knowledge should be managed in order to facilitate such a continuous renewal.

Knowledge Management
and Continuous Renewal

Continuous renewal (Chakravarthy, 1996; Chakravarthy, Lorange, and Cho, 2002) can be best understood through a simple framework (see figure 16.2). The dimensions used here are an extension of what is used in figure 16.1. After a successful restructuring, the firm begins to identify markets in which it can grow and to build the competencies that it needs to compete successfully in these markets. Protecting and extending this new franchise clearly has to be the firm's primary challenge. However, if it is engaged solely with this strategy, the firm may soon need another restructuring, because what is an attractive market today will become competitive and mature over time. Moreover, the distinction of a firm's competencies can erode as the latter are imitated or replaced by a firm's competitors. In order to sustain its performance, a successful firm must (1) pursue new market opportunities continuously, by first leveraging its available competencies; and (2) build new platforms of competencies to fuel future growth, but doing so by first strengthening the firm's competitive advantage in existing markets. The emphasis has to be on deliberate and controlled experiments: evolution rather than revolution as the preferred mode for corporate transformation.

Knowledge Management

Underlying the above framework for continuous renewal is a closely aligned approach to knowledge management. We see knowledge as synonymous with a firm's distinctive competencies, with the possible exception of hard-to-procure

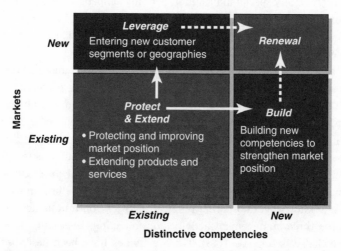

Figure 16.2 Continuous renewal. *Source:* Adapted from Chakravarthy (1996).

tangible assets such as raw materials, plant and equipment, and logistical infrastructure, or intangible assets such as reputation and brand equity that are accumulated over time (Prahalad and Hamel, 1990). We view any competence that can be learned as knowledge.

Nonaka (1994) defines knowledge as *justified true belief*. He argues that knowledge cannot be equated with truth, even though the purpose of learning may in fact be to seek the truth. Given the complex and dynamic environments confronting many businesses today, the "truth" about how to compete successfully may be hard to discern. We define knowledge as *beliefs that guide organizational action*; it is causal understanding that may or may not fully reflect the realities of the environments a firm faces. Knowledge can be superficial or deep. Thus it may be mere insights and heuristics that provide an understanding of the effectiveness of past actions (Fiol and Lyles, 1985), or be more tangible routines to guide organizational actions (Levitt and March, 1988; Nelson and Winter, 1982). Corporate renewal requires the entire spectrum of knowledge, from the tacit to the well articulated.

Furthermore, we see two broad types of knowledge: *resource conversion* and *market positioning*. *Resource conversion knowledge* refers to the ability of a firm to use generic resources, which are also available to its competitors, to create distinctive products and services through product and/or process innovation. The patents, copyrights, and trade secrets that a firm owns are the most articulated aspects of its resource conversion knowledge (Friedman, Landes, and Posner, 1991). The hunches, speculations, and beliefs that are the forerunners to a successful patent or copyright application, or a well-established trade secret, are also part of this knowledge base, albeit more tacit. The ability of a firm to see opportunities in its environment and avoid threats is another form of knowledge. We call this *market positioning knowledge*. The firm may not have access to any special information over its competitors, yet be able to see patterns in this information that others cannot. Superior market positioning knowledge is a combination of rich sensing, sensible boundary management, and effective stakeholder management (Spender, 1996).

Knowledge management is about three key activities: building, protecting, and leveraging both resource conversion and market positioning knowledge (Chakravarthy, 1996, 1997). Assuming that a firm has already built distinctive knowledge, protecting and extending that knowledge is the first step in its striving for renewal. If the firm can then leverage its distinctive knowledge base and apply it to new market opportunities, it ensures growth. But no knowledge base can be distinctive forever, and a firm's moves into new markets will eventually call for new knowledge. The firm must seek to build new knowledge. Corporate renewal calls for continuous iterations between the three management activities of protecting, leveraging, and building knowledge (see figure 16.3). These activities have been described more fully in Chakravarthy, McEvily, Doz, and Rau (2003). Each impacts the firm's

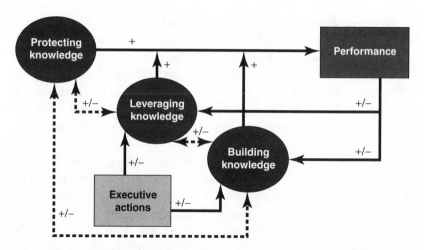

Figure 16.3 The dynamics of knowledge management. *Source:* Adapted from Chakravarthy, McEvily, Doz, and Rau (2003).

performance. We provide a brief summary here, and illustrate these activities with the help of the three examples that were mentioned in the introduction.

Knowledge Protection

Protection encompasses activities that seek to maintain the proprietary nature of a firm's knowledge stock. This includes seeking legal protection, such as patents and non-compete agreements, designing policies to limit employee turnover, and educating employees about the types of knowledge they should not share with their peers in other organizations (Appleyard, 1996). In addition, firms can take a variety of actions to shape the characteristics of their knowledge base in an effort to slow imitation. Three characteristics of knowledge have been repeatedly linked to the height of imitation barriers: tacitness, specificity, and complexity (Dierickx and Cool, 1989; Reed and DeFillippi, 1990; Doz, Santos, and Williamson, 2001; McEvily and Chakravarthy, 2002).

Tacitness refers to the *personal nature* of knowledge (Nonaka and Takeuchi, 1995; Teece, Pisano, and Shuen, 1997). The more tacit a firm's knowledge, the less employees can communicate it freely to suppliers, customers, or their peers, who might deliberately or inadvertently share information with the firm's competitors. Often such knowledge is valuable only in the specific context of a firm (Barney, 1992; Arora and Gambardella, 1994). *Specificity* is the loss in value that occurs when a resource or information is applied in a new context. Competitors that lack contextual knowledge may be unaware that new knowledge has been created, and, even when they are aware, may find it difficult to copy this knowledge without experiencing the specific context in which it was applied. *Complexity* increases with the number of constituent elements in a knowledge set, and is high when the relative importance of these elements to a knowledge set is more equal. The cost of knowledge transfer increases with complexity (Dierickx and Cool, 1989; MacMillan, McCafferty, and Van Wijk, 1985). Tacitness, specificity, and complexity increase "stickiness" of knowledge (McEvily and Chakravarthy, 2002). Sticky knowledge resists identification and imposes a high cost on rivals seeking to access it (Zander and Kogut, 1995; Szulanski, 1996; Von Hippel, 1998).

Consider the case of Best Buy. Its new customer-centered initiative has been announced publicly, yet the company is confident that it can protect the distinctive *market positioning* knowledge it has built. First, this knowledge is *specific* to the merchandise and customer segments that Best Buy has targeted. With the possible exception of Circuit City, none of its competitors has this specific retail experience. True, standard operating procedures are being developed in the company's experimental (or lab) stores in order to roll out customer-centeredness across all Best Buy stores. But a lot of this new knowledge will continue to be *tacit*, transferable only through direct apprenticeship in these lab stores. Also, complementing these procedures are other practices, such as training employees in the new approach, tailoring internal systems to support customer-centeredness, launching special vendor management initiatives, developing a "servant leadership" style at all levels of management, and building a new corporate culture based on customer-centeredness. Within Best Buy, being a "servant leader" means that the role of senior management is to set the broad vision and create a supporting context in which store managers can articulate the needs of their customers and enact strategies to serve these needs. The decision-making power will swing substantially to lower echelons of management. The one closest to the customer will carry more influence in decision-making. The role of top management will be to serve these managers. Customer-centeredness is thus also a *complex* knowledge. Together, the specificity, tacitness, and complexity of Best Buy's customer-centered knowledge provide it with protection against imitation by competitors. As the company's CEO, Bradbury H. Anderson put it:

> I have always believed the social system is the most significant competitive advantage that a company can have. Social system and culture are crucial for delivering a new strategy. Our bet is that our social system will trump that of our competitors.

Knowledge Leveraging

Leveraging is applying existing knowledge to new ends. This has two advantages: (1) it maximizes the return on that knowledge, and (2) it can accelerate the knowledge articulation process by providing more application opportunities. By providing different but related application opportunities, leveraging allows not just the repetitive honing of that knowledge, but also its enrichment and synthesis with other knowledge resources in response to new needs or problems. In other words, leveraging can help with knowledge-building.

Pearson provides an illustration of knowledge-leveraging. As noted earlier, the company sought to extend its strengths in content to applications and services. It acquired the U.S. company NCS in 2000 to help in this endeavor. NCS earned $630 million in revenues that year from its four divisions: Assessment & Testing, Data Management Solutions, NCS Learn, and Government Solutions. Assessment & Testing was the single largest processor of student assessment tests for K–12 (kindergarten to twelfth grade) in U.S. schools. The company also offered a wide range of data management products and services, particularly for schools. Through NCS Learn, the company was the only provider of a full suite of administrative software to help teachers and administrators keep attendance records, grades, and test scores, and manage state curriculum requirements. NCS was also a significant supplier of services to government entities, with a primary focus on the U.S. federal government and its agencies.

Soon after the acquisition, Pearson's education division began exploring opportunities for leveraging the joint *resource conversion* and *market positioning* knowledge portfolio of the parent and its new acquisition. One of these new initiatives, called NCS4Schools, sought to provide the next generation of software aimed at the school market. The revenue potential for NCS4Schools was estimated to be in excess of a billion dollars, if all of the potential synergies within the Pearson family could be exploited. Designed as a daily destination, the NCS4Schools solution sought to provide tools that enhanced learning and teaching, as well as administration and communication among teachers, administrators, parents, and students—all online. For example, a student having academic difficulties could take an online test to assess his or her competence, have a remedial curriculum and content designed for him or her, and have ongoing progress monitored by parents, teachers, and administrators—all within a single Pearson portal. The proposed system aimed at integrating the software, Web technology, and testing/assessment knowledge of NCS with the content and curriculum knowledge of other Pearson businesses to create unbeatable value in the K–12 educational market. In addition, the interfaces that NCS had established with school administrators were seen as a useful complement to Pearson's contacts with teachers. The NCS4School initiative was also potentially a template for Pearson to build other self-help educational programs on the Web for people seeking to earn trade and professional licenses.

Knowledge-Building

Knowledge is built when units within the firm or the organization as a whole gains new understanding. Comprehension may develop through deliberate efforts to learn something, such as through experimentation, or as a by-product of activities that have other outcomes. In either case, learning requires some type of feedback, the ability to observe the effect or outcome of one's efforts. While experience and choice create opportunities for learning, knowledge is generated only when this is accompanied by reflection and abstraction.

New knowledge is developed when individuals in an organization see a cognitive association (Hedberg, 1981) between their action and its consequences. When this individual knowledge is communicated to others in the organization, it becomes a loose heuristic, or method of discovery, that helps guide their actions (McCaskey, 1982). This heuristic per se may not lead to successful action (Reitman, 1964), but over time the cause and effect underlying a heuristic are better understood, and are codified as a script for action. A script retains knowledge of expected sequences of behaviors, actions, and events (Gioia and Poole, 1984). It provides cues to an organization's members on how to act in a given context. When a script can unambiguously specify what action should be taken under a prescribed condition, it is called a tight script. Rules and standard operating procedures (Cyert and March, 1963; Levitt and March, 1988; Nelson and Winter, 1982) are examples of tight scripts. A tight script improves the efficiency with which the organization responds to a threat or opportunity.

Dr. Reddy's moves into generics are a good illustration of this multistage knowledge-building process. By 2001 generic drugs represented a $40 billion market opportunity for the company, one that was also growing at 10 percent to 12 percent each year. In the United States, the Drug Price Competition and Patent Restoration Act of 1984 gave generic drug manufacturers new opportunities. This law permitted generic drug manufacturers to file Abbreviated New Drug Applications (ANDAs) for generic versions of all pharmaceutical products approved after 1962. The first ANDA filing by Dr. Reddy's was in 1997.

An ANDA filing did not have to wait until the patent on a drug was set to expire. The generic competitor could submit what the industry called a Paragraph IV application, claiming that the patent being challenged was invalid or unenforceable, or would not be infringed by the generic drug that the filer sought to introduce. The law allowed the patent holder to sue the applicant within forty-five days of such a filing, in which case it automatically got a thirty-month stay. If the patent holder lost the lawsuit during this period or no decision was available from the courts at the end of it, the FDA could approve the ANDA and give the first generic applicant a 180-day exclusivity period to start marketing its drug. Dr. Reddy's spent several million dollars in 2001 fighting Eli Lilly's patents on the 40-milligram dose of the blockbuster antidepressant drug Prozac. After a six-month court battle, Dr. Reddy's finally prevailed and won the right to market its generic drug exclusively for six months. The company achieved $68 million in sales in the exclusivity period, at a gross margin estimated in excess of 90 percent.

While the rewards from a successful patent challenge could be huge, there were risks as well. Each bioequivalence study cost the company anywhere from $500,000 to $2 million, with the risk that this would be to no avail if the FDA did not grant approval or the patent holder was able to sue successfully and block the launch of the generic drug. As of early 2003, eleven of Dr. Reddy's ANDAs had been approved and the firm had successfully marketed these products. The company was awaiting decisions on twenty-three additional applications, seventeen of which involved patent challenges.

Dr. Reddy's had progressively built the technical and legal knowledge on when to file an ANDA and how to manage the risks involved in the patent challenge game. This new knowledge was initially tacit, and held by the company's U.S. lawyers and senior scientists. The company is now articulating that knowledge and complementing its core team with Indian lawyers and scientists to help with the back office research.

Performance Can Affect Both Knowledge-Building and Leveraging

A firm's own performance can drive the need for knowledge-building and leveraging, but may act on these in opposing ways. For example, superior performance may provide the resources that are needed to invest in knowledge-building (Chakravarthy, 1986); however, this can also lead to complacence, thus lowering the urge to overcome the organizational and political barriers that inhibit leverage. Conversely, continued poor performance can increase motivation within the firm to share and leverage all of its available knowledge in new and innovative ways. But limited resources and preoccupation with short-term results can deter efforts at building new knowledge.

Executive Actions

Executive actions must provide the proper balance in this complex dynamic, helping the firm to go beyond knowledge protection to leveraging and building knowledge. We devote the rest of the chapter to examining critical executive actions that can help achieve such a balance and thus help in corporate renewal.

Executive Actions for
Corporate Renewal

We highlight three executive actions that are important to corporate renewal: *setting a daring vision, making flexible strategy commitments,* and *balancing organizational power.*

Daring Vision

A daring vision (Hamel and Prahalad, 1989) can be very useful for shaking up a complacent organization. It recalibrates the meaning of "superior" performance and changes the reference group of peers. The performance bar is set higher. Ryuzaburo Kaku, the former head of Canon, famously proclaimed: "Today Mount Fuji, tomorrow Mount Everest." Implicit in this succinct statement was a signal to the organization that what was adequate knowledge for scaling Mount Fuji would be inadequate for scaling Mount Everest. A stretching ambition can help improve both knowledge-building and knowledge-leveraging.

In the case of Pearson, after successfully restructuring and revitalizing the company through several acquisitions and divestitures, its CEO Scardino launched a renewal effort based on the slogan "beyond content." She explained:

> We think it's not enough to be just a content company. You have to be able to provide the applications and services to match the content, to help the customer use your content. There's very little content that is not a commodity right now.

This new vision has been the driver for Pearson to acquire new competencies in software development and Web-based distribution of interactive content. It has strengthened its position as one of the leading providers of high school and college textbooks by building skills in testing. As noted earlier, applying existing knowledge to new contexts can create new knowledge.

In the case of Dr. Reddy's, the firm stood at a crossroads in early 2003. Its three legacy businesses—(1) active pharmaceutical ingredients (API) for drug companies worldwide, (2) branded formulations sold exclusively in weak patent regime countries in the Third World, and (3) generic drugs sold in North America and Western Europe, generated most of its $400 million revenues and $77 million profits. With a market cap of $1.5 billion, a return on equity of 19 perent, and a P/E ratio of 19, Dr. Reddy's was one of the top financial performers in the industry.

However, competition was heating up in all of its major businesses, and Dr. Reddy's was looking for new ways to maintain its momentum and achieve nonlinear and explosive growth in the future. The company announced its daring vision of becoming a "discovery-led global pharmaceutical company." A more immediate goal was to become a $1 billion pharmaceutical company by 2008. This would require aggressive growth in the emerging specialty drug business and growing new capabilities for new drug discovery. Moving away from its heritage of imitating the discoveries of industry leaders, Dr. Reddy's sought to be an innovator in its own right. As in the case of Pearson, this new vision became the inspiration for the company to build three new knowledge sets: R&D skills for new drug discovery and specialty adaptations/substitutes for existing drugs under patent, the marketing know-how for selling these in the developed markets of North America and Western Europe, and the skills required both to manage and to protect its own intellectual property as well as to challenge that of current patent holders. The top management team at Dr. Reddy's, led by its CEO, G. V. Prasad, realized that business as usual would eventually lead to the company's decline. It actively sought to build new knowledge before the company's existing knowledge lost its competitive advantage.

Best Buy provides an even more persuasive account of the power of a daring vision in managing a firm's knowledge. Its top management team, led for a long time by its founder, Richard M. Schulze, and more recently by his successor, Bradbury H. Anderson, has reenvisioned the company six times since the mid-1980s. Each new vision, called a "concept" within the company, was an invitation to build new knowledge and/or to leverage it into new markets. These concepts were

- Concept I, the superstore (1983–1988)
- Concept II, the warehouse (1989–1994)
- Concept III, the hybrid model (1995–1998)
- Concept IV, the service store (1999–2000)
- Concept V, the modular store (2001–2002)
- Concept VII, the customer-centered store (2003–).

The first Best Buy Concept I superstore opened in 1983 in Burnsville, Minnesota, focusing more on inventory turnover and larger volume than on unit margins. This allowed the firm to build the know-how and skills that were needed for it to be a discount retailer. Best Buy grew to 100 stores by 1988 with this vision. That year, a regional rival, Highland Superstores, initiated a price war. Even though Best Buy had joined a buyers' cooperative to improve its power over vendors, it could not match the aggressive pricing policies of the much larger Highland. The company faced bankruptcy.

Schulze and his team decided to survey Best Buy's customers on what appealed to them the most. The results were sobering. The average customer, especially women, disliked the shopping experience in a Best Buy Concept

I store. She felt intimidated by the salespersons (who were paid on commission) and was often forced to buy more expensive items under the pretext that the product originally asked for was not in stock. Stung by the findings of its survey, Best Buy introduced its Concept II store in 1989: an everyday low-price consumer electronics warehouse. During the period 1989–1994, sales exploded from $500,000 to nearly $5 billion. The number of stores grew to 151. Over the years Best Buy built new operational know-how and skills for running one of the most efficient retail chains for distributing consumer electronics.

Concept III (1995–1998) and Concept IV (1999–2000) stores helped improve the company's profitability while sustaining its impressive growth trajectory. Concept III required the firm not only to acquire new knowledge that was needed for selling higher end merchandise, without sales pressure but with more involvement by Best Buy's salespersons in the selling process. Concept IV extended Best Buy's product-focused knowledge to installation and onsite service of its products. Concept V, introduced in 2001, was aimed at keeping up with the rapid technological innovations in the consumer electronics and computer industries, while helping customers tie old and new products together. Then in 2003, the company introduced Concept VII, intentionally skipping Concept VI to signal that the new concept was a radical departure from the company's history of being product-centered. The new approach was customer-centered. Best Buy's marketing team helped define five new segments that were based more on consumer needs and behaviors and less on demographic characteristics (as had been the case in the past). The new challenge was to create knowledge for reengineering the customer experience and addressing the specific needs within each segment and its subsegments.

Flexible Commitments

Strategy is about commitments (Ghemawat, 1991), and yet it is also about learning. The knowledge on which a firm commits to a strategy may not be as distinctive as first assumed, or it may lead to newer opportunities that are far more attractive. Commitments have to be flexible as well. This may sound like an oxymoron, but this is precisely what the continuous renewal framework that was proposed earlier (see figure 16.2) is all about.

The transformation journey of Dr. Reddy's is a good example of how commitments can be kept flexible. The company was founded to make active pharmaceutical ingredients (API). It then began selling branded formulations in India and other developing countries that had weak patent regimes by copying the chemical constituents of products sold by the world's leading drug companies. It added generic drugs to its portfolio soon thereafter, still playing the imitation game. Only recently has its launched its own specialty drugs and begun licensing its discoveries to other pharmaceutical companies (see figure 16.4). Each new move has brought the company into a new market

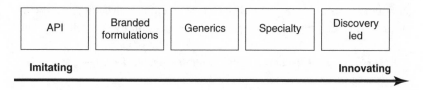

Figure 16.4 The transformation journey of Dr. Reddy's.

(product/geographic expansion). Dr. Reddy's has changed its business model several times as it has moved along the spectrum from being a chemical company to being a full-fledged pharmaceutical major player. All through this journey it has kept building new knowledge (see figure 16.5).

In figure 16.5, the relative sizes of the circles denote the level of competence required in each business, and the shaded part shows the current capability of Dr. Reddy's. Being an API supplier required manufacturing competencies; selling branded formulations in developing countries called for strong sales and marketing skills in these countries; generics demanded competencies in managing intellectual property (IP skills); and specialty and new drug discovery required R&D capabilities, as well as strong IP and marketing skills in developing countries. A successful company has to strive continuously for new market opportunities and new capabilities. If these capabilities can be cumulated and leveraged, as Dr. Reddy's has attempted to do, success can be enduring.

The important point to note here is that acquisitions, alliances, and organic growth are all legitimates modes for managing knowledge and driving

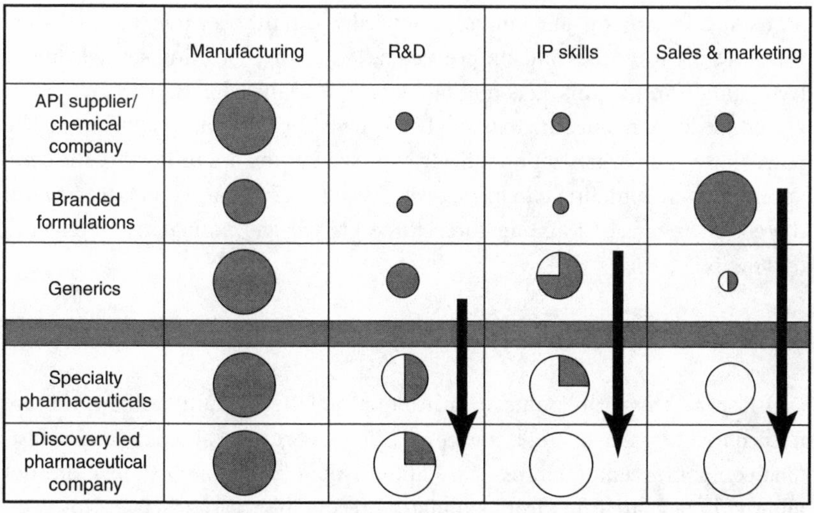

	Manufacturing	R&D	IP skills	Sales & marketing
API supplier/ chemical company	⬤	•	•	•
Branded formulations	⬤	•	•	⬤
Generics	⬤	⬤	◕	◑
Specialty pharmaceuticals	⬤	◑	◕	◯
Discovery led pharmaceutical company	⬤	◕	◯	◯

Figure 16.5 New market opportunities and new capabilities at Dr. Reddy's.

continuous renewal; but their effectiveness is enhanced if they are orchestrated within the principles of continuous renewal that were stated earlier:

1. Pursue new market opportunities continuously, first leveraging available competencies, and
2. Build new platforms of competencies to fuel future growth, but only after strengthening the firm's competitive advantage in existing markets.

Some firms, such as Best Buy, have relied primarily on organic growth for their renewal. On the other hand, Pearson has relied on acquisitions, and Dr. Reddy's, on alliances, to complement organic growth in their renewal journey. The emphasis has to be on deliberate and controlled experiments, with evolution rather than revolution as the preferred mode for corporate transformation. The challenge here is to ramp up speedily when the experiment is a success, and to exit decisively when it is a failure. The very nature of their turbulent business environments requires Dr. Reddy's, Pearson, and Best Buy to venture into projects with a low probability of success. Timely exits have been crucial to their survival and growth. It is useful to have clear Go/No Go criteria before launching an experiment, and also to have the discipline to apply the criteria firmly despite the emotional pleas of managers driving these initiatives. A failed idea does not mean the manager executing it is also a failure. Making this simple distinction can go a long way toward exiting failed experiments quickly.

Balancing Organizational Power

We described three distinct types of knowledge management activities—protecting, leveraging, and building knowledge—in the previous section. When a firm seeks to go beyond its preoccupation with protecting knowledge to leveraging it in new markets and building new knowledge to help fuel future growth, it faces what Christenson (1997) calls the innovator's dilemma. The power base in an organization is likely to be skewed toward protecting the core. Leveraging and building can be neglected as a result. While each is important, there can be tensions among these three knowledge management activities (see figure 16.3).

Knowledge-Building versus Leverage

Consider a firm with multisite operations. Relatively tight frameworks are needed to leverage existing knowledge in such a firm. Local operations in fast-food companies, chain stores, gas stations, retail banks, and the like are not allowed to deviate much from standard (presumably best) practice. However, exhaustive specification of procedures, and strict adherence to them, can stifle learning and the building of new knowledge. In general, organizational practices that are helpful for "exploiting" available knowledge are not very conducive for "exploring" new knowledge (March, 1991). A key challenge for top management is to create a "tight-loose" process for knowledge leveraging, leaving enough freedom for learning to take place but imposing sufficient communality and sharing to leverage best practice.

This was the challenge that confronted Best Buy when it sought to introduce customer-centeredness. It had to balance the economic opportunity that customer-centeredness represented with the scale efficiency and standardization that product- centeredness offered. The primary competence of Best Buy has been its ability to procure, ship, and sell large volumes of merchandise at competitive prices. Its operating rules and procedures for its 600-plus stores reflected this knowledge. However, the new customer-centered strategy would require the company to give more autonomy to its stores. Within the broad framework set by the company's corporate office, each store manager would now have the discretion to influence merchandising, signage, and marketing communication as appropriate to the customer segments served by his or her store. This new knowledge had to be built while leveraging the operational excellence that a product-centered strategy had helped perfect.

Knowledge Protection versus Knowledge-Building

Routines are the result of a satisfactory compromise between stakeholders in an organization, and they implicitly reflect the relative credibility and relative power of various categories of stakeholders (Leonard-Barton, 1992). A shift in the relative criticality of knowledge may threaten the balance of power in the organization and question the continued validity of existing knowledge. Dominant groups and coalitions are committed to existing knowledge, in order to perpetuate their greater influence within the organization. These commitments may also extend to powerful outsiders, such as important customers who have vested interests in the continuation of the firm's current business portfolio and technological trajectory. These forces lead firms to favor protection of existing knowledge rather than the building of new knowledge. It is striking, for example, to see how IBM masterfully achieved "architectural" control over mainframes in the 1960s and 1970s, but let Microsoft and Intel take such control away from IBM in personal computers in the 1980s. It thus lost its early lead in the subsequent explosive growth of personal computers. To encourage effective knowledge-building, management needs to shake up existing patterns of behavior, values, and tacit mind-sets.

In the case of Best Buy, in order to pursue customer-centeredness, there had to be a noticeable shift in power from the corporate office to the retail stores. For example, product assortment in the stores was historically modified five times a year. The merchant and the general merchandise teams would meet, decide what they wanted, and communicate their decisions to the field for implementation. Local stores did not have a say in the process. This had to change. Newcomers to Best Buy's executive team had mixed reactions to this change. Some had been brought in specifically to strengthen corporate functions. The company's CEO, Brad Anderson, realized that he had to shift the power pendulum away from corporate executives toward midlevel managers in the field and in the stores. He began giving these managers more of a voice in key corporate decisions. At the same time, he encouraged his senior executives to voice their dissent openly. In the give-and-take of these debates and discussions, a more balanced approach that blended the virtues of both the old and the new organization emerged, with a broad buy-in from the entire organization.

In the case of Dr. Reddy's, the challenge was to create a power balance between the core of the organization, devoted to API and branded formulations; and the new initiatives centered on generic drugs, specialty drugs, and new drug discovery. Dr. Reddy's has chosen to balance power by moving the headquarters for the latter businesses to the United States, bringing in high-priced talent from outside and staffing half of its management council in 2003 with non-Indians representing the new businesses.

Knowledge Leverage versus Protection

Knowledge leverage and protection can also be in conflict. Effective protection of knowledge often requires segregating or embedding knowledge within the organization, while leverage demands integration and articulation. Groups and individuals may prefer to hone their skills on local problems, and small groups will try to deepen their local knowledge rather than articulate and transfer it to other parts of the organization. Moving skills and knowledge from the individual to the collective level requires the articulation of the knowledge (or a collective apprenticeship) and its diffusion to other units (Hedlund and Nonaka, 1993). However, articulation of knowledge is unlikely ever to be fully feasible, because knowledge cannot be captured entirely in explicit procedural knowledge. Direct diffusion of tacit knowledge and skills is also possible, but their transfer is likely to place a greater burden on the transferrer (Szulanski, 1996). Articulation of knowledge makes it easy to transfer it internally, but also leaves it vulnerable to external pilferage. Additionally, characteristics of knowledge that protect it from imitation can hinder its transformation and recombination, making leveraging difficult (Galunic and Rodan, 1998; McEvily and Chakravarthy, 2002).

At Pearson, a good illustration of this tension involved the NCS4Schools initiative that was described earlier. The NCS business group that managed this project was keen on perfecting and protecting the knowledge it was developing. On the other hand, the concern within Pearson was that not enough attention was being paid to connect this application with products delivered by other Pearson Education business groups. These businesses were focused on knowledge leverage, and saw the NCS project team as being overly "insular." The head of Pearson Education, to whom NCS and all of these business units reported, saw this tension as healthy. He expected his business group managers to sort this out among themselves, noting:

> If the business group heads consistently show poor judgment, I will replace them; but as long as they run their businesses well, I will defer to their judgment.

Underlying this remark was the firm belief that dilemmas were healthy, and effective managers should show good judgment in balancing the resulting tensions. In addition, through their personal leadership style, senior executives can help maintain the right balance. They have to demonstrate the fine art of always caring for the unchosen—the neglected aspect of knowledge management within the firm, whether it be protecting, leveraging, or building knowledge.

Conclusions

We have demonstrated that knowledge management is an important aspect of corporate renewal. Managing knowledge requires the balancing of knowledge protection with knowledge-building and leverage on a continuous basis. There are three key executive actions for achieving this balance:

- Setting a daring vision
- Using a strategy architecture that supports flexible commitments
- An organizational architecture that tries to balance the tensions in knowledge management.

Leonard-Barton (1992) perceptively observed that core competencies of a firm tend to become core rigidities because of top management's failure to build new knowledge and make old knowledge obsolete. We have argued here that periodic revisioning is an important prerequisite to renewal. The more daring the vision, the greater the chance that the limitations of a firm's current core competencies will be exposed. The Best Buy and Dr. Reddy's examples both support this hypothesis. Further, they show that the old competencies need not be discarded, but can provide useful building blocks for new strategies. We called this approach one of making flexible commitments. Both Best Buy and Dr. Reddy's have leveraged their low-cost heritage even as they have sought to differentiate their product portfolios. Competencies take a long time to build, and instead of waiting until they become rigidities and then discarding them, it is important to seek opportunities where these competencies can become the second and third lines of defense. Nevertheless, as newer competencies begin to shape the firm's competitive advantage, there is no denying that there will be an associated shift in the firm's power structure. In the case of Best Buy, for example, the power balance had to shift more in the direction of store managers. In Dr. Reddy's the process chemists had to play second fiddle to the inventors of new chemical entities. Core competencies become core rigidities because the associated managerial elite refuses to give up its power base. In both companies, the CEO actively managed this shift in power. As the three examples (Best Buy, Pearson, and Dr. Reddy's) show, the three executive actions (periodic revisioning, experimenting through flexible commitments, and rebalancing the power structure in an organization) must be well coordinated to ensure the continuous renewal of the firm.

References

Appleyard, M. (1996). "How Does Knowledge Flow? Interfirm Patterns in the Semiconductor Industry." *Strategic Management Journal* 17 (Winter special issue): 137–154.

Arora, A., and Gambardella, A. (1994). "The Changing Technology of Technological Change: General and Abstract Knowledge and the Division of Labor." *Research Policy* 23: 523–532.

Baden-Fuller, C., and Stopford, J. (1994). *Rejuvenating the Mature Business: The Competitive Challenge.* Boston: Harvard Business School Press.

Barney, J. (1992). "Integrating Organizational Behavior and Strategy Formulation Research: A Resource-based Analysis." In P. Shrivastava, A. Huff, and J. Dutton, eds., *Advances in Strategic Management,* vol. 8, pp. 39–62. Greenwich, Conn.: JAI Press.

Chakravarthy, B. S. (1986). "Measuring Strategic Performance." *Strategic Management Journal* 7: 437–458.

Chakravarthy, B. S. (1996). "Flexible Commitments." *Strategy and Leadership* 24: 14–20.

Chakravarthy, B. S. (1997). "A New Strategy Framework for Coping with Turbulence." *Sloan Management Review* 38(2): 69–82.

Chakravarthy, B. S. (2004). "Regaining Relevance Lost." In S. W. Floyd, J. Roos, C. D. Jacobs, and F. W. Kellermanns, eds., *Innovating Strategy Processes,* pp. 247–251. London: Blackwell.

Chakravarthy, B. S., and Bourgeois, H. (2004). "Best Buy: Staying at the Top." IMD Case 3-1430.

Chakravarthy, B. S., and Gargiulo, M. (1998). "Maintaining Leadership Legitimacy in the Transition to New Organizational Forms." *Journal of Management Studies* 35(4): 437–456.

Chakravarthy, B. S., and Jha, A. (2003). "Dr. Reddy's Laboratories: Chasing a Daring Vision." IMD Case 3-1234.

Chakravarthy, B. S., Lorange, P., and Cho, H. (2002). "The Growth Imperative for Asian Firms." *Nanyang Business Review* 1(1).

Chakravarthy, B. S., McEvily, S. K., Doz, Y., and Rau, D. (2003). "Knowledge Management and Strategic Advantage." In M. Easterby-Smith and M. A. Lyles, eds., *Blackwell Handbook of Organizational Learning and Knowledge*. London: Blackwell.

Chakravarthy, B. S., and Thompson, S. (2003). "Pearson: Not Content to Be a Content Company." IMD Case 3-1100.

Christensen, C. M. (1997). *The Innovator's Dilemma: When New Technologies Cause Great Firms to Fail*. Boston: Harvard Business School Press.

Cyert, R. M., and March, J. (1963). *A Behavioral Theory of the Firm*. Englewood Cliffs, N.J.: Prentice-Hall.

Dierickx, I., and Cool, K. (1989). "Asset Stock Accumulation and Sustainability of Competitive Advantage." *Management Science* 35(12): 1504–1511.

Doz, Y., Santos, J., and Williamson, P. (2001). *From Global to Metanational: How Companies Win in the Knowledge Economy*. Boston: Harvard Business School Press.

Fiol, C. M., and Lyles, M. A. (1985). "Organizational Learning." *Academy of Management Review* 10(4): 803–813.

Friedman, D. D., Landes, W. M., and Posner, R. A. (1991). "Some Economics of Trade Secret Law." *Journal of Economic Perspectives*, 5: 61–72.

Galunic, D. C., and Rodan, S. (1998). "Resource Recombination in the Firm: Knowledge Structures and the Potential for Schumpeterian Innovation." *Strategic Management Journal* 19(12): 1193–1201.

Ghemawat, P. (1991). *Commitment: The Dynamic of Strategy*. New York: Free Press.

Gioia, D. A., and Poole, P. P. (1984). "Scripts in Organizational Behavior." *Academy of Management Review* 9: 449–459.

Hamel, G., and Prahalad, C. K. (1989). "Strategic Intent." *Harvard Business Review* 67: 63–76.

Hamel, G., and Prahalad, C. K. (1994). *Competing for the Future*. Boston: Harvard Business School Press.

Hedberg, B. L. T. (1981). "How Organizations Learn and Unlearn." In P. Nystrom and W. Starbuck, eds., *Handbook of Organizational Design*. Oxford: Oxford University Press.

Hedlund, G., and Nonaka, I. (1993). "Models of Knowledge Management in the West and Japan." In P. Lorange, B. Chakravarthy, J. Roos, and A. Van de Ven, eds., *Implementing Strategic Processes: Change, Learning, and Co-operation*, pp. 117–144. Oxford: Blackwell Business.

Leonard-Barton, D. (1992). "Core Capabilities and Core Rigidities: A Paradox in Managing New Product Development." *Strategic Management Journal* (special issue, *Strategy Process: Managing Corporate Self-Renewal*) 13: 111–127.

Levitt, B., and March, J. (1988). "Organizational Learning." *Annual Review of Sociology* 14: 319–340.

MacMillan, I., McCaffery, M., and Van Wijk, G. (1985). "Competitors' Responses to Easily Imitated New Products—Exploring Commercial Banking Product Introductions." *Strategic Management Journal* 6: 75–86.

March, J.G. (1991). "Exploration and Exploitation in Organizational Learning." *Organization Science* 2: 71–87.

McCaskey, M. B. (1982). *The Executive Challenge: Managing Change and Ambiguity.* Boston: Pittman.

McEvily, S., and Chakravarthy, B. S. (2002). "The Persistence of Knowledge-Based Advantage: An Empirical Test for Product Performance and Technological Knowledge." *Strategic Management Journal* 23(4): 285–305.

Nelson, R., and Winter, S. (1982). *An Evolutionary Theory of Economic Change.* Boston: Belknap Press of Harvard University Press.

Nonaka, I. 1994. "A Dynamic Theory of Organizational Knowledge Creation." *Organization Science,* 5: 14–37.

Nonaka, I., and Takeuchi, H. (1995). *The Knowledge-Creating Company: How Japanese Companies Create the Dynamics of Innovation.* New York: Oxford University Press.

Prahalad, C. K., and Hamel, G. (1990). "The Core Competence of the Corporation." *Harvard Business Review* May-June: 79–91.

Reed, R., and DeFillippi, R. J. (1990). "Causal Ambiguity, Barriers to Imitation, and Sustainable Competitive Advantage." *Academy of Management Review* 15(1): 88–102.

Reitman, W. R. (1964). "Heuristic Decision Procedures, Open Constraints, and the Structure of Ill-defined Problems." In M. Shelly and G. Bryan, eds., *Human Judgments and Optimality,* pp. 282–315. New York: Wiley.

Spender, J. C. (1996). "Making Knowledge the Basis of a Dynamic Theory of the Firm." *Strategic Management Journal* 17 (special issue): 45–62.

Szulanski, G. (1996). "Exploring Internal Stickiness: Impediments to the Transfer of Best Practice within the Firm." *Strategic Management Journal* 17(Winter special issue): 27–43.

Teece, D. J., Pisano, G., and Shuen, A. A. (1997). "Dynamic Capabilities and Strategic Management." *Strategic Management Journal* 18(7): 509–533.

Von Hippel, E. (1988). *Sources of Innovation.* New York: Oxford University Press.

Zander, U., and Kogut, B. (1995). "Knowledge and the Speed of Transfer and Imitation of Organizational Capabilities: An Empirical Test." *Organization Science* 6(1): 76–92.

Glossary

active empathy Empathy is the attempt to put yourself in the shoes of the other, understanding his or her particular situation, interests, skill level, successes, failures, opportunities, and problems. Active empathy means that you proactively seek to understand the other. You care for the other through active questioning and alert observations: you practice conversational dialogue rather than advocacy, taking a listening and questioning attitude. Since there are numerous barriers to dealing with emotional issues in an organization, a broad acceptance of the emotional lives of others is crucial for establishing good working relationships—and good relationships, in turn, lead to effective knowledge creation. (*chapter 6*)

ambiguity Ambiguity is one of the conditions that enhances the knowledge-creation process, since it evokes fluctuation which triggers organization members' creativity. Fluctuation is a condition in which individuals or members of an organization expand their understanding when facing changes, gaps, or uncertainty. Ambiguity can prove useful, at times, not only as a source of a new sense of direction, but also as a source of alternative meanings and a fresh way of thinking about things. On the other hand, however, causal ambiguity—that is, inadequate understanding of the reasons for the success or failure of a practice—can be one of the most important barriers to the internal transfer of a best practice. (*chapter 4*)

analogy An analogy is a method of clarifying how two ideas or objects are alike and not alike. In this respect, analogy is an intermediate step between pure imagination and logical thinking. It is much more structured than a metaphor in making a distinction between two ideas or objects. Analogies are often used in a dialogue conducted to articulate tacit knowledge.

ba *Ba* (place, field) means the right context—one that fosters emerging relationships within microcommunities, across group boundaries, throughout an organization, whatever it takes to unleash tacit knowledge. *Ba* is essentially a shared space that serves as a foundation for knowledge creation. The concept of *ba* unifies the physical spaces, virtual spaces, and mental spaces involved in knowledge creation. (*chapter 1*)

barriers to knowledge creation Individual and organizational barriers are inherent in knowledge creation: lack of understanding, lack of agreement, lack of a common language, company myths, failure stories, and rigid procedures. Many barriers to knowledge creation crop up regardless of managerial style, simply because the process depends so much on the vagaries of human relationships and differing intellectual capabilities. As for organizational barriers, there are four severe barriers to knowledge creation in a group setting: (1) the need for a legitimate language, (2) organizational stories, (3) procedures, and (4) company paradigms. (*chapters 4 and 5*)

black-boxed know-how and technologies *See* KNOWLEDGE PROTECTION.

care To care for others is to help them learn; to increase their awareness of important events and consequences; to nurture their personal knowledge while sharing their insights. The concept of care matters most in an organization when those in charge provide a context in which knowledge is created and shared freely. The five dimensions of mutual trust—active empathy, access to help, lenience in judgment, and courage—enhance a high level of care in organizational relationships; if they are lacking, relationships are characterized by a low level of care. Knowledge creation can take very different paths, depending on the extent to which care is present. Under the condition of low care, a process of seizing characterizes individual knowledge creation, and most social knowledge creation occurs through transacting. In other words, individuals try to seize knowledge from others without sharing it with others and knowledge creation is formed in transactions (trading in business relationships or interests). When care is high, however, knowledge-creation processes reflect strong relationships. Individuals create knowledge through bestowing their insights, and groups will create social knowledge through what we call indwelling. *See also* IN-DWELLING. (*introduction*)

chaos   Chaos is a condition in which our habitual, comfortable state of being is interrupted and we are given an opportunity to reconsider our fundamental thinking and perspective. Chaos is generated naturally when the organization faces a real crisis, such as a rapid decline of performance due to changes in market needs or significant growth of competitors. It also can be generated intentionally when the organization's leaders try to evoke a "sense of crisis" among organizational members by proposing challenging goals. This intentional chaos, called "creative chaos," increases tension within the organization and focuses the attention of its members on defining the problem and resolving the crisis. The benefits of "creative chaos," however, can be realized only when organization members have the ability to reflect upon their actions. Without reflection, chaos, rather than enabling knowledge creation, tends to lead to "destructive" chaos. (*chapter 1*)

combination   Combination is a process of systematizing concepts into a knowledge system. This mode of knowledge conversion involves combining different bodies of explicit knowledge. Individuals exchange and combine knowledge through such media as documents, meetings, telephone conversations, or computerized communication networks. Reconfiguration of existing information through sorting, adding, combining, and categorizing of explicit knowledge (as conducted in computer databases) can lead to new knowledge. Knowledge creation carried out in formal education and training at schools usually takes this form. An MBA education is one of the best examples. In a business context, the combination mode of knowledge conversion is most often seen when middle managers break down and operationalize corporate visions, business concepts, or product concepts. At the top management level of an organization, this mode is realized when midrange concepts (such as product concepts) are combined with and integrated into grand concepts (such as corporate vision) to generate a new meaning of the latter. *See also* SECI MODEL. (*chapter 1*)

communication   Communication—sharing or exchanging information or ideas—is an indispensable action for organizational knowledge creation, and its importance is boundless. Appropriate communications in response to situations are necessary, and managing communication is one of the most important tasks for managers in business organizations. Through the organizational knowledge creation process, communication is practiced under various conditions (e.g., face-to-face or in cyberspace) and in diverse ways (e.g., conversation, dialogue, imitation, observation). (*chapter 3*)

community Communities are naturally forming social organisms characterized by common interest and generalized mutual aid, rather than any particular productive aim. In contrast, a team is a mandated work group with a specific productive goal. In communities, people share their own experiences. Sharing experiences with colleagues in the organization is the first process of organizational knowledge creation. In a community, individual knowledge might be tacitly shared, as the example of community of practice shows. Sharing tacit know-how in the apprentice system is a concrete example of a community of practice. Communities for sharing knowledge can be created virtually. Discussion forums on the Web can also function as a community for knowledge- and experience-sharing. Creating and using virtual as well as real communities is especially useful for companies that operate in more than one geographical region. (*chapters 6, 8, and 15*)

community of practice In communities of practice, people exchange ideas and learn together. Members of a group learn through participating in the practices of that group and by gradually memorizing jobs—as in an apprenticeship system. It differs from an enabling context in that a community of practice is a place in which members learn knowledge that is embedded there, and its boundaries are firmly set by the task, culture, and history of that community. Membership in a community of practice is fairly stable, and it takes new members time to become full participants. (*chapters 4 and 15*)

concept justification Concept justification is the process of determining whether newly created concepts are truly worthwhile for the organization and society; it is similar to a screening process. Since knowledge is defined as justified true belief, new concepts created by individuals or teams need to be justified at some point in the knowledge-creating process. Unlike individuals, organizations must conduct justification in a more explicit way to check whether the organization's intention is still intact and to ascertain if the new concepts meet the needs of customers or society at large. The most appropriate time for the organization to conduct this screening process is right after the concepts have been created. (*chapter 6*)

context Context is the set of circumstances that provides sense to knowledge and information. Both information and knowledge are context-specific in that they depend on the situation and are created dynamically in social interaction among people. According to Berger and Luckmann (1966), people interacting in a certain historical and social context share information from which they construct social knowledge as a reality, which in turn influences their judgment, behavior, and attitude. (*chapters 1, 4, and 6*)

conversation   Conversation is the most natural and commonplace of human activities; at the same time, it is one of the best means for sharing and creating knowledge. Good conversations are the cradle of social knowledge in any organization. Through extended discussions, which can encompass personal flights of fancy as well as careful expositions of ideas, individual knowledge is turned into themes available for others. Each participant can explore new ideas and reflect on other people's viewpoints. And the mutual exchange of ideas, viewpoints, and beliefs that conversations entails, allows for the first and most essential step of knowledge creation: sharing tacit knowledge within a microcommunity. In productive microcommunities, conversations can unleash the creative powers of individual participants and fuel knowledge creation beyond the capabilities of a single mind. Conversations are an arena for creating social knowledge in contemporary business settings. Conversations that take place in business organizations usually have one of two basic purposes: they either confirm the existence and content of knowledge, or they aim to create new knowledge. (*chapters 6 and 15*)

creative fusion   The sources of needed know-how and expertise are often separated functionally, physically, geographically, and cognitively. But such diverse perspectives are essential for creativity. Such diversity enables creative abrasion—intellectual disagreements that help a group identify assumptions and avoid premature convergence on a particular solution. And if creative abrasion is well managed—that is, if debate is encouraged but also closed down at some point to enable progress—the result is creative fusion, the combination of different perspectives that leads to innovative products and services. In fact, creative fusion occurs when different mental worlds collide and then coalesce around an innovation. *See also* REQUISITE VARIETY. (*chapters 4 and 9*)

cross-leveling of knowledge   The interactive and spiral process does not end once an archetype has been developed. The new concept, which has been created, justified, and modeled, moves on to a new cycle of knowledge creation at a different organizational level, and is termed cross-leveling of knowledge. Organizational knowledge creation is a never-ending process that upgrades itself continuously. Cross-leveling of knowledge takes place both intraorganizationally and interorganizationally. Intraorganizationally, knowledge that is made real or that takes form as a certain level of organization (e.g., in a project team located in the United States) can trigger a new cycle of knowledge creation, expanding horizontally and vertically across the organization (e.g., in a project team located in Japan). And in intraorganizational cross-leveling, knowledge vision will act as a control mechanism on whether or not knowledge should be cross-fertilized within the company. Interorganizationally, knowledge created by the organization can mobilize knowledge of affiliated companies, customers, suppliers, competitors, and others outside the company through dynamic interaction.

dialectics According to Hegel, dialectics is the creation of a synthesis by reconciling thesis and antithesis or rejecting what is not rational and retaining what is rational. For Hegel, knowledge begins with sensory perception, which becomes both more subjective and more rational through a dialectic purification of the senses, and at last reaches the stage of self-knowledge of the "Absolute Spirit" (Russell, 1961). In organizational knowledge creation theory, dialectics instills a creative way of thinking in the organization, and can raise the quality of dialogue among team members in the concept creation phase. (*chapter*

dialogue In dialogue, people develop a shared context for getting knowledge from information that involves personal relationships. People discuss how to interpret facts, which facts are important, and why they are important. When people share information, they ask questions, provide examples, and make predictions about implications. This dialogue increases tacit knowledge for each of them, especially when it is face-to-face. Dialogues tend to be more intensive and focused than conversations because they usually center on a specific problem or issue, with the purpose of finding a solution. (*chapters 1, 5, and 8*)

east/west dichotomy Two opposed approaches to organizational knowledge creation are those between Western and Japanese (Eastern) companies. Epistemologically, Westerners tend to emphasize explicit knowledge, and the Japanese tend to stress tacit knowledge. Ontologically, Westerners are more focused on individuals, while the Japanese are more group-oriented. (*chapter 1*)

embedded knowledge Companies are arranged along a continuum of knowledge intensity. At the low end are companies with simple products or services (e.g., fast-food chains, companies manufacturing and selling glass jars and other containers). At the high end are companies that sell knowledge (e.g., consulting and law firms, software developers, and biotech research companies). It is these firms for which embedded knowledge is most critical. Developing the knowledge is what leads to competitive and financial success in these knowledge-intensive companies. Knowledge that exists in a certain place is called embedded knowledge. A company with a high level of knowledge is a good example of the place where knowledge is embedded. Only those who belong to the place (or community) can learn and use this knowledge. (*chapters 4 and 7*)

East/West Dichotomy

	European Style	Japanese Style
Objective	Pursuit of superior performances	Adaptation to changing needs
Product appeal	Function (e.g., high-speed performance)	Image and quality
Product concept creation	Clear-cut decision at the initial stage, adhered to throughout the ensuing stages	Vague at the initial stage, modified and altered in ensuing stages in accordance with changes in needs
Flow of activities	Sequential approach	Overlapping approach
Ensuing process	Specific design targets fixed at the initial stage are pursued under a strict division of labor	Close coorperation among all departments concerned during the development
Organization	Organization according to function and often under a project leader with limited authority	Matrix- or project-team-type organization under a project leader with authority over the entire process from planing to production to sales
Strengths	Conducive to a relentless pursuit of superior performance, function, and high quality	Shorter lead time (3–4 years), high quality, and attuned to needs in the market
Weaknesses	Longer lead time (7–8 years), high development costs	Risk of compromise on a low level; not conducive to an all-out pursuit of surperior performance

empathic design   Empathic design is the creation of product or service concepts based on a deep (empathic) understanding of unarticulated user needs. It can be deployed to augment the development of product enhancement, and its techniques are most useful in the process of creating new product concepts. There are three important characteristics that set empathic design apart from other forms of market research: (1) The product concept is based on observed customer behavior (versus espoused behavior, self-reported behavior, or opinions). (2) Empathic design is usually conducted through *direct interaction* between those who have a deep understanding of the firm's technological capabilities (product developers such as engineers and designers) and the product users. (3) Empathic design tends to draw on existing technological capabilities that can be redirected or imaginatively deployed in the service of new products or markets. (*chapter 9*)

enabler   Enablers are slogans that put knowledge-enabling into practice. They help to increase dissemination of information throughout an organization and to dismantle the barriers to communication. The enabler connects most closely with relationships and care in the organization. Five knowledge enablers are "Instill a Vision," "Manage Conversations," "Mobilize Activists," "Create the Right Context," and "Globalize Local Knowledge" (Von Krogh, Nonaka, and Ichijo, 2000). (*chapter 6*)

enabling   Knowledge-enabling is a set of organizational activities that positively affect knowledge creation. It includes facilitating relationships and conversations, as well as sharing local knowledge across an organization or beyond geographic and cultural borders. At a deeper level, however, it relies on a new sense of emotional knowledge and care in the organization. This concept comes out of the idea that controlling and managing knowledge creation is almost impossible because of its fragility. This enabling concept supports knowledge creation and emphasizes that the relationships in the organization are the most important factor in knowledge creation. (*chapter 6*)

enabling context   An enabling context is a shared space that fosters emerging relationships: a place in which knowledge is shared, created, and used. An enabling context is not necessarily a physical space. Rather, it combines aspects of physical space (such as the design of an office or dispersed business operations), virtual space (e-mail, intranets, teleconferences), and mental space (shared experiences, ideas, emotions). It is a network of interactions determined by the care and trust of participants, and can be changed easily. The members of an organizational who interact in an enabling context come and go, so it has a here-and-now quality that can spark real innovation. *See also* BA. (*chapters 1 and 6*)

epistemology in the Japanese perspective   Three traits—oneness of humanity and nature, oneness of body and mind, and oneness of self and other—have formed the foundation of the Japanese view of epistemology. Oneness of humanity and nature creates an essential epistemological pattern for the Japanese to think visually and manipulate tangible images, and gives them a flexible view of time and space. Oneness of body and mind reflects the Japanese view that knowledge means wisdom, which is acquired from the perspective of the entire personality. Japanese epistemology tends to value the embodiment of direct, personal experience. And oneness of self and other is related to the Japanese view that human relationships are collective and organic. It is within this context of an organic worldview that the Japanese emphasize subjective knowledge and intuitive intelligence. Therefore, the Japanese perspective is tactile and interpersonal. (*chapter 1*)

epistemology in the Western perspective   In Western epistemology there has long been a tradition separating the subject who knows from the object that is known. Rationalism and empiricism are two great epistemological traditions in Western philosophy. The former argues that true knowledge is not the product of sensory experience but of some ideal mental process. In this view, knowledge can be attained deductively by appealing to mental constructs such as concepts, laws, or theories. In contrast, empiricism claims that there is no a priori knowledge and that the only source of knowledge is sensory experience. In this view, knowledge is derived inductively from particular sensory experience. Despite the fundamental differences between the two approaches, Western philosophers have generally agreed that knowledge is "justified true belief." Westerners have a sequential view of time, and grasp the present and forecast the future in a historical retrospection of the past. Western epistemology tends to accord the highest values to abstract theories and hypotheses that have contributed to the development of science. (*chapter 1*)

explicit knowledge   Explicit knowledge can be expressed in words and numbers, and is easily communicated and shared in the form of hard data, scientific formulas, codified procedures, or universal principles. In the view of the organization as a machine for information- processing, which is deeply ingrained in the traditions of Western management, it is necessary that knowledge be explicit—formal and systematic. (*chapter 1*)

externalization   Externalization is a process of articulating tacit knowledge into explicit concepts. It is a quintessential knowledge creation process in that tacit knowledge becomes explicit in the forms of metaphors, analogies, concepts, hypotheses, or models. This mode of knowledge conversion is typically seen in the process of concept creation, and is triggered by dialogue or collective reflection. A concept is frequently created by combining deduction and induction. *See also* SECI MODEL. (*chapter 1*)

globalizing local knowledge   Globalizing local knowledge indicates dissemination across many organizational levels; in other words, its main purpose is to spread knowledge organizationally. It emphasizes breaking down the physical, cultural, organizational, and managerial barriers that often prevent effective knowledge transfer in a multinational corporation. The ultimate goal of globalizing local knowledge must be to enhance the capacity for social action, competence, and successful task performance. The process includes three phases: triggering, packaging/dispatching, and re-creating. Companies globalize local knowledge when they leverage their locally developed knowledge (i.e., collect and disseminate for use throughout their organization knowledge developed in their local offices, branches, factories, marketing units, and other divisions. (*chapter 13*)

hegemonic effect   One company or a group of companies (A) with the only source of particular tacit knowledge engages in knowledge-sharing with another company (B) based on expected returns; when those returns are satisfactory for A, future transactions with other companies (C) to achieve similar returns are avoided. This typically happens when suppliers work closely with customers, tapping their tacit knowledge in order to provide future solutions to customers' problems. Once a company has successfully shared tacit knowledge with a given supplier, it is unlikely to continue such exchanges with other firms. (*chapter 8*)

indwelling   Indwelling is about commitment to an idea, to an experience, to a concept, or to a fellow human being. In developing shared tacit knowledge, the challenge for individuals in a microcommunity is to shift from a commitment to one's own interest to that of the group. A high-care organization allows for the expression of emotions, "fuzzy" logic, and ideas that are not rigidly specified; and individuals will share their tacit knowledge at the same time they refine it. They will create knowledge while bestowing it on others, and their colleagues will do the same. Rather than trying to deal with a task alone, the individual will aim for maximum leverage of other people's knowledge. This process of mutual bestowing of knowledge leads to the kind of social knowledge creation that is the source of radical innovations: indwelling. An authoritative source for the term is in Polanyi and Prosch (1975), who suggest that indwelling is a concept that can be understood as a dramatic shift of perspective: from looking at the concept to looking with others at the concept.

information and data   Information is data put in context; it is related to other pieces of data. As Gregory Bateson notes, "Information is a difference, which makes a difference" (Bateson, 1973, 1979). Information is about meaning, and it forms the basis for knowledge. (*chapter 1*)

information technology   Information technology is helpful, perhaps indispensable, in modern corporations. Effective use of information technology makes knowledge-sharing speedy and broad-based. This infrastructure provides an electronic knowledge space or cyber *ba* for firms; however, firms cannot rely only on information technology to generate knowledge or innovations. (*chapter 7*)

innovation   The essence of innovation is to re-create the world according to a particular ideal or vision. And the creation of new knowledge is as much about ideal as it is about ideas. Thus, innovation is not just about putting together diverse bits of data and information. It is a highly individual process of personal and organizational self-renewal. The personal commitment of the employees, and their identity with the company and its mission, become indispensable. (*chapters 3, 8, and 16*)

internalization Internalization is a process of embodying explicit knowledge into tacit knowledge. Members of an organization have a deeper understanding of newly created organizational knowledge (its process, its justification criteria, a new paradigm supporting the new knowledge), thus internalizing that knowledge. This mode of knowledge conversion is carried out through re-experience, sharing a mental model, or learning by doing. For explicit knowledge to become tacit, it helps if the knowledge is verbalized or diagrammed into documents, manuals, or oral stories. Documentation helps individuals to internalize what they experience, thus enriching their tacit knowledge. In addition, documents or manuals facilitate the transfer of explicit knowledge to other people, thereby helping them experience the experiences of others indirectly. *See also* SECI MODEL.

IT and knowledge management Contemporary knowledge management tends to rely on easily detectable, quantifiable information. Thus firms often mistake building a sophisticated information system for knowledge management. If knowledge equals information, much of this makes sense, and information technology becomes the key enabler. However, unlike information, knowledge is not always detectable; it is created spontaneously, often unpredictably. Therefore, storing knowledge and transferring it electronically from one part of the company to another is difficult. Information systems are of limited usefulness in facilitating a group's commitment to a concept, sharing emotions tied to tacit experience, or embodying the knowledge related to a certain task. (*chapter 7*)

justification criteria Criteria to justify new concepts through checking whether they follow organizational intentions and meet the needs of society at large are called justification criteria in the theory of organizational knowledge creation. The normal justification criteria for business organizations include cost, profit margin, and so on. But justification criteria can be both quantitative and qualitative. They need not be strictly objective and factual; they can also be judgmental and value-laden. Organizational intention is the most important criterion. (*chapter 6*)

kata The word *kata* means "model way." It includes both explicit and tacit knowledge, and understanding it is very difficult. There are no clear judging criteria for *kata*, and pursuing excellency of *kata* (skill) is a never-ending journey. The same thing can be said of companies; they have their own model (*kata*) that is appropriate for knowledge creation. And companies owning *kata* are competitive. "The Toyota Way" is a good example of a company's *kata*. It combines explicit and tacit knowledge among its workers in the unique way that Toyota has developed over the decades. In order to learn *kata* such such as "the Toyota Way," people need hands-on coaching on the job; this takes much time, so long-term human resources development is important for companies. (*chapters 1 and 8*)

know-how, know-what, know-who, know-why   Know-how is the contextually based, interdependent, and noncodified tacit knowledge that must be built in its own context. It puts explicit knowledge to work. Know-what is explicit knowledge that can be codified, for example in a manual, a patent, a description, or a set of instructions. Know-how is skill-based processes; know-what is facts; know-who is interpersonal networks as well as information about who knows what in an organization (e.g., a company's Yellow Pages); and know-why is cause-and-effect relationships. (*chapter 4*)

knowledge   Knowledge is justified true belief, individual and social, tacit and explicit. An individual justifies the truthfulness of his or her beliefs based on observations of the world; these observations, in turn, depend on a unique viewpoint, personal sensibility, and individual experience. Therefore, when somebody creates knowledge, he or she makes sense out of a new situation by holding justified beliefs and committing to them. Under this definition, knowledge is a construction of reality rather than something that is true in any abstract or factual way; it is a uniquely human process that cannot be reduced or easily replicated. Groups of people, as well as individuals, hold tacit and explicit knowledge that allows for competent collective action. (*chapter 1*)

knowledge activists   Knowledge activists are the knowledge proselytizers of the company, spreading the message to everyone. They are essential for cross-leveling of knowledge, since they are responsible for energizing and connecting knowledge creation efforts throughout a company. Knowledge activists play three roles—catalysts, coordinators, and anticipators of the future value of knowledge—and serve six purposes: (1) initiating and focusing knowledge creation; (2) reducing the time and cost necessary for knowledge creation; (3) leveraging knowledge creation initiatives throughout the corporation; (4) improving the conditions of those engaged in knowledge creation by relating their activities to the company's bigger picture; (5) preparing participants in knowledge creation for new tasks in which their knowledge is needed; and (6) including the perspectives of microcommunities in the larger debate on organizational transformation. (*chapter 6*)

knowledge-brokering   Knowledge-brokering can be defined as a process to connect individuals needing knowledge to sources of knowledge through personal mediation. Basically, the role of knowledge brokers is very similar to that of knowledge activists; the main difference is that knowledge brokers are formally assigned to this task. In some companies, knowledge brokers are called knowledge advisers. (*chapter 15*)

knowledge conversion Knowledge conversion is a social interaction between tacit knowledge and explicit knowledge that creates and expands human knowledge. Tacit knowledge and explicit knowledge are mutually complementary entities. They interact with and interchange with one another in the creative activities of human beings. This conversion is a social process between individuals and is not confined to an individual. Knowledge conversion gave rise to the SECI model. *See also* SECI MODEL. (*chapter 1*)

knowledge creation Knowledge creation differs from general knowledge management by its focus on the tacit dimension of knowledge. It can be defined as a discipline arising from the general field of knowledge management, and describes processes, tools, and techniques to provide organizations with new knowledge, and to engage in a process of knowledge socialization, combination, externalization, and internalization (Nonaka, Von Krogh, Voelpel, and Streb, 2005). (*chapter 1*)

knowledge-discarding Knowledge may become obsolete, for instance, when new technologies are developed or changes happen in the environment that make knowledge appropriate for the previous technologies or in the previous environment obsolete. In that case, members of the organization should not hesitate to discard old knowledge and start to create new knowledge that is appropriate in the new environment. However, old knowledge dies hard, especially in companies which have had a long history of using that knowledge successfully for gaining and sustaining competitive advantages. This issue is dealt with in the literature as "organizational forgetting" or "organizational unlearning." *See also* KNOWLEDGE MANAGEMENT. (*chapter 8*)

knowledge-exporting The more companies collaborate with other companies, the more knowledge can be exported to these partner companies. For example, in "design-in" in the automotive industry, suppliers are involved in the early phase of new car development so that appropriate parts are developed efficiently, effectively, and fast. Suppliers may thus get access to manufacturing know-how of a partner automotive company. In the export of knowledge outside the organization, therefore, suppliers cannot be ignored. Since knowledge constitutes the source of competitive advantage, companies should not forget to continue to create new knowledge in order to increase their knowledge-based competence. At the same time, they should examine what can be shared with business partners and what cannot. (*chapter 1*)

knowledge-importing   The "ability of a firm to recognize the value of new, external information, assimilate it, and apply it to commercial ends is critical to its innovative capabilities.... Successfully absorbing technological knowledge from beyond the periphery of the firm is as important a managerial activity as integrating it across internal boundaries.... Companies seek to acquire knowledge from outside when strategically important technical expertise is unavailable or inadequate internally" (Leonard-Barton, 1995).

knowledge management   Discussions of strategic management of knowledge assets tend to focus on creating and sharing the knowledge assets. However, a more holistic view of knowledge management is required. Holistic knowledge management consists of four main activities: creating, sharing, protecting, and discarding. *Creating*: Companies should be knowledge-creating, trying to generate new knowledge well ahead of competitors. *Sharing*: After successfully creating new knowledge within a company, it has to be shared among the firm's members across regions, businesses, and functions. *Protecting*: The firm's knowledge assets must be kept out of the hands of competitors. *Discarding*: Companies need to reflect on whether their knowledge is outdated. In some cases, it may be necessary to discard existing knowledge and promote new knowledge creation. Indeed, without discarding old knowledge, the creation of new knowledge is difficult to initiate.

knowledge managers and knowledge officers   Managers who direct the organization's knowledge creation process and have responsibility for the results are knowledge managers. They manage the process somewhat more removed from the daily operation, deciding which projects to create and fund, and establish the required management systems. The concept of the knowledge manager comes from the idea that knowledge is both a resource and an output, and is created by individuals and also by organizations.

Knowledge officers can be seen as the formal institution of knowledge managers. A knowledge officer is a manager who has an explicit responsibility for all dealings with knowledge in a company. Knowledge officers are usually fairly high-ranking executives—with the highest-ranking being called chief knowledge officers (CKOs)—and have a variety of duties: They can craft a company's vision for knowledge creation, set up knowledge management systems, implement information technology platforms, establish the value of the firm's intellectual capital, and design compensation systems that will push the development of expertise. Through these roles, the knowledge officer is responsible for maintaining stable knowledge management in a firm. (*chapters 2, 3, and 6*)

knowledge protection   Since knowledge is an important source of the competitive advantages of a firm, it must be protected. Such protection can include intellectual property rights and increasing the complexity of a product or service to make imitation by competitors difficult. Further measures include hiding precious corporate knowledge in a black box. An example would be intentionally avoiding the public articulation of a corporation's unique tacit knowledge. Since knowledge is created by talented managers, human resource management to retain them plays an important role in avoiding the outflow of knowledge from a firm. *See also* KNOWLEDGE MANAGEMENT. (*chapters 6, 8, and 16*)

knowledge reuse   Reuse of knowledge, one way of transferring knowledge within organizations, is essential for leveraging knowledge assets. It is essential in several situations. Perhaps the most obvious case is that of physically dispersed operations that must duplicate production processes for competitive, quality, or regulatory reasons. Local plants must duplicate every detail of the model plant. No change in the specification of a plant can be made without approval of a central corporate committee. Franchises such as McDonald's face a similar knowledge transfer challenge, since they must replicate the products and processes of the original business. (*chapters 4 and 7*)

knowledge-sharing   Sharing knowledge in an organization or a network is a trigger and a first step of knowledge creation. Knowledge tends to be local, sticky, and contextual; thus much of knowledge remains tacit. Therefore, when knowledge is shared interpersonally or in a network, it slowly moves from one individual to another through communication, especially face-to-face, and co-work such as conversation, discussion, or doing something together. In the theory of organizational knowledge creation, tacit knowledge is shared through the deep socialization of a project team or a microcommunity of knowledge, typically through direct observation, direct observation and narration, imitation, experimentation and comparison, and joint execution. *See also* KNOWLEDGE MANAGEMENT. (*chapters 3 and 6*)

knowledge transaction cost   When knowledge is shared across businesses, functions, and geographical regions, knowledge transaction costs emerge. When knowledge is not clearly articulated, the transaction cost is high. Therefore, companies should generate an effective infrastructure for sharing knowledge effectively and efficiently. Hard infrastructure, such as an IT-based knowledge-sharing system, is indispensable. However, if it is not accompanied by soft infrastructure, such as a culture of sharing knowledge across business boundaries and good social relationships among people working in different business, functional, and regional units, knowledge transaction costs will not be lowered despite the hard infrastructure. (*chapter 2*)

knowledge transfer Moving knowledge across organizational boundaries to provide sustainable competitive advantage throughout a company or organization is called knowledge transfer. In a process of knowledge transfer, knowledge that can be easily packaged for shipment is explicit knowledge, because tacit individual knowledge is more "sticky"; it usually remains with its local business unit. Therefore, it is necessary for receivers to understand the context in which packaged explicit knowledge (e.g., a document) is created. (*chapters 4 and 5*)

knowledge vision Knowledge vision is the vision that encompasses the types and contents of knowledge to be created, and thereby provides clear direction to members of the microcommunities within an organization. Thus, it is a supportive vision to knowledge creation firmly connected to an advancement strategy. The knowledge vision is more of an ongoing process than a written document; it is lived by everyone in the organization rather than formally codified. Labeling the streams of knowledge related to the vision in language easily understood by everyone in the organization is important. *See also* VISION. (*chapters 1, 6, and 8*)

knowledge worker Workers with knowledge acquired in higher education are called knowledge workers. They are the professional corps of engineers, scientists, medical doctors, writers, software designers, and other creative thinkers. In the field of management, as early as in 1959 Peter Drucker used the term "knowledge worker" for the first time, in his book *Landmarks of Tomorrow*, saying that knowledge workers play a major role in the knowledge society. The concept of knowledge worker is derived from the idea that knowledge is a resource which is owned by knowledge workers as a form of capital. As for the difference between a knowledge worker and a knowledge manager, the former is an owner and a user of his or her own knowledge, while the latter is a coordinator or a promoter of knowledge creation. (*introduction and chapter 7*)

knowledge-based competencies of a firm Competencies such as technological know-how, product design, marketing presentation, understanding of the customer, personal creativity, and innovation are intellectual and intangible. These knowledge-based competencies are the key resource of modern corporations. It is said that knowledge is the source of the highest-quality power: the economic and producing power of a firm lies more in knowledge than in its hard assets, such as land, plant, and equipment. (*introduction and chapter 8*)

language   It is said that language has two functions: as an instrument of communication and as a vehicle of thought. Language is essential for sharing knowledge and creating new concepts. Externalizing knowledge is implemented through expressing shared practices and judgments by means of language, and a common language is the basis for good knowledge flow. A figurative language using metaphors and analogies is useful for absorbing personal knowledge, and thus is particularly important for concept creation. (*chapters 4, 6, and 9*)

learning   According to Robert Reich, learning is the new coin of the realm in a knowledge-based economy. It is widely agreed that learning consists of two kinds of activities: obtaining know-how in order to solve specific problems based upon existing premises and establishing new premises to override existing ones. Knowledge creation happens when these two kinds of learning interact and form a dynamic spiral. *See also* SPIRAL OF ORGANIZATIONAL KNOWLEDGE CREATION. (*chapters 13 and 16*)

mental models   Johnson-Laird put forward the concept of "mental model," in which human beings create working models of the world by making and manipulating analogies in their minds (Johnson-Laird, 1983). Mental models such as schemata, paradigms, perspectives, beliefs, and viewpoints help individuals to perceive and define their world. Mental models thus represent cognitive tacit knowledge, and it is essential for knowledge creation to share individual mental models. However, mental models can be barriers to knowledge creation because they are fixed images or concepts within an individual or an organization, and thus are difficult to break when the market situation or the pattern of establishing competitive advantage changes. *See also* BARRIERS TO KNOWLEDGE CREATION. (*chapter 4*)

metaphors   A metaphor is a distinctive method of perception. It is a way for individuals grounded in different contexts and with different experiences to understand something intuitively through the use of imagination and symbols. No analysis or generalization is needed. Through metaphors, people put together what they know in new ways, and begin to express what they know but cannot yet say. Thus metaphors are highly effective in fostering direct commitment to the creative process in the early stages of knowledge creation. Metaphors make tacit knowledge expressible, and they are essential for externalization and creating concepts. (*chapter 9*)

microcommunity   A microcommunity is a small, productive work community to create knowledge. For new tacit knowledge to emerge through socialization, the group must be small: five to seven members. In a microcommunity, members have face-to-face interactions, and gradually get to know about each other's personalities, fields of interest, possible agendas, and forms of behavior. Tacit knowledge is shared between members through interactions, and good knowledge flow can occur in a community. A microcommunity of knowledge has more potential to evolve over time rather than being project- or deadline-driven; thus it will develop its own rituals, language, practices, norms, and values. *See also* BA. (*chapter 6*)

middle-up-down management   The management model of the knowledge creation process, which puts middle managers at the center of knowledge management, is called "middle-up-down management." It best communicates the continuous iterative process by which knowledge is created. Simply put, knowledge is created by middle managers, who are often leaders of a team or task force, through a spiral conversion process in which they take the initiative to involve both the top and the front-line (i.e., bottom) employees. This model is one of the most effective ways of managing creative chaos. It is enabled by positioning middle managers at the intersection of the vertical and horizontal flows of information within the company. (*chapter 1*)

organization theory and knowledge   The Western organizational theory developed on the basis of Barnard's attempt to synthesize the scientific and humanistic views of management (Barnard, 1938). The two streams pursued divergent paths, with the scientific approach advanced by the information-processing paradigm and the science of strategy, and the humanistic approach by the garbage can model, the theory of organizational sense-making, and studies of organizational culture. There seem, however, to be three shortcomings with this line of thought. First, most of these studies have not paid enough attention to the potential and creativity of human beings. Second, the human being, in most cases, is seen as an information processor, not as an information creator. And third, the organization is portrayed as passive in its relation to the environment, neglecting its potential to change and create. (*chapters 1 and 6*)

organizational arrangements for knowledge creation   In order to solve the problem of how companies create a coherent enabling context, one that fits both their knowledge vision and their business strategy, an organizational arrangement for knowledge creation is essential. The right context for knowledge creation must be accompanied by the right organizational structure. Since companies' strategic objectives sometimes compete with each other, it is not appropriate to pursue all of them by means of the same management or structure. Therefore, organizations should develop specific structural arrangements that can provide the right contexts for various objectives. In the theory of knowledge-enabling, four organizational structures are mentioned that correspond to strategic objectives: (1) a cross-divisional unit for risky but strategically very important projects (new business, new knowledge); (2) a task force for new product development; innovation independent of everyday operations (existing business, new knowledge); (3) a platform/virtual network for new business that depends on alliances or partnerships (new business, existing knowledge); and an empowered division for process innovation (existing business, existing knowledge). (*chapter 6*)

organizational culture   The concept of organizational culture is proposed in terms of a humanistic approach to management. Peters and Waterman (1982) stated that each excellent company has created its own unique "corporate culture," which determines how the company thinks and behaves; it is promoted by sharing of values among employees. Schein (1985) argued that culture is a learned product of group experience, while Pfeffer (1981) stressed the importance of beliefs. Organizational culture can be seen as consisting of beliefs and knowledge shared by members of the organization. In the theory of organizational knowledge creation, tacit knowledge forms one part of organizational culture when it is shared by organizational members. (*chapters 2 and 8*)

paradigms   A paradigm consists of shared goals, values, and norms of an organization that are coherent and constitute its worldview. Paradigms become ingrained in an organization; they define the themes talked about in management meetings, the language used, the key stories told, and the routines followed. Paradigms also determine the legitimacy of personal knowledge within an organization. Company paradigms can be the most fundamental and all-encompassing organizational barrier to knowledge creation; they have the power to make or break knowledge creation. When it becomes a barrier to knowledge creation, the mechanism is the same as a mental model. *See also* BARRIERS TO KNOWLEDGE CREATION; MENTAL MODELS. (*chapter 1*)

perspective Perspectives are views that influence individual knowledge; knowledge depends on an individual's perspective. Everything known to an individual is attached to a particular perspective of observation, so if people change their perspective, knowledge of a phenomenon also changes. Though changing perspectives is a natural function of human cognition for individuals, it is essential for a business organization to acknowledge that there is a range of perspectives among individual workers. If business organizations cannot acknowledge a wide range of perspectives—if they fix their perspective—it is difficult for their members to observe phenomena in new ways. In such a situation, perspectives are barriers to knowledge creation. *See also* BARRIERS TO KNOWLEDGE CREATION. (*chapters 4 and 6*)

product development Product development is knowledge creation in existing businesses; it is an innovation independent of daily operation. It must bring together representatives from a number of different functions and areas in an intensive yet flexible way, and their interactions create new knowledge in the form of new products. New product development often becomes a firm's main strategic objective. In this case, task forces or project teams are the structural arrangements that best enable knowledge creation. (*chapter 3*)

prototype The prototype is a tangible form of the concept, and it is achieved by combining existing concepts, products, components, and procedures with a new concept—in other words, combining new explicit knowledge with existing explicit knowledge. Building a prototype is a self-regulating, playful phase in which the participants assemble things at hand and make them into a new object without losing track of the original concept. (*chapter 6*)

recontextualization One of the most difficult challenges in bringing knowledge in from the outside is seeing its relevance in the first place. Knowledge becomes valuable because of its relationship to a particular context, and in order to bring it inside, the boundary spanner must identify the link between the knowledge and its context, separate the two, and anticipate the value of the recontextualization. Therefore, recontextualization means putting the knowledge back into the context of the firm in which it was created. To develop the ability to recontextualize and gain value from external knowledge management, managers must leverage their internal networks of social capital not only for straight transfer of knowledge, but also for dialogue about knowledge that may not seem immediately relevant. (*chapter 5*)

redundancy Redundancy is the existence of information that goes beyond the immediate operational requirements of an organization's members. In business organizations, redundancy refers to intentional overlapping of information about business activities, management, responsibilities, and the company as a whole. Sharing redundant information promotes the sharing of tacit knowledge, because individuals can sense what others are trying to articulate. In this sense, redundancy of information speeds up the knowledge creation process. Redundancy also spreads new explicit knowledge through the organization so that employees can internalize it. On the other hand, redundancy of information increases the amount of information to be processed, and can lead to the problem of information overload. (*chapter 1*)

relationships Relationships are important for knowledge-sharing and creation of an enabling context. In order to share personal knowledge, individuals must rely on others to listen and react to their ideas. Constructive and helpful relations enable people to share their insights and freely discuss their concerns. Thus, only through good relationships can the sharing of tacit knowledge happen, making such knowledge available to a larger group of people and creating an overall enabling context. Good relationships purge a knowledge-creation process of distrust, fear, and dissatisfaction, and allow organizational members to feel safe enough to explore the unknown territories of new markets, new customers, new products, and new manufacturing technologies. (*chapters 1, 13, and 15*)

requisite variety Internal variety within an organization that matches the variety and complexity of the environment in order to deal with challenges posed by the environment is called requisite variety. It helps to advance the knowledge spiral. The organization's members can cope with many contingencies if they possess the requisite variety, which can be enhanced by combining information differently, flexibly, and quickly, and by providing equal access to information throughout the organization. (*chapter 1*)

routine A routine generally is an unvarying or habitual method of procedure. Routines are the result of a satisfactory compromise among stakeholders in an organization, and they implicitly reflect the relative credibility and relative power of various categories of stakeholders. Thus, for example, over time teams develop rules and routines that limit the team's ability to deviate from preconceived directions of action and move into innovative new actions. (*chapters 1 and 7*)

SECI model   The fundamental model of the theory of organizational knowledge creation is the SECI model; SECI stands for the initials of four modes of knowledge conversion: socialization, externalization, combination, and internalization. In this model, knowledge originates in individuals who convert it into explicit knowledge and turn it into organizational knowledge through the four knowledge conversion phases: (1) from tacit knowledge to tacit knowledge, called socialization; (2) from tacit knowledge to explicit knowledge, or externalization; (3) from explicit knowledge to explicit knowledge, or combination; and (4) from explicit knowledge to tacit knowledge, or internalization. (*chapter 1*)

serendipity   Serendipity is the occurrence and development of events by chance, in a happy or beneficial way. In a business organization, it corresponds to unexpected technological discoveries or unexpected events that may affect development of a particular stream of knowledge. Companies should keep their knowledge vision open and flexible, and make the process one of feedback and learning, in order to accept the results of serendipity.

social capital   Social capital is the value that results from the intangible resources found in relationships between people. People can draw upon these relationships to help them achieve something of value to themselves. Individuals, teams, and organizations can all have social capital. Social capital is the set of assets in networks of personal relationships that can be valuable to achieve specific objectives. It exists entirely in relationships between parties. (*chapter 15*)

social network   Social networks are mutually beneficial connections over time. They are personal connections that go beyond business relationships. Individuals within them follow through by responding to people quickly, keeping commitments, and actively reciprocating by giving in order to receive. (*chapter 15*)

socialization   Socialization is a process of sharing experiences and thereby creating tacit knowledge such as shared mental models and technical skills. An individual can acquire tacit knowledge directly from others without using language. Apprentices work with their masters and learn craftsmanship not through language but through observation, imitation, and practice. In the business setting, on-the-job training uses basically the same principle. The key to acquiring tacit knowledge is experience. Without some form of shared experience, it is extremely difficult for one person to project herself or himself into another individual's thinking process. *See also* SECI MODEL. (*chapter 1*)

spiral of organization knowledge creation An organization cannot create knowledge by itself. It has to mobilize tacit knowledge created and accumulated at the individual level. This mobilized tacit knowledge is organizationally amplified in what is called the knowledge spiral, in which the interaction between tacit knowledge and explicit knowledge becomes larger in scale as it moves to higher knowledge levels. This spiral of organizational knowledge creation starts at the individual level and moves up through expanding communities of interaction, crossing sectional, departmental, divisional, and organizational boundaries. *See also* SECI MODEL. (*chapter 1*)

stickiness of knowledge "Stickiness of knowledge" is the difficulty of separating knowledge from its source. Some knowledge is extremely context-specific, and therefore not useful elsewhere. Knowledge can also be culturally sticky, in that the organizational culture does not encourage knowledge-sharing. Procedures, routines, and assumptions that are commonplace in one culture may be inappropriate, insensitive, or ineffective in another. (*chapter 4*)

story Stories, of which all organizations have various kinds, can become barriers to organizational knowledge creation. They constitute organizational memory or a commonsense understanding of how things work that allows individuals to regulate their own behavior. Such stories help people orient themselves in terms both of bonding with others (whom to bond with and when) and of understanding the organization's value system. Yet stories can be barriers to new knowledge creation, since they make it difficult for individuals to express contradictory ideas. Organizational stories and company myths can reject new knowledge and direct attention elsewhere. Stories may highlight the differences between new knowledge and knowledge that already exists, thereby making the new seem less legitimate. Therefore, organizational stories may be both enablers of and barriers to knowledge creation. *See also* BARRIERS TO KNOWLEDGE CREATION. (*chapter 4*)

strategy and knowledge creation   Placing knowledge creation as a part of a strategic framework is important for practice of an organization's knowledge creation. Creating new knowledge and effectively using the knowledge that already exists in an organization are core elements of business strategy. There are essentially two types of strategies: survival and advancement. Survival strategies secure current company profitability, focusing workers on rapid and effective knowledge transfer across the business. In contrast, advancement strategies emphasize future success and improved performance, which focus workers on creating new knowledge for future sustainable competitive advantage. Advancement strategies are necessary for knowledge-creating companies, yet a careful balance between advancement and survival strategies is important. When companies are getting started with knowledge creation, it is important to create an advancement strategy that explains the rationale for this process in terms of establishing new sources of competitive advantage and by broadly outlining how knowledge creation should happen in the company. (*chapter 8*)

tacit knowledge   Tacit knowledge is personal knowledge embedded in individual experience, and involves intangible factors such as personal belief and perspective, and the value system; it is not easily visible and expressible, and thus is hard to articulate with formal language and to communicate. Subjective insights, intuition, and hunches fall into this category. Tacit knowledge can be segmented into two dimensions. The first is the technical dimension, which encompasses the kind of informal and hard-to-pin-down skill or craft captured in the term "know-how." The second is the cognitive dimension, which consists of schemata, mental models, beliefs, and perceptions so ingrained that we take them for granted. (*chapter 1*)

trust   Trust is a foundation of the good relationship essential for knowledge creation. One person's trust in some ways compensates for the knowledge he or she lacks. Individuals cannot help others grow and actualize themselves unless they trust them to add value to their learning process. Trust is also reciprocal. In order to accept one person's help, the other person has to believe in his or her good intentions. (*chapters 6 and 15*)

uncertainty   The word "uncertainty" characterizes our current world. We are facing an economy in which the only certainty is uncertainty. Times of uncertainty often force companies to seek knowledge held by those outside the organization. Coping with uncertainty is a matter of life or death for companies, and knowledge involved with uncertainty is the key factor of management in this world of uncertainty. (*chapter 8*)

values   Individuals and organizations have their own value systems; and value systems create the criteria of justification for knowledge creation. In a knowledge creation process, this value system evaluates, justifies, and determines the quality of knowledge the company creates. An organization's value system is established as a knowledge vision by top management or by knowledge officers. *See also* JUSTIFICATION CRITERIA. *(chapters 1 and 8)*

vision   Vision is not only foresight about a future state, but also vision of one's present situation, since companies need to envision a future based on their current condition, and even on some sense of the past. A corporate vision presented as a strategy by a leader is organizationally constructed into knowledge through interaction with the environment by the corporation's members, which in turn affects the firm's future business behavior. *(chapters 1, 6, and 8)*

wisdom   Wisdom is required for a caring manager to understand and integrate the needs of workers. A caring manager must understand the needs of his or her group, the company, and society. He or she must integrate these needs in such a way that individuals can contribute to the creation of social knowledge while also learning and expending knowledge on their own. *(chapters 4, 6, and 8)*

References

Barnard, C. I. (1938). *The Functions of the Executive.* Cambridge, Mass.: Harvard University Press.

Bateson, G., (1973). *Steps to an Ecology of Mind.* London: Paladin Books.

Bateson, G., (1979). *Mind and Nature: A Necessary Unity.* New York: Bantam Books.

Berger, P. L., and Luckmann, T. (1966). *The Social Construction of Reality: A Treatise in the Sociology of Knowledge.* Garden City, N.Y.: Anchor Books.

Johnson-Laird, P. N. (1983). *Mental Models.* Cambridge, Mass.: Harvard University Press.

Leonard-Barton, D. A. (1995). *Wellsprings of Knowledge: Building and Sustaining the Sources of Innovation.* Boston: Harvard Business School Press.

Nonaka, I., and Takeuchi, H. (1995). *The Knowledge-Creating Company, How Japanese Companies Create the Dynamics of Innovation.* New York: Oxford University Press.

Peters, T. J., and Waterman, R. H. (1982). *In Search of Excellence: Lessons from American's Best-Run Companies.* New York: Harper & Row.

Pfeffer, J. (1981). "Management as Symbolic Action: The Creation and Maintenance of Organizational Paradigms." In L. L. Cummings and B. M. Staw, eds., *Research in Organizational Behavior,* vol. 3, pp. 1–52. Greenwich, Conn.: JAI Press.

Polanyi, M., and Prosch, H. (1975). *Meaning*. Chicago: University of Chicago Press.

Russell, B. (1961). *A History of Western Philosophy*. London: Unwin Hyman.

Schein, E. H. (1985). *Organizational Culture and Leadership*. San Francisco, Calif.: Jossey-Bass.

Von Krogh, G., Ichijo, K., and Nonaka, I. (2000). *Enabling Knowledge Creation: How to Unlock the Mystery of Tacit Knowledge and Release the Power of Innovation*. New York: Oxford University Press.

Index

Note: Page numbers in *italics* indicate figures or tables.

ARPA net, 203
Arrow, Kenneth, 5
artificial intelligence and expert systems, 99–100, 104
assimilation of local knowledge, 217–19
asynchronous meetings, 111
Athanassiou, Nicholas, 69–82
AT&T, 201, 208
attitudes, listening and questioning, 275
Augier, Mie, 198–212
AUO (AU Optronics), 136
AU Optronics (AUO), 136
Australia, R&D investment in, 183–85, *186–87*, 188–89, 192–94
automation
  of decision making, 99–100, 104–6, 108
  of dispute resolution, 105
  of structured transactions, *98*, 98–99
automotive industry, 178–79, *182*, 182–83. *See also* Toyota
autonomy, 28, 165–71, 172, 200, 244, 269. *See also* motivational solutions to social dilemma

ba (place)
  knowledge assets from, 25
  and knowledge creation process, 23–25
  leaders' development of, 28
  microcommunities and, 88, 276, 279, 284, 287, 290, 292
  overview, *18*, 23–25, 276
  Toyota's creation of, 88–89
  W. L. Gore's creation of, 243–44, 246, 248
Barnard, C. I., 293
Barney, J. B., 189
barriers to change, 13
barriers to knowledge creation
  mental models as, 292
  narrow relevance bandwidth, 217, 218, 219, 223, 225–26
  overview, 276, 294, 296, 297
  preconceived ideas, 22, 203, 294
barriers to knowledge imitation, 60, 137, 259–60, 297
barriers to knowledge transfer, 59–61, 63, 230–32, *231*, *238*
basic research, 200–201, 206, 210*n*2
Bateson, Gregory, 284
bathtub metaphor for value of R&D, 180
BBA (Bush Boake Allen), 155–56
beliefs, 258. *See also* knowledge; values
Bell Labs, 201–2, 205, 208

Berger, P. L., 278
Best Buy
  customer-centered initiative, 260, 265–66
  empowering midlevel managers, 269–70
  overview, 256, 269, 271–72
  reenvisioning process, 265–66
Bettis, R., 143*n*4
biotechnology industry, 185, 188–89, *190–91*, 206, 263
black-boxed know-how and technologies, 135, 137–38, 140–41
blogging, 108
boards of directors' information problems, 229–32, 236
Boer, P., 189
boundary-breaking sessions, 133–34
boundary spanners, 75, 79–80, 295
BPM (business process management), 106
brand equity, 151, 176, 192–93, 196*n*6, 266–67, *267*
Brazil, 6
BRICs (Brazil, Russia, India, and China), 6
British Petroleum, 252*n*10
broadband technology, 202–3
Brown, Hobson, Jr., 242–43
Brown, John Seely, 241
BT AdvisorSpace system, 99, 103–4
Büchel, Bettina, 44–56
Buckman Labs, 58, 130
Burt, Ron, 37
Bush Boake Allen (BBA), 155–56
Business 2.0, 37
business process management (BPM), 106

call center technology, 103–4, 107
Canon, 20
capital investment to R&D investment ratio, 178–79. *See also* R&D investment, empirical analysis of
capitalism, 198–99
capitalized development in software firms, 177
Capital One, 110–11
care, level of, 7, 171, 276, 299
career management, 222, 226
Carothers, Wallace, 202
Casey, Jim, 242
causal ambiguity, 60, 275
cause-and-effect relationships, 286
CEOs. *See* managers/management, senior

Cerf, Vinton, 203
CG silicon development, 137–38
Chakravarthy, Bala, 254–74
Chandler, Alfred, Jr., 91
change
 barriers to, 13
 to external environment, 5–6
 as impetus for advancement strategies,
  132
 mindset regarding relationships, 74–78
 in organizational norms, 243
 as requirement for spiral effect, 140–41
 technological, 210n1
 See also knowledge activists/activities
chaos, 250–51, 277, 292
chemical industry, 182, 182–83
Chesbrough, Henry, 206
chief knowledge officers (CKOs), 34–35,
 36–37, 41–42, 289
China, 6
Christenson, C. M., 268
Cisco Systems, 110
Citigroup, 4, 101, 105
citizenship behavior, 165
CKOs (chief knowledge officers), 34–35,
 36–37, 41–42, 289. See also
 managers/management, senior
Clarke, Dave, 113
clients. See customers
closed networks, 49–50, 50
cognitive association, 262
cognitive tacit knowledge, 143n4, 292,
 298
Cohen, Don, 240–53, 241
Cold War, 203–4
collaboration
 alliance arrangements, 76–77,
  125–26, 206, 267–68
 creative fusion from, 59
 in R&D, 206
collaboration model for work
 transactions, 98, 98–99
Collabrys, 154
collective/common good, 159, 161, 162,
 164–65, 168–70
collective cultures, 73
Collomb, Bertrand, 222
combination, 17, 22, 160–61, 277, 296
commitment
 active, from all members, 27–28
 flexible, 266–68, 267, 271
 indwelling, 276, 278, 284
 to justified beliefs, 15, 86–87, 258,
  278, 286
 via video connection, 252n10

common good, 161, 162, 164–65,
 168–70
communication
 electronic systems, 37–38, 53, 108,
  130, 278
 of experts with novices, 61, 65, 66
 with external contacts, 52–53, 76–78
 externalization of tacit knowledge,
  16–18, 283, 296
 of justification criteria, 94
 listening and questioning, 275
 managing, 87–89
 overview, 277
 and perception of procedural fairness,
  169–70
 and prosocial intrinsic motivation,
  170–71
 stories, 64, 130, 297
 technology improvements, 53, 108,
  130
 of values, beliefs, and business
  methods, 129
 of vision, 86–87, 90
 See also conversations; dialogue;
  language; relationships
communities
 conditional cooperation in, 170
 and knowledge spiral, 297
 microcommunities, 88, 276, 279,
  284, 287, 290, 292
 overview, 278
 perceived fairness in, 168–70
 and prosocial intrinsic motivation,
  164–65, 166–67, 168–71
 socially appropriate behavior, 171,
  242
 See also relationships
communities of practice, 241–42, 278
Compaq Computer, 207
competence, feelings of, 167–68
competency. See core competencies
competitive advantage
 gaining and sustaining, 8, 121, 126,
  128–30, 138
 and knowledge creation, 160–61
 overview, 141–42
 and problem with patents, 137
 profit centers versus, 163
 and R&D, 177, 201
 of Seven-Eleven Japan, 20
 sources of, 124, 127
 from survival and advancement
  strategies, 124, 126–27
 Toyota's, 128–29
competitive knowledge, 123, 124

monetary compensation, 36, 122–23, 166, 167–68, 171, 172
nature of, 15–16
perception of social relatedness, 168–71
and performance reviews, 36, 41, 66, 237
and performance support, 102–3, 106–9
problem-solving skills, 134–35
training expenses, 177
utilizing self-assertion and modesty, 21
See also incentives; knowledge workers; motivational solutions to social dilemma; socialization
enablers
creating the right context, 90–92
globalizing local knowledge, 92–93
instilling a knowledge vision, 86–87
leadership development as, 93–95
managing conversation, 87–89
mobilizing knowledge activists, 89–90
overview, 85–86, 281
role of, 83–85, *84*
enabling, 131, 282
enabling context, 85, 90–92, 282, 293
enjoyment-based intrinsic motivation, 164
environment
equitable, 247–48
overview, *18*, 26
reshaping, 14–15
stable versus uncertain, 132
epistemology, 15, 29, 217, 281, 282–83
equitable environments, 247–48, 251
equity, equality, and need, 168–69
essential dialogues, 21
ethnography and empathic design, 152–54
EVA (economic value added), 194
evolution
from assimilation to accommodation, 218–19
of i-mode service, 15–16
of industry, 125–26
of organization and environment, 26
evolutionary economists' theory, 13–14
eWorkforce initiative at Intel, 111
executive actions for corporate renewal, 264–71. *See also* managers/management, senior
existential questions, 21–22
expat flow, 222
experience-based knowledge, 155
experimental software, 108

experimenting and relevance bandwidth, 217, 218, 219, 223, 225–26, 262
expertise location systems, 37, 240
expert model for work transactions, *98*, 99, 101–2
expert systems and artificial intelligence, 99–100, 104
explicit knowledge
as common good, 161
converting to tacit knowledge, 22
and dialogue process, 22
ease of transfer, 61, 63–64, 290
internalizing into tacit knowledge, 285
and knowledge conversion, 17, 287
making knowledge vision into, 87
overview, *18*, 22, 283, 286
from personal relationships, 72
reconfiguration of, 277
sharing with external contacts, 70, 78–79, 80–81
Western emphasis on, *280*, 281
See also knowledge transfer; sharing knowledge; tacit knowledge
exporting knowledge to partner companies, 288. *See also* collaboration
external contacts/networks
assigning team members to, 53
early stages to maturity, 50–52, *51*
integrating, 78–81
leveraging, 70, 74–78, *75*
managing the interface, 52–53, 70, 78–81
overview, 48, 69–70, 78–81
productivity/network density balance, 48, 49–52, *50*, *51*
quality of, 70–74
synthesis with internal, 26
value of, 52
external environment, 5–6
externalization, 16–18, 283, 296. *See also* communication
external knowledge management, social capital for, 46–48, *47*, 70–74, 78
external partners, 41–42, 288. *See also* collaboration
extra-role behavior, 165
extrinsic and intrinsic motivation, 164–65

failures
admitting, 218
of boards of directors, 231
communities of practice, 241–42
methods for exiting quickly, 268
utilizing, 226

group knowledge, 35, 37, 38, 40–41, 270

groups
  commitment to interest of, 284
  communities of practice, 241–42, 278
  focus groups, 147
  incentives for, 40–41
  innovation and creative fusion, 59
  Intel's eWorkforce initiative, 111
  Japanese emphasis on, *280*, 281
  microcommunities, 88, 276, 279, 284, 287, 290, 292
  social power of, 242
  technology for, 97–98, 109–16, *111*
  tension in, 270–71
  thematic groups, 58
  See also *ba*; task force/project team structure; teams

growth
  acquisitions, 256, 261, 264, 267–68, 268
  and corporate transformation process, 254
  and knowledge-discarding, 142
  of sales, 184, *190–91*
  value chain premise and, 141, 256
  See also advancement strategies; corporate renewal; vision
guided experiences, 65–67
GVO, 153

Hand, J., 185
Hayek, F. A., 23
Healy, P., 185
Hegel, G.W.F., 280
Hegelian dialectic thinking, 21
hegemonic effect, 129–30, 284
Heidegger, M., 23
Hewlett-Packard, 242
high-care organizations, 276, 284
Highland Superstores, 265
Hippel, Eric von, 150, 155–56
Hitotsubashi University, 9
holistic knowledge management, 83–96, 85, 130–31, 142, 288. See also discarding knowledge; knowledge management; protecting knowledge assets; sharing knowledge; strategic management of knowledge; *entries starting with* "knowledge"
Holtshouse, Dan, 109, 116n3
Honda, 19, 21–22
Hong Kong, R&D investment in, 183–85, *186–87*, 188–89, 192–94

horizontal coordination across local units, 223
Howe, C., 185
HRM. *See* human resources management
hub and spoke management style, 225
human beings, 15–16, 293. *See also* employees; knowledge workers
human capital, 148–49, 176, 196n6
humanistic view of management, 293
human resources management (HRM)
  cool hunting, 155
  countering knowledge loss, 58–59
  differences between manual and knowledge workers, 160–61, 166
  and feedback processes, 167–68
  and international expansion, 220–21, 222, 224
  kata from, 286
  overview, 158, 172
  and pay for performance compensation, 166, 167–68, 171, 172
  prosocial preference in hiring, 170, 243
  See also incentives; knowledge workers; motivational solutions to social dilemma; protecting knowledge assets

IBM, 4, 40–41, 269
IBM Credit, 105
Ichijo, Kazuo, 3–10, 83–96, 121–45
IDC, 39
IDEO, 153
Idinopolus, Michael, 38
IKEA, 143n6
imagination, analogy and, 275
IM (instant messaging), 111, 112, 115
incentives
  advancement, 226, 241, 243, 248
  for knowledge-sharing by external sources, 70
  monetary, 36, 122–23, 166, 167–68, 171, 172
  and organization culture, 36–37
  positive career impact, 226
  profit-sharing and stock purchase plans, 247–48
  shifting from individuals to groups, 40–41
  structural, 162–63
  symbolic, 167–68
  See also motivational solutions to social dilemma

managers/management (*continued*)
  on independent board members, *231,*
    231–32
  and international expansion, 221
  longevity of, 241
  organizing intellectual confrontation
    in global arena, 224–25
managers/management, traditional
  actionable information, 126
  efficiency and productivity versus
    conversations, 245
  knowledge management versus, 7, 88
  pay for performance compensation,
    166, 167–68, 171, 172
  structural solutions to social dilemma,
    162–63
mandates for relationships, 74–75, *75*
manual workers' teamwork, 159–60
market positioning knowledge, 13,
    125–26, 138, *257*, 258, 260, 261.
    See also survival strategies
market research
  and corporate transformation,
    254–55, *255*
  developer/designer roles, 152–54,
    154–55
  empathic design from, 152, 281
  as justification process, 17
  limits of inquiry, 147–49
  metaphors and consensus mapping,
    151
  niche positioning, 138
  nontraditional, 149–52
  overview, 146–47, 156
  practice versus logical analysis, 22
  user roles, 154, 155–56
Marshall, Alfred, 5
Matsushita, 178
Maznevski, Martha, 69–82
McDonald's, 57
McEvily, Sue, 254–74
McKinsey company, 4
McKinsey Quarterly, 38
mental accommodation, 217–19
mental models, 203, 292, 294. *See also*
    barriers to knowledge creation
mental rehearsal, 218, 219, 221–23
mentorship. *See* socialization
mergers and acquisitions (M&A), 178,
    181
metaphor elicitation technique, 151
metaphors, 88, 151, 180, 292
microcommunities, 88, 276, 279, 284,
    287, 290, 292
Microsoft, 109

Microsoft Share Point, 38
middle managers, 27–28, 53, 90, 125,
    292
middle-up-down management, 27, 292
Mind of the Market Laboratory at
    Harvard Business School, 151
mission, defining, 22–23, 27
mistakes, well thought-out, 226. *See also*
    failures
monetary compensation, 36, 122–23,
    166, 167–68, 171, 172. *See also*
    incentives
motivational solutions to social dilemma
  autonomy of knowledge workers,
    166–67
  creating social relatedness, 168–71
  extrinsic motivation, 164
  fostering feelings of competence,
    167–68
  overview, 163, 172
  prosocial intrinsic motivation,
    164–65, 166–67, 168–71
  self-determination theory, 163–71
  structural, 162–63
Motorola, 152
multi-user domain (MUD), 61
Myers, S., 185

Nakano, Makoto, 176–97
narrow net versus wide net networks,
    74–75, *75*
NASDAQ, 183–84, 185
National Cooperative Research Act
    (1984), 206
natural science versus social science, 14
NCS, 261
NCS4School initiative, 261, 270–71
need, equity, and equality, 168–69
NEEDS (Nikkei Economic Electronic
    Databank System) database,
    181–82
Nelson, R., 25
neoclassical economic theory, 15
net operating profits after taxes
    (NOPAT), 194
networks
  closed, 49–50, *50*
  dense, 46, 49, *51*, 51–52
  electronic communication system for,
    130
  internal, 80
  interpersonal, 70–71, 286
  knowledge, 46, 49, *51*, 51–52, 58
  knowledge-brokers, 47–48, 287
  for new business, 293

wide net versus narrow net, 74–75, *75*
See also external contacts/networks;
relationships; social networks
neutrality and perception of fairness,
169–70
new technology. *See* technological
improvements
niche positioning, 138
Nikkei NEEDS (Nikkei Economic
Electronic Databank System)
database, 181–82
Nishida, Kitaro, 23, 24
Nokia, 222, 226, 252*n*9
Nonaka, Ikujiro, 3–10, 13–31, 33,
160–61, 258
NOPAT (net operating profits after
taxes), 194
Novartis, 40, 111
NYSE (New York Stock Exchange),
183–84

objectives
connecting knowledge management
to, 34–35, 41–42
driving objectives, *18*, 19–20
new product development as, 294
supportive structural arrangements
for, 24–25, 293
See also globalizing local knowledge/
learning; strategy; values; vision
objectivity and subjectivity, 16–17, 24–25
observation, 22–23, 65–66, 152–54. *See
also* customers; socialization
Ô coefficient, 196*n*3
O'Dell, Carla, 33, 109, 116*n*3
Ogilvey & Mather, 234
Ohlson, J., 194
Ollila, Jorma, 226
Olsson, P., 193
Olympus, 19
open innovation model, 206, 208
open style management, 225, 226, 246
Oracle, 122
order entry systems, 102
ordinary least squares. *See* R&D
investment, empirical analysis of
organic network of meanings, 24–25
organizational arrangements for
knowledge creation, 293
organizational barriers, 276
organizational capital, 176, 196*n*6
organizational culture
alignment pyramid, 234–35, *235*, 237
alliance arrangements, 76–77,
125–26, 206, 267–68

changes in norms, 243
citizenship behavior, 165
culture of innovation, 5–6, 95
firm politics, 238
and globalizing local knowledge, 93
incentives and, 36–37
and knowledge-sharing, 87, 240
overview, 293
perspective, 39–41
processes for globalizing local
knowledge, 216, 220, 222–23,
224, 225–26, 227
and prosocial motivation, 164–65
ratio of pay for least and most senior
members, 247–48
and scripts for action, 262–63
social aspects of, 36
transparency, 225, 226, 246
trust-building, 241–43
values within, 223
See also corporate renewal; human
resources management; incentives;
managers/management; values;
vision
organizational forgetting, 288. *See also*
discarding knowledge
organizational knowledge, cross-leveling,
140–41, 279–80, 287
organizational knowledge creation
theory, 280, 293
organizational power, balancing, 268
organizational structure, 91–92, 293.
See also strategic management of
knowledge
organizational unlearning, 288. *See also*
discarding knowledge
Orlikowski, Wanda, 34
Osterloh, Margit, 158–75
Oswald, D. R., 193
outside-in learning. *See* globalizing local
knowledge/learning
outsourcing R&D, 206

packaging/dispatching, 284
paradigms, 22, 203, 294
participation, 169
partner organizations, 41–42, 288
Partners HealthCare, 101–2
patents, 127, 137, 262–63
pay for performance versus prosocial
motivation, 166, 167–68, 171, 172.
See also incentives; motivational
solutions to social dilemma
PBR (price-to-book ratio), 181, 183–84,
185, 188, *190–91*, 193–95

and social capital, 17, 46–48, *47*,
    49–50, *50*
  user involvement, 154–56
  See also external contacts/networks;
    task force/project team structure
professional service firms, 233, 234.
    See also product/process/service
    development
profitability
  contemporary theories, 14
  importance of, 123, *124*, 143*n*5
  of intangible investments, 176–77,
    189, 192, 193
  inventory cost versus opportunity
    loss, 20
  and survival strategy, 298
  See also R&D investment
profit centers, 163
project teams. *See* task force/project team
    structure
Prosch, H., 284
prosocial intrinsic motivation, 164–65,
    166–67, 168–71. *See also*
    incentives; motivational solutions to
    social dilemma
protecting knowledge assets
  black-boxed know-how and
    technologies, 135, 137–38,
    140–41
  knowledge-building versus, 269–70
  knowledge leverage versus, 270–71
  and managing knowledge-based
    competence, 84
  overview, 142, 288, 289
  retaining personnel as, 121–23, *124*
  strategies for, 127–31, *259*, 259–61
  unique knowledge, 127–29,
    137–38
prototype, 294
Prusak, Laurence "Larry," 5, 32–43, 33,
    142*n*3, 241, 249–50
psychological constraints on knowledge
  accessibility, 40–41
psychological research, 149
public knowledge, 130
publicly held companies
  emphasis on profit versus social
    capital, 250–51
  governance of, 236–38
  shareholders' value, 179–83, *180*,
    182, 183–85, *186–87*, 188–89,
    192–94
publishing knowledge management
  information, 33
pure imagination, analogy and, 275

qualitative justification criteria, 286
qualitative market research, 149–52
quality movement, 42, 64–65
quantitative justification criteria, 286

RAND Corporation, 203
rationalism, 283
Rau, D., 259–60
RCA (Radio Corporation of America),
    135–36
R&D activity, 200–201
R&D and the economics of knowledge
  changing nature of R&D, 204–5
  "distributed" approach to industrial
    R&D, 205–7
  early developments in, 200–204
  industrial R&D expenditures by
    funding source, 208, *209–10*
  innovation and knowledge production
    activities, 199–200
  overview, 198–99, 207–8
  R&D value diagram, 179–80, *180*,
    188–89
R&D capability, 179–80, 189
R&D investment, 176–81, *180*
R&D investment, empirical analysis of
  of global firms, 183–85, *186–87*,
    188–89, 192–94
  of Japanese firms, 181–83, *182*
  knowledge-intensive industries, 185,
    188–89, *190–91*
  limitations to analysis, 196*n*6
  science-based industries, 185–88
  summary, 188–94
  valuation model, 194–95
R&D project stages, 189
receptors for comprehension, 61
reciprocity, norms of, 49, 167–68
reconfiguration of explicit knowledge,
    277
recontextualization, 79–80, 216,
    221–22, 295
recreating, 284
redundancy, 28, 295
regression results. *See* R&D investment,
    empirical analysis of
Reich, Robert, 291
relationships
  in enabling context, 93, 282
  individual equals firm aspect of, 78–79
  and intrinsic motivation, 170–71
  level of care, 276
  leveraging, 70, 74–78, *75*
  personal, 70–72, 170–71
  prioritizing, 94

relationships (*continued*)
quality of, 73–74, 233
at Sharp's Kameyama plant, 141
social capital in, 72–78, *75*, 296
with stakeholders, 70
tactics for building, 37–38
See also communication; external
contacts/networks; networks
relevance bandwidth, 217, 218, 219,
223, 225–26
remuneration process, 36, 166, 167–68,
171, 172. *See also* incentives
renewal. *See* corporate renewal
renewal of self, 25
replication, strategy of, 57–58
repositories, knowledge management,
100–101
requisite variety and creative fusion, 28,
59, 154, 279, 295. *See also* diversity
research, 200–201, 206. *See also* market
research; *entries beginning with*
"R&D"
residual income model (RIM), 180, 193,
195
residual income (RI), 195
resource-based theory, 13
resource conversion knowledge, 258,
261
response bias, 147
restructuring, 254–55, *255*. *See also*
corporate renewal
return on equity (ROE), 181–84, *182*,
188
return on investment capital (ROI/ROIC),
54–55, 189
reusing knowledge, 57–58, 79–80, 99,
289
revisioning process, 265–66, 271–72
RI (residual income), 195
rigidity as knowledge barrier, 60
RIM (residual income model), 180, 193,
195
ROE (return on equity), 181–84, *182*,
188
ROI/ROIC (return on investment capital),
54–55, 189
role-specific portals, 103–4
role-specific software, 103–4, 107–8
Roos, J., 125
Rousseau, D., 252n6
routines, 25, 296
rules of thumb, 64, 86
Russell Reynolds, 242–43
Russia, 6
Rustichini, A., 166–67

Salas, Alvarro, 246
sales growth, 184, *190–91*
Salomon Brothers, 234
sample surveys, 147
Samsung Electronics, 136–37
Sankyo, 178
satisfying relationships, 73–74, 80–81
scaling, 134
Scardino, Marjorie, 256
Schein, E. H., 293
Schön, D. A., 219
Schulze, Richard M., 265–66
Schumpeter, Joseph, 26, 198
science-based industries, R&D
investment in, 185, 188–89,
190–91, 202–4
scientific view of management, 293
SC Johnson Professional (SCJP), 153
scope "creep," 36–37
script for action, 262–63
search technology improvements, 37,
38, 39–40
SECI MODEL, 17, 160–61, 296
self-determination theory, 165–71
self-help educational programs, 261,
264
selfishness. *See* motivational solutions to
social dilemma
self-renewal through *kata*, 25
senior management. *See* managers/
management, senior
sensory perception, 280
serendipity, 296
servant leaders and leadership, 260
service firms, 234. *See also* product/
process/service development
Seven-Eleven Japan, 20, 22–23, 26
shared context in motion, 23–24
shareholders' value, 179–83, *180*, *182*,
183–85, *186–87*, 188–89, 192–94.
See also R&D investment
Share Point software, 38
sharing knowledge
about customers, 60
and *ba*, 40, 88–89, 243–44, 246, 248
of best practices, 4, 131
with external contacts, 70, 78–79,
80–81
globalization and, 224
knowledge vision as guide to, 87
microcommunities and, 290
overview, 288, 290
project transparency and, 226, 246
and redundant information, 295
and social capital, 251

value of, 80, 127

See also embedded knowledge; explicit knowledge; intangible assets; knowledge transfer

tacit knowledge sharing

challenges, 85, 290

overview, 278, 284, 288, 290

in personal relationships, 71–72

as socialization, 61, 65, 66, 292

with stories, 64

See also communication

tactile perspective, 282

Taiwan, R&D investment in, 183–85, *186–87*, 188–89, 192–94

Takeda, 178

Takeuchi, Hirotaka, 5, 33, 160–61

target receivers, receptors in, 61

task force/project team structure

action learning within, 93–94

building *ba* in, 23, 28

and cross-leveling of knowledge, 140–41, 279–80, 287

cross-regional and cross-functional, 90–91, 93–94, 95n2, 139–40

European versus Japanese style, 280

and knowledge transfer, 54–55, 290

middle managers' role in, 292

for new product development, 90–91, 95n2, 139–40, 243–44, 293, 294

Sharp's example of, 90–91, 95n2, 139–40

for strategic planning, 222, 224

tension within, 270–71

See also groups; product/process/ service development; teams

Taylor, Frederick, 159

teams

boundary-breaking sessions, 133–34

and communities of practice, 241–42, 278

composition of experiment teams, 226

diversity in, 134

innovation independent, for new product development, 293

interfacing with external constituents, 45–46

joint knowledge work, 160–63

of manual workers, 159–60

and norms of reciprocity, 49

overview, 158–60, 278

for process innovation, 293

sharing knowledge in, 290

See also groups; task force/project team structure

technical constraints on knowledge accessibility, 40

technical know-how, 115–16, 130, 298

technological improvements

in communication, 53, 108, 130

and economic predictions, 210n1

history of, 200–207

leakage of, 205, 208, 210n3

search capability, 37, 38, 39–40

Sharp's lead in LCD, 86, 90–91, 138–41

social networking, 37–38, 53, 108, 130, 278

See also Web utilization; *entries beginning with "R&D"*

technology for individuals and small groups, 97–98, 109–16, *111*

technology for organizations

for automated decision-making, 104–6

automation of structured transactions, *98*, 98–99

expert model for work transactions, *98*, 99, 101–2

expert systems and artificial intelligence, 99–100, 104

history of, 99–106 *passim*

integrating, 108–9

overview, 97–98, 115–16

performance support, 102–3, 106–9

portals, 103

product life cycle management system, *98*, 99

role-specific software, 103–4, 107–8

technology-oriented valuation of R&D, 176–77

Teece, David J., 179, 198–212

thematic groups, 58

theories of firm differences, contemporary, 13–14

theory of knowing, 217

theory of knowledge-creating firms, 14–17, 26–29. *See also* dynamic model of knowledge-creating companies

theory of organizational knowledge creation

justification criteria, 17, 86–87, 89, 94, 286, 299

SECI MODEL, 17, 160–61, 296

spiral concept, 17, 140–41, 160–61, 296, 297

See also sharing knowledge; tacit knowledge

thinking
 cognitive tacit knowledge, 143n4,
  292, 298
 dialectical thinking and action, 21–22
 and perspective, 26, 148, 277, 294
 See also logical thinking
Thomke, S., 155–56
3M, 166, 246–47
360° feedback instruments, 53
Tierney, T. J., 233
tight scripts, 262
time limitations of directors, 230
Tokyo Stock Exchange, 178
Tokyo Stock Exchange, First Section
  (TSE1), 181, *182*
tool kits for customer innovation, 155–56
total debt/total equity capital (DE ratio),
  186, 190–91
Toyota
 communication as core competence,
  88–89
 competitive cost advantage of, 128–29
 employees' problem-solving skills,
  134–35
 essential dialogues at, 21
 knowledge activists at, 89–90
 R&D to capital investment ratio, *178*
 success of, 4
Toyota Way 2001, 4, 89, 129, 286
tragedy of the commons, 159, 170. *See
  also* motivational solutions to social
  dilemma
transaction cost economic theory,
  13–14, 40–41, 290
transaction model for work transactions,
  98, 98–99
transferable relationships, 73, 74, 77, 79
transparency in global venues, 225, 226,
  246
transport equipment industry, *182*,
  182–83
travel and transportation industry, 106
triggering, 284
trust
 between client and knowledge-
  intensive provider, 233
 from conversations, 88–89, 245–46
 in dense networks, 49
 fair treatment and, 168–71
 Frío Aéreo's example of, 245–46, 250
 overview, 298
 and physical proximity, 62
 social capital from, 241–43, 245–47,
  251
 3M's example of, 246–47

W. L. Gore's example of, 243–44, 246,
  248
 See also social capital
trust-based constraints on knowledge
  accessibility, 40, 41
trust relationships, 240–41
truth, 15, 16
TSE1 (Tokyo Stock Exchange, First
  Section), 181, *182*
t-statistics, *182, 186, 190–91*
Tumo, Ilkka, 252n9

uncertainty, 13–14, 49, 210n1, 275,
  298. *See also* innovation; product/
  process/service development; R&D
  investment
Unipac Optoelectronics, 136
unique knowledge, protecting, 127–29,
  137–38
United Kingdom, 183–85, *186–87*,
  188–89, 192–94, 230. *See also
  specific U.K. companies*
United States, 183–85, *186–87*,
  188–89, 192–94. *See also specific
  U.S. companies*
UPS (United Parcel Service), 241, 242
U.S. Department of Defense, 202–3, 204,
  210
U.S. GAAP (generally accepted
  accounting principles), 177
U.S. government support of R&D, 202–3,
  204, 207, 208, *209–10*, 210
users. *See* customers

value, shareholders', 179–83, *180, 182,*
  183–85, *186–87*, 188–89, 192–94.
  See also R&D investment
value chain premise, 141, 256
value chain relationships, 74, *75,*
  75–76, 78
values
 articulating, 129
 and beliefs, 129, 258, 298
 changes in, 243
 diversity as a value, 24, 59, 134, 154,
  279
 overview, 19, 298, 299
 prosocial intrinsic motivation based
  on, 164–65
 providing reasons for decisions, 223
 and social capital, 242
 synthesis of, 22–23
 See also commitment
van Alstyne, Marshall, 37–38
venture capital industry, 206–7

Vey, Meredith, 109, 116n3
video connections, 252n10
virtual conversations/relationships,
    37–38, 249–50
vision
    communication of, 86–87, 90
    connecting planning, knowledge
        management, and, 34–35
    and corporate renewal, 264–66
    embedding, 27–28
    leadership's role in, 27
    niche positioning, 138
    overview, *18*, 18–19, 290, 299
    revisioning process, 265–66, 271–72
    and serendipity, 296
    at Sharp, 138–41
    See also objectives; values
von Hippel, Eric, 150, 155–56
von Krogh, G., 125

W. L. Gore and Associates, 242, 243–44,
    246, 248
WACC (weighted average cost of capital),
    194
WalMart, 248
Waterman, R. H., 293
weak versus strong relationships, 72–73,
    74–78, *75*
The Wealth of Nations (Smith), 5
Weaver, Warren, 204
Web sites, 9
Web utilization
    broadband technology, 202–3
    for communication, 37–38, 53, 108,
        130, 278
    for consumer participation in design,
        155
    as example of thinking without limits,
        148

mouse track data, 153–54
psychographic profiling and lifestyle
    segmentation, 154
role-specific portals, 103–4
self-help educational programs, 261,
    264
for surveys, 112–13
thematic groups, 58
weighted average cost of capital (WACC),
    194
Weiss, Leigh, 32–43
Wellsprings of Knowledge (Leonard-
    Barton), 5, 33
Wenger, Etienne, 241
Western epistemology and knowledge
    creation, *280*, 281, 283
whistle-blowers, 165
why? question five times, 64–65, 89,
    135
wide net versus narrow net networks,
    74–75, *75*
Winter, Nelson, 58
Winter, S., 25
wisdom, 299
Working Knowledge (Davenport and
    Prusak), 5, 33
Work-Out system at GE, 4
work processes, utilizing technology for,
    98, 99, 101–2
World Bank, 38, 58, 64
The World Is Flat (Friedman), 6
Worldscope database, 183, 185, 188,
    196n3
World War II, 202

Xerox Corporation, 109, 152–53, 155,
    205

Zaltman, Gerald, 151